"*Outdoor Environments for People* is essential reading for anyone who wants to create better places for people. This wonderfully insightful and illustrated book should be required for students in landscape architecture, architecture, planning, as well as allied fields of environmental psychology and human ecology. The book's creative hands-on exercises and projects show designers how to apply the readings to a variety of settings."

Dr. Robert L. Ryan, *FASLA, Professor and Department Chair, Department of Landscape Architecture and Regional Planning, University of Massachusetts Amherst. Co-author,* With People in Mind: Design and Management of Everyday Nature

"This book is a fantastic addition to the analogue of literature in the field of environment-behavior studies. It takes long-established theoretical concepts familiar to all those who value understanding the relationships between people and place in design and repositions their relevance in relation to contemporary contexts, communities, and challenges. It offers students in design, planning and architecture a fabulous resource, both theoretical and practical, and demonstrates the strength of evidence-based design."

Dr. Kate Bishop, *Associate Professor, School of Built Environment, University of New South Wales, Sydney, Australia. Co-editor,* The Routledge Handbook of Landscape Urban Research *and* The Routledge Handbook of People and Place in the 21st Century City

"Every project requires a thoughtful approach towards human-environment design. *Outdoor Environments for People* is a timely primer for developers, architects, landscape architects, and urban planners. This book is a foundational piece for every professional library."

Marq Truscott, *FASLA, Landscape Architect, Developer, Educator, and past ASLA Vice President for Education*

"*Outdoor Environments for People* draws upon theory from a wide range of disciplines and uses this to inform suggested ways to design outdoor environments for people. It explains and acknowledges past and future family, social, cultural, technological changes, together with the increasing issue of climate change and how these should influence the process of design and the outcome of that process. It explores perceptions, environmental behaviors and needs of users of outdoor environments though the cycle of different stages of life while also addressing issues of inclusion and gender. The text is supported by a range of informative illustrations. This inspiring book is essential for all students of landscape architecture and practitioners, of even a few years, would benefit from this as part of their continuing professional development."

Helen Woolley, *FLI, FRSA Professor of Landscape Architecture, Children's Environments and Society, and Head of Department of Landscape Architecture at the University of Sheffield, England*

Outdoor Environments for People

Outdoor Environments for People addresses the everyday human behavior in outdoor built environments and explains how designers can learn about and incorporate their knowledge into places they help to create. Bridging research and practice, and drawing from disciplines such as environmental psychology, cultural geography, and sociology, the book provides an overview of theories, such as personal space, territoriality, privacy, and place attachment, that are explored in the context of outdoor environments and, in particular, the landscape architecture profession. Authors share the impact that place design can have on individuals and communities with regard to health, safety, and belonging.

Beautifully designed and highly illustrated in full color, this book presents analysis, community engagement, and design processes for understanding and incorporating the social and psychological influences of an environment and discusses examples of outdoor place design that skillfully respond to human factors. As a textbook for landscape architecture students and a reference for practitioners, it includes chapters addressing different realms of people–place relationships, examples of theoretical applications, case studies, and exercises that can be incorporated into any number of design courses. Contemporary design examples, organized by place type and illustrating key human factor principles, provide valuable guidance and suggestions. *Outdoor Environments for People* is a must-have resource for students, instructors, and professionals within landscape architecture and the surrounding disciplines.

Patsy Eubanks Owens is an Associate Dean of Human and Social Sciences and a Professor of Landscape Architecture at the University of California, Davis. She holds a Bachelor of Landscape Architecture from the University of Georgia and a Master of Landscape Architecture from University of California, Berkeley. Her research focuses on the relationships between people and the outdoor environment including the role of the physical environment in the development, health and well-being of youth, and methods for youth and adult engagement in design and policy development.

Jayoung Koo is an Associate Professor of Landscape Architecture at the University of Kentucky. She holds a Bachelor of Science from Korea University, a Master of Landscape Architecture from Seoul National University, a Master of Environmental Management from Yale University, and a PhD in Geography from the University of California, Davis. Her research focuses on recreating landscapes to enhance and sustain the overall health of communities and built environments at various scales and perspectives, focusing on sustainability, resilience, and community development and design.

Yiwei Huang is an Assistant Professor of Landscape Architecture at Purdue University. She holds a Master of Landscape Architecture from the University of Massachusetts, Amherst, a Master of Urban Design from the University of Michigan, Ann Arbor, and a PhD in Geography from the University of California, Davis. Her research focuses on cultural competency and design, visual-driven participatory methods, and the relationships between the outdoor environment and the everyday geography of traditionally marginalized urban communities.

Outdoor Environments for People

CONSIDERING HUMAN FACTORS IN LANDSCAPE DESIGN

Patsy Eubanks Owens, Jayoung Koo, and Yiwei Huang

LONDON AND NEW YORK

Cover design and art © 2023 by Lauren Frances Owens
Instagram: @laurenfrances

First published 2024
by Routledge
4 Park Square, Milton Park, Abingdon, Oxon OX14 4RN

and by Routledge
605 Third Avenue, New York, NY 10158

Routledge is an imprint of the Taylor & Francis Group, an informa business

© 2024 Patsy Eubanks Owens, Jayoung Koo, and Yiwei Huang

The right of Patsy Eubanks Owens, Jayoung Koo, and Yiwei Huang to be identified as authors of this work has been asserted in accordance with sections 77 and 78 of the Copyright, Designs and Patents Act 1988.

All rights reserved. No part of this book may be reprinted or reproduced or utilised in any form or by any electronic, mechanical, or other means, now known or hereafter invented, including photocopying and recording, or in any information storage or retrieval system, without permission in writing from the publishers.

Trademark notice: Product or corporate names may be trademarks or registered trademarks, and are used only for identification and explanation without intent to infringe.

British Library Cataloguing-in-Publication Data
A catalogue record for this book is available from the British Library

Library of Congress Cataloging-in-Publication Data
Names: Owens, Patsy Eubanks, author.
Title: Outdoor environments for people : considering human factors in landscape design / Patsy Eubanks Owens, Jayoung Koo, and Yiwei Huang.
Description: Abingdon, Oxon; New York, NY : Routledge, [2023] | Includes bibliographical references and index. |
Identifiers: LCCN 2023010518 (print) | LCCN 2023010519 (ebook) | ISBN 9781138296435 (hbk) | ISBN 9781138296442 (pbk) | ISBN 9781315100036 (ebk)
Subjects: LCSH: Environmental psychology. | Landscape architecture. | Human behavior.
Classification: LCC BF353 .O84 2023 (print) | LCC BF353 (ebook) | DDC 155.9--dc23/eng/20230624
LC record available at https://lccn.loc.gov/2023010518
LC ebook record available at https://lccn.loc.gov/2023010519

ISBN: 9781138296435 (hbk)
ISBN: 9781138296442 (pbk)
ISBN: 9781315100036 (ebk)

DOI: 10.4324/9781315100036

Typeset in Bembo and Mundial
by KnowledgeWorks Global Ltd.

Every effort has been made to contact copyright-holders. Please advise the publisher of any errors or omissions, and these will be corrected in subsequent editions.

Dedication

We dedicate this book to our families who have supported us in this journey. Your love, inspiration, and faith in our abilities have kept us moving forward. We also dedicate our work to our instructors and colleagues, past and present. Their encouragement and wisdom has guided each of our careers. In particular, we greatly appreciate the influence and mentorship that Mark Francis provided to each of us. Lastly, this book is for all the people who believe in the benefits and importance of outdoor places.

CONTENTS

Acknowledgments — *xiii*
List of Tables — *xv*
List of Figures — *xvii*
Preface — *xxiii*

INTRODUCTION — 1

SECTION I: THEORY AND RESEARCH ON HUMAN–ENVIRONMENT RELATIONS — 5

1 HUMAN FACTORS IN CONTEXT — 7

What are human factors in design? 7
Why do human factors matter in design? 9
Situating human factors in the design process 11
Situating human factors in the societal context 13
Understanding landscape values 19
Potential exercises and project 24

2 PEOPLE–PLACE RELATIONSHIPS — 27

Proxemics and personal space 27
Territoriality 34
Crowding and privacy 38
Affordances 42
Health and well-being 44
Place attachment 49
Safety and security 53
Wayfinding 56
Conclusion 59
Potential exercises and project 59

SECTION II: UNDERSTANDING COMMUNITIES AND PEOPLE — 65

3 PEOPLE AND CULTURE — 67

Introduction to culture   67
General findings   71
Applications to design   77
Developing cultural competency   82
Conclusion   84
Potential exercises and project   85

4 THE LIFE-CYCLE STAGE AND PLACE — 89

Environments for children   89
Places for adolescents   95
Worker needs and workplace design   101
Designing for older adults   105
Potential exercises and project   109

5 A SPIRIT OF INCLUSION — 113

Inclusion in outdoor environments   113
Roles and responsibilities of designers   118
Beyond requirements   124
Steps toward inclusive design   130
Conclusions   131
Potential exercise and project   131

6 GENDER AND PLACE — 133

Background   133
Gender differences   139
Gender identities, sexual orientations, and public spaces   145
Gender-inclusive design   148
Conclusion   149
Potential exercise and project   150

SECTION III: DESIGN APPLICATIONS — 151

7 VISUALIZING PEOPLE AND BEHAVIOR — 153

Historical context   153
Reading the landscape   154
Observing, documenting, and analyzing behavior   156
Community and participatory mapping   159
User-employed photography   162
Scored walks   165
Post-occupancy evaluations and the case study method   166

Digital sources and methods   168
Conclusion   170
Potential exercises and project   171

8 ENGAGING PEOPLE IN THE PROCESS — 175

Roots of community engagement in design and planning   175
Beyond legal obligations   178
Benefits and challenges of community participation   180
Participation strategies   183
Conclusion   187
Potential exercises and project   188

9 CASE STUDIES IN PEOPLE PLACES — 191

Introduction   191
A place for relaxation and restoration   191
A place for gathering   197
A place for inclusivity and equity   202
A place for learning and playing   207
Reflections and discussion   211

SECTION IV: LOOKING AHEAD — 213

10 PEOPLE AND CHANGE — 215

Sustainable planning, design, and people   215
Health and well-being   222
Virtual influences in design   228
Conclusion   233
Potential exercise and project   234

REFERENCES — 235

Index   *259*

ACKNOWLEDGMENTS

During our journey of researching and writing this book, we sought advice from trusted experts in the people–environment field. Many scholars provided their insight and wisdom by reviewing early versions of chapters. We greatly appreciate their willingness to contribute their valuable time and knowledge as well as their own experience teaching human factors in design to this book. Our expert readers often directed us to overlooked relevant research and identified gaps in our explanations. We hope that they will see their suggestions reflected in the finished product.

We would like to thank fellow educators and researchers Adina Cox and Ben Shirtcliff, Iowa State University; Karen Franck, New Jersey Institute of Technology; Lynne Manzo and Jeffrey Hou, University of Washington; Robert Ryan, University of Massachusetts, Amherst; and Cory Parker, Elizabeth Boults, and David de la Pena, University of California, Davis (UC Davis). We also thank Julie Stevens, Iowa State University; Kurt Culbertson, Design Workshop; and Matluba Khan, Cardiff University, for sharing information on their design projects, and the many scholars and professionals who generously granted us their permission to include their images and tables. Furthermore, we greatly appreciate Lauren Owens working with us to explore cover alternatives and to develop the final design.

We thank our many graduate and undergraduate students who have provided assistance with literature reviews and illustrations and for providing feedback on exercises and projects throughout the years. In particular, we would like to acknowledge Purdue University undergraduate Yuan Zhang for her help with illustrations. In addition, UC Davis graduate students Mariah Cosand, Marissa Coyne, Nermin Dessouky, Farnaz Feizi, and Mina Rezaei contributed research and reviews of early drafts; University of Kentucky students Carson Ann Adams and Amanda Reese, and Purdue student Chole Kennedy helped with locating images and references; and Gabi Kirk, a doctoral student at UC Davis, provided her copy-editing expertise.

Lastly, we thank the staff at Routledge for their encouragement, patience, and support throughout this endeavor. We are particularly appreciative of their confidence in this book.

LIST OF TABLES

1.1	Hester's user-needs checklist (adapted from Hester, 1984)	23
2.1	Comparison of sociopetal and sociofugal spaces	31
2.2	Types of territories according to Altman (1975)	35
2.3	Design considerations for physical activity and restoration (Ryan, 2012)	48
2.4	Wayfinding communication strategies in the outdoor environment	60
3.1	A comparison of five cultural groups' use and attachment to Independence National Historical Park (Low et al., 2002)	80
4.1	Developmental functions of play (Gray, 2017; Piaget, 2013)	90
4.2	Essential characteristics of play (Gray, 2017)	90
4.3	The evolution of the playground in the United States (adapted from Cranz, 1982; Frost & Worham, 1988; Verstrate & Karsten, 2015)	92
4.4	Key elements of a universally designed playground (adapted from ASLA, n.d.b.)	96
4.5	Projections of the older adult population: 2020–2060 (Vespa, Medin, & Armstrong, 2020)	105
4.6	Relationship of physical design features to healthy aging according to existing literature (adapted from Mather & Scommegna, 2017)	108
4.7	Design considerations for outdoor spaces for Alzheimer's patients and other older adults (adapted from Lovering, 1990)	110
5.1	Brief historical timeline of standards and legislation addressing accessibility in built environments in the United States. (U.S. Access Board, n.d.; Goltsman, Gilbert, Wohlford, & Kirk, 1993)	121
7.1	The different components of a POE method used in assessing outdoor spaces (adapted from Marcus & Francis, 1998)	167
8.1	A summary and comparison of NEPA and CEQA processes (adapted from CEQ & OPR, 2014).	176
9.1	Overview of this chapter's case studies	192
9.2	VanPlay's five phases of engagement and content development (adapted from Vancouver Board of Parks and Recreation, 2018)	203
10.1	Examples of potential physical and social environment impacts due to projected societal shifts	216

LIST OF FIGURES

0.1	An illustration of Bronfenbrenner's socio-ecological model in the landscape. Image credit: Patsy Eubanks Owens and Yiwei Huang.	3
1.1	A socio-ecological model. Adapted from Eisenmann et al. (2008).	8
1.2	People sit where there are places to sit as illustrated by this image from *Social Life of Small Urban Space* (Whyte, 1980).	10
1.3	Incorporating human–environment research into the design process. Adapted from Zeisel (2006).	12
1.4	Gates and paving design at the Mexican Heritage Cultural Center in San Jose, CA, by artist Victor Mario Zaballa. Image credit: Juliet Flower MacCannell.	14
1.5	The two-parent household in decline in the United States (Pew Research Center, 2015).	16
1.6	The butterfly wings painting in Nashville is a popular Instagram photo spot. Artist and credit: Kelsey Montague.	18
1.7	The places people value are influenced by their interests and experiences. The place on the left might be valued by a fly-fisher while a motorcyclist would likely prefer the place on the right. Images are from an unpublished research project examining public values of forest lands.	20
1.8	Drawings by adults recalling places important to them during their teenage years. One recalled spending time with friends in a secluded place and another remembered basketball courts and green space close to their home. Images are from an unpublished workshop.	21
2.1	Interpersonal distances. Adapted from Hall (1990a).	28
2.2	Social distance circles in Mission Dolores Park, San Francisco, CA. Image credit: Joey Parsons.	32
2.3	Social distancing at the Fort Mason farmers' market, San Francisco, CA. Image credit: Sarah Owens Izant.	33
2.4	Adolescents claiming territories at high school. Image credit: Patsy Eubanks Owens.	36
2.5	Comparing territoriality at two co-housing locations (plan views adapted from McCamant & Durrett, 1994). Image credits: Liz Stevenson (top) and Patsy Eubanks Owens (bottom).	38
2.6	Illustrated diagram of social density and spatial density.	40

2.7	A planter wall (left) and boulders (right) provide seating options at Levi Strauss Plaza, San Francisco, CA. Image credit: Patsy Eubanks Owens.	43
2.8	Photograph taken by an adolescent girl of a place she liked to go to get away. Image credit: Patsy Eubanks Owens.	46
2.9	The tripartite model of place attachment (Scannell & Gifford, 2010a).	49
2.10	Village concept – informed by the community's sacred structure, Manteo, NC. Drawing and image credit: Patsy Eubanks Owens.	52
2.11	Safety and security principles – Jacobs (1961), Newman (1972), and CPTED.	54
2.12	Designing to accommodate desired gathering activity at a school. Adapted from Crowe (1991).	55
2.13	Environmental cues (path, edge, district, node, and landmark) inform an individual's wayfinding plan (from point A to point B and to point C). Additional wayfinding features can support the travel experience.	57
3.1	Giant umbrellas (closed and open) in the plaza outside al-Haram Mosque in Medina, Saudi Arabia. Image credit: Jamila Khan.	70
3.2	Floating water markets in Thailand. Image credit: Li Chen.	71
3.3	Colorful market umbrellas at a *tianguis* in Mexico City. Image credit: Yiwei Huang.	72
3.4	The Hall of Prayer for Good Harvest and its surrounding landscape at the Temple of Heaven, Beijing, China. Image credit: Fong Chen, retrieved from Wikimedia Commons.	73
3.5	The daily Promenade at Plaza Mayor in Salamanca, Spain. Image credit: Patsy Eubanks Owens.	73
3.6	Visitors enjoying the upper terrace in Park Guell, Barcelona, Spain. Image credit: Yiwei Huang.	75
3.7	Prohibitions on activities are common at public parks in the United States (Rogers, 2018).	75
3.8	A distinctive sidewalk pattern in the *calçada portuguesa* tradition in Curitiba (left) and Rio de Janeiro, Brazil (right). Image credit: Patsy Eubanks Owens.	77
3.9	Participants engaging in the "design buffet" during an intergenerational workshop (Hou, 2013).	82
3.10	Developing cultural competency levels relevant to designing outdoor environments. Adapted from Center for Community Health and Development (n.d.).	83
3.11	An example of Instagram posts featuring "street markets" illustrate the visual richness of this assignment. Image credit: Yiwei Huang.	86
4.1	Children using loose parts in their play. Image credits: Yiwei Huang (left) and Amy Wagenfeld (right).	91
4.2	Musical instrument in a "Learning through Landscapes" schoolyard. Image credit: Learning through Landscapes.	94
4.3	A play area design that incorporates natural elements located in Nadaka Park, Gresham, Oregon. Designer: Moore, Iacofano, and Goltsman. Image credit: Billy Hustace Photography.	94
4.4	Photograph taken by an adolescent girl of her view to Mt. Diablo (California) – a place she liked to go to "get away." Image credit: Patsy Eubanks Owens.	98

4.5	Photograph taken by an adolescent girl of her favorite place to hang out at school. Image credit: Patsy Eubanks Owens.	98
4.6	Esplanade Youth Plaza in Fremantle, Australia. Photo courtesy: City of Fremantle.	100
4.7	In transit deserts, residents often walk greater distances to access bus stops. This graphic depicts James Robertson's 21-mile daily commute to work. © Martha Thierry – USA Today Network.	103
4.8	The Charles Schwab campus in Austin, Texas provides welcome opportunities to be outside and in the presence of nature. Courtesy of Charles Schwab. Image credit: Brandon Huttenlocher/Design Workshop Inc.	104
5.1	North Beach playground offers inclusive features for toddlers and young children, including a range of sensory design features. Image credit: Yi Ding.	114
5.2	At Brooklyn Bridge Park, signs welcome everyone and list rules at a picnicking area (left) and provide guidance on appropriate ages at a play area (right). Image credit: Patsy Eubanks Owens.	115
5.3	A skateboard park sign in Bowling Green, Kentucky, listing activities and behaviors allowed and not allowed. Image credit: Jayoung Koo.	116
5.4	Skateboarding impediment designs in Millennium Square in Sheffield, England (left) and San Francisco, CA (right). Image credits: Woolley et al. (2011) (left) and Patsy Eubanks Owens (right).	117
5.5	Varied path options along the Scioto Greenway and River in downtown Columbus, OH, allow accessibility to the waterfront while providing inclusive and broad user opportunities. Image credit: Jayoung Koo.	118
5.6	Range of disabilities Americans are living with as of 2019. Image credit: U.S. Census Bureau (2021).	120
5.7	A redesign of the main entrance to Hunt Hall, University of California, Davis, occurred during building renovations. Previously stairs were the only access to the main entrance (left) while a new landing and ramp were added to comply with ADA requirements (right). Image credits: University Archives Photographs: 1915–1980: AR-013, Archives and Special Collections Library, University of California, Davis (left), and Patsy Eubanks Owens (right).	122
5.8	An example of the types of outdoor accessibility requirements provided in *Outdoor Developed Areas* (adapted from Access Board, 2014).	122
5.9	Campground site plan including designated wheelchair accessible sites distributed throughout the site exceeding federal requirements (Brown et al., 2021). Image credit: National Park Service.	123
5.10	Example of users and abilities that can be addressed through inclusive, accessible, and universal design approaches.	126
5.11	Increased accessibility through (a) lighting during evening hours, (b) seating with armrest and back, (c) trees offering shade, (d) wide pathways for conversation with less conflict in Woolwich Square, London, United Kingdom (Dillon & Green, 2019b). Image credit: Gustafson Porter + Bowman.	127
5.12	The Indianapolis Cultural Trail (Indiana) offers a wide inclusive corridor for pedestrians, cyclists, people with disabilities (left) and segments of delineated paths for cyclists and slower travelers such as pedestrians (right). Image credit: Margaret Klondike.	127

5.13	Inclusive designs can create safer and more comfortable ways for people to travel such as a lift for bus access in Curitiba, Brazil (left) or raised garden beds and space for assisting personnel in an outdoor learning environment in California (right). Image credits: Mario Roberto Duran Ortiz Mariordo, retrieved from Wikimedia Commons (left) and Tahereh Sheerazie (right).	128
5.14	Design features such as an outdoor xylophone with Braille (left) and a cable guide with Braille signage (right) welcome and guide visitors with visual challenges in Watertown Riverfront Park, Watertown, MA. Image credit: Solomon Foundation.	128
5.15	Signs in multiple languages in a San Francisco, CA, playground offering inclusive experiences for varied users. Image credit: Patsy Eubanks Owens.	129
6.1	Americans see gender differences exist but hold varied opinions as to their origins (Pew Research Center, 2017).	135
6.2	Crocker Plaza catchment area difference between men and women showing women travel shorter distances to get there (Mozingo, 1989).	137
6.3	Of the 34 countries surveyed, 74% said gender equality was very important (as indicated on this map) and 94% said it was important (Pew Research Center, 2020).	138
6.4	Differences between gender in sports participation is less restrictive than in the past but discrepancies remain. Image credit: Yiwei Huang.	140
6.5	Dark, empty, under-maintained spaces may be perceived as unsafe by people of varied gender identities. Image credit: Yiwei Huang.	142
6.6	Moms and female caregivers are frequently seen in playgrounds with children. Image credit: Yiwei Huang.	143
6.7	As shown in earlier studies (e.g., Mozingo, 1989), men and women continue to claim different territories in parks (Huang & Napawan, 2021). Image credit: Yiwei Huang.	144
6.8	The number of Americans identifying as LGBT is rising (Pew Research Center, 2017).	146
6.9	Dupont Circle, a traditionally gay neighborhood in Washington, DC, recognizes the LGBTQ+ community through rainbow-colored crosswalks. Image credit: Yiwei Huang.	147
7.1	A site sketch and reflection submitted for a design assignment. Image credit: Aina Smart Truco.	155
7.2	An example of a data collection form and the resulting behavior mapping of children in a residential setting (Sanoff & Coates, 1971).	157
7.3	Digitizing behavior mapping data helped increase understanding of gender separation at one urban plaza (Huang & Napawan, 2021).	157
7.4	Behavior mapping showing dynamic patterns of spatial occupancy. Maps from left to right present daily occupancy on a weekday afternoon during poor weather, a weekend afternoon during very good weather, and a daily weekday in the early afternoon during good weather (Goličnik, 2005).	158
7.5	A student's behavior observation sketch using pen and colored markers to capture activities during one specific moment (left). Image credit: Sonia Shoji-Jeevanjee. In the "Bodies in Motion" exercise, a student used Adobe	

	Illustrator to incorporate photo clips and notation to convey behavior (right). Image credit: Isabella Jimenez.	158
7.6	Cognitive maps of Los Angeles as perceived by the predominant ethnicities in different neighborhoods – white residents in Westwood, Black residents in Avalon, and Latino/a residents in Boyle Heights (Los Angeles Department of City Planning, 1971). Retrieved from Hayden (1995).	161
7.7	Members of the Sactown Heroes documented through photographs, videos, and text what they like and do not like in their community during the Youth Voices for Change project. Image credit: jesikah maria ross.	163
7.8	Scored walks were used during the Runyon Canyon master planning process to gain knowledge from the nearby residents and to increase their understanding of the place. Image credit: Randy Hester.	165
7.9	PPGIS mapping, based on 728 survey responses, documents the typical boating routes and existing recreational activities in Franks Tract (Milligan, Kraus-Polk, & Huang, 2020).	169
7.10	Social media data was used to understand park use and users' emotional connections during different seasons (Zhang & Song, 2019).	171
8.1	The police killing of George Floyd prompted the creation of a memorial in his honor by community members. The memorial is located at the intersection of Chicago Ave and E 38th St in Minneapolis, Minnesota. Image credit: Fibonacci Blue, retrieved from Wiki Commons.	177
8.2	The various manifestations of community-driven design efforts (Wilson, 2018).	178
8.3	An example of group facilitation and visual note taking. Image credit: Randy Hester.	180
8.4	Diagramming daily patterns – the archetypes and idiosyncrasies – of a community. "Newsing at the post office" in Manteo, North Carolina (Hester, 1987).	181
8.5	The Public Sediment Project: Alameda Creek Atlas includes participatory tools for community members which are available in multiple languages and on social media networks (SCAPE, 2019). Image credits: N. Claire Napawan, Brett Snyder, and Beth Ferguson.	185
8.6	A design review for a senior housing project conducted at the site enabled residents to participate. Image credit: Yiwei Huang.	186
9.1	The Iowa Correctional Institution for Women (ICIW) master plan (Stevens, Toews, and Wagenfeld, 2018). Image credit: Hunter and Fangman.	193
9.2	Multipurpose outdoor classroom design plan (Hamerlinck et al., 2015). Image credit: Julie Stevens.	195
9.3	Community effort during the building process (Hamerlinck et al., 2015). Image credit: Julie Stevens.	197
9.4	Davis Central Park community workshop ("Central Park and Davis Farmer's Market," n.d.). Image credit: Mark Francis.	199
9.5	Central Park Master Plan (Francis & Griffith, 2011). Image credit: CoDesign Inc.	200
9.6	Central Park in 2005 (Francis, 2010) and 2018. Image credits: Mark Francis (left), Yiwei Huang (right).	200

9.7	A special powwow performance on Central Park's main lawn (left) and the weekly inclusion of bounce houses (right). Image credit: Yiwei Huang.	201
9.8	Novel forms of community engagement. Image credit: Copyright © 2018 by Design Workshop, Inc. for Vancouver Board of Parks and Recreation.	204
9.9	Equity approaches to mapping initiative zones. Image credit: Copyright © 2019 by Design Workshop, Inc. for Vancouver Board of Parks and Recreation.	205
9.10	Tulatoli Primary School before and after the design interventions (Khan, 2017). Image credit: Matluba Khan.	208
9.11	Design plans showing the school's outdoor environment before and after the intervention (Khan, McGeown, & Bell, 2020).	209
9.12	Tulatoli Primary School academic performance comparisons: Differences in mathematics and science attainment between the treatment group (students using the outdoor environment for learning), the comparative group (students at this school not using the outdoor environment for learning), and a control school (a school in the region without outdoor learning) (Khan et al., 2020).	210
9.13	Behavior mapping showing student activities before and after the design intervention (Khan, 2017).	210
10.1	Common features of transit-oriented developments include a transit station near public open spaces and quality pedestrian-focused environments with mixed land use of medium to high density. Image credit: U.S. Government Accountability Office.	218
10.2	Complete streets consider all users by including designated lanes or areas for vehicles, bicycles, service providers, and pedestrians. Image credit: Boston Transportation Department.	220
10.3	Washington Canal Park in Washington, DC earned recognition as a SITES Platinum level pilot project in 2013. Originally used for school bus parking, the OLIN Studio and collaborators designed a public park for the site which embraced sustainable principles and emphasized user experience. Image credit: OLIN (left) and OLIN/Sahar Coston-Hardy (right).	221
10.4	A rendering of a future transit stop in a mixed-use neighborhood which will accommodate walking, cycling, and driverless vehicles (Hilburg, 2018). Image credit: Kohn Pedersen Fox Associates.	222
10.5	Atlanta BeltLine Eastside Trail near Ponce City Market connects people to parks and destinations around the urban greenway. Image credit: Christopher T. Martin.	224
10.6	A person using the Pokémon GO app (augmented reality) for recreation in the outdoors. Image credit: Jayoung Koo.	226
10.7	Diagram of augmented reality and virtual reality where design is simulated over a physical environment (AR) or communicated through virtual tools (VR).	229
10.8	Using AR, a B&O Railroad Museum (Baltimore, Maryland) visitor explores elements of a three-dimensional model through an iPad camera. The camera app provides more detailed information on buildings and other features. Image credit: HighRock/highrock.com.	231
10.9	Community members experience design alternatives through a virtual reality (VR) headset during a presentation by students. Image credit: Jayoung Koo.	232

PREFACE

Our belief is that landscape designs that embrace an understanding of human factors will more fully contribute to the use and enjoyment of places. We also hold that such places have additional benefits for the individuals who use them and for society as a whole. Our goal in writing this book is to share information on these human factors and relate it to the design of outdoor environments. We intend for this text to be used in landscape architecture classrooms and offices. We also hope that other disciplines, such as planning, urban design, and architecture, will find value in the book. Along with providing an overview of theories and research on people–environment relations, we discuss implications for the design process and lessons for spatial design. Our intent is to complement existing publications that focus on various aspects of the social and psychological influences of environments or are directed at other audiences. Books focusing on environment–behavior relations often reach environmental psychologists while others target architectural applications. Earlier books focused on people and outdoor space design provide an excellent foundation for our continued exploration of the current influences on outdoor spaces and their design. Readers are encouraged to question, apply, and challenge the assumptions and findings shared and join us in the pursuit of promoting and creating better places for people.

INTRODUCTION

I had the privilege of taking Clare Cooper Marcus's "Social Factors in Landscape Architecture" course when I was a graduate student. My timing was off since Clare was on sabbatical that year, but luckily her former student and my future colleague, Mark Francis, made the trip from UC Davis twice a week to teach the course. Clare, an emeritus professor of architecture and landscape architecture at UC Berkeley, was the initiator and instigator of integrating human factor considerations into design curricula. This book builds upon the knowledge I gained in that course and teaching similar courses at Virginia Tech and UC Davis in the following years, conducting my own research, and leading community-based projects. Like Clare and Mark, I have relied on the books and articles from others for my course reading lists and references. It was during my time co-teaching with my fellow author Jayoung Koo that the idea of writing a dedicated book on human factors in design took root. We asked Yiwei Huang to join us and contribute her expertise on cultural competency and professional applications. Little did we realize how long that journey would take – teaching obligations, administrative duties, family matters, and a global pandemic threw wrinkles into our timeline; however, the delays allowed us to incorporate new research into our writing as well as reflections on how the role of outdoor spaces has evolved in recent years. Along with building upon years of research, we also offer ideas and interpretations as a starting point for continued discussion and future research. We do not claim to share all the relevant research in this book or to hold all the answers about people and environment interactions. We do intend for this book to serve as a starting point for classroom and office discussions, to encourage new perspectives on the meaning of places and how they function for different people, and to promote new questions and research directions.

The book has four main sections – theory and research on human–environment relations (Chapters 1 and 2), understanding communities and people (Chapters 3–6), design applications (Chapters 7–9), and looking ahead (Chapter 10). The chapters are organized and suitable for classroom delivery with each warranting one or more lectures; however, they can also be read independently or consulted for information on specific topics. With most chapters, we have included potential exercises or projects to illustrate the concepts presented and to give readers an opportunity to experiment with the concepts in real-world situations. Students, instructors, and practitioners are also encouraged to develop their own exercises to apply the information learned. In addition, we encourage readers to pursue their own research to confirm, dispute, or contribute to the existing body of human and social factors research. Most of all, we hope that seasoned and aspiring designers will find value in applying this knowledge to the places that they help to create, preserve, and protect.

DOI: 10.4324/9781315100036-1

We have used the terms human–environment and people–environment interchangeably and have not drawn distinctions between them. We also use both social and human factors to describe the focus of this work. While arguments could be made that social factors relate to larger social groups or communities and their interactions and human factors relate to individual experiences and preferences, we have not addressed those differences here. Our focus is intended to encompass both approaches with specific attention to how these factors influence the physical landscape and its design. For those readers unfamiliar with human–environment studies, we have italicized some of the key terms and included definitions within the text. An index is also provided so that readers can easily locate multiple mentions of concepts.

The first two chapters provide theoretical and societal context with particular attention to design relevance. In Chapter 1, "Human Factors in Context," we use Bronfenbrenner's socio-ecological model as a framework for acknowledging and examining human–environment relations at all scales. Like the landscape architect's professional expertise, our focus is not limited to site design but includes intimate and individualized environments as well as larger scale communities and regions. Building upon Bronfenbrenner's original diagram of nested circles, we strive to illustrate the realms in which designers can and should consider human–environment relations (see cover drawing and Figure 0.1) Instead of neatly defined boundaries between these spheres, we see a fluid movement of people between one setting and the next. In addition, we include various environmental elements such as nature, agriculture, transportation routes, and other land uses. While not reflective of all communities, the drawing is offered as a framing for understanding where these interactions occur. The first chapter continues with a reflection on societal influences on user perceptions and design priorities. Chapter 2, "People–Place Relationships," is an overview of various theories and research focused on human–environment relationships. In general, the chapter progresses from the innermost circle of Bronfenbrenner's model to the outer or community sphere. Topics covered include personal space, territoriality, crowding and privacy, affordances, health and wellbeing, place attachment, safety and security, and wayfinding. For each topic, a brief introduction, key findings, and applications to design are provided.

The following four chapters focus on various populations and the research relevant to their use and experience of outdoor environments. Chapter 3, "People and Culture," sets the stage by providing an overview of the influence of culture on the physical form of places and the artifacts within them as well as why understanding culture is important to the creation of contemporary places. Instead of focusing on the specific uses or items that may or may not be found in certain places, we focus on ways to examine, question, and understand people's roles in shaping a place, with focused attention to how designers can develop cultural competency. Chapter 4, "The Life-Cycle Stage and Place," provides examples of how a person's age or role in life influences their spatial needs. The environments of children, adolescents, adult workers, and older adults are discussed. Chapter 5, "A Spirit of Inclusion," focuses on how designers can create places that welcome people with different abilities and ages, and from diverse backgrounds and economic classes. In addition, a brief history of accessibility requirements, guidelines, and resources are provided. The last chapter in this section, Chapter 6, "Gender and Place," introduces the reader to various ways in which gender and gender identity have shaped environments and how they can influence a person's use or perception of a place. We provide contemporary context for this discussion and draw upon both historical and more current studies.

FIGURE 0.1 An illustration of Bronfenbrenner's socio-ecological model in the landscape. Image credit: Patsy Eubanks Owens and Yiwei Huang.

The third section includes three chapters focusing on including human–environment considerations in the design process and the design. Chapter 7, "Visualizing People and Behavior," presents ways that the designer can document and convey human factors information graphically. Methods that can be used during various design stages and for different project scales are described and include reading the landscape, behavior observations, participatory mapping, photography, guided walks, case studies, and digital tools. Chapter 8, "Engaging People in the Process," provides ideas and techniques for gathering information and ideas, as well as building community ownership for a place once the designer has left and the project has been built. Our premise is that engaging people is more than holding a meeting and sharing alternatives. This chapter provides a brief review of the history of community participation in design and discusses strategies that can be incorporated from site analysis to implementation. The case studies in Chapter 9 illustrate how the research, theories, and practice can be integrated into the design process. Four case studies were selected to illustrate different types of people-focused designs and design processes. We looked at projects that have received recognition for their focus on people rather than traditional award-winning criteria such as aesthetics. We have included more recent projects and others that have a long-standing record of use and love by their community.

The last chapter, "People and Change," is offered as a starting point as much as a conclusion. Some recent influences on the shape of the physical landscape and how people use it are discussed and shared as examples of how place design is continually evolving. While not a comprehensive examination of these influences or any number of other innovations, adaptations, or advances, we intend for these ideas to spur discussion among aspiring and established practitioners. Designers are continually challenged by shifts in activities and interests of populations and by the advent of new design tools and technologies. The consideration of human factors in the design of outdoor environments is essential for creating relevant and meaningful places. Within that context, designers can and should lead the future shape of our physical landscapes.

– Patsy Eubanks Owens

SECTION I: THEORY AND RESEARCH ON HUMAN–ENVIRONMENT RELATIONS

1
HUMAN FACTORS IN CONTEXT

This chapter introduces and defines the concept of human factors in design with particular attention given to the social, psychological, and cultural dimensions of the built environment. Why human factors are a necessary consideration when designing outdoor environments is addressed as well as how the inclusion of person-centric criteria can create more sustainable and supportive environments. Next, the chapter situates human factor considerations into the various phases of the design process – inventory, analysis, design development, and design implementation – as well as some of the societal contexts that currently influence design and planning decisions. This discussion includes a review of how demographic shifts, family structures, technology advances, and climate change have altered the practice and priorities of these professions. In closing, the reader is challenged to understand their own landscape values and how those values inform their design decisions. The intention is to make these influences known in an effort to prepare designers to be more sympathetic to and understanding of the desires of others.

WHAT ARE HUMAN FACTORS IN DESIGN?

For the purposes of this book, human factors in design are framed as a range of human and environment interactions and influences. These interactions and influences occur in both directions: The environment influences a range of human outcomes such as behavior, emotional response, and social interactions; likewise, humans influence the physical environment. The influence of place design on activities that occur in a space, the emotional implications of these interactions, and the role of culture in the activities and visual characteristics of a space are a few examples of why understanding the implications of human–environment relations is critical for designers.

The terms *human factors* and *human–environment relations* describe work that focuses on the human experience of place and the human dimensions of environments as they relate to design and their implications for design professions. These terms are intended to capture the broad range of research and practice in this area. Human factors in this text are intended to be inclusive. Research and applications related to social, psychological, cultural, or other factors fall under this umbrella. Likewise, the interplay between people and the physical environment in all of its many forms is of concern to designers. While these terms provide a broad umbrella for the design underpinnings discussed in this book, other terms such as "environment-behavior" are used here, and by other scholars and practitioners, to describe this work (for more examples, see Devlin, 2018). Stokols and Altman (1987) define environment–behavior study as the examination of the mutual relations between the socio-physical environment at all scales and human behavior at all levels of analysis, and the utilization of knowledge thus gained in improving the quality of life through better informed environmental policy, planning, and design. Such study focuses on "the interdependence of social and physical environmental systems and explicitly includes both environmental and human factors" (p. 1360). Acknowledging this human–environment relationship occurs at various scales, Bronfenbrenner's socio-ecological model (1977) provides a useful framework for understanding where these interactions occur (see Figure 1.1). In the following chapters, human–environment influences are discussed at these various scales ranging from the individual to the community level. These influences have internal and external origins as well as internal and external manifestations. For example, individuals seek privacy, but so too do couples and even groups. An internal manifestation may be that an individual needs privacy in order to mentally "put things in order," while an external manifestation may be a group claiming a space through their behavior. Using the socio-ecological model provides a basis for the designer to both evaluate existing built environments regarding the influences on individuals and groups, as well as a scaffold for proposing design improvements.

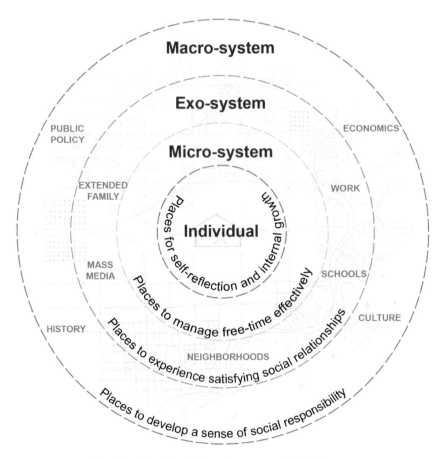

FIGURE 1.1 A socio-ecological model. Adapted from Eisenmann et al. (2008).

The study of human–environment relationships has its roots in multiple disciplines. Notably, psychologists researching animal behavior have informed much of the understanding of human behavior. In particular, experimental psychologists have focused on the relationships between the environment and behavior for decades (see, e.g., Stokols, 1977). While this research and its disciplinary foundations are discussed in the next chapter, understanding the early influences of this research on design professions is useful here. The first gathering of multidisciplinary researchers concerned with environment–behavior relationships occurred in June 1969, convened by architect Henry Sanoff, a North Carolina State University professor emeritus (Wener, 2008). This first meeting of the Environmental Design Research Association (EDRA) spurred ongoing collaborations between academics and practitioners from disciplines such as environmental psychology, anthropology, sociology, architecture, landscape architecture, and planning. In Europe, like-minded individuals also began convening successful conferences around the same time and subsequently the sister organization, the International Association of People-Environment Studies, was founded in 1981 (IAPS, 2021). The overarching goal of these organizations and their members was, and continues to be, to "bridge the gap" between research and practice. Accomplishing this goal includes understanding how this perspective informs both the theories underlying human–environment research as well as the education of designers and planners, with the purpose of improving the quality of life for everyone. The early works of these scholars clearly recognize disparities between individuals with regard to access (in terms of proximity, affordability, and social acceptance) to supportive built environments. Thus, the field of human–environment studies has long aimed to consider and represent the needs of multiple populations. Currently, terms such as social justice and inclusion are used to describe the need for designing for populations that may not have the political capital to advocate for their concerns.

At first, designers applied knowledge uncovered by researchers from other disciplines to their professional work. Beginning in the late 1960s, it became more common for academics in professional programs such as architecture, urban design, landscape architecture, and planning to conduct their own research independently or in collaboration with others. The journal *Environment and Behavior* is published in cooperation with EDRA and is an excellent resource for locating some of these early studies as well as contemporary research. It was also around this time that these professional programs began to add courses or coursework on environment–behavior to their curricula. Currently, it is not unusual for these programs to include research faculty with expertise on human factors in design; however, the frequency of these faculty experts is not as common as many in this field believe is warranted. Along with advanced degrees in design disciplines, doctoral programs in Environmental Psychology, Geography, and other allied disciplines attract designers interested in environment-behavior research. The pursuit of the question, "how can knowledge of human behavior inform the places we create," continues to animate the work of such scholars, and the contents of this book.

WHY DO HUMAN FACTORS MATTER IN DESIGN?

Why merge the work of psychologists, sociologists, designers, and others? Just as the research of botanists and engineers contributes to better practices and products in landscape architecture and architecture writ large, research on people and cultures can positively inform design decisions. Psychologically supportive and culturally aware decisions will likely improve the places where people live, work, and play. For example, past and current research contributes to topics such as the significance of access to nature, safe routes to schools, and accessibility. In turn, these improved places lead to an increased quality of life. The premise of enhancing the quality of life is at the core of design professionals' work. For example, licensure for landscape architects in the United States includes a responsibility to protect the health, safety, and welfare of the public. Landscape architects should understand the human factor implications of this obligation to maintain and expand this role. Professionals create better products when they have a better understanding of how people use environments, why they use them, and the social and psychological impacts of these places on people.

In the film and accompanying book, *Social Life of Small Urban Space*, William Whyte captured the movements of people on the streets and plazas of New York City (1980), in order to learn how and why people use the places they do. Whyte suspected people would sit where there was sun – while often true, designers of public plazas often overlooked another finding, seemingly obvious: People will sit where there are places to sit (see Figure 1.2). This conclusion demonstrates how our built environments hold many other directives, benefits, miscues, and unaccommodating characteristics.

Landscape architecture and architecture education programs seek to ensure that graduating students have a command of design principles such as scale and balance, and design knowledge on topics such as history, construction material and techniques, and design process. An understanding of human–environment relations and how this informs the design process

FIGURE 1.2 People sit where there are places to sit as illustrated by this image from *Social Life of Small Urban Space* (Whyte, 1980).

and design products are just as necessary. Although it is impossible for all designers to fully understand everything about every community or every individual for whom they will design, research is presented here to inspire future designers to question what they do not know and what they need to know, in order to produce an appropriate and successful design.

Knowledge of human–environment relations also contributes to creating sustainable and resilient communities. In order to achieve social sustainability, designs must be responsive and appropriate to the communities in which they are located. Social sustainability requires that environments, whether created, improved, or protected, meet the needs and desires of those accessing these places; that is, these places need to be supportive both now and in the future. While the term sustainability has gained a great deal of attention both in the design professions and the public more generally since the mid-1990s, much of the focus has been on the environmental component of the sustainability quotient. Sustainability, however, also relies on addressing the social and economic components of design and planning decisions. Meadows (1998) states that "sustainable development is a social construct, referring to the long-term evolution of a hugely complex system – the human population and economy embedded within the eco-systems and biogeochemical flow of the planet" (p. 7). In addition, sustainability is forward-thinking: "sustainable development ... meet[s] the needs of the present without compromising the ability of future generations to meet their needs" (WCED, 1987, p. 54).

The sustainable and supportive quality of a place derives from an understanding of both the global and unique human–environment relations at play in a particular locale. Culture often informs how individuals and groups interact with their environments and will be discussed in more detail in Chapter 3. Likewise, individual characteristics can inform perceptions and activities (see Chapters 2, 4, and 6). Individuals contribute to producing a long-lasting design by building upon cultural context and the unique characteristics of a place. In addition, environments must be adaptable, either by individual users on a short-term basis or by the greater community for long-term purposes. Applying an understanding of human factors may make such adaptability more fluid or possible. For example, while urban sidewalks were originally designed to provide a safe place for people to walk, many have evolved to provide a place to rest, to gather with others, to sell goods, or to enjoy a cup of coffee. While designers cannot anticipate all the future iterations of a place, allowing for adaptations will contribute to a more sustainable environment.

SITUATING HUMAN FACTORS IN THE DESIGN PROCESS

Understanding when and how human and social factors need to be considered in the design process is important. While design processes vary by the individual, most designers employ some version of getting to know their project site and its context, developing (or interpreting a given) design program, generating design concepts and alternatives, and developing construction directives. Knowledge of human factors research should be applied throughout this design process and to the methods used in gathering and interpreting site-specific information (see Figure 1.3).

Having a basic understanding of human–environment relation principles informs analysis of a project site and its context. Along with examining a site for characteristics such as drainage

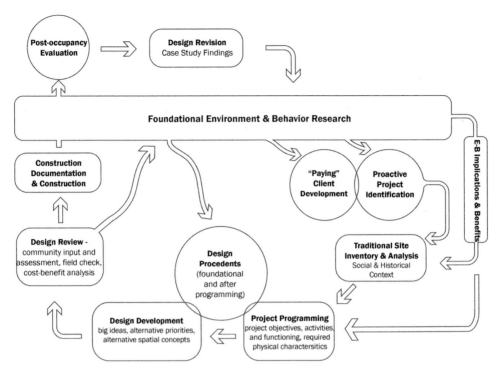

FIGURE 1.3 Incorporating human–environment research into the design process. Adapted from Zeisel (2006).

patterns, vegetation types, location, and health, and sun patterns, the designer must look for indications of existing and potential uses and identify missing anticipated uses. The concept of *affordances* can help designers interpret how a built environment might be used as compared to how the designer intends it to be used. For example, when a designer recommends locating a tree next to a playground, they might be thinking this would provide shade for parents to watch their children play. The children, however, may think the tree is great for climbing; a student may think it is a good place to sit to read; and someone else may be most interested in picking the tree's fruit. The place – in this instance the tree – presents differing affordances or possibilities for each park user. Affordances are explored in more detail in the next chapter.

Understanding affordances and designing for various experiences adds richness to places. A *design program* is a collection of experiences and opportunities that the designer intends to incorporate into a place design. Examining and understanding the population characteristics of a community can inform this design program. Even elements that at first seem straightforward may have unique needs for the local population. For example, community members may say that they want a basketball court. The city includes this on their list of program elements forwarded to the designer. What is not clear, however, is who will use this court and how. Is the court for a junior basketball program, for a nearby senior living community, or for a late-night basketball league? All of these potential scenarios place different demands on the design of the basketball court and adjacent areas. In addition to questioning elements proposed for a site, the designer should understand the context of the project. Are there more children in the neighborhood, or more elderly? Are certain activities not supported, that could be? Are there anticipated changes for the neighborhood population that might impact the design program?

The resulting design should anticipate and respond to both likely users and uses. Chapters 7 and 8 discuss approaches to informing design products such as observing, mapping, and soliciting input from future users.

Along with the site analysis and design generation phases, the design's construction may integrate and respond to local community values and skills. Local materials may contribute to both lower construction costs and a design that is reflective of and appropriate to the community. Unique cultural motifs and materials can be incorporated into features and construction methods. The gates and paving design at the Mexican Heritage Cultural Center in San Jose, California, provide one example (see Figure 1.4). The design is based on the Mexican folk art of *papel picado* and was proposed by a local artist, Victor Mario Zaballa, to celebrate the heritage of many nearby residents. Projects such as this bring local relevance to the design. Likewise, incorporating local expertise into design decisions and implementation is a launching point for building place attachment and symbolic ownership, two people-environment concepts that will be discussed in the next chapter.

SITUATING HUMAN FACTORS IN THE SOCIETAL CONTEXT

The societal context in which design occurs changes constantly, and designers need to be aware of how these changes might impact the places in which they work and that they create. As of this writing, the COVID-19 pandemic of 2019–2021 as well as the social justice protests prompted by the killing of George Floyd in May 2020 (and many other persons of color previously) had, and continue to have, profound impacts on how public places are used and modified. During the COVID-19 pandemic, more people began to use trails, sidewalks, parks, and other outdoor amenities close to home as they looked for recreation and escape while working from home. They also used city streets, plazas, and parks to voice their frustration and aspirations for social justice reform. Restaurants and other businesses created innovative ways for people to dine outdoors or wait in line while safely keeping their distance from others. Cities rethought expanses of lawn to help users separate themselves from others, and quickly reclaimed underused streets for pedestrians, runners, bicyclists, diners, and notably, as a statement of support for protesters such as the designation of the Black Lives Matter plaza in Washington, DC. While the influence of these two simultaneous events warrants a greater examination than provided here, together they illustrate the importance of understanding the societal context of design decisions. The following paragraphs provide a snapshot of some of the current influences that will likely impact design and planning decisions now and in the coming years. The topics discussed here include demographic shifts, family structure changes, technological advances, and climate change implications. Other future projections relating to design are discussed in Chapter 10.

Demographic change

The population of the United States is changing. In particular, age distributions among the population have shifted and the racial composition has become more diverse. As baby-boomers have aged, the median age of the population is increasing; that is, there are more older residents now than in earlier decades (U.S. Census, 2019). Currently, designers are catching up to the needs of this age group as they approach their retirement years with different

FIGURE 1.4 Gates and paving design at the Mexican Heritage Cultural Center in San Jose, CA, by artist Victor Mario Zaballa. Image credit: Juliet Flower MacCannell.

expectations from previous senior cohorts. For example, many current seniors lead a more active lifestyle than prior generations. They are likely to want multiple and varied options for their recreational pursuits. Likewise, senior housing options of the past might not meet the demands of the new cohort. Those entering retirement currently may wish to remain in their current homes longer, may wish to move closer to children or grandchildren, or may want to move to an urban area with more amenities. It is a critical responsibility of designers to understand these demographic age projections (in terms of both numbers and interests) in order to appropriately plan for these changes. In addition, US demographics in respect to racial and ethnic composition have changed significantly in the last few decades and are projected to continue to remake communities. While urban areas have typically had more ethnically and racially diverse populations, immigrant settlement into the suburbs increased in the 1990s and is now the norm (Singer, 2013). The addition of these new residents has been welcomed by some areas as they offset declining populations, while other locations struggle with how to accommodate and support these populations while preserving the sense of community held by long-time residents.

Family structure

Family structures and composition in the United States have been changing rapidly since the mid-20th century. Though frequently depicted in the television shows of the 1950s and 1960s, the nuclear family of a dad, stay-at-home mom, and children has decreased in recent decades (see Figure 1.5). While 87% of children lived in a two-parent household in 1960, only 62% are in this type of family arrangement today (Pew, 2015). Today, one-fourth of children in the United States now live with a single parent. In addition, the percentages of children growing up in single-parent households vary significantly between racial and ethnic groups. For example, 54% of black children live with a single parent. Another shift in family structure that has occurred over the last half-century is the addition of women to the workforce. While less than half of mothers worked in 1975, about three-fourths of all mothers currently work full time today. These changes impact the built environment in many regards. For example, when an adult is not around to provide supervision, families are less likely to let their children roam the neighborhood and play with friends after school. Additionally, work environments are adapting to the needs and desires of the female workforce. It is crucial to remember, however, that these types of family structure changes are not static. As noted in the Pew Research Center report, the characteristics of families are very fluid and there is no longer a dominant family structure. These shifts in families, along with more companies allowing or encouraging their employees to work from home, will alter the activities and users of residential neighborhoods. Perhaps as more adults start working from home, for instance, more children will be allowed to explore their neighborhoods.

Technology

Technological advances over the past two decades have altered how we use our free time, find our way through unfamiliar places, communicate with others, and learn about our environments. Computers and cellphones are found in most, if not all, households in the United States (Pew Research Center, 2021). Connectivity options for and reliability of these devices have improved. Wi-Fi and broadband networks allow improved Internet connections away from home, school, or the office. These devices have altered the engagement of people with

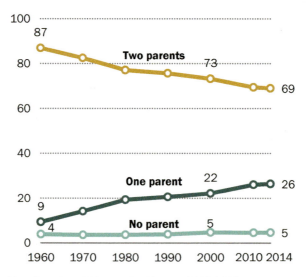

FIGURE 1.5 The two-parent household in decline in the United States (Pew Research Center, 2015).

the built environment in prolific ways, influencing how we connect with others, how we spend our time, how we get around, and how we perceive (and record) the visual quality of a place.

Whether through Facebook, text messages, or any one of numerous other digital communication methods, technology has altered how people correspond with one another. Eighty-four percent of teenagers say that they use their phones to connect with other people (Schaeffer, 2019). Interestingly, those youth who are likely to socialize with friends on their phones are also likely to do so in person (Jiang, 2018). Many adults (70%) stay in contact with others through Facebook and other social media applications such as YouTube, Instagram, and Pinterest (Perrin & Anderson, 2019). These technologies make it possible for people to connect with family members or friends, or others with similar interests no matter where they live. Social media has also made the connections with people with shared political or social agendas possible. In a number of cases, such as the Arab Spring, #MeToo, and #BlackLivesMatter movements, virtual connections prompted widespread activism, which moves between the digital and the physical public realm.

Computers and cellphones have also influenced how people spend their free time. In addition to using these technologies for communications, many people use these devices for other entertainment purposes. Access to games, movies, shopping, and more are limitless online. This access means that a person can pursue these activities at home and may no longer need to venture into the public realm. The long-term implications for this change in use patterns need to be considered when creating places. For example, should outdoor places support online and computer-based activities? In addition, the COVID-19 pandemic has likely increased the comfort for some individuals of engaging in these and other online activities (such as remote learning), as their wariness toward engaging in physical, real-time interactions increased. Conversely, staying at home for an extended period may reinforce the need to have face-to-face interactions at work and school, and highlight the need for experiences in nature and the outdoors.

Furthermore, technological advances have dramatically altered map-making and map-reading. While the basic principle of representing a landscape through visual means still applies, the methods of how maps are created, delivered, and interpreted are vastly different from less than two decades ago. (Google Maps was launched in February 2005.) Created through satellite imagery and aerial photography, today's digital maps are extremely accurate and easily updated. Such maps are revised and annotated knowingly and unknowingly by users. For example, traffic accidents and driving times are adjusted in real time based on the movement of individual cell phones. While online mapping applications provide a wealth of information, they have also decreased the ability of individuals to read a map. Instead of orienting the map viewer with a north arrow pointed to the top of the screen (following the accepted orientation of maps in printed form), the map rotates to allow the user to follow along as the route changes. Instead of reading a static visual map, audio narration provides step-by-step guidance to a destination. This guidance, however, does little to help the user to understand the context of their trip – the river that is nearby, the small town just off the highway, or the National Forest up the road. This unfortunate lack of awareness and understanding of nearby geography is likely to have implications on populations' understanding and appreciation of the physical environment.

Lastly, technology has changed how we look at and record visual experiences of the world around us. With the advent of the digital camera and then the cell phone camera, many gained the ability to conveniently photograph and share anything and everything. Previously, taking a photograph prompted consideration of whether or not to waste precious film, or to pay for developing and printing. The ability to take digital photos has reduced many of those concerns; other than the original purchase of equipment, the photography process is nearly free, and the financial risk is minimal. This, in combination with social media platforms such as Instagram, has allowed and encouraged people to more widely experiment with photographing food, friends, themselves, and landscapes to share with anyone. This activity has also influenced how the photographer experiences places. When visiting a place, for instance, for some the pursuit of the perfect photograph for an online post is perhaps a higher priority than the experience of the visit itself. Public and private entities have aimed to satisfy this desire by creating photo-worthy settings (see Figure 1.6).

Climate change

Finally, climate change is predicted to have profound far-reaching impacts to physical and social environments. Designers must consider how their work might reduce the impacts of climate change and might need to adapt in the future. Along with altering plant, animal, and insect

FIGURE 1.6 The butterfly wings painting in Nashville is a popular Instagram photo spot. Artist and credit: Kelsey Montague.

habitats, expected shifts in temperature and precipitation will transform human habitats. Some communities have already been displaced by rising sea-water levels. In addition to the loss of individual homes, the history and culture of these communities will likely vanish. Typically, marginalized communities, due to race, ethnicity, age, or income, are expected to be the ones to experience the greatest displacement and loss from climate change (see, e.g., Chappell, 2018; Climate Central, 2019). In many instances, these communities live in less desirable and more vulnerable low-lying areas, with limited resources to plan for and counter projected losses.

In addition, climate change's impacts to human health, infrastructure, and livelihoods are expected to be significant. Along with immediate health threats generated through catastrophic weather events such as flooding and fires, it is expected that disease spread may increase, and new diseases may emerge. Public networks for transportation, energy, and communication are also at risk. Thoughtful planning may help to alleviate the extent of the interruption of those services or propose alternatives in case of disruption.

Understanding societal context is paramount to providing a responsive and appropriate design recommendation. The four topics discussed here are some examples of how societal changes influence the use and perception of environments. Much of this impact is clearly evident, such as the ubiquitous cellphone use in public spaces. Other impacts are less visible but widespread. For instance, many children now return home from school to an empty house. Instructed to go in and lock the door, they are cut off from their neighbors and nature. Instead, they find a new community online and recreation through a keyboard. Many older residents may not be interested in living in a dedicated senior community, or they may look for communities that cater to active individuals. Ethnic enclaves, historically found in major cities, are developing in suburban and rural locations as a response to a desire to bring up children in safe environments and to be part of a greater community; however, new residents are not being fully integrated into many long-established and tight-knit communities. Societal context contributes valuable information to design decisions. Whether it provides vital information on existing residents, the site, the activities likely to be engaged in at the project location (now or in the future), or who to involve in the decision-making process, context is critical.

UNDERSTANDING LANDSCAPE VALUES

As a precursor to understanding the human factors associated with a specific community or project site, the designer should take an assessment of their personal values and how they might influence their understanding of a place or their design recommendations. An individual's values influence how they perceive, use, and feel about places. For example, a person's home can usually tell you a great deal about the person's values. Even when taking into consideration variations in available funds, decisions about a home's location, architectural style, landscape style, and even the paint color can tell you about the owners. Each designer is influenced by their own experiences and should actively examine and consider their own biases in this regard. Landscape values are formed over a person's lifetime; they may change, but they are often based on previous experiences as well as familial and cultural settings. Evidence has shown that a designer's values are often misaligned with those of non-designer populations (Hester, 1984b). It is therefore imperative that aspiring designers explore their own values and their biases early in their education and careers.

Value formation

An individual's landscape values are formed over time through a number of influences. Early on, an individual's values are most likely influenced by their family and the culture in which they are raised. A person growing up in a densely populated city has very different expectations of their surrounding environment than does someone growing up on a farm. Likewise, these experiences may have either a positive or a negative influence on that individual's values. Someone growing up in the city may not feel comfortable in the quiet of the countryside. Conversely, a young girl growing up in a rural community may have a dream of living in a home with a sidewalk out front one day. This dream is inspired more by what was not present in the early environment than what was. Particular cultural settings can also influence how an individual perceives and values place. Certain cultures may assign different values to similar landscapes or environments. For example, residents of one community may appreciate the adjacent forest land because of its beauty and recreational value, while those in another community may appreciate the income harvesting this timber provides to their family. Likewise, cultures associated with various countries and ethnicities use and value places in differing ways. Chapter 3 will provide more information on how culture shapes human–behavior interactions.

Subcultures, such as gender and age, can also play a role in someone's value of a place. A classic study by Rapoport (1969) examined men's and women's domains in East London. These realms consisted of the places, people, and activities that were most significant in each person's life. Rapoport found that even though they had similar backgrounds, experiences, and economic classes, and lived in the same community, these men and women had very different perceptions of what comprised their personal environments. For the women, the most meaningful domain was the home, and also extended to the shops she visited, her daughters, and the street. For the men, the home dwelling was not significant. The focus of their lives was work, the pub, and football. Similarly, age can influence which landscapes and associated activities are valued more or less. Children are more inclined to value places where they can explore, adolescents where they can get together with their friends, and young adults where they can engage in a particular activity. Chapter 4 explores more of the unique landscape value characteristics associated with age.

Life experiences and one's educational background also influence an individual's landscape values (see Figure 1.7). Annual visits to one's grandparents, or a special vacation to a faraway place, may hold lasting memories of a specific landscape or place characteristics for a person. Whether this memory is something particular – like the smell of the Rose of Sharon tree at a grandparents' home – or more general – like the fun associated with playing in the grass – designers may find themselves trying to recreate these memories in the places they design. Past educational opportunities also inform values. Someone who has learned about the story of Valley Forge, a military encampment during the Revolutionary War, may during their visit appreciate the

FIGURE 1.7 The places people value are influenced by their interests and experiences. The place on the left might be valued by a fly-fisher while a motorcyclist would likely prefer the place on the right. Images are from an unpublished research project examining public values of forest lands.

rolling fields and small cabins more than someone who merely sees the current landscape. Someone who has studied the habitat of certain animals or plants may appreciate land set aside as a reserve, versus someone who just sees the land as untamed vegetation. Recent attention in school curricula to environmental topics such as climate change, water conservation, and recycling makes a notable impact on the values youth assign to the protection and restoration of places (Heft & Chawla, 2005).

Uncovering landscape values

As noted previously, understanding one's landscape values is essential for a designer. This understanding allows the designer to be aware of intentional and unintentional influences on their design decisions. In addition, understanding the values of those who will be using a place is vital in order to respect and reflect those values in the design. Numerous methods exist to uncover the values of the designer or the resident, including interviews and behavior observations. Later chapters feature these techniques and others to understand values and behavior; a brief focus here is on the method of environmental autobiography.

Clare Cooper Marcus, a professor at University of California, Berkeley, in the College of Environmental Design, designed an assignment in the 1970s for her landscape architecture and architecture students to explore their personal environmental experiences (2014). The students began by recalling and writing about a favorite childhood place, followed by other places that still hold meaning for them. This environmental autobiography assignment provided insight into the types of places that were meaningful during their childhoods, and also served to generate discussion around the implications of such places for broader society (see Figure 1.8). Around the same time, other design faculty used similar techniques to elicit students to remember significant environments in their lives (e.g., Helphand, 1979; Horwitz & Klein, 1978; Rivlin, 1978). They and others shared their experiences at academic conferences, and over the past four decades, numerous educators have adopted and adapted the technique.

The environmental autobiography has also been used to gather information about clients' past environments and experiences (e.g., Israel, 2003; Marcus, 1995). Others have employed the

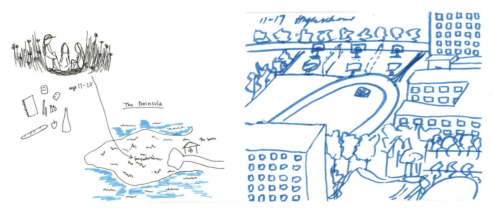

FIGURE 1.8 Drawings by adults recalling places important to them during their teenage years. One recalled spending time with friends in a secluded place and another remembered basketball courts and green space close to their home. Images are from an unpublished workshop.

technique to increase the empathy of adults for the needs of children (Hester, 1979). Still others have used it to explore the environmental influences of famous architects (Israel, 2003). While not explicitly explored by Marcus in her retrospective article, the environmental autobiography is a beneficial method for designers to become more sympathetic to the values of their clients. Recalling influential past environments and what made those places important provides direct information about clients' preferences for certain types of places or place characteristics. With this knowledge, the designer can then knowingly include or eliminate those qualities from the designs they propose.

Value-based criteria

Landscape architecture professor Randy Hester developed a user-needs checklist that identifies the criteria people use to determine whether or not a place meets their needs (Hester, 1984b). This list is based on the criteria frequently used and taught in design programs, as well as the criteria used by someone deciding which park, plaza, or other open space to visit (see Table 1.1). Hester tested these criteria with two groups – park users and designers. He found significant differences in how these groups prioritized these criteria.

Hester's user-needs checklist provides a comprehensive summary of the types of criteria people use when deciding whether or not a location is appropriate for their desired activity. While it cannot be assumed that all potential visitors to a place will have the same priorities, the list does provide designers with a general understanding of which criteria are considered during the decision process. Future research might tease out differences in criteria between age groups, genders, cultural groups, or locations, but at this time, those differences, if there are any, are not known. Hester's study does, however, provide insightful information on the differences between the designer and the non-designer. While visitors to a site might be concerned with who else will be there, how convenient it is to get to, and whether or not it will cost anything, the designer is likely to focus on how the place looks and what activity spaces are included in the design. These differences in priorities illustrate the possible, if not frequent, misalignment between what people want and what they get as it relates to the outdoor environment.

So why does this difference between what the designer and the non-designer prioritize matter in determining whether a place meets their needs? These differences illustrate a difference in values between the designer (who will be making decisions about what should be included in a design, how it will function, and what it will look like) and the values of the people wanting to use the place. Knowingly or not, the designer makes decisions that reflect how they think others should behave in a place and how they will feel in a place. For example, a design might encourage someone to stop and enjoy a view by providing seating directed at an overlook, or it might discourage stopping by not providing any seating or shade. These designer-imposed values dictate the behavior of others. Likewise, the designer's aesthetic preferences typically guide decisions relating to design style, materials, and composition.

Zeisel (1974) proposed that three principles can guide design decisions: Freedom, need, and fit. *Freedom* is the idea that the physical environment should maximize the opportunity of individuals to decide how to use or manipulate a space. Allowing people to move chairs and tables in public plazas meets this principle. *Need* is more than what the users say they need or want but is instead an understanding of how a place should function to meet their behaviors and accompanying implications. For example, individuals who will stop and sit on a bench to

TABLE 1.1 Hester's user-needs checklist

Concepts	General users' rank	Designers' rank
☐ **People to do activity with or without**	1	6
with – to interact, friends, to watch without – to get away, seek privacy, avoid overcrowding		
☐ **Appropriate activity settings**	2	1
the location – how close to houses, to the woods site characteristics – paths, open, wooded		
☐ **Relatedness through interaction with nature**	3	4
physical aspects – to feed the ducks, to smell the flowers psychological aspects – to get yourself together, to put the world in perspective		
☐ **Safety**	4	3
physical safety – location, barriers, signs, lighting, maintenance social safety – supervised, formal and informal activities		
☐ **Aesthetic appeal**	5	2
style, visual unity, cleanliness		
☐ **Psychological comfort**	6	7
emotional release, social reinforcement, balance between old and new choices		
☐ **Symbolic ownership**	7	9
frequency of use, participation in acquisition or design, legal ownership is ambiguous, personalized by use, person lives close by		
☐ **Physical comfort**	8	5
site factors – weather, temp erature, pollution facilities – transportation, drinking fountains, benches		
☐ **Convenience**	9	8
distance from home, functional distance		
☐ **Policy on use**	10	12
enabling or restrictive		
☐ **Cost to use**	11	–
admission and transportation		
☐ **Cost of construction**	–	10
☐ **Definition of space**	–	11
☐ **Construction methods**	–	13

Source: Adapted from Hester (1984b).

have their lunch are also likely to need a place to dispose of their litter. Lastly, Zeisel describes *fit* as the condition of matching the behavioral and perceptual opportunities provided by a place with the needs of the user. This fit is beyond the functional needs, and should respond to behavioral, symbolic, and aesthetic desires as well. While the lay person and the hiring public agency or private organization relies on and seeks out the designer's professional knowledge in these areas, the personal preferences of those who will be using the place are frequently not considered. It is imperative that the design acknowledge and integrate the values of the potential users to create a place that will fit the needs and desires of both paying and non-paying clients, to hopefully become a place with greater meaning.

POTENTIAL EXERCISES AND PROJECT

An indoor exercise
Construct your own environmental autobiography

Your early experiences, both positive and negative, likely shaped your landscape values and influenced how you perceive environments. As described previously, your environmental autobiography can help you, as a future designer, understand why certain places from your past hold significance for you. Having this understanding will make you a better designer. You will become more aware of the types of places and the specific characteristics of places that are important to you. You can then transfer this knowledge into the places you create and increase your awareness of how and when you might be imposing your preferences on others. This in-class exercise is intended as a starting point to exploring your personal environmental background. The in-class exercise may be followed by a formal recording and analysis of places throughout your life. As discussed previously, this exercise is based upon the environmental autobiography that Claire Cooper Marcus (2014) developed for her beginning landscape architecture and architecture students.

Materials and setting needed:

Drawing paper
Crayons or colored markers
Writing surface
A quiet place to reflect

Steps:

Close your eyes and think back to a place that was significant to you when you were growing up. Let's begin with a place from the time you were between 6 and 10 years old. The place you recall can be any kind of place: A place you went to every day or a place that you only visited once; a place with other people or not; a place close to home or far away.

1. Once you recall a place, keep your eyes closed and think about the place. What did it look like? What did you do there? What sounds do you hear and what odors do you smell? What does being in this place mean to you?
2. After you feel like you have a good recollection of the place, open your eyes. Using the paper and crayons or markers, draw this place. How you represent this place does not matter; you

can sketch all or part of the place, draw a bird's-eye view or something more abstract. What is important is that you record your memory of the place on the piece of paper.
3. Once everyone in the class completes their drawings, pin them on a wall or spread them on a table so that everyone can see. Ask for volunteers to talk about these places and why they were meaningful to them.
4. Discuss with the class any characteristics that these places had in common and those that differed. For example, did students identify places with nature or were the places more urban, or did they recall places where they could be with their friends or places where they could be alone?
5. Once everyone who wants to share has had an opportunity, each student should think about if and how this past environment influenced their decision to study design. Also, think about and discuss how this past experience has influenced any design decisions they have made; that is, have you been trying to recreate this place or an experience you had in this place in your design work?

After class:

Outside of class, either on your own or under the guidance of your instructor, repeat this exercise for other places that hold significance for you. It is helpful to think about these places in relation to different periods in your life. What places were meaningful to you when you were a small child, a teenager, or now when you are in college? Write a story or description to go along with each of these places as well as the one you recalled during class. This is *your* environmental history so share it how you think is best.

After you have completed remembering and recording the places that have been significant to you, think about what your ideal place would look like and what you could do there. In a drawing and in writing, record the characteristics of this ideal place that are critical for you. Write a reflection on how your past experiences and places inform who you are as a designer.

An outdoor exercise

Subjective appraisal. Conducting a subjective appraisal will allow you to tap into your own senses to learn about a place. Landscape architecture programs typically instruct students how to conduct an objective site analysis. This exercise guides you to explore a site subjectively and by using your senses. Before beginning, you will need to determine the site to be examined. This may be a site assigned by your class instructor or one that you have selected.

Materials needed:

Sketchbook
Pencil

Steps:

1. You should go to your site alone. When you first arrive at the site, you should find a place to sit where you are comfortable. Do not engage in any conversations, draw, or take notes. Spend a few minutes relaxing and just "being" in the place.

2. Take a moment to think about each of your senses and then record what you are experiencing through each of your senses. There is no right way to record this data – you may develop your own method for doing this. Two options you can consider are to write a poem or maybe a story as if this place could speak ("I smell like summer." or "I love having the children run and laugh on me"). You should spend about five minutes on each sense. The following questions are suggestions to get you started.
    a. *Sight*: What can you see? What attracts your attention? Is your view enclosed or open? What seems to be the mood of the people in the space? Record your feelings about what you see. Do the sights make you happy or sad? Is the space relaxing, exciting, uncomfortable, etc.?
    b. *Hearing*: With your eyes closed, what do you hear? Are the sounds from inside the space or outside the space? Are they pleasing or irritating?
    c. *Touch*: Touch the space with your hands and body. What textures, temperatures, or qualities do you discover? Can you feel air movement or temperature changes?
    d. *Smell and Taste*: Close your eyes and smell. Does it smell fresh, stuffy, old, or new? Are there things to taste, such as items from a nearby food cart?

Back in class:

If more than one student conducts a subjective appraisal at the same location, their experiences should be shared. What was similar and what was different about the perceptions of those conducting the appraisals? What information gained from the appraisal can be applied to design recommendations? What are other ways in which this information might be used? For example, the subjective appraisal could be used to introduce others to the site during a community meeting.

A potential project

Conduct an evaluation of a student housing site. Select an on-campus housing area to evaluate. Applying Hester's user-needs criteria described above, either in teams or individually, you should visit the location and conduct an assessment of the outdoor places at this housing site. Which of the user-needs criteria are most important to this student team in determining if this location is a successful design?

Next, you should imagine that you live in this location and answer the questions – What is the thing I like most about living here? "Are any of the characteristics I identified in my initial assessment mentioned in response to this question?"

Why do you think these differences exist? How could a designer gain this understanding before developing a design? Alternatively, you can ask current residents these questions.

Based on what you learned, what was important to the residents and how does that compare to what you think the designer was trying to achieve? Develop a list of recommended changes or prepare a revised design.

2
PEOPLE–PLACE RELATIONSHIPS

In order to understand how human factors influence the use of physical environments and how those factors might inform the places designers create, this chapter provides a theoretical foundation drawing upon research from many disciplines, including environmental psychology, anthropology, and sociology. The role of the environment on topics such as individual, group, and community perceptions; activities and use patterns; and well-being is examined. Understanding these basic principles is key to creating environments that allow humans the ability to feel comfortable in, build attachment to, or establish long-lasting meaning in a place.

Each of these subjects warrants an entire book – indeed, numerous books and articles have been written on these topics. For each issue discussed, an overview of the literature is discussed, key findings particularly relevant for landscape architects and other designers are highlighted, and how each theoretical background can be applied to the creation of outdoor environments is provided.

PROXEMICS AND PERSONAL SPACE

Background

In the 1960s, the anthropologist Edward T. Hall coined the term *proxemics* (1990a) to describe interrelated theories of and observations on how people use space, specifically how it reflects an individual's or group's culture. While Chapter 3 focuses on cultural influences and implications for outdoor spaces, Hall's work provides an important foundation for understanding human–environment relationships. Proxemic research challenges the notion that all people will respond (physically or emotionally) in the same manner to similar situations, while also identifying common human reactions and expectations. As noted by Hall, these behaviors are rooted in biology and physiology.

An understanding of both *personal space* and *territoriality* first came about by studying animals (e.g., Allee, 1938; Hediger, 1955; Howard, 1920). In the 1960s and 1970s, researchers began asking if these same theories also applied to humans. This early work established the foundations of current thinking. Hall (1990a) described four distances related to interactions among the same species: intimate, personal, social, and public (see Figure 2.1). The factors that influence the use of each zone are described under key findings.

DOI: 10.4324/9781315100036-4

Intimate <18"

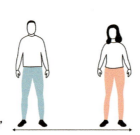
Personal 18" - 4'

Social 4' - 12'

Public >12'

FIGURE 2.1 Interpersonal distances. Adapted from Hall (1990a).

These interpersonal distances or zones are not fixed in a geographical location (Sorokowska et al., 2017). Instead, they move with individuals and groups. Environmental psychologist Sommer (1969) described *personal space* as the distance that an organism typically places between itself and other organisms. As a term commonly used by the general public, everyone understands what it means to have someone "get into their personal space." Designers, however, need to have better awareness of what this actually means, how personal space may differ for each individual, and how understanding the dynamics of interpersonal relationships influences design decisions. Everyone carries around their own personal space bubble. That bubble is not static – for instance, it changes as a person gets older or as they change environments.

Nonconformance to interpersonal distances can be perceived as a threat to others, cause anxiety, or, at a minimum, be seen as awkward and inappropriate (Perry, Nichiporuk, & Knight, 2016). In contrast, the use of appropriate distances leads to feelings of comfort and safety (Kaitz, Gar-Haim, Lehrer, & Grossman, 2004). Individuals who perceive a violation of interpersonal distance norms may respond in several ways. They may attempt to adjust the distance by changing their own positioning, confront or ask the violators to change their position, or flee the situation.

Key findings

Our understanding of proxemics and specifically personal space relates to the characteristics of individuals, the relationships between the individuals, and the settings in which the interactions occur.

An individual's characteristics impact the size of their personal space as well as how others interpret that space. Qualities such as age, gender, and cultural upbringing have been demonstrated to influence the size of the space a person carries with them. In addition, others have noted that external factors and experiences may make a person more or less comfortable with close physical contact (Perry et al., 2016). Therefore, the distances discussed here are not universal; rather, they are presented as a starting point for designers to consider when creating gathering places and furnishings.

Characteristics of individuals

Age. Studies have typically found that the size of an individual's space "bubble" varies with age and that age is a significant predictor of intimate and personal space distances. While there are periods in early childhood when a child might exhibit a fear of strangers and strong preference for their caregiver, research has found that younger individuals are more likely to get closer to and be comfortable with closer distances to others (Rands & Levinger, 1979). As a general observation, children often seem to not have a personal space bubble and do not recognize the interpersonal distances of others.

Gender. Early studies on interpersonal distances seemed to indicate that women have smaller personal space bubbles than men; however, later studies have challenged that notion. Recent research instead suggests that women's personal space appeared smaller because they are more frequently invaded and challenged. One study found that women generally prefer greater distances (Sorokowska et al., 2017). While further research is warranted to fully understand gender differences, including new research examining other gendered populations, respecting the likelihood of gendered variations is important.

Culture. Early research on proxemics indicates that variations exist between geographic locations and cultures. Early findings by Hall (1990b) noted that Latin American and

Mediterranean Arab populations preferred closer interpersonal distances while Americans and Europeans preferred greater distances. However, some studies have noted significant variation within Latin American countries (Shuter, 1976). Others have noted variations in interpersonal distances due to climate instead of culture (Sorokowska et al., 2017). Social distances were greater in colder climates even among people in the same country. Lastly, interpersonal distances transfer with individuals when they move and may persist for years. With a highly mobile global population, designers can expect to find people with different cultural backgrounds sharing outdoor spaces.

Other characteristics of individuals. Influences on interpersonal distances remain the subject of ongoing research. Physical characteristics of individuals, such as how they are dressed, their size, and even the props they carry, appear to influence the distances at which others feel comfortable or feel like they can intrude into the other person's personal space. In one study, the dress of an individual intruding into another's personal space to ask for donations influenced the likelihood that a person would positively respond by contributing to their charity (McElroy & Morrow, 1994). Individuals approached by a person in professional attire, as compared to casual clothes, donated more. Anecdotal experiences shared with the authors confirm similar patterns. One university faculty member, a petite woman, noticed the distances at which others would move out of her way depended upon whether she was in a dress and heels, or jeans and sneakers. The less formal her attire, the closer the approaching person would get before moving over. Another Black university colleague shared that he is more accepted and less likely to be questioned by strangers when walking if he is carrying his musical instrument or briefcase. Such variations warrant additional research.

Other considerations

Relationships and familiarity. Studies indicate that pre-existing relationships influence the size of comfortable distances. Distances tend to be closer between those with positive relationships and those with previous negative interactions prompt greater distances.

Type of setting or situation. The type of setting can signal appropriate behavior and influence the distances which individuals place between themselves and others. For example, expectations and acceptance of distances in a classroom are very different from that in a bar. Variations in noise and light levels, along with expected activities, impact accepted distances. High noise levels and low light levels will typically bring people closer together.

Marking and defending personal space. Understanding the level of comfort or discomfort someone experiences when a stranger sits behind them or next to them is particularly important when designing public spaces since there lies a high probability of strangers sitting in close proximity in these areas. Research findings have varied regarding whether personal space is a consistent distance to our sides and to our fronts and backs (Ashton & Shaw, 1980; Hayduk, 1983; Leventhal, Schanerman, & Matturro, 1978). For designers, this distinction can inform seating configurations such as providing options for users of a space to face away from those they do not know. People convey their comfort level with having others nearby through strategies such as claiming nearby space with personal items, holding up a book or newspaper, or simply turning one's back to the person (Sommer, 1969).

Application to design

Designers have the opportunity and responsibility to create places that provide comfortable and appropriate distances. Understanding the unconscious expectations people have for distances for certain activities will help the designer to decide how much space to leave for activities such as a public speech, outdoor instruction, or solo reflection. Along with space allocations and configurations, such knowledge can inform the layout and design of site furnishings, vegetation, and other design components.

Hall (1990a) describes two types of spaces, those that keep people apart (*sociofugal*) and those that bring people together (*sociopetal*) (see Table 2.1). Understanding these two basic principles is a good place to start for the designer. Neither type of space is better than the other, but each has a role to play in the creation of public places. As Hall notes, "what is desirable is flexibility and congruence between design and function so that there is a variety of spaces, and people can be involved or not, as the occasion and mood demand" (p. 100).

TABLE 2.1 Comparison of sociopetal and sociofugal spaces

		Characteristics	Examples
Sociopetal space	Washington Square, San Francisco, CA	Places that bring people together	Plaza, parks, sidewalks with cafes and other seating
Sociofugal space	Salesforce Park, San Francisco, CA	Places that discourage interaction between strangers	Linear arrangement of benches, separated seating areas

Image credit: Patsy Eubanks Owens.

Along with informing the configuration of outdoor spaces, these *sociopetal* and *sociofugal* principles can guide designers in the design and placement of site features. Research has typically shown that individuals sit face-to-face when in a competitive situation and next to one another when in cooperative settings (Sommer, 1965). Alternatively, research focused on leadership and group decision-making suggests that seating at right angles is the most conducive to productive and nonthreatening relationships. Therefore, seating at right angles might be a better choice for encouraging friendly conversations with others, while a linear bench with enough length to ensure comfortable distancing would be a better choice for someone desiring to sit alone.

In addition to understanding proxemics and the role it plays in how individuals locate themselves in relation to others, additional factors such as the level of lighting or shade, the positioning of seating relative to adjacent buildings or plantings, or the viewing position of the user can encourage or discourage a person's choice to use a space. These factors may also be dependent upon other conditions in that particular location. For example, walking along the sunny side of the street is likely preferred in a cooler climate as opposed to a hot one. Since many factors influence a user's preferences, the designer is challenged to provide multiple alternatives so that individuals can find the best location, whether to ensure their comfort and privacy or to pursue interactions with others. In addition, the advent of new uses necessitates a consideration of how they impact place design. For example, does ubiquitous cell phone use result in a need to create spaces where someone can temporarily claim a private place (and cause less annoyance to others) in our public spaces?

In addition to personal space, designers need to be cognizant of the distances associated with the other three zones: *intimate*, *social*, and *public*. Notably, social and public distances took on elevated meaning during the COVID-19 pandemic and concurrent Black Lives Matter protests beginning in 2019. While some people questioned the use of "social distancing" as the appropriate name for the six-foot distance between individuals recommended by public health officials during the pandemic, this naming is aligned with the definition Hall developed. Recommended distancing inspired creative applications in public spaces, such as the demarcation of social distance zones in parks or changing shopping line formations at farmers' markets and grocery stores (see Figures 2.2 and 2.3). In addition, public outcry against police violence

FIGURE 2.2 Social distance circles in Mission Dolores Park, San Francisco, CA. Image credit: Joey Parsons.

FIGURE 2.3 Social distancing at the Fort Mason farmers' market, San Francisco, CA. Image credit: Sarah Owens Izant.

and systemic racism and in support of the Black Lives Matter movement saw a reclaiming of public spaces for public demonstrations. Much like the Civil Rights and anti-Vietnam War protests of the 1960s, the use of public streets, plazas, and parks for protests and expressions of support provides an important lesson and example for how these public places provide a physical home for the democratic principle of free speech.

TERRITORIALITY

Background

The concept of *territoriality* is a close cousin of personal space. While personal space bubbles and other principles of proxemics are attached to the individual, territories are geographically fixed. We do not take them with us; instead, they are locations where you can leave and return to, and they can belong to more than one person.

As noted previously, early work on territoriality began with observing the behavior of birds, and was defined as "behavior by which an organism characteristically lays claim to an area and defends it against members of its own species" (Hall, 1990a, p. 7). Birds define their territories through song and feather displays. Humans define their territories through physical demarcations and may also use verbal signals to others. In animals, territoriality plays an important role in regulating population density and, therefore, access to the resources needed for survival (Hediger, 1955, as cited in Hall, 1990a, p. 8). For humans, territoriality is the means by which people can control and influence resources and other people (Sack, 1986). It is a spatial means to exert control and is a form of spatial behavior. Unlike in animals (where territoriality has a biological basis), territoriality in humans is more socially and geographically based. Populations (those controlling and being controlled), as well as place and time, influence human territories. Territories can change over time (short-term and long-term) and can take on new and varied meanings dependent upon the populations involved. Territories can also be temporary. For example, your "ownership" of your class studio desk goes with your course enrollment.

Territories can be very large, such as a country, or very small, like your studio desk. These territories exist where we live or where we spend time. Many researchers have discussed and defined territories in terms ranging from the most private to the most public (Porteous, 1977). Altman (1975) proposed three types of territories – primary, secondary, and public – which are used here to provide a framework for designers (see Table 2.2).

Key findings

Territories, like interpersonal distances, vary with age, gender, and culture. Children's territories are greatly influenced by their caregivers while older persons' territories may be impacted by changes in their mobility. Historically, men (both older and younger) have been given greater freedom to explore their surroundings while women have been relegated to closer to home. Although many US women left their families and farms behind to move to cities in the late 19th and early 20th centuries, the advent of suburban development during the 1950s and later consigned women back to the home (England, 1993). Cultural norms also present or deny opportunities for any number of population subgroups to engage in certain places. These conditions are important for designers to understand since, as discussed in Chapter 1, our opportunities to visit and explore places influence our landscape values.

Researchers in various locations have studied the territories of children (McKendrick, 2000). The extent of a child's territory typically grows as the child ages. In addition, some research indicates that boys are typically given a larger range to explore while girls stay closer to home; this is likely influenced more by the caregiver's control than the young person's desires

TABLE 2.2 Types of territories according to Altman (1975)

	Territory type	Characteristics	Examples	Methods of marking	Additional references
A private backyard	Primary	Places used every day exclusively by a specific individual or group and are clearly identified; others must be invited to enter	Homes; places of work or study	Permanent or semipermanent additions such as fencing, plant borders, furniture placement, or decorative elements	Taylor and Stough (1978)
A shared courtyard	Secondary	Extension of primary territories; the size is influenced by relationships with others	May be limited to the immediate area next to an apartment or could extend for several neighborhood blocks	Less clear or more open for interpretation; may be guarded by shared "owners"	Appleyard and Lintell (1972)
Public outdoor dining	Public	Places that are used temporarily; still offer a sense of control	These may include: a. stalls – physically defined space like a bench, chair or table b. use space – less defined like a picnic blanket c. turn – a space occupied while waiting	Strategically placing their personal belongings	Altman (1976) and Zeisel (2006)

Image credits: Patsy Eubanks Owens and Haven Kiers.

PEOPLE–PLACE RELATIONSHIPS   35

(Matthews, 1987). Research also suggests that the territories of all children have reduced in size over recent generations (Gaster, 1991; Louv, 2008). Many of the societal changes discussed earlier, such as changes to the family structure and the increased presence of technology, have likely contributed to these smaller youth territories. Fewer adults in the neighborhood, an absence of adults at home, and outside safety concerns lead caregivers to direct youth to stay inside when they return home from school (Owens, 2020). The intent to limit independent exploration by youth is prevalent in the United States. Adults, spotting children playing unsupervised at a neighborhood park, have called the police, and their parents cited for child neglect (Sneed, 2014). Challenging this notion, one mother decided that her nine-year-old son could navigate the New York City subway system alone and documented his trip in a newspaper article (Skenazy, 2008). Her actions not only prompted an outcry against her "bad parenting" but also generated interest in "free-range parenting," an alternative to the constant surveillance employed by many current parents. In addition, the availability of cell phones may grant some youth more freedom. Parents may express more comfort in letting their children go places if they have a cell phone with them. The ability for either party to reach the other quickly and tracking apps available on smartphones lead to this reassurance.

As children get older, understanding territorial bounds becomes an important means for knowing where to find their friends and places to avoid. High school students have reported the importance of having places at their school where they know they can find their friends. A picnic table at the edge of the quad and the steps to the band room are the types of places students have claimed for their friendship groups (see Figure 2.4). Conversely, youth also describe avoiding certain areas because they do not like the activities of the youth there, or that they feel threatened by those youth (Owens, 2005). Some have also made similar observations about their neighborhood or city (Owens & Hafer, 2004).

FIGURE 2.4 Adolescents claiming territories at high school. Image credit: Patsy Eubanks Owens.

Territories can also be formally and informally claimed by any number of groups. Soccer teams may sign up to use the same city field week after week; therefore, it begins to feel like their home field. A group of cricket players may gather at the same park weekly, so others start to expect to see them there. We also see evidence of immigrant or diaspora communities seeking and claiming public spaces. The need to have a place to gather with others with similar cultural backgrounds is strong. In one community, some neighbors were disturbed by a group of men gathering in the park after dark. After meeting with neighbors and talking with youth, the designers learned that the men were of Russian descent and got together in the park after dinner to talk – something that was culturally important for them to do. While Rishbeth and Rogaly (2018) discuss the importance of sitting outside for residents in southeast London, more research is needed to understand the importance of these types of territories for various populations and to develop alternatives for how they might be incorporated into the existing fabric of communities.

Lastly, understanding the role of territoriality in outdoor environments is critical to creating places where people feel safe and like they have control. Undefined or poorly demarcated spaces are more likely to prompt conflicts between users or uses. For example, a housing area that has a common area open to a public street is more likely to invite nonresidents to use the space than one that has a simple separation such as plantings or a change in paving. If a territory is invaded by others that do not have permission to enter, several scenarios are possible. Those who claim ownership of the territory may confront or challenge the uninvited visitor(s). They may ask the visitor to leave or negotiate the terms of their leaving (i.e., this is a private courtyard, please leave when you finish your coffee). In some circumstances, the person who staked claim to an area may leave if an uninvited person joins them. For instance, park benches are frequently abandoned when someone else sits down.

Application to design

The concept of territories and territoriality has direct implications for the design of private and public spaces. Providing clear visual and physical designations of places that people can claim that they own or that belong to others can help to prevent unintentional intrusions into others' territories. These design signals can also contribute to increasing the comfort people have in places and their place attachments, which will be discussed later in this chapter ("Place attachment" section).

Oscar Newman (1972) proposed territoriality as one of the elements needed to create defensible spaces. He suggests that the delineation of spaces would encourage nearby residents to assume more responsibility for these spaces, thereby leading others to not intrude into them. Newman recommends that residents have spaces close to their individual homes that they can personalize and control. Such spaces indicate to others that someone cares and looks out for the place. They also provide an opportunity for residents to become invested in where they live and to develop a sense of control over their space.

The design of two co-housing projects in California illustrates this idea. One design provides ample space adjacent to each home for residents to personalize and use, while in the other, residences open directly onto a common area (see Figure 2.5). During a class field trip to each of these sites, students received markedly different receptions from residents. At the first

Southside Co-housing, Sacramento, CA

Muir Commons Co-housing, Davis, CA

FIGURE 2.5 Comparing territoriality at two co-housing locations (plan views adapted from McCamant & Durrett, 1994). Image credits: Liz Stevenson (top) and Patsy Eubanks Owens (bottom).

housing area, residents warmly greeted students. Neighbors waved and said hello from their raised decks or patios. At the second, a resident immediately confronted the students and told them that visitors were not permitted. This resident was very displeased to hear that a fellow resident had invited the group. At the time the physical design of the second community provided little separation of individual homes from the shared outdoor space; however, residents have since added plantings and other elements to create more privacy outside their front doors. The design of each project potentially led residents to feel either in control of their home territory or not.

Designers should understand and build upon what is known regarding territoriality. In private and semipublic settings, designs can provide for opportunities to personalize and claim places. In public settings, design clues, such as a change in paving materials, the addition of architectural elements, or the use of plantings, can indicate appropriate behavior and promote increased comfort and control.

CROWDING AND PRIVACY

Background

Crowding and *privacy* are concepts that help explain why individuals or groups may feel comfortable in a space or not. Crowding refers to someone feeling uncomfortable in a space because of the presence of others. Privacy is the feeling of having exclusive control over an area, either temporarily or permanently. Neither of these concepts have fixed physical requirements or characteristics but are instead determined by the individual's psychological state in a particular situation. Does a person feel like they are in a crowded situation or like they have privacy?

Crowding is often confused with density, but the two are actually very different. Density is a physical characteristic defined as the number of people per space measurement, for example, number of residents per acre. Planners and designers often refer to and consider density in their work. They may consider the density of a city or neighborhood when making decisions about locating new parks or other community amenities, or when evaluating housing quality. However, density measurements do not accurately determine the degree of crowding experienced by residents. Stokols (1972) delineated a basic difference between density (the physical spacing of people) and crowding (a negative psychological state that may or may not accompany dense spacings). Crowding occurs when a person has more interaction with others than they desire. Crowding can occur when there are two people in a space if one of them experiences the sense that the other is encroaching upon them. Conversely, a lack of crowding may be perceived even when there are many people present. In some instances, larger numbers of people are expected and desired. A lack of people may actually lead to more uncomfortable feelings than the presence of more people. For example, an event planned for 100 may feel uncomfortable if only 20 people attend. In this case, fewer people do not promote more comfort, and more people would not have felt crowded.

Privacy, like crowding, is related to the psychological state of an individual and may not necessarily be related to a setting's physical characteristics. Privacy is the need or desire to be alone, but this does not necessarily mean to be by oneself. Others have identified four types of privacy: *solitude, intimacy, anonymity*, and *reserve* (Westin, 1967). Solitude describes the desire to be alone. Intimacy refers to privacy for close relationships such as with a spouse. Anonymity is that situation where an individual does not want to be recognized by others. Reserve is the desire to control how much interaction takes place with others.

Key findings

Crowding Understanding the impacts of crowding on individuals, as well as the mechanisms for preventing or alleviating crowding, is important for designers and planners. Crowding has been shown to have direct correlations with psychological stress, while density does not (Evans, 2001). Some communities have high population densities, but the residents do not experience crowding. With this in mind, two types of density can lead to crowding: spatial and social (see Figure 2.6). In *spatial density*, the population stays the same, but the space they occupy decreases in size. Imagine a family of four moving from a 2,500 square foot home to a 1,200 square foot home. This decrease in overall space available would mean each member of the family would likely experience feeling like they had less space. *Social density* is where the space size stays the same but the number of occupants of that space increases. Imagine this same family staying in their 2,500 square foot home, but now grandparents move in. The space available to each person is reduced and the occupants may be impacted. Studies on spatial and social density often describe the size of spaces and populations, while measuring the effects on an individual's experiences is more difficult and less reported (Neuts & Vanneste, 2018).

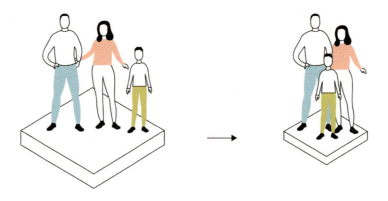

Spatial Density

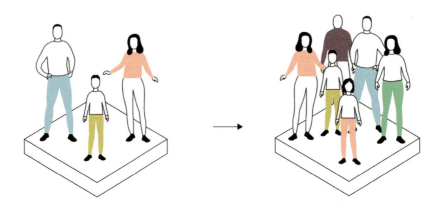

Social Density

FIGURE 2.6 Illustrated diagram of social density and spatial density.

Studies on crowding conducted in different settings, such as schools and prisons, show increases in negative affect and physiological stress in situations where the social density for the population was increased (Baum & Paulus, 1987; Evans, 2001; Paulus, 1988). Inmates or students sharing standard cells or a resident hall room with more individuals exhibited more negative effects than those sharing with fewer individuals. Similarly, Hall (1990a) notes that early studies comparing the size of space available to individuals (i.e., the spatial density) produced evidence that social pathologies, such as crime, and physical pathologies, such as illness, are linked to reduced available space. Similar-sized homes that housed more individuals showed a doubling in these pathologies. Evans (2001) found that crowded home environments interfered with the development of socially supportive relationships in that setting.

Crowding is not defined by a single spatial dimension or a specific number of occupants. Crowding is different for each person and varies from one situation to the next. The most important take-away from the existing research is that a clear link exists between the increased incidence of mental and physical stresses and their accompanying harm. The design of the physical environment can play a role in lessening or eliminating those damaging effects. For example, Wachs and Gruen (1982) found that having the ability to get away and be alone, even briefly, may reduce some of the negative impacts of crowding in residential settings.

Privacy People need privacy, but the amount and type of privacy needed vary between individuals. One setting may enact privacy for one person but not for another. Specifically, some people have a greater need or preference for privacy than others. People with a high privacy preference may report that they do not have enough privacy even when they have more than an individual with a lower privacy need (Marshall, 1972). Some studies also indicate that there may be differences in the privacy preferences of men and women. One study found that women had higher preferences for family intimacy and friend intimacy than men; however, men had significantly higher desire for isolation than women (Pedersen, 1987).

People generally use four behavioral mechanisms to achieve privacy (Altman, 1976). The first, *verbal behavior*, is where the person seeking to be alone tells an intruder to "go away." Such behavior is commonly not only experienced in a family setting but can also occur in public situations. The second, *nonverbal behavior*, involves a signal to others that one does not want to be disturbed. Reading a book or wearing headphones are some common clues used to indicate someone does not want to be disturbed. The third behavior, *exerting one's personal space*, involves using body language to signal that they want to be alone. Turning one's back to someone else is an obvious indication that a person does not want to talk. Lastly, *territorial behavior* is used as a temporary or permanent message to others to keep away. Claiming or demarcating space with objects, such as a blanket and umbrella at the beach or a fence at your home, indicates the space that you have claimed for yourself or for those with whom you want to share privacy.

Application to design

The environmental conditions and characteristics of crowding and privacy have implications for design, planning, and place making. Design plays a role in creating appropriately sized places for anticipated activities and participants to thereby avoid the feeling of crowding. Likewise, design can create opportunities for users to create privacy. For example, one study found that distance from, visibility to, and noise from neighbors directly influenced perceived privacy (Marshall, 1972). Designers should also consider changing societal conditions and their influence on crowding and privacy expectations. Changes in residential patterns which indicate more people moving away from where they grew up may create a need for opportunities to meet others – or they may lead people to seek privacy from strangers. Increases in random violence or targeted attacks may make people more fearful of crowded public places. Designers need to be conscious of changes in public and individuals' perceptions. The COVID-19 pandemic vividly illustrated the role that societal events have on perceptions of what is acceptable and what is a safe distance from others.

AFFORDANCES

Background

Perceptual psychologist Gibson (1979) developed the concept of *affordance* to describe the perceived functional significance of environmental features for an individual. Greeno (1994, p. 338) succinctly describes affordance as "whatever it is about the environment that contributes to the kind of interaction that occurs," while Heft (2001) expands by explaining that such properties are both objectively real and psychologically significant.

Affordances allow us to understand the physical, psychological, social, and cultural opportunities made available for an individual by an environment. They allow us to consider the fit between an individual and a particular environment, as "… the existence of an affordance implies a fit between animal and environment" (Withagen & Michaels, 2005, p. 606). Because all individuals are different, it is important to understand whatever it is about them as the agent that contributes to the kind of interaction that occurs; as Greeno terms it, the agent's "ability" (1994). For example, a concrete seat wall may be perceived by one teenager as a place to sit with a friend, whereas a young skateboarder could see it as an object to jump over or grind along its edge. Affordance is in the eye (and capabilities) of the beholder.

Researchers have classified affordances by type (e.g., functional, socio-cultural, and emotional, see Mäkinen & Tyrväinen, 2008) and by level of interaction (from avoidance of people to being with others, e.g., Clark & Uzzell, 2002). In studying young children, Kyttä (2004) notes how social and cultural factors affect the actualization of an affordance beyond the physical characteristics of the environment. She proposes that there are three subsets of affordances: *promoted action, constrained action,* and *free action*. The placement of an affordance into one of these categories depends upon social or cultural factors. Promoted actions are socially encouraged or allowed, constrained actions are those activities that are discouraged or limited, and free actions are those that are selected independently and may be either socially promoted or constrained.

Costall (1995) further describes how people can influence the affordance of places. Other people are involved in constructing, defining, explaining, policing, and maintaining environments. Therefore, their decisions affect the affordance of a place for others. For example, the addition of "skate stops" to the previously described seat wall would alter the affordance of this environment for some, but not for others. While an affordance relates to an activity that is perceived to be possible, some researchers have focused on *actualized affordances*, or in other words, activities in which a person actually engages (Heft, 1988; Reed, 1996). Owens (2017) also uses the concept of affordances to analyze the ability of an environment to meet the developmental needs of adolescents, or its *developmental affordance*. For example, a young person may or may not perceive a place as affording the opportunity to spend time with their friends, an important developmental task during adolescence.

Key findings

An important aspect of affordances is that every person perceives a place's opportunities and constraints through their own lens. What might seem like an ideal place to sit and have lunch for one person may be seen as too hot, noisy, or crowded by someone else. The designer must understand and navigate the many possible interpretations of the places that they create. The designer often begins with a vision for how they would like to see a place used and then proposes the forms, materials, sizes, etc. that they think will facilitate that desired activity. Often, a design solution is successful in its interpretation and use by others. When an urban plaza includes benches, for instance, it is likely the designer intended for users to sit on these benches (and they do); however, the designer may not have intended for the benches to be used as a bed by someone who is homeless or to post advertising for a real estate agent promoting their business. While it is impossible for a designer to anticipate all the different permutations of how their design will be interpreted and used, a realistic assessment of these potential uses is needed.

In addition, designers must consider activities that may be desired but that the current or proposed environment does not facilitate. In understanding a project site, designers often look to understand how a place is currently used so that the proposed design will allow those activities to continue. It is more difficult, however, to understand and project uses that are not currently present but that are likely desired. Designers should consider the missing affordances at a site or in the community more generally.

Application to design

While findings on affordances provide very broad generalizations of how a designer might approach a project, there are specific tasks that can be undertaken to both incorporate varied affordances into a design and to interpret how others might perceive them. Individual designers have their own design process or approach to developing design ideas and proposals; therefore, it is impossible to give one right way to incorporate affordances into a design. Some designers take an intuitive approach to a project, while others are systematic and deliberative. However, at some point, all designers begin to decide the elements and activities that will be included in their proposal. The description of these elements, or the project program, provides an opportunity to define and describe how the components of the proposed design might be used. A place to sit and have lunch as described earlier can be defined by the designer as a place comfortably sized for two people, whereas other places might be better for a larger group (see Figure 2.7). The designer needs to go beyond simply deciding to incorporate a place to eat

FIGURE 2.7 A planter wall (left) and boulders (right) provide seating options at Levi Strauss Plaza, San Francisco, CA. Image credit: Patsy Eubanks Owens.

lunch to instead understand and determine the qualities of that place and how others might interpret how it can be used.

HEALTH AND WELL-BEING

Background

The physical environment, particularly the outdoor environment, plays an important role in an individual's health and well-being. The places we inhabit can provide opportunities for restoration, escape, and comfort. Across all populations, research has linked the conditions of the physical environment to healthy outcomes and conversely, when conditions are not supportive, to poor outcomes. Early research in the field of environmental design linked a patient's ability to see nature as a positive factor in healing from surgery (Ulrich, 1984). More recent studies have shown that the supportive and moderating effects of nature have a wide range of influences on a person's psychological, social, and physical health (Evans, 2003; Frumkin, 2001; Kuo, 2015).

The last two decades have brought a greater understanding of the role outdoor environments, and in particular nature, play on psychological and cognitive health. Access to and even just views of nature have been shown to moderate stress in children (Wells & Evans, 2003) and adults (Cohen, Underwood, & Gottlieb, 2000) as well as improve positive cognitive functioning such as the ability to concentrate and learn (Kaplan, 1995; Li & Sullivan, 2016). Others have noted that contact with natural landscapes might contribute to developing resilience and buffer the effects of multiple adversities (Wells, 2000). Nearby nature was also found to be connected with lower rates of depression (Maas et al., 2009), higher self-discipline in girls (Faber Taylor, Kuo, & Sullivan, 2002), and enhanced self-confidence in children (Chawla, Keena, Pevec, & Stanley, 2014).

Other human characteristics of the outdoor environment influence psychological health. The provision of welcoming public areas, safe neighborhoods, and maintained streets are among the physical characteristics also likely to support psychological health. For example, places where adolescents feel like they belong and have a role in decisions have been shown to be important (Owens, 1988). In another study, Evans, Wells, and Moch (2003) found that women experienced different levels of loneliness and a sense of territorial control depending on whether they lived in a low-rise or high-rise building.

The physical environment also contributes to forming healthy social settings and relationships – *social health*. Places that encourage or allow interactions among occupants show evidence of creating positive outcomes for individuals. These supportive contexts can play a role in developing the social capital of individuals (Wells & Rollings, 2012) and in mitigating the effects of adversities, such as poverty or illness (Norris, Stevens, Pfefferbaum, Wyche, & Pfefferbaum, 2008). In a study of natural schoolyards, Chawla et al. (2014) found that children experienced several positive outcomes, including control over social interactions and a sense of competence. Natural learning environments create "feelings of competence and supportive relationships" (p. 11), which in turn lead to greater resilience in difficult situations. Kuo, Sullivan, Coley, and Brunson (1998, p. 843) found that in one public housing development "the more vegetation in a common space, the stronger the neighborhood social ties near that space." The role of such neighborhood connections and the building of social capital on an individual's social health have garnered research attention in recent years. The ability to confidently navigate community social networks has been shown to have tremendous positive health implications (Ziersch, Baum, MacDougall, & Putland, 2005). Owens, LaRochelle, Nelson, and Montgomery-Block (2011) found that building social capital through the use of visual media (photographs and videos) among youth countered adult perspectives and led to the reprioritization of community actions. Other positive outcomes of a healthy social environment may have implications beyond the individual and contribute to community success.

Finally, *physical health and well-being* have been linked to certain environments. As noted earlier, views of natural settings have been shown to contribute to faster recovery rates in surgery patients, but further physiological benefits of nature and other environmental characteristics are also at play. The presence of nature has been shown to have a positive impact on multiple health indicators including lower blood pressure, stronger immune systems, and generally lower levels of ailments (Hartig, Evans, Jamner, Davis, & Gärling, 2003; Li & Sullivan, 2016; Wells & Rollings, 2012). Views to green areas or access to natural spaces have even been shown to reduce the symptoms of attention deficit and hyperactivity disorder (Taylor, Kuo, & Sullivan, 2001). Kuo (2015) provides a comprehensive review of the literature linking health with the physical environment.

Key findings

Several findings relating to the connections between health and well-being and the built environment are particularly relevant for designers. Places that provide (1) restoration and promote resilience, (2) pleasing aesthetic qualities, and (3) characteristics that support recreation and engaging with others contribute to positive health outcomes.

People find opportunities for *reflection and restoration* in many types of places, from a shade tree in one's backyard, to a bench in a small park, to an overlook at a national park (see Figure 2.8). Restorative places are commonly comfortable, safe, quiet, and awe inspiring; they often provide a separation from others and an absence of distractions. In addition, the presence of nature or water in various forms can contribute to making a place restorative. Finally, restorative environments often have a view. The ability to think about one's problems and gain perspective is often associated with a setting that provides a view to a distant place. Appleton (1975) identified prospect refuges, or places where a person could look out and feel protected, as being important to humans. However, people value views differently based on characteristics such as age. While adolescents in one study frequently and enthusiastically indicated that the ability to look out and not be seen was why they liked a place, adults in the same study valued views but did not care if they were seen by others (Owens, 1988).

The *aesthetic and physical qualities* of a place can influence how comfortable someone feels and have been linked to different aspects of health. Along with views, as noted above, visual qualities such as relief and quiet fascination (Kaplan, Kaplan, & Ryan, 1998) and light levels can contribute to restoration. Other physical characteristics such as lower vehicular volumes have been linked to fewer mental health issues independent of neighborhood residents' income (Evans & Kantrowitz, 2002; Leventhal & Brooks-Gunn, 2000; Wandersman & Nation, 1998). Physical cleanliness can be an important aesthetic quality; one study showed young people

FIGURE 2.8 Photograph taken by an adolescent girl of a place she liked to go to get away. Image credit: Patsy Eubanks Owens.

recognize clean sidewalks, no litter, and a lack of graffiti as indicators that their community cares (Owens, 2010). Other studies identify connections between the physical environment and psychological health indicators, such as knowing one's neighbors and feelings of safety (Ziersch et al., 2005), in addition to links between aesthetic qualities (sidewalk conditions, lighting, and traffic) and increased physical activities, such as walking and jogging (Razmjouei, Tehrani, Alibabaei, Tanjani, & Razmjouei, 2017).

Places that provide opportunities for *physical and social activity* also contribute to a person's well-being. While these activities are commonly included in master plans for parks or other public spaces, the role they play in promoting health is not always at the forefront of a designer's thoughts. Often designs are developed with attention to decreasing walking distances instead of encouraging an enjoyable walking experience. The suburban cul-de-sac design is often cited as an example of planning that, while easing driving makes walking less convenient and discourages physical activity (Brownson, Boehmer, & Luke, 2005). Similarly, the typical suburban home layout with an attached garage has been cited as a reason that neighbors do not get to know one another (Abass, Andrews, & Tucker, 2020). New Urbanist communities seek to incorporate design elements such as parks, paths, and front porches in an effort to reclaim some ways that neighbors might get to know one another (Lund, 2003).

Application to design

Designers and planners have numerous opportunities to incorporate health-promoting places and features, from advocating for land use or transportation planning that encourages healthy behaviors and supportive systems, to the design of small-scale, easily accessible recreational or restorative places. Ryan (2012) describes several ways in which designers can contribute to promoting physical activity and creating restorative settings (see Table 2.3). While these lists are independent of the other, a restorative setting can support physical activities and physical activities can be restorative. Building upon these lists, designers should consider the multifaceted ways that design can contribute to all forms of health. While not exhaustive, some of the means available to the design and planning profession include promoting accessibility and mobility at the community scale; incorporating visual and physical access to nature; creating secure and intimate spaces; and integrating multisensory experiences in the places they design.

Accessibility and mobility. Some community configurations are more conducive than others to incorporating healthy behaviors into daily life. Current attitudes and patterns, such as reclaiming city streets for pedestrian use and the emergence of autonomous vehicles, hint that prioritizing cars over pedestrians is decreasing. However, challenges to incorporating convenient access to recreation, restoration, and social engagement persist in lower density residential areas. While increased moves to online work and shopping have decreased the need for physical facilities, the need for nearby options remains, as they provide venues for social interactions. Furthermore, the lived experiences of various populations need to be heeded in transportation and planning decisions. Allen's (2017) research in New Orleans provides strong evidence of the impact poor planning can have on marginalized and less politically connected communities, causing lower-income workers to have long, difficult commutes to low paying jobs. (For more discussion of issues surrounding the design of work environments, see Chapter 4.)

TABLE 2.3 Design considerations for physical activity and restoration (Ryan, 2012)

Physical activity settings	Restorative settings
Plan an environment that makes physical activity seamless	Consider the view from the window
Create a more pedestrian-friendly environment	Borrow off-site views
Seek partnerships with public health professionals	Provide small-scale and intimate spaces
Provide connections to larger open-space networks	Provide enclosures
Plan for an appropriate length of onsite walkways and bikeways	Reduce noise pollution; encourage quiet
Design playgrounds for all ages	Provide seating
Plan for sports facilities and recreation fields	Focus on beauty and the importance of aesthetics
Provide support facilities (e.g., drinking fountains, bicycle racks)	Design for multisensory experiences
Promote gardening as a physical activity	Provide water for a sensory experience
Maintain recreation facilities and structures	

Visual and physical access to nature. Designers and planners also have opportunities to incorporate both visual and physical access to nature. The preservation and incorporation of green spaces, whether large parks, small gardens, or street trees, can provide opportunities for people to interact with plants and animals. Occurrences of nature close to home are particularly important for those populations that do not have either the physical or financial access to larger protected natural areas. As uncovered by Faber Taylor et al. (2002), even views of nature can have positive health benefits, and therefore should be incorporated into the site planning of housing and other land uses. Ryan (2012) notes that the Japanese routinely "borrow" views from adjacent properties and have developed skills in screening unpleasant views, a practice called *shakkei*. In addition to the restorative benefits of access to nature, parks and wilderness lands provide excellent settings for physical activities and exercise.

Secure and intimate spaces. The inclusion of small-scale, intimate spaces within public spaces can be particularly useful for people looking for privacy. The opportunity to reflect, sort through concerns, and escape distractions are important components of a restorative environment. These places should feel protected, safe, and under the control of the person occupying the space. They should be quiet and without unpleasant, noisy distractions. In addition, they need features that allow a person to stop and rest, such as benches, ledges, rocks, or other elements that can provide acceptable stopping points.

Multisensory experiences. Ryan (2012) and others identify the role that multisensory experiences contribute to mental restoration. While pleasing aesthetics and beautiful scenes are qualities that support restoration, places and experiences that engage the other senses can also be particularly satisfying. Smells, sounds, touch, and taste can all contribute to positive experiences. Evans (2003) identifies several studies (Frumkin, 2001; Kaplan & Kaplan, 1984; Kaplan et al., 1998; Ulrich, 1991) that indicate that these experiential elements do not have to come from nature, but can also be architectural features (e.g., fountains, fireplaces, or sculptures) that promote curiosity and fascination. Lastly, designers have an opportunity to entice visitors to a place to slow down, enjoy the experience, and engage their senses. Many individuals miss the potential healing powers of the landscapes they visit. Instead, their focus is often on capturing a photograph to share on social media. To counter this tendency, New Zealand has launched a tourism campaign that encourages visitors to create their own experiences rather than recreate the experiences of others (Picheta, 2021).

PLACE ATTACHMENT

Background

Although populations and individuals have a long history of allegiance to places, the study of *place attachment* and aligned concepts such as place identity, rootedness, and sense of place did not begin until the middle of the 20th century. These concepts are deliberated thoroughly by others (e.g., Lewicka, 2011; Manzo & Devine-Wright, 2021); therefore, this section focuses on how place attachment concepts can inform place making by designers.

The three-part framework described by Scannell and Gifford (2010a) captures the dimensions of these concepts most relevant to the design profession (see Figure 2.9). The first dimension,

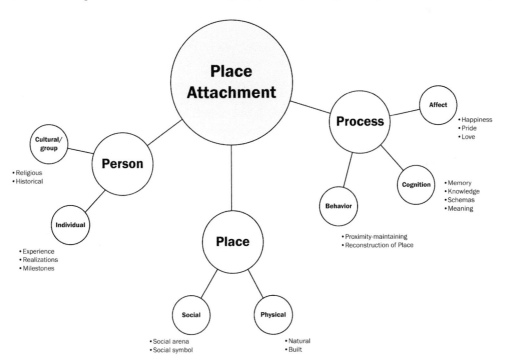

FIGURE 2.9 The tripartite model of place attachment (Scannell & Gifford, 2010a).

the *person*, refers to the individual or group that holds meaning of and connection with a place. This meaning or attachment may be developed through experiences or have cultural or religious significance (Mazumdar & Mazumdar, 1993).

The second dimension, the *psychological process*, relates to human–psychological interactions connected to attachment. Emotion, identity, and behavior are the three aspects of this process (Scannell & Gifford, 2010a). Emotion refers to the bond that a person feels toward an environment and has been identified and described as the "love of place" (Tuan, 1974). While in many instances the emotions attributed to place attachment are positive, they can include emotions ranging from positive to negative and also ambivalence (Di Masso et al., 2019; Manzo, 2005). On the other hand, place identity, as named by Proshansky, Ittelson, and Rivlin (1970), describes the close affiliation between an individual's memories, values, and preferences and representative places. Lastly, behavior refers to how individuals maintain a physical connection to a place, return to a place, or seek a similar place. This type of attachment, or place dependence, is based on the physical features or amenities of a place (Stokols & Shumaker, 1981).

The third dimension, *place*, includes social and physical spaces at a range of scales – home, neighborhood, and city. Many researchers have stressed that place attachment must have a social element and is frequently conflated with the ideas of "sense of community" (e.g., Perkins & Long, 2002) or "sense of place" (e.g., Tuan, 1974). Social elements may include communities of interest (shared lifestyles or interests) or communities of place (geographic proximity) (Nasar & Julian, 1995). In addition, the realm of place attachment may be associated with the particulars of the physical features of a place without consideration of the social aspects. The type of place or specific elements, built or natural, contained within a place may contribute to feelings of connection or attachment.

Key findings

Place attachment is an important consideration for design and planning professionals in two overarching regards: (1) in the recognition of and respect for places that hold meaning; and (2) in the creation of places that are likely to instill connections and meaning for individuals, groups, or communities. Understanding existing place attachment has implications for maintaining or improving existing conditions for people. Removing or altering existing valued physical characteristics or qualities may lead individuals with prior knowledge of a place to become detached from or less concerned for that place, or it might disrupt existing community behaviors and patterns. For example, the unknowing removal of a tree that is decorated at Christmas time could lead community members to suffer sadness or anger and could prompt the community to find another place for future celebrations or discontinue them.

The creation of new places which will have meaning for people is a powerful responsibility of designers. Manzo and Devine-Wright (2021) describe two processes, place creation and place intensification, that address how designers' and planners' efforts can enhance or undermine place quality. Decisions that stimulate or improve community use and experience can actively contribute to people–place attachment. In addition, place attachment can play an important role in community stewardship (Manzo & Perkins, 2006). Conversely, decisions that misunderstand, ignore, or weaken existing features or uses can lead to a decline in the importance of that place to those that previously held the place in high regard.

Opportunities and obligations to consider place attachment in planning and design are numerous and varied. Place attachment theories have been utilized in a number of planning and design areas such as natural resource and recreation management (Kruger, Hall, & Stiefel, 2008), disaster preparedness (Mishra, Mazumdar, & Saur, 2010), and housing policy (Manzo, Kleit, & Couch, 2008). Implications of place attachment theories are both broad in scope and scale and have small-scale applications. In one study, youth expressed a preference for well-kept streets, which contributed significantly to feelings of pride in their community (Owens, 2010), while other studies have noted how people's knowledge that a natural hillside was protected made them feel better (Owens, 1988).

Application to design

Understanding and mapping places of attachment is an important addition to traditional site analysis. This analysis requires a thorough knowledge of the patterns, behaviors, or histories of a population; therefore, the guidance of those with immediate knowledge is critical. The landscape architectural practice and writings of Hester (1985) provide one model, *sacred structure mapping*, for collecting such stories and respecting them in design recommendations (see Figure 2.10). Hester's sacred structure mapping documents the places or elements that a community is unwilling to give up for change. These places are not sacred in the religious sense, but rather in the context of the daily lives of people. This mapping often reveals places that are not necessarily the most beautiful or refined, but instead are places that hold special meaning because of memories of past events, personal investments, historical significance, or even simply daily patterns.

When identifying a community's sacred structure, the designer must seek to understand not only what places are important but also why they are important. This understanding can then inform design recommendations and projected use patterns. Community members should be engaged in consciously determining the social and emotional value of these places, as well as the role these places will play in the future. This community understanding and commitment is critical for long-term success following the designer's departure. The exploration of place attachment by designers can also catalyze participation and inform a more socially responsible design. Ruggeri (2021) more fully discusses how place meanings and attachments can inform the participatory design process.

For those communities that are new, have frequent resident turnover, or that have seen an influx of new residents, identifying a sacred structure is likely to be more difficult. The designer can play a role in helping to create places that will reflect the desires and anticipated patterns of new occupants. Additionally, in many instances, a community may have independent or overlapping sacred structures. Populations of different ages, cultures, or interests may have clearly established patterns of use that are divergent from one another but are no less important. Recognizing these variations in design decisions can strengthen a sense of belonging and attachment for all residents. The process of developing this sense of ownership and the accompanying caring for places by nearby residents is within the designer's realm, particularly through participatory design approaches discussed in Chapter 8.

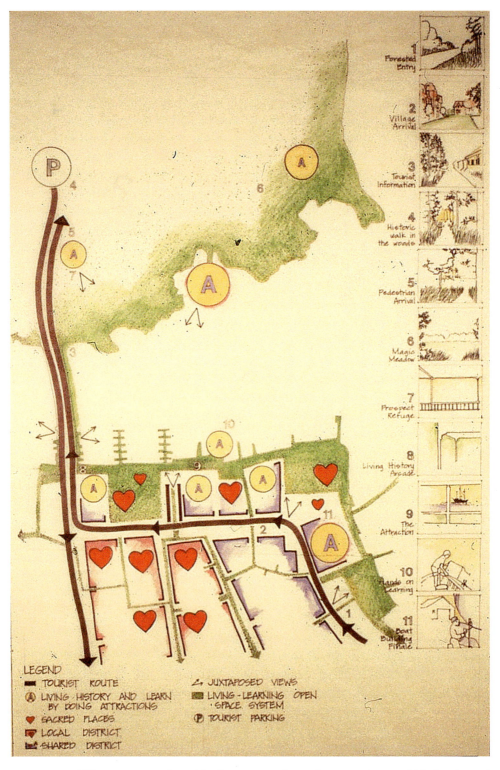

FIGURE 2.10 Village concept – informed by the community's sacred structure, Manteo, NC. Drawing and image credit: Patsy Eubanks Owens.

SAFETY AND SECURITY

Background

One of the key tenets of professional licensure is to protect public health, safety, and welfare; therefore, the landscape architect has a responsibility to consider community and user safety in the places they design. Licensing requirements include measures of competency in designing features that will not cause or will prevent physical harm, such as consistent step heights and handrail placements. However, designers should also consider the influence of their work on perceptions of safety, and, in turn, how that impacts people's comfort and sense of belonging. Safety in the built environment falls into two broad categories: *actual safety* and *perceived safety*.

Actual safety refers to a susceptibility to physical danger or harm. These may be threats posed by design characteristics such as vehicular and pedestrian conflicts, uneven or slippery walking surfaces, blocked sight lines, or inadequate or missing lighting. Any of these or other factors could lead to physical injury. In addition, certain design decisions or indecisions can impact the likelihood of criminal activity, and with that an increase in incidences of theft or bodily harm. Areas with poor natural surveillance or the inadvertent creation of visually and physically isolated areas may become locations of such criminal activities.

Perceived safety refers to how safe a person feels in a place. This feeling may or may not be aligned with actual safety, but nonetheless it can significantly impact one's comfort in and use of a place. Factors influencing this sense of safety include physical and social characteristics as well as past experiences and associations. Some physical features that can make a place feel less safe are low lighting levels, blocked views, and the presence of litter. Social characteristics include the presence or absence of certain types of other people or people engaging in certain types of activities. Preconceptions of a place's safety or previous associations with a place may also lead users to avoid it. In addition, an individual's personal characteristics, such as size, build, and gender, can influence whether they feel safe or not.

Designers must consider both the actual and perceived safety of the places they create. Along with assisting in keeping people safe from physical harm, designs can contribute to people feeling more secure.

Key findings

The theory of crime prevention through environmental design (CPTED) gained recognition in the 1990s and proposed numerous ways that design could deter unwanted behaviors and increase legitimate place uses and feelings of security (Crowe, 1991). The validity of this theory has been questioned by some who note that it does not adequately address the safety perceptions and concerns of women (Pain, 1991) and that it privileges some populations over others (Angeles & Roberton, 2020). The principles, however, are widely applied and include six realms to consider: *activity support, image/maintenance, territoriality, access control, surveillance,* and *target hardening* (Moffat, 1983). Territoriality and aspects related to access control are discussed earlier in this chapter; therefore, the following discussion focuses on the other facets of CPTED.

Activity support encourages an increase in users and uses that are more likely to be accepted by the public. As noted earlier, the presence of others with characteristics similar to oneself can make a place feel safer, just as the presence of activities deemed illegitimate or individuals perceived as questionable can make a place feel unsafe. A city plaza with many users in the evening feels safer than a place that is empty, but a city plaza with only a scattering of skateboarders may feel uncomfortable for a parent with their young children.

The *image or visual quality* of a place, as well as the care it receives, can influence feelings of safety. Evidence of regular maintenance or beautification, such as swept sidewalks, new paint, or the planting of flowers, indicates that someone is looking out for a place. Conversely, the presence of trash, graffiti, or unmaintained features provides an indication that no one cares for the place (e.g., Li & Nassauer, 2020). This understanding has contributed to communities implementing programs to immediately address graffiti as well as other forms of destruction. One notion, the broken window theory, went so far as to propose that when signs of disorder are not addressed, they prompt additional damage – one broken window leads to more broken windows (Wilson & Kelling, 1982). While this theory has been challenged, signs of disorder that raise concerns for one's safety and security have been shown to have an impact on mental health (O'Brien, Farrell, & Welsh, 2019).

Two additional CPTED principles are *surveillance* and *target hardening*. Jacobs (1961) introduced the idea of community surveillance or "eyes upon the street." She argued that informal surveillance – people within or looking into a space – is important to make people feel safer. This notion has evolved to include a reliance on more sophisticated and formal means of watching public behavior, such as the now ubiquitous closed-circuit video monitoring of roadways, plazas, and parks (Norris, McCahill, & Wood, 2004). While there is evidence to show that these cameras can deter crime, they can also give people a false sense of security and raise concerns regarding privacy. Although the idea of *target hardening* preceded the attacks in the United States on September 11, 2001, this date was a turning point for increasing efforts to block access to sensitive or vulnerable areas. Site designs now frequently incorporate walls, bollards, vegetation, and other features to prevent easy access to select locations, while also offering experiences of safe and secured places.

Application to design

In considering how safety and security concerns influence design decisions, the work of Jacobs (1961) and Newman (1972), as well as the CPTED principles, together provides much guidance (see Figure 2.11). The challenge is to consider and apply this advice to the creation and re-design of places. All types of places – residential and recreational, public and private – experience increases in both actual and perceived safety when these principles are followed.

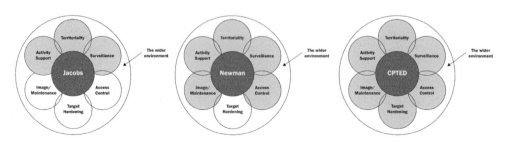

FIGURE 2.11 Safety and security principles – Jacobs (1961), Newman (1972), and CPTED.

A few examples illustrating how three of these – surveillance, activity support, and visual quality – can be actualized in designs are provided.

The main premise behind *surveillance* is that there are people looking out for other people. Design can make it easier (whether formally or informally) to keep an eye on nearby activities. The designer needs to consider the activity patterns of both observers and participants. For example, at a playground, a caregiver needs a place where they can wait comfortably and have a view of the children. In other settings, such as downtown streets or plazas, observers and participants likely do not know one another; however, a similar dynamic still contributes to a sense of safety. Walking along a street with shop windows, door openings, and informal seating is likely more comfortable for the walker than a street with blank facades and little or no activity. Urban renewal projects in the United States during the 1950s, 1960s, and 1970s, which had many negative effects, impacted surveillance through the replacement of small shops with large faceless buildings which moved activity from the street to the interior of buildings.

Recommendations around *activity support* and safety vary somewhat between Jacobs, Newman, and CPTED guidelines. While Jacobs promotes continuous activity, where people are out and about, Newman's defensible space guidelines focus on having a clear separation of different uses. For Jacobs, the more activity taking place, the more people who are watching. For Newman, designated areas for specific activities will result in fewer conflicts. Earlier CPTED writings (e.g., Crowe, 1991) focused on designing to support activities in which people want to engage, as compared to designing to prevent or promote certain uses. This distinction is evident when considering school or public plaza designs. As Crowe illustrates, school officials often blame crowded hallways on students that stop to chat with their friends, whereas a design that provided for these impromptu gatherings would accommodate this desired activity and simultaneously relieve the hallway congestion, defusing potential conflict (see Figure 2.12). Similarly, many cities have waged ongoing battles with skateboarders who use smooth paved plazas for practicing, performing, and gathering. Instead of penalizing or preventing this activity, attention to designing plazas to support this use in conjunction with other uses might be more prudent. Before deeming an activity inappropriate, designers, along with the property owners and managers, should consider how to make the activity legitimate and welcomed.

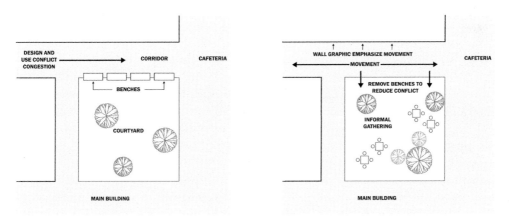

FIGURE 2.12 Designing to accommodate desired gathering activity at a school. Adapted from Crowe (1991).

The *visual quality* of a place certainly has an impact on perceptions of safety. The CPTED principles refer to these characteristics as the image and maintenance of a place. The way a place looks, the materials used, and the maintenance required are central to design recommendations. Pavers that crack, drains that clog, and plants that die immediately convey that no one is caring for the place, nor the safety of those in it. Considerations for how places will age and who will take responsibility for upkeep are important. Newman suggests that in shared residential areas, opportunities for personalization and control can empower residents to take on some of these responsibilities. Likewise, in many cities, shop owners frequently clean adjacent sidewalks or decorate with potted plants. Attention to the visual quality is also important in natural and park settings. Along with the unwanted presence of litter, heavily vegetated areas with a lack of visibility or poorly maintained plantings can cause concerns for safety.

Designers have an ability and responsibility to create places that are safe. This safety includes addressing considerations that might contribute to physical harm such as uneven walking surfaces and also qualities that make a place feel unsafe such as poor maintenance. Perceptions of safety can vary between individuals; therefore, the designer needs to engage residents to understand their experiences and expectations of the landscape in question.

WAYFINDING

Background

Wayfinding is related to environmental imagery, cognitive mapping, and spatial orientation. Distinctive features of an environment help people create a mental image of a place and find their way around. Wayfinding is a spatial problem-solving skill in which people orient themselves by relying on designed or natural environmental information (Arthur & Passini, 2002; Passini, 1992). The concept emerged from studies of neuropsychology, migration of animals, and how Indigenous people navigate around their environments (Lynch, 1960; Passini, 1992). Traditionally, people found their way around relatively unmarked routes by understanding geographic orientation, cardinal directions, and distinctive visual objects. Natural or cultural landmarks such as a river, steep hill, or significant structures helped travelers become familiar with their routes and supported their experiences. In other instances, sailors and explorers used cues in the environment that were intentionally placed or naturally existed, such as lighthouses, constellations, or other landmarks to navigate (Lynch, 1960; Morville, 2005; Passini, 1992).

Lynch first used the term *wayfinding* in his seminal work *The Image of the City*. He explained that the skill of orientation may not necessarily be an instinct of mobile species but is instead "a consistent use and organization of definite sensory cues from the external environment" (Lynch, 1960, p. 3). Later, Passini defined wayfinding as "spatial problem solving [which] includes perceptual and cognitive phenomena and the various ways a person can relate to the spatial environment and to destinations; it involves memory and learning, all essential in explaining how people find their way" (1992, p. 46). Passini further specified the difference between spatial orientation and wayfinding by describing spatial orientation as "a person's ability to mentally determine his position within a representation of the environment made possible by cognitive maps" (p. 35). Lynch found that people develop cognitive images of their cities that represent their "generalized mental picture of the exterior physical world" (1960, p. 4).

Such mental images strategically link how people perceive the landscape to how they move about their environments.

These cognitive or mental maps represent the physical environment in simplified forms; actual distances may be distorted, visual components may be schematic, and features may be included or omitted. Select map elements may have particular meaning for the person creating them, but maps may also include non-existing elements (Golledge, 1999; Passini, 1992). Furthermore, a person may clearly produce a reflective image of the physical environment in their cognitive maps, but this does not mean that they also have a clear sense of orientation. Therefore, people also need the ability to orient themselves in the environment (built or natural) to be successful at wayfinding.

Key findings

Researchers have found that the legibility and readability of a landscape positively influences user satisfaction and positive perceptions. Good wayfinding practices through recognizable features, natural or designed, can help lessen the fear, frustration, or stress of navigating through unknown places and confirm a positive perception of known places (Kaplan et al., 1998). Conversely, disorientation in an environment can be heightened with the feeling of being lost and contribute to people avoiding unfamiliar places (Arthur & Passini, 2002). Therefore, "people will be more eager to explore areas when they feel oriented and confident that they can find their way around, and their general anxieties are lessened" (Kaplan et al., 1998, p. 49).

Based upon studies in three cities, Lynch found that people's mental maps had five distinctive yet similar recognizable elements – *paths*, *edges*, *districts*, *nodes*, and *landmarks* (Lynch, 1960) (see Figure 2.13). These elements contribute to one's ability to find their way across numerous locations. For example, another study in Australia found that cognitive maps created by tourists

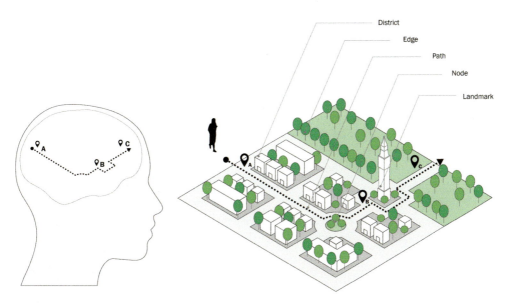

FIGURE 2.13 Environmental cues (path, edge, district, node, and landmark) inform an individual's wayfinding plan (from point A to point B and to point C). Additional wayfinding features can support the travel experience.

in a small destination city included paths, districts, and landmarks (Walmsley & Jenkins, 1992). The longer a tourist visited, the more elements they recognized.

King and de Jong (2016) suggest that there are two important themes in wayfinding: *legibility* and *continuity*. Streets and cities need to be legible in terms of context, network, and markers, and there needs to be consistency in features and their design. In addition, they identify five factors for successful wayfinding routes: connectivity, hierarchy, interconnectivity, proximity, and redundancy. *Connectivity* describes routes that are uninterrupted, allowing for reduced travel distances. *Hierarchy* provides a clear framework of prominent features or landmarks such as schools, major roads, religious institutions, or parks. *Interconnectivity* guides users who are transferring between different modes of travel, such as from parking to walking or sidewalk to subway. *Proximity* locates starting points and destinations close to each other in order to simplify wayfinding. Lastly, *redundancy* includes multiple routes and options when possible as well as repeated wayfinding features. These key findings reinforce the notion that wayfinding is not merely about signage, but also is an inclusive approach to designing and planning that facilitates the understanding and comprehension of a place.

Application to design

Designers have a significant role in enhancing people's wayfinding experiences in outdoor environments. Outdoor environments should be designed to guide and direct people between origin and destination or within the boundaries of the destination. Such design considerations enable users to quickly perceive places as comfortable, friendly, and welcoming, even when environments are unfamiliar. Designers should consider at least four factors when creating a wayfinding system: the user, the image of a place, the overall framework, and communication strategies. These factors can be applied at various scales.

User. User characteristics and how they will be traveling need to be considered when making wayfinding decisions (King & de Jong, 2016). Are users predominately residents or tourists? Are they likely to be families, young adults, or seniors? Each of these populations and others would necessitate different design responses. To increase user comfort and awareness, wayfinding design needs to adhere to user-friendliness as much as design sophistication. Modes of travel are also important since they will influence visibility of landscape features and user experience (e.g., Transport for London, 2007).

Image of a place. When done well, wayfinding should reflect local identity and help to enforce the image of a place (Gibson, 2009). Sometimes referred to as "branding," a clear image can convey the significance of place heritage and integrate into place design. Gibson notes that a branding scheme should be holistically and systematically addressed, coordinated, and applied in conjunction with wayfinding efforts to create a coherent experience overall. Wayfinding features, whether small-scale design elements or prominent landmarks, can contribute to a person's understanding of where they are.

Overall framework. Designers can play a significant role in a person's wayfinding experience through planning and designing outdoor environments with clear spatial organization and environmental information that enhances user experience (Passini, 1992). Attention to the legibility and navigability of the landscape can be applied to various settings, natural to urban, and to different scales. As noted by Walmsley and Jenkins (1992), the city-level legibility of an area should be fostered, and city layout should facilitate easier orientation. Depending upon the scale, a hierarchy of alternative routes and layering of destinations may be appropriate. Wayfinding features may not only guide users directly but can also help them explore and be pleasantly surprised.

Communication strategies. Effective wayfinding systems should enhance how a space is experienced without destroying the character of the place. Furthermore, people can better identify places and their locations when wayfinding signage systems are successfully paired with designed outdoor elements as explicit communication tools which help users navigate through both unfamiliar and familiar environments (Arthur & Passini, 2002; Lee, 2016; Passini, 1992). Wayfinding features need to provide information in varied formats to assist people in reaching their destinations. Locating information at or close to decision-making points is crucial for travelers to make timely decisions. "Information at the wrong place is as good as no information at all" (Arthur & Passini, 2002, p. 34). Wayfinding systems that incorporate maps can also promote exploration and lessen general confusion (Kaplan et al., 1998). Lastly, repetition in sign designs, symbols, and intervals can assist the user. Signs have different purposes (e.g., identification, orientation, directional, and regulatory); however, sign styles and forms should complement each other and be clearly recognizable (see Table 2.4).

Wayfinding considerations can make a place and the experience of it memorable. It is important to create accessible and safe places while celebrating local identity and providing opportunities to explore. A successful wayfinding system will provide recognizable cues as well as comfort in the outdoor environment.

CONCLUSION

The need to understand and acknowledge the interrelationship between people and the environments in which they live is not new. Hall (1990a), drawing upon his own and others' previous research, noted that in the people–environment relationship, each shapes the other. People determine the composition and organization of built environments. Environments mold human interactions and provide comfort or distress to populations. His work challenges architects, planners, and others to respect the power of places to shape people in order to "avoid catastrophe" (p. 6). While not all poor design decisions will lead to catastrophe, designing environments for people can create places that allow people to explore, socialize, restore, and thrive.

POTENTIAL EXERCISES AND PROJECT

An indoor exercise

A sacred space. Think about a place that has special meaning for you – a place that you would be upset if it changed without your input. This can be a place that you go to often or infrequently. It can be a place you go to alone or with others.

Describe what makes this place important to you.

TABLE 2.4 Wayfinding communication strategies in the outdoor environment

	Type	Location	Function	Examples
Identification	Gateway sign	Main entrance to locale	• Welcomes visitors and users • Sets tone regarding image of place • Conveys historical and cultural significance	
	Entry sign	Entry point to park, subarea, district or neighborhood	• Welcomes visitors and users • Conveys identity of park, subarea, district, or neighborhood	
	Banners	Along streets, paths, or corridors using existing poles	• Conveys the identity of the area • Announces events	
	Landmark	Featured locations	• Focal point • Distinctive attraction	
	Interpretive sign	Near important locations or significant features	• Focal point • Stopping or resting point	
Orientation	Information and orientation kiosk	Starting or decision-making points	• Overview of area showing points of interest • Information on distances, routes, and travel times • Other contextual information for reference	

60   PEOPLE–PLACE RELATIONSHIPS

	Directory	Starting or decision-making points of location such as the entrance to a district or subarea	• Provides a listing of points of interest • Free standing or in combination with a map	
	Distance or mile markers	Consistent intervals between starting and destination points; free-standing or incorporated into other types of features	• Informs distances from a known starting point • Simple indication of distance from or to one's next location	
Directional	Directional signs	Decision points such as landmarks and intersections	• Assist users with navigation • Visible for pedestrian and vehicular travelers	
Regulatory	Regulatory	Entry points and edges of regulated area	• Indication of what is or is not allowed • Unobtrusive, but large enough to be visible • Enhances, not disrupts, the experience	

Image credits: Patsy Eubanks Owens, Jayoung Koo, and Yiwei Huang.

PEOPLE–PLACE RELATIONSHIPS 61

Review what you have written and identify the following:

- Is the place uniquely important to you or is it also important to others?
- What are the experiences that informed your attachment to this place?
- What are the physical characteristics of this place that make it sacred to you?
- What are the emotions that this place generates for you?

Share and discuss your thoughts with a classmate, friend, or family member.

Outdoor exercises

Mapping your territory. The place where we live often includes private, semipublic, and public spaces. How are these types of spaces created in the place you live?

1. Draw a plan of the place you live (residential hall, apartment, house).
2. Indicate the private spaces in blue, the semipublic or transition spaces in yellow, and the public spaces in red.
3. Was it easy to determine which spaces fell into which categories? Why or why not?
4. Do you feel your private territory is clear and respected by others? If not, what changes would make the "ownership" of these spaces clearer?
5. Do you feel like the boundaries of the public area are clear? How are these boundaries formed?

Personal space boundary exercise. Everyone has their own personal space. The size and shape of this space is influenced by many factors. This exercise is intended to give you a sense of how personal space varies between individuals, how it is protected, and how people cope with intrusions.

1. Divide the whole class into three groups.
2. Go to a public space where there are seating areas, such as an outdoor eating or gathering place, and preferably with a high volume of people. Once at the place, each group will engage in one of these behaviors:
   - The first group should find a place to sit and see if people come to sit close to you,
   - The second group should intentionally sit next to a stranger,
   - The third group should sit next to each other at whatever distance feels comfortable.
3. Share your experience with your classmates. Were you comfortable? Do you think the people you were sitting close to were comfortable? Why or why not? How did people respond to you sitting by them? Did they change their behavior or "mark" their territory?

Alternative. Conduct a similar experience as you are walking. Notice how close someone gets to you before they change to the other side of the sidewalk. Does what you are wearing or what props you are carrying (i.e., briefcase, musical instrument) make a difference?

A research project

Affordance observations on children's playground. In this chapter, we talked about affordance theory (Greeno, 1994; Heft, 1988; Kyttä, 2004). This theory has been used to understand the different types of physical characteristics of outdoor environments and how those support different activities. For example, a flat, smooth surface affords an opportunity to walk, bike, run or skateboard.

For this project, you are asked to study an existing children's playground. Through site visits and observations, identify the current affordances available at this location and whether these are actualized by the users. That is, how are the users using this flat, smooth surface?

Please keep those questions in mind while observing:

1. What activities are afforded by this playground? (These may not be limited to affordances for children.)
2. Which of these anticipated activities do you observe and which ones do you not see?
3. What are the unexpected activities that are occurring?
4. Has the environment been adapted by the children for these activities? If so, how?
5. What lessons can you learn from your observations that would be helpful in the design of other play areas?

Be sure to record your observations including the date, time of day, weather. Explain your observation procedure – how long did you observe, where did you sit, how did you record the information. Describe your observations generally and then provide a more in-depth discussion of at least three observed activities as they relate to affordance theory. Discuss how your observations might inform play area design.

SECTION II: UNDERSTANDING COMMUNITIES AND PEOPLE

3
PEOPLE AND CULTURE

This chapter provides an overview of how cultural background influences an individual's preferences for, comfort with, and often-seen use patterns for various types of environments. While each community and its residents are unique, some culturally linked behaviors in outdoor settings have been identified. Patterns and behaviors common to multiple cultures as well as characteristics unique to certain cultures are explored. In addition, a more comprehensive discussion of developing a culturally sensitive and responsive approach to design is included. As society and specific communities become increasingly diverse, recognizing and celebrating cultural differences can contribute to the creation of rich and relevant public spaces.

INTRODUCTION TO CULTURE

What is culture and why is it important?

As addressed in Chapter 1, it is important to understand how culture informs individuals' and groups' interactions with their environments. The qualities of a place are derived from people–environment relations at various scales, from site-specific to global. Culture is one lens through which society influences the creation and use of designed outdoor environments. People have differently sculpted environments as places for civic, productive, social, or religious functions based on distinct cultural influences. These environments and the cultures that shape them rarely remain stagnant; rather, they evolve or change completely over time. In addition, cultural upbringing also influences how people use outdoor places and often varies from one location to another.

Culture can be defined as "the customary beliefs, social forms, and material traits of a racial, religious, or social group" and "the characteristic features of everyday existence .... shared by people in a place or time" (Merriam-Webster, n.d.). The definition of culture as "[a] complex whole which includes knowledge, beliefs, arts, morals, laws, customs, and any other capabilities and habits acquired by [a human] as a member of society" (Tylor, 1871, p. 1) has been adopted by the United Nations Educational, Scientific and Cultural Organization (UNESCO, n.d.). Both definitions imply two ways of understanding culture, one as a "way of life" and the other as expressive arts and representational practices (Rana & Piracha, 2007). Traditionally, culture is shared by people of the same or similar ethnicity, language, nationality, or spiritual beliefs. A person's age, gender, social status, and familial structure can also influence the construct of culture, making it diverse and complex.

Currently, the term culture encapsulates many aspects of people's daily lives: how they dress, what they eat, how they talk, and what they do. In the planning and design disciplines, researchers and designers use "culture" to describe how people use places based on their activities and behaviors; it is not limited to describing certain racial, ethnic, or religious groups or their norms. In this sense, culture is related more to politics, urban transformation, and demographic change, among other broader societal changes, than it is to communal characteristics or trends (Amin, 2009). Culture is ever evolving, and as such so are the cultural influences on the use and design of outdoor environments.

With globalization and increased mobility, people can readily meet and live with others with different cultural backgrounds to their own. Trans-global migration has become more convenient and trans-cultural influences have become more accepted than in the past. In addition, popular media, such as television and film, and social media provide opportunities for different cultures to be exposed to one another. This increased exposure may contribute to a greater curiosity and understanding of other cultures. In countries with increased immigration rates like the United States, the population includes diverse ethnic backgrounds (Frey, 2020). Culture helps identify who residents are, how they express themselves as individuals and as members of society, and how they use spaces based on shared foundations. Therefore, when building outdoor environments such as shared or public spaces, designers should be aware of and competent in the cultural norms and needs of different groups and communities.

The characteristics of culture

Cultures and environments simultaneously influence and shape each other; therefore, it is critical that the design of outdoor environments considers the culture of nearby residents and site users. While all cultural aspects are important to consider in design, this chapter focuses on race and ethnicity-related influences. Other cultural considerations such as age (Chapter 4), inclusion, (Chapter 5), and gender (Chapter 6) are discussed in respective chapters. With that said, designers should avoid stereotyping racial, ethnic, or religious cultures and their characteristics. The nature of culture defies a one-size-fits-all approach. Aspiring designers should remember some key qualities of culture: it is ever-changing; it is not spatially bounded; it is geographically influenced; it occurs at various scales; and it is spiritual. Each of these characteristics is briefly discussed below.

Culture is ever-changing Cultures are not stagnant collections of artifacts attached to particular racial, ethnic, or religious groups. Cultural associations with particular groups can change both temporally and geographically, with certain cultures dominating at varying times. For example, different periods have seen the influence of Christians in Europe and the Americas, and Muslims in Europe and Asia. Our current transnational world exhibits a strong dispersal and intermixing of cultural influences. Geographically, cultures settle and evolve in different locations. Due often to political conflict or ostracism, disadvantaged groups relocate, taking their cultural characteristics with them. For example, many Hmong communities immigrated to the United States during the 1970s following the Vietnam War. Because of their close family ties, they tended to settle near one another and brought many religious and other traditions with them. Cultures' temporal and geographic shifts may bring new conflicts between different cultures, or different cultures may find that they can coexist without issue. Such shifting of cultures crosses regional and global boundaries. Cultures may also be passed on to subsequent generations (directly and indirectly), while also changing and evolving. In the current age of globalization, cultural assimilation and the dominance of certain cultures bring about considerations for respecting and sustaining cultural diversity. Globally dominant cultures frequently exploit vulnerable societies, and some cultures, such as Indigenous cultures, are dismissed, dispersed, or diminished (Smith, 1990).

Culture is not spatially bounded Cultures are not bound to a set geographic location. As noted above, where certain cultures are found may change over time and they may also disperse over geographic settings. When travel and global communication was more limited, the distribution of cultures was also more restricted. With increased globalization, cultural enclaves are likely to have numerous locations instead of being limited to the traditional or historical home of a particular culture. While the physical environment may influence cultural groups to migrate to a particular location, other factors influencing that decision include interpersonal relationships (as with the Hmong) and opportunities for employment or leisure. In addition, cultures reside in the nonphysical realm. Whether through online communities, or in-person communities outside the home such as religious, hobby, or recreation-based groups, individuals have opportunities to seek out and share experiences with similar minded people. Such cultures may reside in the virtual world, but they may also travel from one place to another, such as a bird-watching group that goes to different locations.

Culture is geographically influenced The formation of culture relies on various factors including physical geography. This geography includes the climate, topography, and natural resources people encounter every day. Those characteristics can influence a person's preferences, activities, and patterns. For example, someone growing up in a forested landscape may continue to prefer landscapes with tree coverage as compared to desert landscapes. Likewise, people growing up near a lake may be more inclined to fish or boat, while people living in prairie regions might be more closely attuned to farming and people living in mountainous areas to hunting. Geography may also influence the patterns of daily lives such as weather patterns determining when crops are planted, outdoor activities halted, or even how close people stand to one another (for further discussion, see Chapter 2, "Territoriality" section). Preferences and behaviors may be deeply rooted in an individual's environmental background and contribute to a shared culture with others of similar backgrounds. A shared geography, however, does not dictate a common culture for all who reside there. Individual beliefs, preferences, and experiences may inform very divergent views.

Culture varies across scales Culture can occur at many scales, including the individual, community, regional, or global levels. For example, young people from any number of communities, countries, or settings (e.g., urban, suburban, or rural) may have a shared youth culture, such as similar interests in recreational activities, music and other entertainment, or societal concerns (i.e., climate change or social justice). Similarly, other commonalities can contribute to shared perceptions and aspirations across scales, such as for women's rights or religious freedom. The manifestation of these cultural attitudes may have an influence on the home or local level (e.g., prompting family members to recycle) as well as across larger areas (e.g., protesting policy inaction on climate change). Cultures may overlap or be embedded, where one can have more than one cultural influence or identity at one time.

Culture is spiritual Cultures often have strong religious underpinnings. These spiritual or religious foundations endure despite changes in social structures, relationships, or other external factors. Formal religious institutions and beliefs have far-reaching influence on the physical landscape and accompanying social networks, as reflected in physical structures for gathering, ceremonies and celebrations, and pilgrimages. Temples, mosques, and churches are clear formal religious architectural representations, while practices such as ceremonies and pilgrimages may only be visible at certain times. For example, the religious processions of *Semana Santa* (Holy Week before Easter) in Spain transform city streets, and *Las Posadas* (a reenactment of Mary and Joseph's search for a room) at Christmas time in Mexico temporarily reshapes neighborhoods in Mexico. Spiritual influences also inform the protection of and celebrations in certain landscapes. This can be seen in the Australian Aboriginal reverence for the sacred mountain of Uluru. After years of being open to climbing by tourists, the Anangu People were successful in reclaiming and protecting the religious significance of the site. Lastly, religious sites, like other cultural landscapes, change over time. An adaptation of a religious landscape is seen in design features that protect worshippers from extreme sun exposure at a mosque in Medina, Saudi Arabia (see Figure 3.1).

Culture in global cities

Globalization and the rise of new information technologies have redefined city spaces, culture, and power dynamics. Currently, a process or event that happens in one location can extend beyond that physical geography, or even into digital space (Sassen, 2000). This intensified transnational and translocal culture and information exchange increases the socio-culture diversity in cities. Moreover, the migration of professional elites and low-income workers also takes place in this global context and contributes to the re-territorializing of new local subcultures (Sassen, 2000).

This transcultural character of global cities brings many challenges to designers and planners as they strive to design with culture. Along with the formation of new subcultures, new forms

FIGURE 3.1 Giant umbrellas (closed and open) in the plaza outside al-Haram Mosque in Medina, Saudi Arabia. Image credit: Jamila Khan.

of behaviors and attitudes emerge and transform with time and context. For example, *cultural assimilation* – the process of minority culture or groups resembling fully or partially a society's dominant group, in terms of values, behaviors, and beliefs – might occur (Spielberger, 2004). Hou (2013) argues that urban places should function as vehicles for cross-culture learning and understanding, and that while migration, diasporas, and translocality might have destabilized existing meanings of places, designers should re-envision placemaking, especially within the context of these shifting cultural terrains.

GENERAL FINDINGS

Historical and cultural uses of spaces

Historically, spaces, especially public spaces, related to and reflected the local culture. Different cultures throughout history have utilized urban centers as gathering places for various purposes such as markets, public gatherings, ceremonies, celebrations, and remembrances for people and events. Today, urban centers around the world share similar historical and cultural roots, as evidenced by similar uses of spaces like *piazzas* (Italy), *plazas* (Spain), *zócalos* (Mexico), *platzes* (Germany), squares (China), *maydans* (Iran), and commons (United States). For example, markets, a type of cultural artifact that continues to exist and adapt with time, reflect the cultural necessity to trade goods and services as part of everyday activities. Markets' varied physical forms and how they reflect local geography and climate, residents, and use patterns can be seen in the street markets in Taipei, floating water markets in Thailand, *tianguis* in Mexico, town hall markets on the east coast of the United States, and more (see Figures 3.2 and 3.3).

Celebrations or rituals have taken place anywhere people gather, whether to express thanks for a productive harvest or to pray for necessary elements such as rain (see Figure 3.4). Historically and currently, cultures also utilize common areas to display power through ceremonial events. These events might include coronations of new rulers, confrontations and conquests, executions, or public protests (see Chapter 2, "Proxemics and personal space" section). Similarly, public areas are used to promote and display innovations, such as the tradition of World Fairs and Expos, or the *La Biennale di Venezia* in Venice, Italy, which promotes advances in the arts and architecture.

Common spaces have also been used for collective needs, including such mundane tasks as grazing animals or getting water – the Boston Common began as a place to feed cattle, and

FIGURE 3.2 Floating water markets in Thailand. Image credit: Li Chen.

FIGURE 3.3 Colorful market umbrellas at a *tianguis* in Mexico City. Image credit: Yiwei Huang.

free-flowing drinking water is found in most Italian *piazzas*. Public spaces are also frequently used for informal social gatherings. Because of their proximity to civic buildings and commercial interests and their visitors, these spaces provide a place for people to linger and see others. The courthouse square in the southern United States has a long tradition of being the location where older men gather, in addition to its more sordid yet prominent history as the site of public executions. In Salamanca, Spain, young men and women have a long tradition of strolling the *Plaza Mayor* in opposite directions so that they can more readily see those of the opposite sex (Gade, 1976) (see Figure 3.5).

Contemporary uses of open spaces

Public urban spaces today are frequently designed for specific uses and controlled so that only acceptable activities are allowed. In many cases, what appear to be public spaces are in fact privately owned and subject to even stricter enforcement. Globally, public open spaces continue to be used for celebrations, event gatherings, and protest; however, organized activities

FIGURE 3.4 The Hall of Prayer for Good Harvest and its surrounding landscape at the Temple of Heaven, Beijing, China. Image credit: Fong Chen, retrieved from Wikimedia Commons.

now often require permissions and approvals prior to the event. Informal gatherings have also become more suspect. In particular, law enforcement or nearby merchants often break up gatherings of certain groups such as homeless people and skateboarders; furthermore, their gatherings or activities are increasingly prohibited by law. In addition, the exchange of goods and ideas now happens in places that are specifically designed for that purpose.

FIGURE 3.5 The daily Promenade at Plaza Mayor in Salamanca, Spain. Image credit: Patsy Eubanks Owens.

Permission to sell goods is required at these designated spaces with specific dates, times, and locations assigned.

Many urban design scholars note that these highly regulated, program-restricted spaces might suppress certain populations' enjoyment. Design responses to these restrictions might support and celebrate multiuse and multicultural activities rather than single-use activities by preferred or dominant populations. Thompson (2002) proposes shifting parks from a "melting pot" model to instead a "salad bowl" approach, wherein parks would allow different cultures to find their own individual expressions instead of designing for a single, predominant user group or use.

Designers and planners should consider whose culture is to be reflected and respected in the creation of a space. This is not an easy task since, as noted earlier, populations and places are constantly evolving. Although challenging, the design process can incorporate and acknowledge differing populations, their preferences, and their likely activities (see Chapter 8 for further discussion). The culture of a place and its people might inform considerations such as the materials used or activities accommodated in the design (see Chapter 1, "Situating human factors in the design process" section). Populations might not even be aware of cultural preferences that have developed over time. For example, throughout much of the United States, the ubiquitous grass lawn, associated with success and wealth, is cherished and replicated without thought. However, climatic conditions are leading some to question the appropriateness of this choice in vegetation. (For a further discussion of the lawn, see D'Costa, 2017). Similarly, acceptable activities may vary from one culture to another. Gathering with other men after dinner in a local park might be commonplace in some communities, while in other places, doing so might raise suspicions. For many years, local youth were allowed to play soccer alongside tourists on the upper terrace of Park Guell in Barcelona, Spain. However, recent restrictions and required ticket purchases have effectively banned this use (see Figure 3.6). Relatedly, many cities in the United States have explicitly prohibited skateboarding in plazas, parks, and on sidewalks (see Figure 3.7).

Culture, behaviors, and use preferences

Many researchers have examined whether people from different cultures have differing perceptions of and appreciation for the same landscape, and whether different design features are needed to support various cultural activities. This research includes studies on landscape preferences and recreational activities, as well as other interests and concerns.

Landscape preferences Beginning in the 1960s, environmental psychologists examined the connection between culture or ethnicity and people's preference for landscape styles and visual values (Sonnenfeld, 1967; Ulrich, 1983; Zube, 1984). Their general findings indicate that when cultures are relatively similar, people may show relatively high agreement on preferences for natural environments. Conversely, when cultures are rather dissimilar, preferences are distinctly less comparable, though in some cases, preferences can be inconsistent within the same culture (Kaplan & Herbert, 1987).

Recreational activities and the use of space Scholars have generally found that people from different cultures are likely to use the same open space slightly differently, though sometimes they might share similar patterns. Rapoport (1980) indicated that use and perception of space vary dramatically for different user groups because of their socio-cultural distinctions

FIGURE 3.6 Visitors enjoying the upper terrace in Park Guell, Barcelona, Spain. Image credit: Yiwei Huang.

FIGURE 3.7 Prohibitions on activities are common at public parks in the United States (Rogers, 2018).

PEOPLE AND CULTURE

(i.e., gender, age, race, income differences, life-cycle stages). Loukaitou-Sideris (1995) explored the cultural differentiation of uses of four urban parks in Los Angeles, CA. She compared patterns of use by African Americans, Asians, Hispanics, and Caucasians, and found that significant differences existed between racial groups in the way they used the park as well as the most-like park qualities. Other scholars have found similar conclusions related to ethnicity's influences on user patterns or preferences for park facilities (e.g., Sasidharan, And, & Godbey, 2005; Tinsley, Tinsley, & Croskeys, 2002).

Core interests and concerns Although research has shown that behavior and use patterns may vary between cultural groups, other studies show that different cultural groups share core interests and concerns for outdoor environment design and management. For example, Gobster (2002) surveyed 898 park users in Chicago and found that, despite ethnic differences, users shared many core interests. These included a core interest in highly participatory activities, shared preferences for natural features, shared concerns for cleanliness and maintenance, and common perceptions about park safety. Similar results have been found by others in different contexts (Jim & Chen, 2006; Özgüner, 2011). Gobster (2002) further suggests that use patterns and preferences could vary within racial groups; hence, it is risky to stereotype and to make statements such as "white people prefer …" or "Black people do …"

The design of outdoor environments should consider users' cultural backgrounds and use patterns; however, due to limitless cultural variations, there is no single outdoor environment design solution that can address everyone's needs and aspirations. Moreover, research findings such as those described previously should not be used to stereotype behaviors or preferences of certain populations. The previous studies' findings may represent a specific population, but should not be applied to all people of a similar background. Instead, designers should aim to design a culturally inclusive and welcoming landscape. To do so, one needs to understand the complexity of the local social context, engage with concerned communities, examine relevant demographic changes, and explore creative engagement methods.

Cultural aesthetics and cultural representation in vernacular landscapes Outdoor environments that reflect traditional cultural influences often present distinctive and unique aesthetics and representation of styles, whether through materials, forms, patterns, or construction techniques. These aesthetics, such as distinctive paving patterns found in cities in Brazil (see Figure 3.8), hold clues to people and their culture. Drawing upon a long tradition of mosaic walks in Portugal, this art form, the *calçada portuguesa*, is found throughout the country and was notably embraced by landscape architect Roberto Burle Marx.

Jackson (1985) discusses cultural influences that can be seen at macro- and micro-scales. At the macro-scale, cultural landscapes reflect political influences as indicated through socially recognized markers and boundaries. At the micro-scale, landscapes present "layers of meaning that are produced by its inhabitants through their everyday lives" (Gieseking, Mangold, Katz, Low, & Saegert, 2014, p. 256). Civic spaces and large city planning frameworks also contain vernacular features (e.g., monuments, fences, and steeples) that hold meaning by those who cherish them (Gieseking et al., 2014). These local or micro-scale places of meaning are described and mapped by Hester (1985) in his work on sacred places (see also Chapter 2,

FIGURE 3.8 A distinctive sidewalk pattern in the *calçada portuguesa* tradition in Curitiba (left) and Rio de Janeiro, Brazil (right). Image credit: Patsy Eubanks Owens.

"Place attachment" section). Like other representations of culture, vernacular landscapes evolve with their inhabitants and their activities. Jackson suggests that the landscape mirrors the cultural character of the everyday lives of the individuals, families, and communities that reside there (Jackson, 1985).

APPLICATIONS TO DESIGN

Strategies for applying culturally relevant information to designing places have garnered less research than those that focus on understanding culture. There are no checklists or guidelines for culturally relevant design for designers to follow. However, several institutions such as the US National Park Service, the UK National Trust, and UNESCO have focused attention on how culture can and should be reflected in the places under their jurisdictions. This section first introduces some institutional organizations and their missions for cultural preservation. Next, prominent principles for incorporating cultural considerations into the design of inclusive places are presented.

Institutional knowledge at a glance

Landscapes reflecting cultural influences are typically historic sites or landforms that denote representative, significant, or celebrated events of the past. These sites include, among others, memorials, preserved wilderness, and vernacular landscapes that are associated with a location's heritage and its corresponding cultures. The meaning of such places may be significant to one or more cultural groups but not to others. This places responsibility on organizations to identify the diverse stories and meanings of these landscapes. In addition, organizational bodies seek to protect and sustain shared natural or designed landscapes for all in the present day and future generations. From an institutional perspective, landscapes of cultural significance are important resources which require preservation, conservation, and restoration. For example, UNESCO World Heritage sites, US National Parks, and UK National Trust sites are designations from these organizations seeking to identify and maintain outdoor environments that reflect varied cultural influences.

UNESCO takes on the important task in today's global environment of protecting landscapes that represent the unique heritage of diverse cultures. As evidence of the organization's regard for cultural diversity, the UNESCO Universal Declaration on Cultural Diversity was adopted in 2001. This declaration acknowledges differences of cultures in an ever-transnational period of time in history (Stenou, 2002). Later, the *Global Report on Culture for Sustainable Urban Development* addressed the differing roles of culture in urban development efforts to further strengthen cultural considerations in a pluralist world (UNESCO, 2016). This report discussed strengthening cultural considerations through a thematic approach to addressing sustainable urban development needs through three themes – people, environment, and policies. Principles that emphasize the human scale, local development, and governance efforts needed to strive for sound environments with culture in mind are presented.

The National Park Service (NPS) and the Cultural Landscape Foundation (TCLF) in the United States and the National Trust in the United Kingdom are representative agencies and organizations that guide and educate others on the importance of cultural representation in our outdoor environments. The NPS, housed within the US Department of Interior, protects and preserves natural and culturally significant lands "for the enjoyment, education, and inspiration of this and future generations" (NPS, n.d.). The Cultural Landscape Foundation, a nonprofit organization, focuses on connecting people to places while identifying the value of and making visible shared landscape heritages; they empower stewards through various educational efforts including projects, programs, publications, and activities (TCLF, 2020). These efforts include maintaining a database of and resources for cultural landscapes and significant historical designs; however, the inclusion of landscapes and monuments with discriminatory and otherwise questionable associations is being debated. The National Trust is a charitable organization in the United Kingdom that has conserved and restored cultural places for their historic interest or natural beauty to serve the broader public. Although open to the public, these significant sites are subject to commercial operations for revenue to support continuing maintenance goals (National Trust, n.d.a, n.d.b).

Organizations such as these aim to protect landscapes that represent and reflect diverse cultures across different scales. Their long-standing efforts provide an invaluable resource for designers, both in terms of the inventory of places they hold and their processes and criteria for designating and celebrating places. By better understanding the history and culture related to a site, designers are well positioned to appropriately represent the varied layers of history and meaning of places of the people who created them (Hood & Basnak, 2015). These institutional precedents can help designers better understand and value the diverse cultural heritages of various outdoor environments.

Principles for culturally inclusive design

As noted earlier, there are no checklists for incorporating cultural considerations into the design of places; however, there are a number of important concepts that can inform the work of designers and planners. This section draws up the work of three designers and researchers – Galen Cranz, Setha Low, and Jeffrey Hou – for those guiding principles. These principles are not definitive or all-inclusive, but instead provide suggestions for designers as they prepare to work with individuals, communities, or regional entities from diverse cultural backgrounds.

Civic space design and use evolve with time The function of parks has always evolved with time and changes depending on social context. In *The Politics of Park Design,* Cranz (1982) categorizes four eras of park development in the United States from the 1850s to the 1970s by examining parks in Chicago, New York City, and San Francisco. Cranz argues that park designs during the different periods reflect the different everyday lives and requirements of people at each time. She identifies that physical features, such as park appearance, landscaping, built structures, and site selection, reveal the complexities of the social and political context in which they were created or built (Cranz, 1982).

For example, "reform parks" were popular during the 1900s to 1930s, aiming to provide space for organized activities as opposed to the unstructured pleasure grounds that were common earlier. The social and political context of reform parks was that of increased personal incomes, earlier retirements, and shorter work weeks. These conditions provided people with more leisure time; therefore, more structured recreational facilities, such as stadiums, golf courses, tennis courts, and picnic areas, were built during this period. The other three park stages – the pleasure grounds, the recreation facility, and the open space system – revealed similar relationships between contemporary culture and the resulting open space designs (Cranz, 1982).

Other scholars share similar findings regarding culture and open space use. Francis (1989) argues that with changes in public life and society, cultures transform the design and management of their open spaces. He notes that malls became an important escape for people living in isolated neighborhoods who spent long periods in impersonal work environments and suffered from other stresses of modern life. The COVID-19 pandemic prompted many communities, both officials and residents, to question local open-space design, such as the prioritization of streets for automobiles and the importance of access to nature. The long-term impacts of this global health crisis on the design of physical environments are unknown. The principle derived from Cranz's work is that designers need to recognize the social and political context within which they are working. Adaptation and flexibility to adjust to current concerns and conditions are critical.

The importance of cultural elements and design features Designers often work on projects that need to appropriately interpret and represent the cultures of people who use the designed outdoor environments. It is often challenging to determine the values that different cultural groups have for a shared space; however, it is imperative that designers fully understand how spaces are being used and what values they hold before any new attempts to create or re-create places.

Low, Taplin, Scheld, and Fisher (2002) present an evaluation of the impact of the Independence National Historical Park redesign in Philadelphia, Pennsylvania, that illustrates this principle. Low's team studied responses and perceptions from five different park-associated cultural groups that lived adjacent to the 55-acre public park. These groups included African Americans, Asian Americans, Italian Americans, Hispanic Americans, and Jewish Americans (see Table 3.1). Low et al. discovered that among these five cultural groups, only one group – Hispanic Americans – continued to frequently use the park after the renovations. Members of this group saw their culture represented in the redevelopment process through events such as

TABLE 3.1 A comparison of five cultural groups' use and attachment to Independence National Historical Park (Low et al., 2002)

CATEGORIES	AFRICAN-AMERICANS	ASIAN-AMERICANS	HISPANIC-AMERICANS	ITALIAN-AMERICANS	JEWISH-AMERICANS
VISITOR USE	Do not visit frequently — too busy, no black history, went in past; infrequent visitation, walk, play in Washington Square	Liberty Bell and Independence Hall main sites visited, visit with guests or on special occasions	Frequent visitation — parade, trysts, work, lunch, bring children to play or out of town guest	Most do not visit, few feel it is not safe, many visited when young, some like scenery	Do not visit frequently, memories of visits, take out of towners, some walkers
MEANING AND SYMBOLS	History and cultural identity; no particular meaning or negative meaning because only for tourists or whites	Clean, safe, organized, peaceful place, "broken bell" represents reality of struggle for freedom	Pretty, quiet place; "too serious," historical place representing struggle for freedom	Some attachment to physical elements, story of immigration, community-making, and Constitution	Liberty Bell is symbolic because of inscription, Declaration of Independence very important
CULTURAL REPRESENTATIONS	Does not represent African-Americans, feel excluded from park because of lack of diversity	Do not expect to be represented, emphasize education, Chinese feel little recognition of city contributions	Puerto Rican Day Parade is a kind of representation, would like to see more exhibits about their culture	Balch Institute represents immigrant groups, park should be for everyone, pretzels, pizza, hoagies	Ambivalent about calling attention to group, Mikveh Israel and Chaim Solomon should be highlighted

Source: Courtesy of the University of Texas Press.

the Puerto Rican Day parade. Members of the Asian American community occasionally used the park because they thought it was clean, safe, and organized; however, they also did not expect their culture to be represented. The other three cultural groups – African Americans, Italian Americans, and Jewish Americans – rarely visited the park after the redevelopment efforts. They thought that their cultures were ambiguously represented in or absent from the park's physical and cultural elements. In particular, African American residents stated that they would not visit the park anymore because, despite their ancestors contributing to the construction of the original park, they could not find any clue telling this story in the redeveloped park design and setting (Low, Taplin, & Scheld, 2005). This study showed that while the redesign might bring revenue from tourists, the omission of culture led certain cultural groups to feel disassociated from and lack place attachment with the site.

Multicultural impacts and culturally sensitive engagement strategies Along with understanding the nature and importance of culture, designers need to understand best practices for engaging different cultural groups. Lessons can be learned from the experiences and challenges of other scholars and practitioners undertaking planning and design projects. Some issues faced by designers include working with populations, such as immigrants or other groups that may not be familiar with common community-engagement practices used by design professions. They may be hesitant to participate in workshops or public meetings, or, if they do attend, may be less likely to voice their opinions, as public expression of personal opinions may not be part of their cultural traditions. Typical engagement methods such as surveys, voting, and majority-win methods may also make some feel uncomfortable and lead to passive acceptance or agreeing with what others say. Other interactions such as volunteering to help may be counter to their upbringing. Hence, innovative engagement methods are an important component of constructing a culturally inclusive design process and final design.

Hou (2013), along with many scholars, recommends varied participatory methods when working with people who share different cultures than that of the designer. While working on a neighborhood strategic plan for the Seattle International District (Washington), Hou explored more culturally inclusive and democratic methods and approaches. Like the Independence National Historical Park project, the International District also served multiple cultural groups, including Chinese, Japanese, Filipino, and Southeast Asian immigrants. In addition, this project was faced with the needs of multiple generations living in the area. The district opened to and served the public since the first wave of Asian immigrants in the 1940s. By 2012, the third generation of these immigrants was one of the most active park user groups. Three different age groups – elderly residents, working adults, and youth and children – all expressed their concerns and needs for the open spaces in their neighborhood. Language barriers and difficulties understanding the concept of citizen participation added more challenges during the neighborhood strategic plan process (Hou, 2013).

Hou introduced two participatory methods in the neighborhood strategic plan project that successfully engaged cultural groups who had mostly been absent during earlier community meetings. First, Hou used a photovoice method, which targeted the primary users of the streets – non-English speaking, elderly immigrants from mainland China, Hong Kong, South Korea, and Taiwan. Following the image soliciting, interviews with residents enlisted bilingual designers who collectively spoke English, Ho'lo Taiwanese, Japanese, and Mandarin. Next, Hou developed the "design buffet" method, an interactive game that allowed residents to freely choose their ideal design elements from provided cut-out photographs (see Figure 3.9). Like in a buffet line, participants are given aluminum trays to collect and then organize the photographs in ways they wanted. The design buffet method provided a means to overcome language barriers and address the concerns of different generations and provided a platform for everyone to express their different opinions and preferences (Hou, 2013).

Many other researchers have also focused on the development of participatory methods for working with people who have different backgrounds and cultures from the designer (see Chapter 7 for more discussion). For example, Nassar and Duggan (2017) share "village talk," a process in which designers walked with local residents to streets, markets, restaurants, mosques, and diwans (town councils) while listening to stories about their everyday life. In this way, the designers learned things from the community residents that they would not learn during typical community meetings. Cadórniga and de la Peña (2017) introduced "*el carrito*," an engagement process that uses a mobile cart. The designers rolled the cart into the public spaces they are investigating and invited those passing by to learn about the project. This allows the designer to reach people who actually use the space, and results in hearing from a much wider diversity of people and gathering more accurate information. Designers can employ any number of creative methods to deconstruct the power dynamics between design expert and citizen, and to establish a conversation with communities from different cultures.

FIGURE 3.9 Participants engaging in the "design buffet" during an intergenerational workshop (Hou, 2013).

These three projects illustrate key principles that should be incorporated into projects by designers. The first principle – designers need to recognize the social and political context within which they work – provides an important foundation to any project. Understanding the historical context of a place as well as more contemporary decisions will inform the role this place has played or will likely play for concerned populations. Next, designers need to understand how spaces are being used and what values they hold for various populations. Designers should seek to uncover the stories these places tell and the significance they hold for people. Lastly, concerted efforts need to be undertaken to engage residents and others in the design process, while understanding that many established methods such as community meetings may not be welcoming or effective in soliciting the input of many audiences.

DEVELOPING CULTURAL COMPETENCY

Developing cultural competency can help designers better understand how and what to address in their outdoor environment design projects to appropriately accommodate culturally diverse user needs. While the idea of cultural competency is relatively new, diverse organizations and individuals are currently bringing attention to its essential elements. Building cultural competency requires advancing through four levels: 1) cultural knowledge, 2) cultural awareness, 3) cultural sensitivity, and 4) cultural competency (Center for Community Health and Development, n.d.). These concepts or stages can be applied to the work of designers or planners and to the organizations in which they function.

The first level, "cultural knowledge," means that designers should know about the cultural characteristics, histories, values, beliefs, and behaviors of various ethnic or cultural groups.

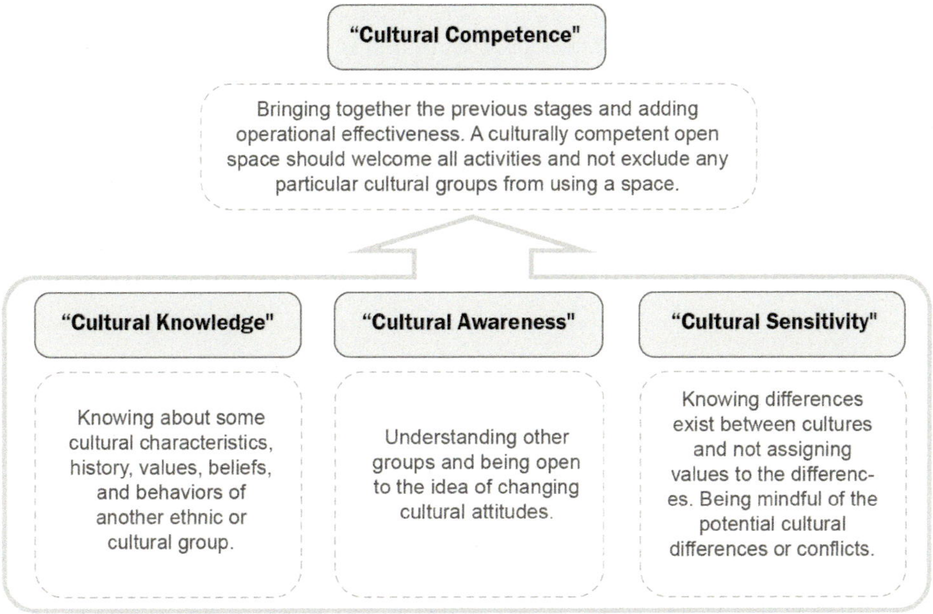

"Cultural Competence"

Bringing together the previous stages and adding operational effectiveness. A culturally competent open space should welcome all activities and not exclude any particular cultural groups from using a space.

"Cultural Knowledge"

Knowing about some cultural characteristics, history, values, beliefs, and behaviors of another ethnic or cultural group.

"Cultural Awareness"

Understanding other groups and being open to the idea of changing cultural attitudes.

"Cultural Sensitivity"

Knowing differences exist between cultures and not assigning values to the differences. Being mindful of the potential cultural differences or conflicts.

FIGURE 3.10 Developing cultural competency levels relevant to designing outdoor environments. Adapted from Center for Community Health and Development (n.d.).

The next level, "cultural awareness," is to understand other groups by being open to the idea of changing cultural attitudes. The third level, "cultural sensitivity," means knowing that differences exist between cultures without assigning values to the differences, such as better or worse, or right or wrong. Designers should be mindful of cultural differences and potential conflicts in case concerns arise. The last level of "cultural competence" brings together the previous levels along with the ability to effectively recognize, address, and operationalize actions (see Figure 3.10). When designers are able to incorporate all the levels of cultural competency, an outdoor environment design can be developed that welcomes many different behaviors, attitudes, and activities while not intentionally or unintentionally excluding any particular cultural groups.

Situating cultural competency in the design process

Cultural influences need to be considered and understood from the start of any outdoor environment design project, regardless of type of use, function, or setting. Early in the design process, designers should be proactive in seeking to understand and to apply cultural values in their work. The designer will need to anticipate behavior patterns, value differences, past experiences, and future aspirations. Most designers start to get to know their client, the project site, and the neighborhood context relatively early in the design process. This stage in the process allows for asking questions and building relationships.

During the inventory and analysis phase of a project, census data or other locally derived demographic information can inform the designer about the area in question. Likewise, examining and understanding a community's cultural characteristics through historical research can reveal past events, conflicts, or decisions that might influence ongoing involvement in a place, or shape the future use and representations of the place. When visiting a project site, designers should be perceptive of the current users and their activities as well as who is missing. Designers should ask, but not rely upon, their clients for demographic and cultural information as well as their experience working with the community. Direct interviews and observations are excellent tools to help inform the designer.

Developing (or interpreting a given) design program provides an opportunity for the designer to begin to apply their understanding of the local community. Demographic characteristics may hint at possible activities or use patterns. Past conflicts or discussions may identify competing interests. Often, community members seek guidance or suggestions from the design professional while also expecting them to understand their specific needs.

The generation of design concepts and alternatives should build upon the understanding gained in earlier design phases. Concepts will likely be more forthcoming once the cultural emphasis is known, and the community consulted. Likewise, resulting designs should anticipate and respond to the likely users and activities and be influenced by various cultural backgrounds. Designers can also influence cultural understanding and change at the micro-level by identifying and incorporating program elements. Most importantly, residents or potential users should identify the stories that they would like the design to tell. Lastly, the performance of spaces should be gauged using post-occupancy evaluation techniques such as behavior observations and interviews. This information will provide guidance for alterations and lessons for future designs.

CONCLUSION

Culture fundamentally informs how individuals and groups interact with their environments. Respecting the unique characteristics of a place and its people is a critical component of creating a long-lasting and meaningful design. Understanding the cultural aspects of people–environment relations includes those for individuals and broader populations, whether based on proximity, shared interests, or similar backgrounds. This understanding should apply to any scale of planning or design decisions and is not limited to small-scale, or local placemaking.

The aspects of culture covered in this chapter should be considered in the creation, renovation, and restoration of built environments. While a great deal of attention has been given to the creation of new facilities (e.g., parks), cultural competency principles also should be applied when focused on the preservation or conservation of environments. Often the rich stories these places hold remain untold or uncelebrated. Acknowledging and resolving past cultural conflicts can be an important element of recognizing disadvantaged cultures and incorporating their ideas and aspirations into a place.

Designers should share their goal of creating rich and relevant environments with the communities in which they work and enlist others in helping them to understand and represent different cultural groups' needs and preferences. Cultural influences and distinctive vernacular landscapes are important assets toward creating vibrant and well-used places. In addition, if a place holds meaning for people, it will likely instill a sense of responsibility and stewardship in those individuals and lead to better care (Scannell & Gifford, 2010b). With culturally relevant consideration and representation, empowered users will continue to cherish and adopt meaningful places for future generations to come.

POTENTIAL EXERCISES AND PROJECT

An indoor exercise

Cultural influences on open space perceptions. Everyone grows up with different cultures and different ways of life. These cultural differences will be evident in their perceptions of outdoor environments. This exercise will help you to become more aware of your own preconceptions of places and the perceptions of your classmates.

Steps:

1. Find a classmate who grew up in a different environment compared to you. For example, if you grew up in a city, find a classmate who grew up in a small town. If you grew up on the East Coast of the United States, you might partner with someone who grew up in the Midwest or on the West Coast.
2. Interview each other about your perceptions and preferences of outdoor environments. What types of outdoor spaces do you prefer? Why do you think this is the landscape that you like best? Talk about places that you remember clearly from your childhood. Why do you think this landscape holds a place in your memory? Discuss any memories you have about unique landscapes you might have seen while on vacation. Think about the everyday landscapes of your childhood. How did you usually spend a typical day? Were there places that you liked to spend time in? Describe these outdoor places – what types of vegetation do you remember from your childhood, how did you feel in this place, was there a view, was the place manicured or more natural?
3. Are there any particular types of environments or environmental features that make you feel more comfortable? Or uncomfortable? Discuss why you feel this way?
4. What are the differences in the places that you and your partner remember? Discuss why you think these differences exist or why they do not.
5. How can an understanding of someone's environmental background influence your future design decisions?

An outdoor exercise

Culture sketch tour. This exercise gives students the opportunity to identify physical representations of culture in an outdoor environment. These representations may be fixed, design features or short-term activities or events. You discuss how this knowledge can be applied to design decisions.

Materials needed:

   Sketchbook
   Pencil/pen

Steps:

1. Before beginning, the instructor should identify a place or places around campus that have diverse cultural elements.
2. The class members and instructor should visit the site as a group. During the site visit, each student should identify and sketch three examples of how culture is represented in this space. These representations may include architectural structures or features, paving or other material choices, vegetation types, observed activities, or other artifacts.
3. Once back to the classroom, you should display your sketches and discuss how each of you saw culture represented in the landscape. What were the observations that others had that you missed? How can these types of culture representations be incorporated into design decisions? Are there representations that should not be incorporated? Why and why not?

A group project

Culture and place. This project allows students to explore the expression of everyday culture in different parts of the world. The presentation, discussion, and review use a public shared platform such as Instagram.

The instructor should identify a topic (e.g., street market) for exploration. A hashtag should be created that is unique to this project (e.g., #LA556_2022_CULTURE). Students should post one or two images related to this topic each day for a set duration (see Figure 3.11). The time allotted for these postings will depend upon the time available in the course and the number of students participating. The intent is to collect a variety of images so a larger class would presumably need less time to develop a sufficient collection. These images may be original

FIGURE 3.11 An example of Instagram posts featuring "street markets" illustrate the visual richness of this assignment. Image credit: Yiwei Huang.

photographs from the student or they may be examples found online or through other sources. A source credit should be provided with each post.

Once everyone has completed their contributions, the images using this hashtag should be reviewed during class. Can the geographic location or culture be identified by looking at an image? If so, what are the visual or design clues that convey the cultural influence? Are there images that more successfully convey culture? What makes it more successful and how was this accomplished? What are the significant differences in these places from one culture to another?

This exercise should inspire students to understand the fluidity and multi-forms of culture. Students are encouraged to use this method when developing a design with and for cultures different from their own.

4
THE LIFE-CYCLE STAGE AND PLACE

This chapter explores how life-cycle stages factor into environmental behaviors, perceptions, and needs. An individual's age, their life-cycle stage, and their roles in life (e.g., do they work or go to school) all influence their spatial needs as well as their understanding of the affordances of public spaces. The human life cycle includes the primary stages of infancy, childhood, adolescence, and adulthood (Armstrong, 2020). This chapter focuses on childhood, adolescence, and late adulthood, as well as the human-environment considerations of working adults. An overview of the societal context and developmental or functional needs related to each age is given, followed by a discussion of activities and types of environments in which they occur. Lastly, an interpretation and application of life-cycle stage research for designers and planners are provided. The intent is to share information that will inform the creation of places that meet the needs of a range of ages; it is not to suggest that environments should be created that cater to only one age.

ENVIRONMENTS FOR CHILDREN

Background

Childhood encompasses a wide range of ages, abilities, and developmental stages. The needs of individuals at each stage and their implications for design are worthy of more detailed investigation and examination than is possible here. Other sources should be consulted to gain more detailed information on the various stages of infancy, early childhood, and middle childhood. The purpose of this discussion is to highlight developmental needs and tasks that closely align with outdoor environments and their design. These developmental needs and tasks include psychological, social, and physical characteristics.

Erikson (1963), Piaget (1951/2013), and others have described the stages of cognitive and social development of an individual, such as trust, autonomy, initiative or purpose, and competency. Erikson's stages of psychosocial development describe the characteristics of normal progression throughout the lifespan. The Centers for Disease Control and Prevention (CDC) and the American Academy of Pediatrics (AAP) also publish developmental milestones for young people (see CDC.gov and AAP.org). Along with cognitive and social skills, those milestones include physical skills such as the ability of infants (0–12 months old) to reach, grasp, and crawl; of toddlers (1–3 years old) to maintain balance, walk, and throw; and of preschoolers (3–5 years old) to run, hop, and catch. The grade-schooler (6–12 years old) continues to develop physical abilities while also increasing the capacity to plan their play, establish a course of action, and make quick decisions (American Academy of Pediatrics, n.d.).

These developmental processes take place in differing environments and generally increase in scale as illustrated in Bronfenbrenner's socio-ecological model introduced in Chapter 1. Development for the infant and toddler occurs at the individual and family levels while later development occurs at these levels plus the community.

Activities and their environments

Children continuously engage in activities that help them to develop their physical, social, and cognitive abilities. Many of these activities are in concert with their daily life tasks, such as eating, dressing, bathing, and sleeping. Others are in conjunction with supplemental undertakings, such as having fun. As discussed in Chapters 1 and 2, even though opportunities for children to engage in unsupervised outdoor play remain important, such opportunities have decreased in recent decades. Designers and planners should consider the inclusion and design of places where children can explore, play, and learn. Existing research on play's purpose is reviewed here, along with an overview of the evolution of formal play environments. A discussion of the role of play in learning and the design of learning environments completes this section.

The purpose of play Gray (2017) and Piaget (2013), among others, describe the developmental functions that play provides for children (see Table 4.1). Playing is something humans have an intrinsic ability to do; however, adults often believe that they need to teach or show children how to play. Such adult intervention can actually remove essential elements of play (see Table 4.2). Certain design characteristics can contribute to making places successful in terms of both developmental opportunities and encouraging child-directed play.

Van Andel (1990) identifies several recurring qualities of places where children like to play: lots of activity, interaction with other children, variety in the environment, natural elements,

TABLE 4.1 Developmental functions of play (Gray, 2017; Piaget, 2013)

Decision making and problem solving
Develop social skills (make friends)
Learn to regulate emotions
Develop interests and skills
Identify and experience joy

TABLE 4.2 Essential characteristics of play (Gray, 2017)

Play must be self-chosen and self-directed
Play needs to be intrinsically motivated ("just because")
Play should be structured by the players (they make the rules)
Play should have an element of imagination

FIGURE 4.1 Children using loose parts in their play. Image credits: Yiwei Huang (left) and Amy Wagenfeld (right).

safety, and enclosed or hidden spaces. Other research reveals a connection between development attainment and the availability of *loose parts* (e.g., sand, water, logs, crates, or tires, which children can move or manipulate) (see Figure 4.1). Haas (1996) found that these elements encouraged the development of both fine and gross motor skills, and even taught children the basics of physics. Maxwell, Mitchell, and Evans (2008) meanwhile witnessed cooperation and negotiation among the children using loose parts. Along with these developmental contributions, natural elements have also been shown to support risky play which contributes to child well-being (Sando, Kleppe, & Sandseter, 2021). Herrington and Studtmann (1998) also describe how natural elements integrated into traditional equipment-based play areas can influence a child's development.

The evolution of playgrounds Prior to the 1820s, much play was undirected and unsupervised, in keeping with the definition of play offered by Gray (2017). Children engaged in work on the family farm or helped with household tasks, but when free time was available, they created their own fun. The notion that children need a designated space to play began to emerge in the late 1880s; the locations, elements, and intent of these playgrounds have varied (see Table 4.3). Motivations for creating playgrounds include promoting health, removing children from the streets, and encouraging learning. The common components of playgrounds – swings, slides, climbing structures – have remained consistent for many years (with the exception of adventure and nature playgrounds).

Playgrounds are a culturally constructed notion and their purpose changes with the issues and motivations of the time. Some researchers question the relegation of play to playgrounds and present arguments for the inclusion of play in other places. In *The Child in the City*, Ward (1990) argues that children should be allowed to play everywhere and not be limited to a park or playground. Torres (2020) contends that children have a legitimate presence in urban areas and on the street, and that this should be considered in the planning of street networks.

TABLE 4.3 The evolution of the playground in the United States

Dates	Early 1800s	Mid to late 1800s	Late 1800s to early 1900s	Mid 1900s	Mid to late 1900s	1943 to present	1970s to present	2000 to present
Type	Outdoor gymnasium	Kindergarten	Sandgarten and manufactured equipment	Manufactured equipment	Novelty playgrounds	Adventure playgrounds	Modular, prefabricated components	Nature playgrounds
Location	New England	Not widespread (Boston, New York City)	Larger cities; then small towns, schools	Widespread	Widespread	Not widespread	Widespread	The Netherlands
Elements	Indoor exercise equipment	Nature (water, plants, animals)	Sand gardens, play equipment, sports fields, play supervisors	Metal play equipment (swings, slides)	Fantasy structures (e.g., ships, western towns, rockets)	Scrap lumber, old tires, concrete pipes, building tools	Wood or powder-coated equipment	Natural features (plants, water)
Intent or motivation	Exercise and health	Child development	Banning of play in the street (NYC); child abuse and neglect	With onset of World War II, steel from play equipment was used in the war effort and play supervisors were not available	Promote imaginative play	Child development	Proliferation of safety standards and liability concerns	Alternative play options, desire to bring children closer to nature, avoid extra costs resulting from safety regulations
Affiliated programs or organizations (if any)	Jahn Gymnastic Association		Child Saving Movement (1865–1900); Playground Association of America (1906)	Works Progress Administration (1935–1943)		European Adventure Playground movement		Spingzaad (https://springzaad.nl/)

Source: Adapted from Cranz (1982); Frost and Wortham (1988); and Verstrate and Karsten (2015).

Others promote the importance of nature experiences for children (Moore, 1997). As noted in Chapters 1 and 2, children's experiences in nature have decreased over the last 40–50 years due to adults' heightened fears, the loss of unclaimed or managed outdoor spaces, the increased use of computers and gaming devices, and an over-scheduling of youth in programmed activities (Owens, 2017). Louv (2008) describes this loss of nature experiences as a "nature-deficit disorder" and, like Moore, argues that exposure to and engagement with nature is important for a young person's healthy development. Moore and Cosco (2000) also propose that children growing up with exposure to nature will develop a love of nature and an understanding of humans' dependence upon it.

Places for play and places for learning Numerous studies show that engaging in physical activity improves cognitive and creative skills and contributes to social and physical development throughout childhood (Ginsburg, 2007). However, many school-aged children (or those in middle childhood) have lost opportunities to play. Some school administrators and policymakers see play, and recess in particular, as a waste of precious instructional time without benefit to students' outcomes and learning. In the United States, the No Child Left Behind Act (NCLB) of 2001 focused attention on annual student assessments in core subjects and led schools to increase class time by removing recesses. Within five years of NCLB's passage, one-third of elementary schools were not offering daily recess (Shammas, 2019). Children's advocates immediately began pushing back and petitioned for legislation that would protect children's recess. Several states, but not all, have subsequently passed laws requiring recess.

Conversely, examples of the integration of children's experiences in outdoor environments with educational activities provide evidence of the myriad benefits of play and outdoor learning. Stine (1997) provides compelling arguments for the creation of outdoor learning places. She notes that outdoor landscapes are ripe with sensory inputs and allow for spontaneous activities, furnishings, and limitless exploration. The Learning through Landscapes program in the United Kingdom takes the outdoor classroom beyond the gardening and science activities sometimes seen in U.S. schools (Lucas, 1995). This program shows how every subject can and should be taught in an outdoor setting (see Figure 4.2).

Application to design

Designing places for children requires understanding specific ages' needs, how they intend to use a place, and how a place might support their development and well-being. This information can be gathered for a particular project and location through a number of methods, including learning from other existing designs, observing the behavior of children at the site to be designed or similar sites, and consulting research relevant to the ages in question.

Examples of places designed for children Some professional offices have expertise in designing children's environments and possess a portfolio of projects from which others can learn. For example, Moore, Iacofano, and Goltsman (MIG) began in the early 1980s around the founders' passion for children's environments (see Figure 4.3). Their office sees the outdoor environment as a teaching opportunity and seeks ways for children of all ages and abilities to engage with the outdoors (MIG, n.d.). In regard to reclaiming streets for play, excellent

FIGURE 4.2 Musical instrument in a "Learning through Landscapes" schoolyard. Image credit: Learning through Landscapes.

FIGURE 4.3 A play area design that incorporates natural elements located in Nadaka Park, Gresham, Oregon. Designer: Moore, Iacofano, and Goltsman. Image credit: Billy Hustace Photography.

examples exist in several European cities (Tranter & Doyle, 1996). The *woonerf* or living yard was first introduced in the Netherlands in the 1970s as a shared space for children, cars, and others. Delineations between automobile and pedestrian spaces are removed and the resulting design creates spaces for social activities. Other examples of similar reclamations of streets for children are common in Germany and Denmark.

Observing children's activities Observations of the activities, participants, and adaptations at places children currently use provide valuable information, such as when activities occur, who participates, and what equipment is used. The designer can apply this knowledge to a new site. Loebach, Cox, and Little (2020) provide a thorough description and analysis of the behavior mapping process as it relates to children's environments, along with example protocols, that are useful for novices and experts in this area. In addition, Cosco, Moore, and Islam (2010) show the direct links between observations of preschooler activity and an outdoor design proposal. Chapter 7 provides more detailed information on behavior mapping and visualization, while the Chapter 9 case study of the Tulatoli school landscape in Bangladesh illustrates the application of many of these theories and methods.

Looking to research Designers can also refer to existing research to inform places they are designing for children. As discussed in Chapter 1, environmental autobiographies can be useful to help designers recall important places from their own childhood. Hester (1979) used this method to help childcare center parents remember what they liked to do when they were young. In the design of an infant garden, Herrington (1997) linked research on developmental goals with her proposed design (e.g., providing a small hammock for developing gross motor skills). Additional research on specific childhood stages may provide guidance on designing for activities that support the completion of developmental tasks during these periods.

There are additional existing resources for designers creating children's environments. The Children's Outdoor Environments professional practice network of the American Society of Landscape Architects (ASLA) provides critical expertise and experience in this regard (American Society of Landscape Architects, n.d.a). Drawing upon successful and professionally recognized designs, key elements of creating inclusive places to play (see Table 4.4) and other resources are offered (ASLA, n.d.b).

PLACES FOR ADOLESCENTS

Background

Youth, young people, and adolescents are terms used interchangeably in this book to describe individuals too old to be considered children and too young to be described as adults. This period of development has been described as the transition between childhood and adulthood, or the preparation for the next stage of life (Hendrey, Glendinning, Shucksmith, Love, & Scott, 1994). Others have made compelling arguments that adolescence is a distinct stage in development, not merely a transition, and deserves recognition as such (Kahn & Antonucci, 1980). The research and design applications presented here support this latter

TABLE 4.4 Key elements of a universally designed playground

Element	Brief description
Multiple forms of play	Contributes to social and motor development; include sensory elements (auditory and tactile elements enhance experiences)
Range of risk	Beneficial for development; allows children and parents to assess risks and abilities
Landform design	Develops motor skills; incorporate changes in topography
Ease of access	Provide multiple options (e.g., steps and slopes) for a range of abilities, visual access, and connections
Non-toxic, non-thorny plants	Select safe plants; incorporate a variety for sensory stimulation
Range of sensory engagement	Incorporate both quiet and active spaces
Materials	Consider the comfort and needs (i.e., navigability and visibility) of children with varied abilities
Accessible equipment	Specialized equipment can expand who can use it; include multiple options for use
Interpretive signage	Clear signage indicates available sensory elements; visual landmarks for orientation
Enclosure	Create a sense of protection; clear delineation of area using landforms, plantings, or fencing
Safe water and sand	Supports sensory experiences; design for child's independent use
Ample seating	Visual access; comfort

Source: Adapted from ASLA (n.d.b).

stance – young people's needs for and use of outdoor environments are different than those of children and adults.

Research on adolescents and the physical environment began with a few studies in the late 1970s (Ladd, 1978; Lynch, 1977) followed by research in the mid- and late 1980s (Conn, 1988; Hester et al., 1988; Owens, 1988) and more recent studies (Chawla, 2002; Loebach, Little, Cox, & Owens, 2020; Owens, 2002; Shirtcliff, 2015). These studies and others explore which places are important to adolescents and why, and how communities do or do not address the needs of youth. In addition, such studies cover the justification and methods for including youth in design and planning decision making. Most of these studies are set in the Global North, while a few notable exceptions (e.g., Chawla, 2002; Lynch, 1977) include multiple cultures and locations (although studies focused on youth in Asian countries and cultures are lacking). Additional research, particularly that which compares youth experiences in diverse settings, is warranted; however, previous studies provide some consistent findings on the reasons youth give for valuing outdoor places and the types of places that are important to them.

Reasons for valuing places

Studies reveal that youth value places where they can be alone as well as places where they can be with others (Owens, 1994). Places where they can be alone are important as they provide opportunities to get away and think about things: adolescents' place in the world, who they are, and what they want to do. Examples include places where youth can be with nature and places where they go for restoration. Places where youth can be with friends or other people are important because such places provide opportunities to engage in conversations and activities. They also help youth to develop their own identity. Places for gathering with their friends and places for recreation provide these opportunities.

Being with nature Many studies have shown that being with nature is a reason young people, particularly those in western societies and suburban areas, give for either going to or valuing a place. Youth find nature in expected settings such as parks and undeveloped agricultural lands, but also at their schools, homes, and in their neighborhoods (Owens, 1988). Research in urban areas as well as suburban and rural areas have uncovered the importance of nearby nature but have also noted that many young people do not have access to nature. Chawla (2002) reports that even when green spaces were not available, youth still mentioned their desire to add more natural places to their communities. Owens (1988, 1994) also notes that some youth might value nearby nature because they know that it is threatened by future development.

Restoration Other studies have shown that teens need places to be alone, places to get away from everyday pressures, and places that help them give order to their world (Kaplan, 1995; Korpela, 1989; Ladd, 1978). However, such private, unsupervised places are often difficult for the teens to find (Ladd, 1978). In particular, youth in urban settings may have more limited access to natural settings which have been shown to be more effective for restoration and recovery (Korpela, 1992). Agricultural lands, a cliff-side view of the ocean, and a summer cottage are examples of places that youth have identified as places they go to get away and to seek peace and quiet (Hester et al., 1988; Korpela, 1992; Owens, 1988) (see Figure 4.4).

Places to be with others An important task of adolescent development is learning to cultivate supportive social relationships. This is the time when many individuals begin to develop meaningful relationships with others outside of their families. In order to do this, young people seek occasions to be with others. While school can provide an important venue for doing this, unsupervised and unprogrammed gatherings are necessary. Like young children's need for unrestricted play, adolescents require opportunities to decide with whom and where to spend time. This often results in youth spending time hanging out with their friends and often occurs in public settings such as shopping areas and parks (Lynch, 1977; Noack & Silbereisen, 1988; Owens, 1988; Owens, 1994). Although this activity is an important component of their development, adults typically see this as an unproductive use of youths' time and believe that it will eventually lead to mischief (see Figure 4.5).

Places for fun Places where young people can engage in recreation and just have fun are also important for their development. Along with affording exercise and social gatherings,

FIGURE 4.4 Photograph taken by an adolescent girl of her view to Mt. Diablo (California) – a place she liked to go to "get away." Image credit: Patsy Eubanks Owens.

FIGURE 4.5 Photograph taken by an adolescent girl of her favorite place to hang out at school. Image credit: Patsy Eubanks Owens.

recreation provides young people with opportunities to develop new skills (including time management skills and leadership skills), their self-identity, and more. Research indicates that reasons for participating in recreational activities vary between individuals and between genders. Some studies have indicated that boys prefer to spend more time playing sports, while girls like to spend time with their friends (Duzenli, Bayramoglu, & Özbilen, 2010).

Application to design

Although design programming for public spaces routinely includes elements and considerations for specific age groups such as children and older adults, activities for adolescents are often avoided. Research shows that designers have been asked to create places that restrict certain youth behaviors such as skateboarding and group gatherings (Owens, 2002). City officials often want to know how to keep teens from hanging out at street corners, shopping strips, parks, or anywhere else they are perceived to be interfering with "legitimate" users. Adolescents, however, are also legitimate users of these spaces and designers should seek to create places that meet their social, physical, and psychological needs. The types of places that fulfill these needs for youth include these aforementioned urban areas (Korpela, 1992; Lieberg, 1995; Owens, 1988) as well as parks (Duzenli et al., 2010; Owens, 1988, 1994), natural areas (Hester et al., 1988; Korpela, 1992; Owens, 1988), places at school (Clark & Uzzell, 2002; Owens, 1988), and home (Korpela, 1992; Noack & Silbereisen, 1988). Some of the design characteristics for each of these place types are reviewed hence.

Young people value *commercial and other urban areas* because these are places where they can hang out with friends and meet new people. Shopping areas that attract adolescents from various neighborhoods offer a level of anonymity that youth value. These are places where they can test out new identities as well as be with friends away from adult supervision. Designs that facilitate these behaviors, such as seating areas for small groups, could provide legitimate places to gather. In addition, attention to including businesses which are youth friendly would be beneficial.

The design of *parks* also presents opportunities to ensure that these places welcome and support adolescents. Youth use parks for sports and other recreational activities and for being with friends. Adolescents also like to watch others. Viewing and gathering areas for non-participating youth should be included. While most research on park elements designed for adolescents has been limited to skateboarding (see Fredericksen, 2002; Jones & Graves, 2000; Owens, 2001), some playground manufacturers have begun to explore products for use by these older youth (see Kompan's playgrounds for tweens and teens – https://www.kompan.us/play/play-systems/galaxy).

Natural and undeveloped areas, including agricultural fields, wooded areas, and beaches are also important to young people. Adolescents like having places to escape to and also where they can be close to nature. Youth particularly value views and prospect refuges, as noted in Chapter 2. One study found that the presence of nature, even when limited, helped female participants "lead more effective, self-disciplined lives" (Taylor, Kuo, & Sullivan, 2002, p. 49). Designers and planners have opportunities to bring natural landscapes into urban or other nature-deficient areas. Recent writings, including *Last Child in the Woods* (Louv, 2008), espouse the idea that children need more interaction with nature; undeveloped lands provide places for this interaction to occur.

Even though young people spend many hours at *school*, they do not often highly value places there. Schools are not viewed as attractive places, nor do they even provide for basic needs such as seating and shelter. When youth describe places at schools as important, they mention the ability to be with their friends or play sports. Youth often comment on their lack of control over where they can go and what they can do at school. In one study, youth mentioned how they felt like school staff assumed they had done something wrong even when they had not (Owens, 2010). Conversely, some youth shared ways that they have helped to improve their school such as picking up litter or planting flowers (Owens, 1988). Designers can play an important role in creating school environments that foster social interactions, a sense of belonging, and recreational opportunities, as well as learning.

Places at *home*, whether their room or the homes of friends, are important to teens. The home environment can have a positive influence on the healthy development of adolescents and their emotional well-being. For instance, one study indicated that girls who engaged in decisions about their room were less likely to engage in suicide ideation (Evans, Owens, & Marsh, 2005). The consistent reporting of the importance of places at home to adolescents illustrates their significance and presents opportunities for designers to create supportive home environments.

Designers and planners have many opportunities to include adolescents' unique activities and needs in the places they create. Many communities in the United States and abroad have begun to create places for skateboarding, but this effort is frequently an attempt to limit the presence of youth in other public places (Malone, 2002; Owens, 2001, 2002). Others, such as the Esplanade Youth Plaza in Fremantle, Australia, and Factoria Joven in Merida, Spain, have been more successful in integrating skateboarding, BMX biking, rock climbing, and parkour into centrally located, family friendly parks. The Esplanade Youth Plaza includes seating and viewing areas which encourage families, tourists, and others to gather and watch (City of Fremantle, n.d.) (see Figure 4.6). Factoria Joven incorporates indoor and outdoor facilities for workshops and unique elements such as graffiti walls for urban art sessions (Katz, 2011).

FIGURE 4.6 Esplanade Youth Plaza in Fremantle, Australia. Photo courtesy: City of Fremantle.

WORKER NEEDS AND WORKPLACE DESIGN

Background

Adulthood includes many variations in lifestyle choices and opportunities. Options may change for individuals throughout their adult years, and vary from one person to the next. Decisions around life partners, children, jobs, and more create different physical environment needs for each person. Each of these issues present unique design considerations and call for reflection from designers and planners. Since most adults will enter the workforce at some point, this section focuses on some of the considerations around workplace design and the needs of workers. A brief history of workplace design and changes in the work are provided followed by a discussion on disparities in the workplace.

History of workplace design: From productivity and efficiency to health and happiness

Finding gainful employment and supporting oneself is a common rite of adulthood. While adults have diverse needs, those associated with work settings warrant particular attention from designers and planners. Along with the actual workplace, designers and planners should consider where an individual lives in relation to their job and the methods of travel between these two locations. While research on indoor workplace design, such as ambient environmental conditions (i.e., light, noise, and thermal comfort), furniture and layout, and worker involvement in decisions (Vischer, 2008), has gained attention in recent years, the following section focuses on aspects relevant to the design of outdoor work environments.

Early approaches to workplace design looked to increase workers' productivity and efficiency. For example, industrial designers specialized in designing machinery and factory layouts that would decrease the time from a product entering an assembly line to when it was ready to ship. This focus, while still present, has been supplemented with attention to worker health and happiness. Recent decades have seen increased focus on keeping employees on the job by decreasing physical and emotional illnesses. In the United States, safety inspections are regular protocol at all places of employment and suggestions for workplace improvements, such as ergonomic checks, are now commonplace. These precautions arise from self-serving motivations since employers lose profits when employees stay home or experience employee turnover. Insurance companies, with the support of the U.S. federal government, frequently motivate employees to participate in wellness programs by offering reduced insurance costs; studies also show that the design of the workplace can have a significant and long-lasting impact on worker health and, in turn, their productivity (Center for Active Design, n.d.). The incorporation of outdoor walking trails, running paths, and social gathering places in the workplace encourages and allows workers to engage in healthy practices.

Changes in the workplace: From agrarian, industrial, service, to technological societies

Where people work, both in terms of geography and job type, greatly varies and is constantly changing. Societies across the world once had predominantly agrarian-based economies with workers living and working on the same land or nearby. With industrialization, more people moved to cities and worked in urban factories. In the United States, this was followed by a shift in the mid-20th century to suburban factories and corporate headquarters.

Mozingo (2016) thoroughly documents the history of the suburban corporate landscape and further explores how this development pattern signified privilege and status. This shift in employment patterns also ushered in a period of designing landscapes for worker enjoyment and health. More recently, companies in the technology sector and related industries have relocated to urban areas where many of their younger employees prefer to live. Many of these companies also provide in-house amenities, such as free meals and gyms, for their employees, to entice them to spend more hours at work. For example, the film production company DreamWorks created a campus atmosphere with gardens and fountains, as well as yoga and art classes (Hall, 2013). With the onset of the COVID-19 pandemic in 2020, patterns of employment adapted rapidly and dramatically. Offices were vacated as employees began working from home, and amenities were reduced or eliminated. Long-term impacts of working remotely are projected to, at minimum, influence many office workers to want to continue to work from home, even after the spread of the virus is under control. However, these altered working conditions do not apply to a large segment of the population. Many adults will continue to work outside their home, particularly those in jobs requiring in-person interactions such as food services and medical support. Design implications arise for both at-home workers and those facing challenges around health and safety at their in-person jobs.

Workplace disparities Occupations and their settings are very diverse. While some jobs are conducted at a desk and in front of a computer, many others are located in factories, stores, restaurants, and more. For these workers, the setting presents issues related to safety precautions or healthy behaviors. Retail, medical, and other service sector jobs generally provide less flexibility for impromptu walks and frequent breaks and put the worker in close proximity to their clients and customers. Limitations on recreational physical activity or restful practices are even more pronounced in blue-collar jobs. Time constraints, limited facilities, and lack of interest by management result in fewer opportunities for blue-collar workers to have healthy recreation and restoration opportunities while at work (Sallis, Burns, Owen, & Veitch, 1997). In addition, many service industry workers cannot afford to live close to their place of employment, so they spend more time and money commuting (Allen, 2014).

The role of design and planning in outdoor workplace environments

Designers and planners can play a role in creating more supportive work environments at two different scales: at the regional or community level, and at the property or site-specific level. While more research is warranted on planning and design considerations, past studies on these environments provide some guidance for creating a workplace that is supportive of healthy behaviors and meets employees' daily needs.

One of the biggest hurdles to overcome in creating supportive work environments is the proximity of jobs to appropriate housing opportunities. Hours-long commutes are commonplace across the United States. Commuters not only have less time for recreational pursuits but also are more likely to suffer from stress caused by traffic delays and demands on their attention (Chatterjee et al., 2020). Studies indicate that lower-income individuals are more likely to have longer commutes to their work (Roberto, 2008). Current land use patterns often situate housing affordable for low-income populations far from the places where they can find jobs. In addition, public transportation options for these communities are frequently limited. Allen (2014) found that many commuters in Baltimore had prolonged travel times and needed

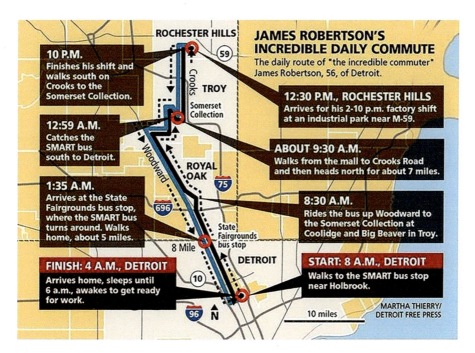

FIGURE 4.7 In transit deserts, residents often walk greater distances to access bus stops. This graphic depicts James Robertson's 21-mile daily commute to work. © Martha Thierry – USA Today Network.

to use several modes of travel to get to their jobs, thereby resulting in "transit deserts" (similar to that of Detroit, see Figure 4.7). Land use planning needs to address both the location of housing in relation to employment and transportation systems to support more distant residential areas, particularly those of low-income populations. Residents that have shorter commutes have more time for recreation or other pursuits; some studies indicate that those workers also have higher job satisfaction (Kneebone & Holmes, 2015).

The creation of outdoor spaces, particularly on suburban corporate campuses, has received some attention as a design response from businesses and designers. Outdoor environments as places for relaxation and recreation in work settings are created with the expectation that employees will be healthier, have fewer days of missed work, and be more productive, as well as have greater satisfaction with their job and therefore be less likely to seek alternative employment. In a privately commissioned study of office employees in Europe, the Middle East, and Africa, Cooper (2014) found that office workers in workplaces that incorporate indoor and outdoor natural elements reported a 13% higher level of well-being and were 8% more productive. Of respondents, 33% were more motivated than those in offices without natural elements. This finding is in keeping with earlier research that shows the presence of nature is effective in reducing stress and offering restoration (Hartig, Mang, & Evans, 1991) (see Figure 4.8).

In line with the desire to reduce insurance costs noted above, many companies seek ways to encourage their employees to exercise. Companies provide changing rooms, showers, and gyms in the interior of some offices, while running and walking trails are incorporated into company properties (Sallis et al., 1997). Some businesses are also able to take advantage of nearby community parks and trails. In addition to increased access to physical exercise, work

FIGURE 4.8 The Charles Schwab campus in Austin, Texas provides welcome opportunities to be outside and in the presence of nature. Courtesy of Charles Schwab. Image credit: Brandon Huttenlocher/Design Workshop Inc.

colleagues may engage in lunchtime walks or group outdoor breaks which can contribute to feelings of belonging and satisfaction with their work environment (Klotz & Bolino, 2021).

Application to design

These research findings have direct relevance to community planning and work environment design. The idea of locating employment opportunities and residential areas in close proximity to one another is not new, but it has received renewed focus during the last few decades. Master planned communities in the United States, which date back as early as 1929 (Radburn, New Jersey) and grew more popular in the 1960s (e.g., Reston, Virginia and Columbia, Maryland), sought to encourage businesses to locate near housing so that residents would not have to travel for work. Unfortunately, despite enticing businesses and companies with diverse skill requirements, such plans typically fell short of meeting the communities' employment needs (Cervero, 1995). Similarly, the goals of New Urbanism as cataloged by the Ahwahnee Principles are to create compact, mixed-use, walkable, and transit-oriented development (Calthorpe et al., n.d.). While some New Urbanist communities have successfully attracted varied work opportunities, they often fall short of meeting the employment needs of all residents (Podobnik, 2011). (For more discussion, see Chapter 10.) Another alternative to the co-location of work and home is the provision of employer-supported transportation. For example, in 2007, Google transported approximately one-fourth of its workforce by private bus to its headquarters (Helft, 2007). These buses provide a free and comfortable alternative to commuting by car.

The need to commute by workers is likely to persist. The incorporation of public transportation into community planning efforts needs further exploration. Alternative transportation modes are of particular importance to lower-income populations and a large number of two-career families. Many dual-career couples find that in order to find a satisfying job, one person must commute (Tryon & Tryon, 1982). This arrangement is especially complicated when factoring in childcare and other home-based responsibilities.

Along with larger-scale planning decisions related to workplace locations, the design of the working facility and its grounds warrants attention to the needs of the individual worker. Designers must understand workers' patterns – what time they arrive, when they leave, how much time they have for lunch, and where and how they spend that time. These patterns can inform how to design the workplace to best support both necessary worker activities and those that would be beneficial to their overall health and happiness. For example, would an earlier commute to work allow the worker to miss the heaviest traffic patterns and get exercise after work? Could an outdoor eating area also be used for small group work meetings? Could views of nature or natural elements be incorporated into the building design? Some businesses have begun to integrate such thinking into their facilities. Chapter 9 features a design for a women's prison that provides places for the staff to escape the demands of the job. BlueCross BlueShield headquarters in Tennessee has pleasant walking paths to entice employees to get outside (Center for Active Design, n.d.). Design professions should further explore other opportunities for and examples of addressing worker needs in workplace design.

DESIGNING FOR OLDER ADULTS

Background

Historically, people over the age of 65 have accounted for a small percentage of the overall U.S. population. However, that age distribution is projected to change dramatically in the coming years. Seniors are expected to outnumber children under the age of 18 for the first time in U.S. history by 2034 (Vespa, Medina, & Armstrong, 2020) (see Table 4.5). Similar trends of aging populations are already the norm in other countries such as Japan, Germany, and Italy. In the United States this population shift is due to the aging baby-boomer population (the youngest of which will reach age 65 in 2030), families having fewer children, and longer life expectancy rates. (These projections were conducted prior to the COVID-19 pandemic and do not reflect the significant loss of life particularly among older populations.) With an aging population, designers and planners need to respond to increased requirements for alternative

TABLE 4.5 Projections of the older adult population: 2020–2060 (Vespa et al., 2020)

Year	Millions of people 65 years and older	Percent of Population
2016	49.2	15
2020	56.1	17
2030	73.1	21
2040	80.8	22
2050	85.7	22
2060	94.7	23

Source: U.S. Census Bureau 2017 National Population Projections

housing types and locations, transportation options, recreational pursuits, healthcare facilities, and other changes to the built environment.

In addition to the shifts toward an older population, understanding the characteristics of this age group is important. Projections indicate several qualities that will likely influence the needs and interests of these seniors. Their *racial and ethnic backgrounds*, their *socio-economic conditions*, their *geographic locations*, and the *presence of a disability* are among the characteristics that are likely to vary as compared to previous older populations (Scommegna, Mather, & Kilduff, 2018).

Racial and ethnic background Older populations are becoming increasingly diverse. While attention has been given to what impact this will have on health disparities between various racial and ethnic groups, less research has focused on the implication for differences in the use of or desires for outdoor environments.

Socio-economic conditions Projections indicate that people with higher education levels and higher income levels will have longer life expectancies (Lynch, 2003). Therefore, some expect these aging populations to have more income available for recreational or other pursuits than did previous generations (Foster, 2016). Others (e.g., Harris, 2007) suggest that inexpensive activities such as walking, biking, and swimming will remain popular among older adults.

Geographic distribution Population studies also indicate that rural and suburban communities have higher concentrations of older populations (Smith & Trevelyan, 2019). These locations typically have fewer health care services and limited alternative or public transportation options as compared to urban areas, and therefore pose access challenges for people as they age. With heavy dependence on automobiles in these areas, older residents become reliant on others for errands when they become unable to drive themselves. As the aging population increases, so will transportation concerns; addressing them will become progressively important for community leaders and planners.

Presence of a disability Lastly, members of this growing senior population are largely expected to have some form of disability (Scommegna et al., 2018). While poor physical, sensory, or cognitive capacity is expected for most, some will experience dementia, or diminished hearing or vision. The design of the built environment, as discussed below, can help accommodate people with these and other disabilities to maintain access to and use of both their home and public environments.

The environments and activities of older adults

The daily patterns of many older individuals revolve around their home and their immediate neighborhood. Although the retirement age has continued to increase, commuting for work has ended for most of these adults. While many older adults continue to engage in intellectual pursuits and community volunteerism, most activities are focused on personal care (e.g., grocery shopping, personal errands, medical care), entertainment (e.g., visiting friends and family, movies, dining out), and recreation. These activities are closely aligned with the navigability of the nearby built environment and the inclusion and design of supportive facilities.

Like children and adolescents, it is impossible to characterize the needs and activities of all older adults into a one-size-fits-all model. Interests and abilities vary per individual; therefore, designers and planners need to consider the specifics of the community and residents of the project at hand. Research does however provide some guidance as to the current and changing patterns of older adults. For example, the percentage of adults over 65 that meet recommended federal guidelines for both aerobic activity and muscle-strengthening exercises more than doubled between 1998 and 2018 (National Center for Health Statistics, 2021). Whether a periodic trip to a local gym, a neighborhood walk, or a tennis match, the provision of nearby facilities to support these activities increases the likelihood of continued participation. Another presumption is that older adults' recreational activities are more varied than those of earlier generations. While previous generations of designers often included shuffleboard courts in parks near senior housing areas, current older residents likely would not be interested in that game. Instead, the recreational preferences they held as younger adults remain prevalent as they age and still maintain abilities. Research on recreation trends indicate activities that are varied and physically demanding are more popular for this age group than for past generations (Cordell & Super, 2000).

Along with individual influences on changes in recreational activities for older adults, variations in family support systems can impact an aging person's daily patterns. Familial relationships of older people may have become less stable due to increases in multiple marriages, geographic dispersal, and financial stress (Silverstein & Giarrusso, 2010). Aging individuals without the support of family are now likely to rely on their neighbors, friends, or community services for assistance with both basic needs and entertainment and recreational activities. Many adults elect to move to senior communities to find the level of support they need. These communities include housing developments for those over 55, independent living associated with senior care facilities, assisted living with meals services and regular care, and skilled-nursing facilities with full care and support. Each of these present unique design challenges and opportunities.

Application to design

Understanding the changes in the needs and activities of older adults can inform designs at different locations and scales such as the community, housing areas, and individual design elements. Overall community planning and neighborhood design can help ensure a more supportive environment for aging adults and all residents. As noted previously, older adults may live in any number of residential areas. The design of these areas is an important contributor to meeting their needs. In addition, research provides important guidance for specific site design characteristics for those seniors with diminished physical and mental capacities. Each of these is briefly discussed.

Community planning The physical, economic, and social features of neighborhoods have been shown to be important factors in the health and well-being of residents (Mather & Scommegna, 2017). Design and planning can positively impact these features. Features such as convenient and safe ways to walk to and access community resources (e.g., parks, libraries, recreation centers) (Clarke, Weuve, Barnes, Evans, & Mendes de Leon, 2015), access to healthy

TABLE 4.6 Relationship of physical design features to healthy aging according to existing literature

Neighborhood physical features	Physical activity	Obesity	Heart disease	Cognitive function
Walkable – More sidewalks and crosswalks; fewer dead-end streets		↓		
Compact – A diverse mix of land uses within walking distance	↑		↓	
Accessible – Barrier-free sidewalks; available public transportation	↑			
Safe – Residents feel safe	↑			
Community Resources – Availability of parks, public spaces, community centers, etc.				↑
Healthy Air – Low concentrations of air pollution				↑

Source: Adapted from Mather and Scommegna (2017).

food (Kaiser et al., 2016), and well-maintained streets and neighborhoods (Boardman, Barnes, Wilson, Evans, & Mendes de Leon, 2012) have been shown to positively impact the health of older residents. Table 4.6 illustrates the impact of various neighborhood physical environment features on different health concerns.

Neighborhood design can increase older adults' accessibility by providing well-maintained sidewalks, connections to desired destinations, and public transportation. Likewise, addressing the perceived and actual safety of older adults will likely increase their physical activity. The design of a neighborhood can also lead to more and better social interactions and individual satisfaction with their living space. One study conducted in Tokyo, Japan found that living close to green public areas positively impacted the life expectancy of older residents (Takano, Nakamura, & Watanabe, 2002). The authors propose that an increase in physical activity outside the home may have improved residents' health.

Residential alternatives for older adults Along with considering the needs of older residents in improvements to all neighborhoods, several residential developments cater directly to the senior population. Senior living communities, often marketed and limited to individuals over 55, have been in existence for several years. Sun City and Trilogy residential developments are examples of this type of development and are located throughout the United States. These communities typically focus on providing recreational amenities such as golf and tennis for the residents. Along with recreation, communities often promote safety measures such as guarded entry and regular security patrols. These communities also encourage and support social interactions at a community club house or through organized activities. While these communities fulfill the desires of a segment of the senior population, not all seniors can afford the high cost of purchasing a property in these communities, while others are not interested in living in an area that is segregated by age.

Over the last three decades another senior housing alternative, "aging in place," has emerged. While nursing homes have been available for many years for older residents that can no longer take care of themselves, the "aging in place" model allows an individual or couple to buy ownership in a complex that will allow them to first live independently, then progress to assisted living and to skilled nursing as needed. These types of facilities can vary significantly in scale. Some are a modest size and include a few independent homes, assisted living apartments, and then a smaller skilled nursing building. Others, however, are on the scale of a small town. They often include the three levels of care but also provide a full complement of support services such as hairdressers, convenience stores, alternative food venues, and multiple recreation options. Assisted living and skilled nursing facilities also are found independently of other housing types.

Specific design considerations Each residential model presents unique design opportunities that are dependent upon the specific population and the climatic conditions of the location; however, a great deal of research has been focused on the design of facilities for Alzheimer's patients and is useful in the design of other elder housing types (e.g., Lovering, 1990) (see Table 4.7). In addition, Marcus (2007) developed an Alzheimer's Garden Audit Tool (AGAT) that is particularly useful for designers undertaking work in this area. The tool is a 74-item checklist that is organized into seven components: location and entry, layout and paths, planting, seating, overall design and details, maintenance, and amenities.

While this chapter focuses on various life cycle stages, the intent is to draw attention to the needs of various ages and not to necessarily promote the separation of these ages in the places that are designed or in a community's planning decisions. Instead, an approach that encourages and supports intergenerational living is suggested. Designers and planners have a responsibility to design for the entire community and to consider expected changes in its population. There are many advantages to designing for diverse ages, as well as diverse racial and ethnic groups. Incorporating housing for older residents near to others may help them to feel like they are a part of the larger community and also provide a support network. Integrating places for adolescents to spend time with their friends or to practice their skateboarding skills within the broader community allows them to practice positive decision making, feel valued by adults in the community, and show off their skills. While some situations may warrant designing for one specific age group, these and other beneficial implications argue for pursuing a multi- and intergenerational approach to most design and planning decisions.

POTENTIAL EXERCISES AND PROJECT

An indoor exercise

Role play – Understanding and addressing the needs of families and individuals in a park design. This exercise challenges you to think about a park's design from the perspective of different family compositions and individuals within families. The intent is to expand your thinking about how various community members use public spaces and how those activities are informed by their life-cycle stage.

TABLE 4.7 Design considerations for outdoor spaces for Alzheimer's patients and other older adults

Issue	Description	Example design considerations
General safety	Accommodation of physical limitations, supervision needs, facilitate sense of control and independence	Enclosure without a sense of confinement
Physical mobility	Movement limitations, decrease in strength and endurance, use of assisting devices (walker, cane, wheelchair)	Walkways: consistent and non-slippery surfaces, clear delineation, resting points Seating: height and incline; hand supports
Visual acuity	Color distinction diminished, sensitivity to glare increased	Adequate and consistent lighting Reduce glare through shading (trees and structures) and non-reflective materials Use contrasting colors (i.e., light furniture on dark ground) but not on ground surfaces except to indicate change in grade
Auditory acuity	Decreased sound discrimination; decreased hearing ability	Avoid locating noise-generating activities close to quiet activities Reduce background noise through walls, heavy plantings Design for close or adaptable seating arrangement
Wayfinding	Poor memory, confusion	Use of patterns and color to reinforce routes Integration of landmarks, distinctive features Views to the features Self-contained loops without hidden spaces
Social interaction	Places for interaction	Multiple, smaller social spaces (seating for four to six people) Seating patterns for conversations
Privacy	Places for solitude and control; essential for maintaining self-regard, self-reflections, and autonomy	Semi-private, one to two-person seating areas

Source: Adapted from Lovering (1990).

Steps:

1. The instructor should divide the students into several groups of differing sizes. Each group should imagine themselves as a whole family. For example, a group of two might be a single-parent family, a group of three a two-parent with one child, a group of four a two-parent with two children, and a group of seven a two-parent, two-grandparent, and three kids.
2. Along with the instructor, students should review the master plan of a nearby park.
3. After a preliminary discussion about the composition of the park, each group should analyze the park from the perspective of their role-playing family composition. Are there amenities in this park for everyone in your family? How often would each family member likely visit the park? Does the park provide adequate spaces for family members to do the things they are likely interested in doing? What other questions does your family have about this park?
4. After this discussion, each group should annotate the existing park master plan with their observations, questions, and suggestions.
5. Each group should present their findings to others in the class. The class should discuss how the findings varied or were similar between the different groups and how this understanding might inform a park design process and the final design.

An outdoor exercise

Observing children's play. Note: Since this exercise likely requires permission to access a private facility, the instructor should gain permission before beginning. Campus locations, such as an on-campus early childhood teaching facility or married student housing, are possible project sites where students might have easier access.

This exercise provides an opportunity for you to observe and understand children's play behavior and to consider how this relates to their physical and social development. These lessons may then be applied to the design of other play environments.

Steps:

1. Identify a play area for observations. This play area might be associated with a daycare center, housing area, or community park. Gather information on the population that this play area serves such as the age of the users, the purpose of the facility (i.e., directed play, free play, educational), the times/days of use, etc. Gain permission from the manager to access the site and to conduct observations.
2. Plan your visit to the play area. Produce a site plan of the area including indicating elements such as surface materials, site amenities (i.e., benches, drinking fountains, storage sheds, vegetation), and access points.
3. Visit the site and observe how children are using the space.
4. Generate a list of observed activities. For each activity, indicate how you think this behavior relates to their physical development and how you think it relates to their social development.
5. Reflect upon your observations and findings. Do you think this play area could be improved in terms of how it supports child development?
6. Describe and discuss what you think these improvements could be with your classmates.

A potential project

Senior housing site visit. Note: Since this exercise requires access to a private facility, the instructor will need to make arrangements with the housing manager prior to students visiting the site.

1. Students should review the readings referenced in this chapter on designing for senior populations and prepare a list of questions specifically related to the needs of older adults for a site visit.
2. Students should visit the project site and conduct a site analysis of the outdoor landscapes with particular attention to the anticipated needs of the senior residents. Depending upon the senior housing project's scale, students may need to divide the site into sub-areas for their site visit and analysis. This analysis should include behavior observations of current activities of the residents, staff, and visitors. The observed behaviors as well as expected, but unobserved behaviors should be documented.
3. Students should provide an analysis and interpretation of their site visit observations. If the analysis occurred across sub-areas, these should be compiled into a comprehensive analysis of the entire site. This analysis should include references to relevant literature.
4. If time permits and the manager and residents are amenable, the students should meet with at least two residents for informal interviews. These interviews should focus on the residents' use of the outdoor spaces and any concerns they may have with the current landscape and on ideas for things they would like available in this landscape.
5. Next, working in small groups, the students should develop recommendations for site improvements. These may include the major re-location of amenities or minor adjustments to design features.
6. Generate a proposed design work within the whole class and share it with the senior housing project visited.

5
A SPIRIT OF INCLUSION

This chapter seeks to instill in the reader an understanding of environments that facilitate and encourage the use of public spaces by all persons, including those with differing physical abilities. Inclusive and exclusionary environments, legitimate and illegitimate uses and users, and the intentional exclusion of certain groups of citizens in public spaces are discussed. Legal responsibilities of designers including a brief overview of the legislation and design guidelines addressing the needs of people with disabilities are provided. The chapter does not provide specific design guidelines but instead provides information on where to find that changing information. Last, how designers can surpass requirements and create places that respect, reflect, and represent everyone's needs and rights to experience the outdoor environment are discussed.

INCLUSION IN OUTDOOR ENVIRONMENTS

Background

Inclusive landscapes are foundations for sound and vital communities which support and strengthen a person's experiences. Inclusive environments make users feel welcomed and comfortable, uplift morale, and offer opportunities to enhance health and well-being. *Inclusivity* can be defined as "the practice or policy of not excluding any person on the grounds of race, gender, religion, age, disability, etc." (Oxford University Press, 2016). However, not all designed spaces welcome all users. Undesired activities or users may be intentionally excluded from a place. Landscapes that exclude are hurtful, can lower self-esteem, and can make people feel lonely or out of place; therefore, inclusive outdoor environments can play an important role for individuals' well-being and social cohesion.

The concept of *inclusion* in planning and design emerged in the 1950s in European countries, the United States, and Japan. Early on, inclusion was addressed through human-factored engineering with attention to removing barriers for people with physical or mental disabilities or limitations. These efforts addressed increasing access to environments, products, and services, with most attention given to wheelchair accessibility. Although the focus was narrow, broader audiences also benefited from the standards that followed (IHCD, 2018). Today, the notion of inclusion in planning and design has broadened to include social factors such as diversity, equality, equity, and social justice. The importance of physical, functional, and usable accessibility remains, while addressing equitable access provides a framework for addressing the needs and visions of all (Heylighen, Van der Linden, & Van Steenwinkel, 2017). Additional aspects of inclusion related to human factors are addressed further in Chapters 3, 4, and 6.

Key findings

Inclusive spaces focus on creating environments that are accessible and usable by various populations and cater to their needs and wants through deliberate design and management. Undesirable users and uses may be controlled and excluded, but this can limit the vibrancy of the space by focusing on desirable persons and ideal uses (Low, Taplin, & Scheld, 2005, in Agyman, 2010). Ideally, inclusive environments do not exclude; they aim to make spatial connections beyond project boundaries for disadvantaged and marginalized populations.

Landscapes of inclusion Potential user populations of inclusively designed spaces are broad, and their needs differ. Inclusively designed spaces can cater to minority, marginalized, or disadvantaged populations, or they may offer opportunities for persons with disabilities, caregivers, the elderly, families with young children, teens, or other members of society. Inclusive designs allow for maximized use. For example, the North Beach Playground in Santa Monica, CA, designed by AHBE | MIG and Patrick Tighe Architecture, reflects the needs of children with limited abilities, their friends and family, and the broader community. Universal accessibility concepts were applied so that children of all abilities can stimulate their imagination and senses. Through inclusive considerations, a broader range of people has access to the locally designed recreation asset (Lutz, 2018; MIG, 2019) (see Figure 5.1). Similarly, Michael Van Valkenburgh Associates, Inc. (MVVA) designed Brooklyn Bridge Park in New York City with diverse park users in mind. Physical, visual, and programmatic connectivity was a guiding design criterion used to welcome a range of ages. The design framework was flexible and accommodated competing users and changing needs by providing broad programmatic opportunities (Brooklyn Bridge Park Development Corporation & MVVA, 2005). Signs posted throughout the park provide information concerning safe and appropriate behaviors (see Figure 5.2).

Varied criteria, considerations, and elements enable the creation of inclusive environments. At a broader scope, inclusive cities are vibrant and thriving places where everyone can

FIGURE 5.1 North Beach playground offers inclusive features for toddlers and young children, including a range of sensory design features. Image credit: Yi Ding.

FIGURE 5.2 At Brooklyn Bridge Park, signs welcome everyone and list rules at a picnicking area (left) and provide guidance on appropriate ages at a play area (right). Image credit: Patsy Eubanks Owens.

choose how and where they want to live, thereby supporting equity and social connections. Meaningfully designed environments addressing people's comfort, safety, connections, discovery, and joy offer healthy, functional, and aesthetically pleasing places. Inclusive designs are also sensitive to community context and may mitigate potential adverse effects of exclusion elsewhere (Goltsman & Iacofano, 2007). Other characteristics of inclusively designed spaces include considerations for convenience and functionality (e.g., proximity to neighborhoods) and how users travel to the places (e.g., walkability, pushing strollers).

Further, detailed considerations for spatial arrangements, site furniture, signage systems, or other design features such as outdoor lights can accommodate the needs and experiences of varied user groups. For example, outdoor environments often include stairs to resolve elevation changes efficiently. While such features can be convenient for those without physical disabilities, they may not be safe or comfortable for families with young children or the elderly (Huang & Napawan, 2021), let alone people with disabilities. However, if space and funding is available, stairs supplemented with ramps can make the experience accessible for people using assisted devices and also inclusive for caregivers and young families pushing strollers.

Landscapes of exclusion Not all shared outdoor environments are inclusive. *Exclusion* of people and uses in the outdoor environments can come about in various and sometimes subtle ways. Spatial features and policies can limit or hinder certain users and uses. Environments can exclude users based on race, ethnicity, or culture (see Chapter 3). It is important to be aware that a designed landscape may unintentionally limit or exclude despite best intentions.

In some instances, these exclusionary design decisions are unintentional, while other times they are deliberate. Some designed outdoor environments discourage certain behaviors or exclude, directly or indirectly, certain targeted communities. For example, in many communities, adolescents and unhoused populations are explicitly or implicitly excluded from using public spaces through signs, designs, policies, and surveillance (Amster, 2003; Owens, 2002).

FIGURE 5.3 A skateboard park sign in Bowling Green, Kentucky, listing activities and behaviors allowed and not allowed. Image credit: Jayoung Koo.

Although such groups may be discouraged from using spaces because of concerns expressed by others, strong arguments have been advanced that they have a right to public space (Mitchell, 2003), and in the case of adolescents this access may play an important role in their healthy development (Owens, 2020). Design solutions may contribute to creating places that can be shared by various populations while addressing other concerns, such as safety.

Adolescents are often assumed to be engaging in troublesome activities and their presence in public spaces is frequently discouraged. This exclusion occurs through the adoption of public policies or designs (e.g., curfew laws, skateboarding, and loitering ordinances) (see Figure 5.3). This age group is often unwelcome and considered inappropriate users of playgrounds, particularly when they are in proximity to younger children, despite that they also want a safe place to play (Owens, 2018). Landscape design practices have discouraged or prevented the use of public areas by teens through practices such as the removal of group seating areas or locating youth-focused amenities away from other public areas (Owens, 2002). For example, skateboarding is an activity enjoyed by members of this age group; however, it is discouraged through the use of skate stops positioned along seat walls and steps (Woolley, Hazelwood, & Simkins, 2011) (see Figure 5.4) or relegated to an inconvenient location. When a skateboarding facility is provided, it is frequently located in an otherwise undesirable location and with the motivation of removing these youths from other public places (Owens, 2001). Therefore, too often, adolescents are being excluded from outdoor environments that would support their healthy social and emotional development and contribute to their becoming engaged and responsible members of society (Owens, 2020).

Another segment of society that is often excluded in public outdoor environments is the unhoused population. With limited alternatives, homeless people spend the majority of their time in both indoor and outdoor public spaces (Parker, 2021). The exclusion of homeless populations can take different forms. Their activities can be controlled through local or state

FIGURE 5.4 Skateboarding impediment designs in Millennium Square in Sheffield, England (left) and San Francisco, CA (right). Image credits: Woolley et al. (2011) (left) and Patsy Eubanks Owens (right).

laws, policing, community actions, and design or programming. Ordinances related to the management of public spaces such as hours of operation may restrict, limit, or prohibit the presence of homeless people in public spaces for extended times. In many instances, unhoused individuals have claimed public rights of way along railroads, roadways, and waterfronts for their temporary shelters. While sometimes tolerated, these accommodations are often disassembled because of community complaints or violation of laws. Designers are often asked by local agencies to include anti-homeless benches or other design features to discourage their prolonged occupancy. Concerns related to the use of public lands by unhoused individuals are not without merit. The health and safety of this population in such living conditions is often dire. In addition, the use and enjoyment of these areas by others may also be jeopardized. Some municipalities have opened designated parks for temporary camping of homeless people while the local government seeks appropriate levels of programs or services before the situation continues to worsen, such as at Beard Brook Park in Modesto, CA (Valine, 2018). Shortly after concerns of increased homeless encampment in the park, Modesto opened a tent city underneath the 9th Street bridge; they provided people with tents and round-the-clock security, and closed the park for revitalization (Howland, 2019a, 2019b).

Design considerations

Inclusiveness in outdoor places should be creative and broad to address the specific needs of some groups that can also benefit others. Peinhardt and Storring state that inclusive public space offers foundations for "sense of attachments and belonging for everyone" (2019a) and offer some principles for creating and managing such spaces (2019a, 2019b, 2019c):

- Design for differing abilities (cognitive, sensory, physical, or developmental) while optimizing features for maximum accessibility,
- Consider gender, age, culture dynamics that reflect differing values but also that make people feel welcomed, safe, and excited,
- Recognize that different populations may have different needs in the same place, and
- Balance between policing, rules, and exclusion.

Designers should identify all potential users at the start of a project. Places should be designed to incorporate shared, overlapping, or complementary uses. This approach is different from

FIGURE 5.5 Varied path options along the Scioto Greenway and River in downtown Columbus, OH, allow accessibility to the waterfront while providing inclusive and broad user opportunities. Image credit: Jayoung Koo.

designing a "multi-use" space since these types of spaces can be subject to conflict by different user groups wishing to engage in conflicting activities. For example, an open, multi-use, grassy field may be used by families with young children and also people who want their dogs to walk or run freely. When each is alone in the space there are no conflicts; however, when they try to use the space at the same time, the experience of each is likely negatively impacted. Policies such as requiring dogs to be leashed, can offset some potential conflicts and allow both groups of users to enjoy the space but not as freely. Inclusively designed places should include alternative features for different activities and movement. Designers may consider ways to offer designated areas where users can coexist safely. For example, inclusive spatial considerations can increase accessibility through widened and gently sloping paths that accommodate varied abilities and needs in a unified way (see Figure 5.5).

Designers need to be aware of and look out for legitimate potential users and uses that may not be represented in current spaces. They should be proactive, have empathy, inquire, and be willing to develop outdoor environments that offer experiences to the broadest user groups possible while preventing any intentional exclusion.

ROLES AND RESPONSIBILITIES OF DESIGNERS

Background

Everyone has the right to access and enjoy shared outdoor environments; however, that opportunity is not available or without challenges for some segments of societies. Although addressing disability requirements is essential, retrofitting environments to meet established standards is an ongoing process. Requirements for accessibility are based on nondiscrimination laws. People with disabilities have a right to access places and services in society (DOJ, 1990). The World Health Organization and the World Bank define *accessibility* as "the degree to which an environment, service, or product allows access by as many people as possible, in particular people with disabilities" (WHO & WB, 2011, p. 301). Here, "*[d]isability* is the umbrella term for impairments, activity limitations and participation restrictions, referring to the negative aspects of the interaction between an individual (with a health condition) and that individual's contextual factors (environmental and personal factors)" (WHO & WB, 2011, p. 4).

A broader understanding of disability and accessibility has increased along with acceptance of those with disabilities. Everyone has a range of physical abilities, where some individuals may have recognized disabilities and others may have unrecognized or undesignated disabilities. Mindsets are shifting from understanding disability and functioning from a medical model or a social model and toward a compromising approach between the medical and social models (Altman, 2001; WHO, 2001). A person's disability is not limited to just their health condition and functioning but is also impacted by social or environmental factors that influence their activities and participation (WHO, 2001). The documentary *Lives Worth Living* directed by Neudel (2011) provides a compelling look at the historical background of the lengthy and resistive legislative progress, negative perceptions, and treatment of what people with disabilities endured prior to the passing of the 1990 federal Americans with Disabilities Act (ADA) in the United States.

Providing comparable experiences of a place to all individuals is an ongoing struggle. Along with independent efforts to make environments open to people with a range of abilities, legislation to require this access has evolved over the last half century. Countries such as the United States and United Kingdom began mandating and implementing accessibility requirements in the early 1970s (Mayerson, 1992; Rydström, 2019). Across various nations and other government entities, provisions addressing accessibility have had a significant impact on design decisions and public experience by influencing practices to creatively offer barrier-free environments. While physical access to public space began to improve in the later part of the 20th century through compliance with regulations and standards, the legal protection to access is not without its limitations and the process is ongoing (Vaughn-Brainard, 2020). Other countries have established their versions of disability laws (Disability Rights Education & Defense Fund, n.d.), addressing the need for guidelines for designing accessible outdoor environments. Since the international Convention on Rights of Persons with Disabilities (CRPD) was adopted in 2006, 185 countries or regional integration organizations have ratified it, with 100 of those also ratifying the optional protocol (United Nations, 2022). However, such provisions are not universal, and not all countries have legal standards set forth that address the outdoor environment settings for people with disabilities.

People may have mobility, hearing, vision, or cognitive difficulties or have difficulty taking care of themselves or living independently (U.S. Census Bureau, 2021) (see Figure 5.6). In the United States, 61 million adults live with some form of disability, which accounts for 26% of the population (Okoro, Hollis, Cyrus, & Griffin-Blake, 2018). Between 2008 and 2019, 4.3% of children in the United States under the age of 18 had a disability, an increase from 3.9% in 2008 (U.S. Census, 2022; Young, 2021). Globally, people with disabilities represented an estimated 15% of the world's population or approximately one billion people in 2011 (WHO & WB, 2011). There are differences between legally documented disabilities and medically defined disabilities. For example, an individual may not be blind medically, but may be considered practically blind for driving purposes. Designers need to consider not only disabilities that are legally recognized but those that may impact a person's experience.

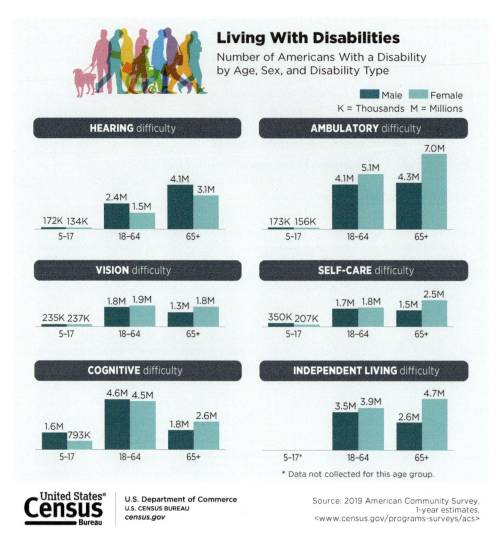

FIGURE 5.6 Range of disabilities Americans are living with as of 2019. Image credit: U.S. Census Bureau (2021).

ADA and other levels of compliance

The legislative efforts in the United States for standardizing structures for people with medically defined disabilities can be traced back to the 1960s. Early architectural standards related to access for physically handicapped people were voluntary (ANSI A117.1) (see Table 5.1). The federal Architectural Barriers Act (ABA) formally came into effect as a law in 1968. Later, the 1990 Americans with Disability Act was passed as a federal-level civil right that protects individuals with disabilities from discrimination. The ADA extended the basic civil rights protections previously granted to underrepresented, marginalized, and disadvantaged peoples to people with disabilities (Mayerson, 1992) and granted them rights equal to others (DOJ, 1990). The guiding standards specify that physical environments must provide access through the removal of barriers, as well as retrofit and make built environments accessible so that everyone has equal access (DOJ, 1994).

TABLE 5.1 Brief historical timeline of standards and legislation addressing accessibility in built environments in the United States (U.S. Access Board, n.d.; Goltsman, Gilbert, Wohlford, & Kirk, 1993)

Year	Standards or legislature	Brief description
1961	American National Standards Institute (ANSI) A117.1	First American national building standard approved to address accessibility issues
1968	Architectural Barriers Act (PL-90-480) (ABA) 3	• First federal law requiring federally funded facilities enable people with disabilities access to them • Required physical access to facilities
1973	Rehabilitation Act (PL-93-112) Section 504	• Required public rights of way and facilities to be accessible to persons with disabilities • Required that people with disabilities have access to federally assisted programs (space made physically accessible or program moved to an accessible location)
1990	Americans with Disability Act (ADA)	• Applies to all new public accommodations, not just those connected to public funding, program accessibility, and readily achievable concepts • State and local government facilities (Title II) • Public accommodations and commercial facilities (Title III)

The ADA cannot be revoked by states or local governments although each state may further strengthen or add guidelines that abide by the federal law to ensure implementation. In the United States, policies, standards, and guidelines for designing built environments such as ordinances and zoning are mostly governed by local jurisdiction; therefore, designers are obligated to comply with the federal regulation while also adhering to local stipulations. The ADA law provides a limited provision for what types of public and private facilities need to comply. Publicly funded projects including buildings and public lands were the first places required to comply. The 1990 ADA was amended in 2008 and further specified requirements that included various recreation facilities, such as playgrounds, swimming pools, and golf facilities, among others. As of 2012, compliance is required of all new construction and alternations of state and local government facilities and accommodations that address and serve the public (DOJ, 2010a, 2010b).

The ADA Accessibility Guidelines address scoping and technical requirements for accessibility to sites, facilities, buildings, and elements for use by individuals with disabilities (DOJ, 1990). The requirements address design, construction, additions to sites, and alterations to sites to the extent required by regulations issued by federal agencies. As an example, the guidelines apply design criteria to outdoor elements such as pathways and sidewalks, parking spaces and connections, curb ramps, site furniture, signs, exterior ramps, and stairways. Communities

FIGURE 5.7 A redesign of the main entrance to Hunt Hall, University of California, Davis, occurred during building renovations. Previously stairs were the only access to the main entrance (left) while a new landing and ramp were added to comply with ADA requirements (right). Image credits: University Archives Photographs: 1915–1980: AR-013, Archives and Special Collections Library, University of California, Davis (left), and Patsy Eubanks Owens (right).

have added many accessible features and public buildings have widened doors and replaced exterior stairs with ramps during renovations (see Figure 5.7). Designers should always check minimum recommended specifications for outdoor recreational areas and facilities such as trail width, slopes, and intersections to ensure compliance with current regulations (Access Board, 2014) (see Figure 5.8).

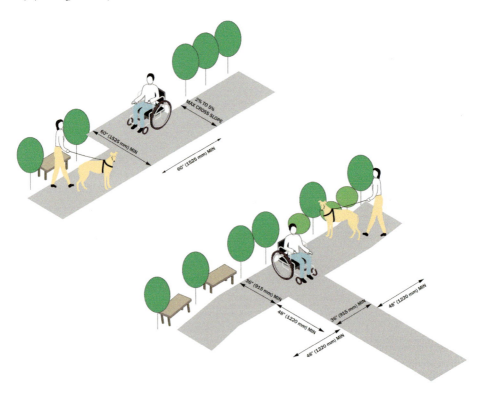

FIGURE 5.8 An example of the types of outdoor accessibility requirements provided in *Outdoor Developed Areas* (adapted from Access Board, 2014).

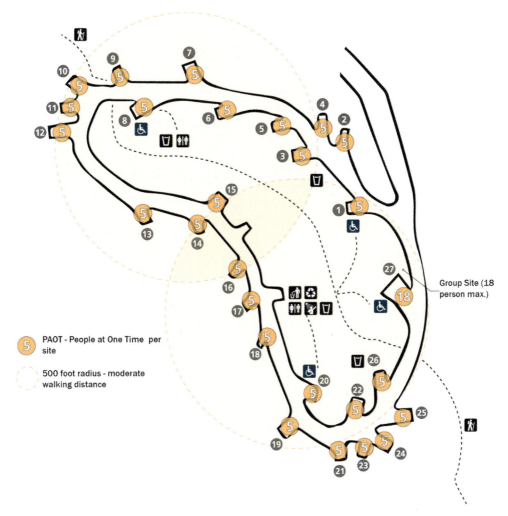

FIGURE 5.9 Campground site plan including designated wheelchair accessible sites distributed throughout the site exceeding federal requirements (Brown et al., 2021). Image credit: National Park Service.

The stipulations of the ADA have advanced the ability of people with disabilities to enjoy the same environmental settings as others and to play a vital role in the community as an independent member (Steinfeld & Maisel, 2012). Different areas may cater to users with varying abilities. For example, standard picnic tables can be adjusted so that people in wheelchairs can also access the feature in multiple ways and not be limited to sitting at the end of the table. Additionally, outdoor environment amenities can be dispersed throughout recreation areas and offer people with disabilities opportunities for inclusive experiences (see Figure 5.9).

Design considerations

Designers have a responsibility to protect the health, safety and welfare of the public, an obligation of licensed professionals, but it is also an ethical obligation (ASLA, 2018). At minimum, by complying with the ADA provisions, designers will be able to provide barrier-free outdoor environments. The regulatory guidelines established grounds for efficient practices that will positively influence inclusive outdoor experiences through design decisions affecting social environments. For example, many communities are installing tactile tiles and beacons at intersection curbs along major roads when bike lanes are added along the corridors. Such renovated intersections improve pedestrian and travel experiences not only for people with disabilities to safely cross the road but also to improve the safety of the broader community.

Complying with the minimal ADA requirements in design decisions not only supports independent living for people with disabilities but also enhances the places where people live, work, and play. Being knowledgeable about accessibility and equity in public spaces, facilities, and services for everyone expands the role of designers to one that addresses an inclusive public good. Since the guidance and regulations regarding accessibility are regularly updated, designers should periodically refer to the U.S. Access Board website (https://www.access-board.gov/), the Department of Justice website (https://www.ada.gov/), and the Department of Transportation website (https://www.transit.dot.gov/regulations-and-guidance/civil-rights-ada/ada-guidance).

BEYOND REQUIREMENTS

Background

While the ADA protects the rights of persons with disabilities, designers have an opportunity to exceed the requirements of regulations. In addition, there are disabilities, physical challenges, and health limitations that people need support with during their lifetime that are not addressed legally. In some cases, although design considerations may be useful, the law does not provide physical space design specifications (Vaughn-Brainard, 2020) but focuses on supportive features such as listening devices for the hearing impaired. Designers, however, can create more functional and welcoming places for those disabilities as well as for their families and caregivers.

Although increasing accessibility in compliance with disability laws can be challenging, when prioritized, needs for the broadest targeted user populations can be supported. These designed environments can be inclusive for all users as well as allowing for future adaptations. With broader notions of inclusivity, more people will have access to and experience welcoming and comfortable outdoor environments. This section focuses on concepts and examples beyond the legal compliance of accessibility and portrays inclusive practices for the creation of outdoor environments.

Key findings

Considerations of inclusivity in design will provide access to more people and to more experiences. A range of users and user groups that would otherwise not be addressed through legal accessibility compliance can benefit from inclusive improvements to the physical environment. Attention to the need for and the means to providing access to places and products continues to evolve and goes by different names in different locations. Terms such as barrier-free design, design for all, inclusive design, and universal design are commonly used (Steinfeld & Maisel, 2012). Among these, universal design and inclusive design concepts are used most frequently and often interchangeably. While *accessible design* is more clearly defined through publications such as the ADA accessibility guide (DOJ, 2010a), universal design and inclusive design are less so. Both terms describe approaches that extend beyond legal compliance, guidelines, or standards, however, who is considered may vary between the two (Heylighen et al.; IHCD, 2018).

Universal design, popular in the United States and Japan, was first introduced by Mace as "[d]esign of products and environments to be usable by all people, to the greatest extent possible, without the need for adaptation or specialized design" (1985 cited in Steinfeld & Maisel, 2012, p. 28). The focus of universal design has been on an individual's right to have access and freedom to use a place or product. In practice, universal design aims to address as many user needs as possible, not just as many users as possible. Accepted principles of universal design include equitable use, flexibility in use, simple and intuitive use, perceptible information, tolerance for error, low physical effort, and size and space for approach and use (NCSU, 2011). Similarly, within the landscape architecture profession, characteristics of universal design include accessibility, comfort, legibility, predictability, and walkability (Dillon & Green, 2019a).

Comparatively, the focus of *design for all* and *inclusive design* in Europe is seen as aspirational or goal-driven more than performance based (Steinfeld & Maisel, 2012). The British Standards Institute defines inclusive design to be "the design of mainstream products and/or services that is accessible to, and usable by, as many people as reasonably possible … without the need for special adaptation or specialized design" (British Standards Institute, 2005 in Steinfeld & Maisel, 2012, p. 29). In recent years, and in the United States in particular, inclusive design and inclusion in public space have gained increased usage most commonly to convey the need to consider marginalized populations or those persons who may traditionally be excluded from accessing or using an environment. In 2001, Rishbeth questioned if landscape designs could be inclusive, particularly in regard to multicultural societies. She suggests that an inclusive approach need not differentiate between different users or define specific areas for those users.

Figure 5.10 illustrates a nested approach to understanding these concepts where inclusive design is the most comprehensive. Inclusive design incorporates the requirement to meet the needs of individuals with disabilities, the desire to accommodate different interests, and an overarching goal of providing a welcoming environment for everyone. While an universal design approach may not address the needs of some segments of society, an inclusive design approach aims to also address the needs of excluded users.

Design considerations

Designing inclusive outdoor spaces requires addressing accessibility in many different forms and for a full spectrum of users. While legal requirements must be met, designs may also encourage and welcome people with diverse interests, needs, and abilities. How a specific design does that is open for interpretation by the designer and in response to the social and environmental context. A few illustrations of how outdoor environments can be made more welcoming, safe, and comfortable are provided. For example, landscape features addressing physical comfort, mobility and sensory issues, and cultural preferences can lead to more inclusive designs (see Figure 5.11).

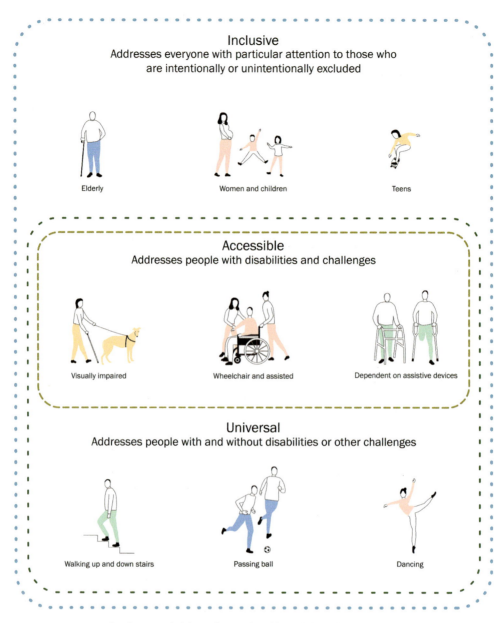

FIGURE 5.10 Example of users and abilities that can be addressed through inclusive, accessible, and universal design approaches.

Providing mobility and access options Open space users, including those relying on assistive devices, may find navigating through some outdoor spaces challenging. Changes in elevation and materials, along with distances, weather conditions, and conflicting uses can create obstacles. Inclusive designs seek to reduce these barriers and improve the access and mobility for all users. For example, wide pathways allow people needing assistance to move through the landscape with a companion while also providing ample space for others (see Figure 5.12). Strategically placed ramps allow people with mobility limitations, such as those who rely on wheeled devices (DOJ, 2010a), as well as caregivers pushing strollers,

FIGURE 5.11 Increased accessibility through (a) lighting during evening hours, (b) seating with armrest and back, (c) trees offering shade, (d) wide pathways for conversation with less conflict in Woolwich Square, London, United Kingdom (Dillon & Green, 2019b). Image credit: Gustafson Porter + Bowman.

FIGURE 5.12 The Indianapolis Cultural Trail (Indiana) offers a wide inclusive corridor for pedestrians, cyclists, people with disabilities (left) and segments of delineated paths for cyclists and slower travelers such as pedestrians (right). Image credit: Margaret Klondike.

to move through a space unimpaired (see Figure 5.13). While gentle slopes may be easier to navigate for some people, stairs with handrails might be better for others (Wolfinbarger & Shehab, 2000). Similarly, a curb cut may be beneficial for people with a range of visual challenges, while they make those with hearing challenges more vulnerable to unheard movements from multiple directions (Heylighen et al., 2017; Vaughn, 2018).

In addition, design features can be flexible and adaptive to meet the needs of different users. For example, fixed seating can be adjusted by offering diverse heights, depths, width, and materials. Other elements such as picnic tables and garden beds can also be adjusted so that varied users can socialize and participate in activities together inclusively (Hale & Provenzan, 2021).

A SPIRIT OF INCLUSION   127

FIGURE 5.13 Inclusive designs can create safer and more comfortable ways for people to travel such as a lift for bus access in Curitiba, Brazil (left) or raised garden beds and space for assisting personnel in an outdoor learning environment in California (right). Image credits: Mario Roberto Duran Ortiz Mariordo, retrieved from Wikimedia Commons (left) and Tahereh Sheerazie (right).

Accommodating for visual and hearing challenges While a great deal of guidance and requirements are articulated for accommodating people with mobility limitations, less advice for designing for people with vision and hearing difficulties is available. These challenges commonly increase with age as well as being innate for others and must be addressed in design decisions. While certain accommodations are required, such as Braille signage, additional features to improve the experience of vision- or hearing-impaired people should also be incorporated.

Considerations for the blind or those with impaired vision may include: (a) using different materials and textures, (b) adapting the environments to maximize vision, (c) installing equipment for aid, and (d) marking terrain clearly (Hale & Provenzan, 2021). For example, ropes with knots can be used to guide users and changes in paving textures can be used to denote particular areas. In one park, an outdoor xylophone with Braille attracts adults and children with limited or no sight to engage in outdoor environments (see Figure 5.14).

FIGURE 5.14 Design features such as an outdoor xylophone with Braille (left) and a cable guide with Braille signage (right) welcome and guide visitors with visual challenges in Watertown Riverfront Park, Watertown, MA. Image credit: Solomon Foundation.

Likewise, the experiences of those with hearing impairments could include visual cues to aid in orientation, or sounds could be experienced through vibrations (Hansel Bauman Architect, 2010; Vaughn, 2018). For example, moving objects or flashing lights can be used to accompany sound-based elements.

Creating a sense of belonging Along with addressing the physical needs for accessing landscapes, design can also be responsive to the cultural and age needs of a community and offer a welcoming and supportive environment. As discussed in Chapter 3, places and their design convey meaning to people. Decisions on materials, shapes, colors, and more may hold particular associations for some groups and not others. Designers should consult with local populations so that they do not inadvertently discourage the use of a place. One effective way to ensure that people with different primary languages feel welcome is to provide appropriate signage (see Figure 5.15).

The design of inclusive landscapes goes beyond addressing legal requirements. Creative solutions for welcoming and accommodating people with different abilities, backgrounds, and interests are needed. While a few examples have been provided, each project and designer will have opportunities to develop new ways to incorporate inclusive goals and features.

FIGURE 5.15 Signs in multiple languages in a San Francisco, CA, playground offering inclusive experiences for varied users. Image credit: Patsy Eubanks Owens.

A SPIRIT OF INCLUSION

STEPS TOWARD INCLUSIVE DESIGN

Designers should develop practices that employ empathy toward populations with unique needs and go beyond legal requirements. Inclusive designs will meet accessibility standards and contribute to meaningful and supportive environments. Some of the characteristics of inclusive designs include engaging with people, proactively complying with requirements, offering alternative functions and access, and creating flexible spaces.

Engage with all potential user groups

Inclusive designs need to start with identifying all potential users and user groups. Designers should invite and engage with users that will likely use and benefit from a space; populations should not be excluded. The designer should be empathetic to the challenges and frustrations people have experienced and seek creative solutions. Targeted audiences should be contacted and asked to partner on projects.

Comply with legal standards and think proactively

Inclusivity should be a foundation for consideration throughout the entire design process. A basic understanding of disability laws and standards should inform the design. Through observations, site analysis, and other modes of inquiry such as user surveys, designers can begin to develop a creative and comprehensive shared design vision. Inclusive design principles can be applied during development of the design program, generating design concepts and alternatives, and developing construction directives.

For example, when visiting a project site, a designer might be more perceptive as to who is using a place or even in identifying a lack of anticipated users. What is the proportion of children, seniors, or people with limited abilities in the neighborhood? What activities or specific users or user groups are currently being unassisted that could or should be? What are any anticipated demographic changes for the adjacent community that might impact the design program? Observing, mapping, and soliciting input from future users can inform final design products (see Chapters 7 and 8).

Offer choices where a single design solution cannot accommodate all users

Depending on the site and project characteristics (e.g., funding, size, terrain), designers may be limited in creating spaces that can be usable and accessible by a range of users with different abilities. However, designers can offer limited accessible areas. For example, certain parts of a public park can be designed to be accessible by the visually impaired or legally blind. The same space may multifunction as a designated space for younger children. Other parts of the same park can be accessible by people with mobility limitations; however, other parts of the park where steep slopes exist may be limited to nondisabled people. While a ramp may not be placed due to site suitability or financial project feasibility, other spaces can be accessible by those using assisted devices.

Design for flexibility

Designers should be open-minded, knowledgeable, flexible, and creative in adapting designs so that all users can be optimally accommodated. People are more likely to choose to live and work in places that provide spatial and programmatic opportunities that are welcoming, safe, and comfortable for their needs.

CONCLUSIONS

Designers have the ability to promote and advocate for inclusive outdoor environments. Design education on accessibility and relevant design principles can play an important role in ensuring that design practitioners have adequate knowledge about the topic. When designers are trained, understand, and practice inclusive design, they have the potential to creatively produce appropriate and successful designs that also comply with legal requirements.

The overall goal of inclusive design is to increase accessibility so a wider population can rightfully use outdoor environments without limitations and frustration. The spirit of inclusiveness can bring about design solutions that address requirements and propose creative solutions. Increased safe and convenient access to designed outdoor environments is the first step toward healthier individuals, families, and communities.

POTENTIAL EXERCISE AND PROJECT

An indoor exercise

Discussion about inclusion and exclusion. Share the first impressions of inclusive and exclusive environments. Everyone has experienced places that they cherish and places that they do not want to revisit. Recall your experiences in places that presented inclusion and exclusion. Instructors can also ask students to bring in a photo of inclusive and exclusive public spaces to prepare for a class discussion.

1. Discuss with your classmates the places where you have experienced a sense of exclusion. What aspects of the public space made you feel that way? What about its design can be changed to lessen such feelings in the outdoor environment?
2. Discuss with your classmates the places where you have experienced a sense of inclusion. What aspects of the public space made you feel that way? What design aspects of the space can be applied to other places? Why do you suggest such ideas or applications?

A potential project
Assessing the built environment

1. Structure
   Each student is encouraged to experience different perspectives of having limited abilities when traveling through public spaces. Students should partner with at least one other person in this exercise. The partners will assist in the travel experience and discuss the designed elements. Determine the landscape to visit – a campus location, park, neighborhood, or commercial area are suggested places to experience using the following assistive devices:
   - Wheelchair
   - Crutches or walker
   - Guide cane and blindfold

2. Route

   Instructors should propose locations and routes that present various challenges and experiences (slopes, pavement materials, path widths, etc.) for students using the assistive devices. Students should take caution while using the devices with their partner looking for dangerous obstacles and situations. When needed, students should feel free to take breaks. Students should take turns using the various assistive devices.

3. Assessment

   After traveling through the landscape, the students should discuss their experience and evaluate the built environment based on their subjective experiences from the following perspectives:

   - Focus on your personal experiences and the special circumstances as you traveled through the landscape (e.g., difficulties, help needed).
   - Focus on the responses from others around you as you traveled through the space (e.g., response to your presence, offering help, responses from drivers, bikers, or people walking by).
   - Focus on what a designer could do to enhance the outdoor setting (e.g., changing slope, expanding width, addressing barriers, including other amenities).
   - Discuss how the experience would have been different for other users (e.g., gender, age, other disability).

6
GENDER AND PLACE

This chapter introduces the ways in which gender and gender identity shape people's use and perception of place. Related terms, the history of gender bias, and social changes and their relationships to gender are briefly introduced. Research and practices related to gendered experiences are presented and discussed along with spatial design implications. Gender disparities and gender equity in the use of public spaces and outdoor settings still need attention and continued research. Using information from this chapter, planners and designers can start to create places that are both gender inclusive and more sensitive to gender differences, resulting in a more equitable and supportive outdoor environment.

BACKGROUND

Definition of gender

Gender is a complicated and under-respected human factor, often not fully understood or considered in design decisions. While place preferences and place use are associated with individual choices, designers also need to understand how gender shapes people's informed preferences and activities. Societies are gradually moving toward a more diverse understanding of gender and gender identity. Contemporary landscapes have evolved, and acknowledgment of all genders in the creation of places is needed. Although gender expression in physical space design is relatively more explicit in westernized cultures, it is found in cultures worldwide. Similarly, disparities between gender expression in urban and rural areas are possible. As designers, it is important to understand gender and its implications for the creation of and reflection on outdoor environments.

Before discussing the relationship between gender and the outdoor environment, the complexity and the evolution of gender definitions is examined. Historically, the general public and research scholars treated "gender" and "sex" similarly, dividing human populations into two gender categories, women and men, or what is generally known as a gender-binary approach (Hyde, Bigler, Joel, Tate, & van Anders, 2019). With time, the definition of gender has evolved, and today, gender has a clearer differentiation with "sex." The World Health Organization (2017) defines *sex* as "the biological and physiological characteristics [that] define men and women," and *gender* as "the socially constructed roles, behaviors, activities, and attributes that a given society considers appropriate for men and women" (para. 1). Due to the long history of researchers treating gender as a dichotomy, much literature shared in this chapter was written based on the needs and perceptions of the two different genders, men and women. Today, some people identify themselves as neither male or female, or as both male and female, with the umbrella terms for such genders as *genderqueer* or *nonbinary* (Richards et al., 2016).

Along with understanding the distinctions between gender and sex, considering sexual orientation can be important in design activities. While the concept of gender identity in society has gained attention, research focusing on the implications of gender identity and sexual orientation on the built environment is limited; therefore and unfortunately, much of this chapter relies on research focused on binary and heterosexual populations. A growing understanding of gender and transgender identities as well as sexual orientation will surely challenge some of the earlier and current concepts and frameworks regarding the design of outdoor environments. Moreover, different cultures may treat gender issues dramatically differently. Such issues in many parts of the world, for example where religious or traditional beliefs prohibit same-sex relationships, may not be comparable to what is elaborated on in this chapter as most of the literature discussed is based on western culture. However, gender inequality exists in every culture, and the concerns, struggles, and distress of women and minority gender identities are noteworthy for discussions beyond this chapter.

With this in mind, general findings, specifically those based on binary situations, are discussed in this chapter. The debate of whether gender differences exist and what these differences mean for their positionalities in society continues to be debated even when focusing on men and women in the United States. Most Americans still believe that men and women differ in various ways, such as how they express their feelings, their physical abilities, hobbies and interests, and parenting (see Figure 6.1). However, the origins of some of these differences, whether biological or societal, are unsettled questions (Pew Research Center, 2017).

Gender bias in the built environment

While gender issues can differ depending on societies, most of the world has long been influenced by a male-dominated hierarchy. One example is in the design of work and public environments. In 1900 in the United States, most women did not work outside their homes. Only 19% of women of working age, and 5% of married women, participated in the labor force (Fisk, 2001; Yellen, 2020). As women were long absent from the workforce, many everyday objects were not gender-friendly as they were designed by and for average-sized males. For example, the shape of the foot for shoe design (Wunderlich & Cavanagh, 2001), the length of automobile seat belts (Schiebinger, 2014), and the height of hand grips in public transportation systems all were designed for the physique of the male.

This gender bias is also represented in how cities were laid out through planning and urban design. Historically, private and public spaces in urban areas have been segregated, gendered, and racialized. Women's roles were focused on domestic familial care as the homemaker taking care of the family, raising children and also as extended caregivers. Such women's tasks tended to concentrate within the prominently "private" spaces of households. The reproduction or familial tasks have strengthened the supportive roles of women in and out of private sphere and continued on to the nurturing professions such as teaching, nursing, administrative support, and similar types of professional roles into which women naturally have advanced (Day, 2000; Franck & Paxson, 1989; Spain, 2014). On the other hand, men have dictated "public" presence

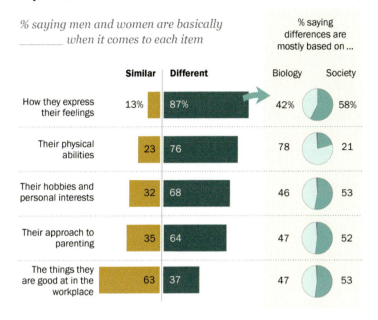

FIGURE 6.1 Americans see gender differences exist but hold varied opinions as to their origins (Pew Research Center, 2017).

and life, partly because they often occupied these spaces and typically spent more time than women outside the home. As a result, patriarchal systems have influenced and shaped much of the everyday public environment and spatial experiences (Scraton & Watson, 1998; Sewell, 2011; Spain, 2014).

Women's relationships to the built environment, especially public open spaces, have evolved since the late 19th century with industrialization and rapid urbanization. Historical events such as the women's suffrage movement, women joining the labor force during the world wars, and the availability of birth control inevitably increased women's roles, activism, and presence beyond home. The emergence of public parks provided opportunities and places for everyone to relax and refresh close to cities, and were not just limited to men (Cranz, 1980). Women started to increase their education attainment and their competitiveness in the workforce (Scraton & Watson, 1998; Spain, 2014). The rise of women's active roles in society challenged the form of the built environment; however, much of women's daily activities in public life were still the extension of domestic responsibilities, and their movements were still restricted (Franck & Paxson, 1989).

Although women's needs have changed in the contemporary context, design and planning practices of outdoor environments have only slowly responded to these changes. For example, Fenster (2005) interviewed women in London and Jerusalem on park and street use. They heard common experiences of avenues, parks, and public transportation rendered unusable because of fear of crime, male domination of the environment, misuse behaviors, and other reasons. In addition, a study of 5,000 women in 1967 found that the journey to work should be differentiated by sex, as the correlations between distance and time for men is not applicable to women due to their different home roles and childcare considerations (Ericksen, 1977). MacGregor's (1996) research supported the notion that women with children tend to make more frequent stops with short trips between spatially dispersed facilities, such as childcare facilities, grocery stores, and children's recreational activities. Hence, their public transit system needs are more complicated compared to men. Although women continue to serve as the primary caregiver, evolving parental roles will likely mean that more men will be transporting their children to daycare and school in the future.

Additionally, women tend to socialize or gather differently in outdoor environments and have varying preferences in such spaces. Some studies point to women having different personal space needs when compared with men (see Chapter 2, "Proxemics and personal space" section) and others note that within the same site, women's territoriality can be smaller than men's (Mozingo, 1989; see Figure 6.2). Mozingo also found that when time is limited, women tend to travel shorter distances for their needs and preferred amenities. In addition, research indicates that the physique of women is different from men and that this sometimes hinders their travel ability (Loukaitou-Sideris, 2005). Such challenges can be overcome when spaces are designed to be accessible (the space itself and the route to it) and when more public spaces are available to women in a more comfortable manner (Franck & Paxson, 1989).

The importance of gender equality and inclusivity

Although the importance of gender equality and inclusivity seems self-evident, an argument needs to be made that it has not been achieved today and that inequities need to be addressed. The recognition of gender equality as a fundamental human right was made by the United Nations more than a half century ago (UN General Assembly, 1948). Their statement noted that gender equality is essential to achieving peaceful and sustainable societal development. The effort to reach gender equality has made some progress but with some difficulty. In the decades since, women have been subjected to many forms of discrimination in education, employment, economic, healthcare, and social activities. The sexual revolution of the 1960s and 1970s drew focused attention to women's autonomy and responsibility for their own bodies, while the passage of Title IX of the Education Amendments of 1972 codified the requirement for federal funds to be used equally for all men's and women's programs. This law continues to have a profound impact on women's access to all programs within educational settings in the United States and to recreation opportunities in particular.

Globally, equality for women is an ongoing goal. At the Fourth World Conference on Women in Beijing, China, an agenda outlining goals and specific actions related to a wide

FIGURE 6.2 Crocker Plaza catchment area difference between men and women showing women travel shorter distances to get there (Mozingo, 1989).

range of concerns including women and poverty, health, education, economy, and power was adopted by 189 countries. Three decades later, this remains the key policy guidance on gender equality (UN Women, 1995). The *Beijing Declaration and the Platform for Action* marked an important turning point for global action toward gender equality. More recently, a Pew Research survey conducted in 34 countries found that a median of 94% of respondents said it was important for women in their country to have the same rights as men, while 45% still

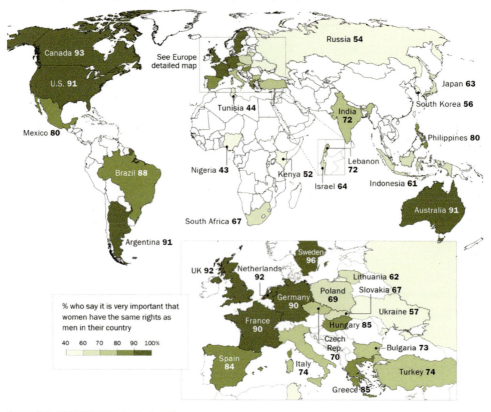

FIGURE 6.3 Of the 34 countries surveyed, 74% said gender equality was very important (as indicated on this map) and 94% said it was important (Pew Research Center, 2020).

believed that men have a better life in their countries than women (Pew Research Center, 2020) (see Figure 6.3).

One of the aspects of gender equality that has received limited attention is whether access to open space and nature is different between men and women. The *Beijing Declaration* (UN Women, 1995) noted that women are "entitled to a healthy and productive life in harmony with nature (chapter IV, section K)" and included objectives of involving women in environmental decisions and integrating their concerns into programs and policies. As noted in earlier chapters, spending time in nature is positively linked to an individual's health and well-being (Capaldi, Passmore, Nisbet, Zelenshi, & Dopko, 2015). Public spaces can and should provide access to the support of nature for everyone. The participation and visibility of women in outdoor environments and public spaces is important; their presence and participation also provides evidence and insight into the level of gender equality in societies (Godtman Kling, Margaryan, & Fuchs, 2020).

GENDER DIFFERENCES

Gender differences reveal themselves in various ways in outdoor environments. Those aspects which are most directly informed or impacted by design decisions are discussed – recreational choices, perceptions of safety and fear of crime, the role of social and cultural ties, and the needs and preferences for specific design features. However, designers should not assume that these are the only gender differences that may inform their work.

Recreational choices

Research on recreation preferences based on gender should inform the design of outdoor environments. Understanding user perceptions and preferences based on gender differences provides valuable information for design decisions yet is often overlooked. The built environment holds many direct and indirect clues of use as well as unaccommodating characteristics that may attract or deter use by different genders. Discerning why people use recreation spaces the way they do and examining the social and psychological impact of these places on different genders can ensure the creation of more accommodating outdoor environments.

Although women often engage in recreational activities in outdoor environments, how these environments support their preferences, comfort, and specific activities has been less intentional. Studies of early 19th century parks and playgrounds indicate that women used outdoor environments for their pleasure, leisure, and recreation. During the Pleasure Garden (1850–1900) and Reform Parks (1900–1930) eras, women were engaged in passive recreation such as strolls, sightseeing, gathering, or picnics. The reform parks enabled women to engage in athletic activities such as lawn tennis, basketball, and bicycling (Cranz, 1980). Furthermore, recreational activities and spaces for the different genders were separated during this period. For example, outdoor gymnastic equipment for men and women were located at opposite ends of a park with a structure or planted vegetation in between. Sometimes, softball, dancing, or yoga classes were offered in separate spaces or different times for the men and women. Although city and county park departments broadened and classified women by age and class (for example, girls, adult women, or working women), park programming remained focused mainly on men (Cranz, 1980).

At a younger age, girls and boys have some distinct differences in how they engage in play. These differences have been recorded in natural and built environments and may be influenced by societal or parental expectations, approval, and individual preferences. For example, boys are often perceived to use significantly more space when playing, while girls are more restricted in their movement. Some research suggests that those variations may be informally reinforced by gender-appropriate behaviors and activities (Kane, 1990). Other studies reviewed by Saegert and Hart (1978) indicate that the spatial range of girls' activities beyond the home is smaller than that of boys. Saegert and Hart (1978) also found that girls' play is less likely to involve active manipulation of the environment. A later review of play research found that play behaviors were influenced by whether or not children played within same-gender or mixed-gender groups (Riley & Jones, 2007). For example, girls playing with girls were less active and boys playing with boys were more aggressive. Societal and familial norms provide guidance for how people should act and likely influence how individuals behave while at play or in recreational settings. For example, Henley (1977) notes that girls are taught to take up less space, to cross their legs, and to smile more often. These types of informal or cultural "rules" likely continue to inform the behavior of adult women in their use of public space.

These societal expectations also influence recreational or formal sports programs available to and participated in by different groups. Title IX made many sports available to girls and women for the first time; however, gendered expectations for certain sports still exist. Hardin and Greer (2009) surveyed 340 college students and discovered that the traditional gender typing of sports remains. Some sports are viewed as more masculine, while others are considered more feminine. At the same time, with increases in gender-equality awareness, there has been a growth in women's sports leagues, a growing participation in male-dominated sports by female athletes, and a change in how women are represented in sports (Chinurum, OgunjImi, & O'Neill, 2014). The funding allocated to women's sports and the promotion of these events to a wider audience, particularly at the professional level, remains inequitable. While sports were historically tied with the masculine domain, this notion is continuing to be challenged and an increase of female participation in all kinds of sports has been seen (see Figure 6.4).

In contemporary public parks and open space systems, gender differences have been observed by some scholars. Hutchison (1994) observed elderly men and women in 13 public parks during the summer in Chicago and found that women and men used the parks at different times of the day. Female groups increased during afternoon (1–4 p.m.) and dinner (4–6 p.m.) hours of the day. Over half of all female groups more likely engaged in stationary activities such as

FIGURE 6.4 Differences between gender in sports participation is less restrictive than in the past but discrepancies remain. Image credit: Yiwei Huang.

using playground facilities, sitting on benches, and picnicking, which relate to gender-based caregiver roles. Among the three types of parks (neighborhood, regional, and waterfront), close to half of the female activity groups were observed in neighborhood parks. On average, female-only groups were larger than other groups – 8.0 persons compared to 6.3 persons for mixed-gender groups and 3.9 for male groups. Females accounted for a higher percentage of the individuals in mixed groups, family groups, and peer groups compared to the males who were most often alone or in peer groups. Krenichyn (2004, 2006) found various reasons women were engaging in physical activity in Brooklyn's Prospect Park. The park was closer to their homes and they were familiar with the other people in the park. The park offered varying exercise opportunities such as changes in the slope of paths and connection to the nearby streets and sidewalks. Women also noted they could access services and amenities such as restrooms and drinking fountains, while experiencing nature. The respondents also found social support from family, friends, and strangers exercising. While gender differences were not noted in this study, the findings contribute to understanding why women were using the outdoor environment. Huang and Napawan (2021) discovered that besides some gender-stereotyped activities, such as square dancing by women or chess playing by men, park users in a San Francisco public square, regardless of gender, conducted similar activities, like poker playing, opera singing, people-watching, and walking. Ho et al. (2005) found that compared to other human factors, gender differences in contemporary park activities and preferences were not as distinctive as in the past; however, the ethnic influences were more significant indicators of park use preferences.

Designers should consider how their work might address gender preferences in activities and how societal expectations might be limiting the use of particular groups. For example, fields and courts designed for one gender would likely limit the use by others. Others have noted that single-use spaces can be easily dominated by one group and cause trouble for others to access them (Grimm-Pretner, 2011). Designers should consider including a range of activities and equipment in public parks to provide flexible settings to allow for self-appropriation by individuals and eliminate the possibilities of domination by certain gender groups.

Safety and fear of crime

In general, for people to be able to enjoy public spaces, they need to feel safe. However, the experiences and perceptions of safety have been shown to vary considerably between men and women. Fear of public spaces is a major concern for women in many parts of the United States and elsewhere. In addition, gay and transgender people often report feeling unsafe in certain public situations. Understanding these different experiences and perceptions of safety is an important prerequisite for designers. While some of these feelings of unsafe conditions are due to interactions with others and outside the scope of the designer's work, the design of a space can contribute to someone feeling more comfortable and safer.

Design characteristics can influence a person's sense of safety. These characteristics include the level of maintenance, sufficient lighting, and social control of the space (Grimm-Pretner, 2011) as well as the presence or absence of other people and the ability to see the surrounding areas (Salmani, Saberian, Amiri, Bastami, & Shemshad, 2015) (see Figure 6.5). Previous research on women's use of public spaces includes the identification of differences between men and women due to perceived safety and comfort levels, the distance to and from destinations during

FIGURE 6.5 Dark, empty, under-maintained spaces may be perceived as unsafe by people of varied gender identities. Image credit: Yiwei Huang.

a limited time frame, and the indirect influences of attire (Loukaitou-Sideris, 2005; Mozingo, 1989). Among the considerations Mozingo (1989) identified, those relating to the sense of safety included preference for places that were located away from the street due to noise levels, crowded conditions, and traffic. The women in this study also preferred seating options that did not put them "on display" and places where they felt more spatial control. These types of perceptions and preferences have implications for physical design decisions.

In a visual preference study of urban community parks visited by visitors and students, Jorgensen, Ellis, and Ruddell (2012) found that social cues (presence or absence of people) and environmental cues (level of concealment) affected fear experiences by women and men. Their recommendations align with other approaches such as Crime Prevention Through Environmental Design (CPTED, see Chapter 2, "Safety and security" section) and the work of Kaplan, Kaplan, and Ryan (1998). The 2012 study suggests several park design considerations and park maintenance interventions to increase feelings of safety and to encourage use by women:

- Some paths should be programmed and managed to have larger numbers of people in sight while limiting paths with less use.
- The design should incorporate natural surveillance opportunities and informal observation by others.
- The design and maintenance of natural features should increase visual access.
- Diverse users and amenities should be encouraged to enhance social opportunities.

Addressing physical design concerns can change existing negative perceptions of a space and increase women's use of an area. For example, design layouts and features that provide a high degree of visual access and support their desired activities will likely encourage more women to frequent a place. In addition, location and accessibility are essential to consider when designing. Parks and other public spaces near homes and workplaces, as well as those with clear, safe access routes, will likely encourage use by women.

Social and cultural ties

The societal expectations placed on women and men can significantly impact what activities a person pursues and what places they use. Gender is not an exclusive factor for understanding and predicting the spatial preferences of individuals but is part of a complex mix of human factors that evolve and develop through a person's lifetime.

A woman's role in society may change throughout her life; it may change through relationships, family obligations, and employment as other factors influence her perceptions, preferences, and uses of public spaces. For example, as a single female, gender influences may have a lesser impact than when she is in the role of caregiver. A woman's preference of outdoor environments begins with her personality and individualized needs and are in turn influenced by experiences, education, and cultural contexts.

Like societal contexts, family and family structures can influence how outdoor environments are used and perceived by different genders. The caregiver's role in the home, which often falls to the woman, may be accompanied with using outdoor places for socializing with other caregivers while their children are occupied (see Figure 6.6). Within a familial structure, married women have further roles and identities that may change preferences toward outdoor environments. As an individual starts to have young children, preferences for outdoor environments may shift to parks with playgrounds while families with school-aged children may prefer more adventurous destinations and formal recreation settings. Although every phase of a family's life cycle influences varying spatial needs and preferences, some researchers proposed that women may still be occupied with caregiver roles and obligated to the ethic of care (Day, 2000; Franck & Paxson, 1989; Miller & Brown, 2005).

FIGURE 6.6 Moms and female caregivers are frequently seen in playgrounds with children. Image credit: Yiwei Huang.

FIGURE 6.7 As shown in earlier studies (e.g., Mozingo, 1989), men and women continue to claim different territories in parks (Huang & Napawan, 2021). Image credit: Yiwei Huang.

During an observational study in San Francisco's Chinatown, Huang and Napawan (2021) found distinct differences in how women and men used a local park. Though many park visitors enjoyed the same activities as mentioned previously, the interviewed female users tended to spend less time in the park compared to male park users, due to family duties such as cooking, part-time jobs, childcare duties, etc. In addition, the territories claimed by the women at the park were smaller than the men's, and the two genders concentrated in different locations in the park (see Figure 6.7).

Designers should observe use patterns in the outdoor spaces they are designing and talk to those users about their preferences. This knowledge, particularly as it relates to gender preferences, can contribute to more successful outdoor environment designs. Environments that acknowledge and reflect the specific context and culture will likely more fully meet the needs of the potential users. In addition, in some circumstances the designer may elect to challenge the status quo and provide gender-neutral or gender-inclusive spaces where people in different stages in their lives are welcomed and their desires considered.

Design features

Along with choices in recreational activities, perceptions of safety, and the influences of culture and society, specific design features and characteristics have been found to be important to women. Scholars have found that men and women tend to respond differently to the same design features and that different genders may have contrasting requirements for a particular feature or function. For example, in Mozingo's study (1989) of urban open spaces in San Francisco, women were more annoyed by the surrounding noise, traffic, litter, and crowded conditions, while the men expressed annoyances over a lack of sun, too many pigeons, too much concrete, and the presence of derelicts. In addition, women noted the lack of benches more often than men, while both groups desired more open spaces. In another study, Virden and Walker (1999) researched how ethnicity, race, and gender related to the meanings of the natural environment and influenced the preference for environmental settings for desired outdoor recreation experiences and found that female university students' meanings and preferences differed from those of males. The female respondents in this study found the forest more threatening, mysterious, and awe-inspiring than men did. This study also asked about preferences in types of environmental settings. Female participants expressed their preferences for seeking an environment that has high visibility of management and law enforcement, and development for visitor convenience (compared to remote natural settings that are preferred by more male participants). Female respondents also preferred places that offer opportunities to spend time with family and close friends.

Sadeghi and Jangjoo (2022) investigated the relationship between the physical characteristics of urban public spaces, specifically streets, and the number of times women were present in them in Shiraz, Iran. They found that the surrounding land use and activities; security, accessibility and permeability; environmental and visual comfort; and facilities and services were important influences on women's presence in urban spaces. More specifically, the physical characteristics of the built environment that significantly correlated to the number of times women were present in the streets included access to public parking, choice of sitting or walking in shade or sun, access to the street through various routes, sufficient light and effective lighting, and beautiful form and facade of buildings. While this study did not examine the choices of men, these findings provide additional insight into considerations of women in this environment.

GENDER IDENTITIES, SEXUAL ORIENTATIONS, AND PUBLIC SPACES

As noted earlier in this chapter, the definition and understanding of gender has changed and is continuing to evolve. People identifying themselves with different gender identities than their assigned gender, those who have a non-heterosexual orientation, or gender minorities, may feel marginalized, like they do not belong in certain public spaces. For example, some businesses, communities, and states have prohibited the use of public restrooms by anyone not conforming to their biological or birth gender; therefore, these individuals are excluded from access to these facilities. This issue has been framed as a matter of individual rights by those supportive of access by transgender individuals and as a public safety issue by those opposing access. While research focused on these public safety claims show that bathroom assaults are exceedingly rare (Hasenbush, Flores, & Herman, 2019), the topic remains highly contested. Individual localities and private businesses are often left to determine how to address the issue of access. Similar decisions are likely to impact amenities and access in the outdoor environment as well.

Persons with non-heterosexual orientations are also frequently targets of hostilities in public places. The first three terms of "LGBT," lesbian, gay, and bisexual, refer to sexual orientations, whereas transgender refers to gender identity (National Academy of Sciences, Engineering, and Medicine (NASEM), 2020). Sexual and gender minorities remain widely stigmatized in current societies in different ways (Herek & McLemore, 2013). Homosexual and bisexual persons report both lifetime and everyday discrimination more frequently than heterosexual individuals (Mays & Cochran, 2001). And sexual minorities are at higher risk of multiple mental health burdens than heterosexuals (Hatzenbuehler, 2009).

Cultural and social norms, education, and popular cultural trends have contributed to the evolution of society's understanding of gender and gender identity. Many organizations started to advance their knowledge in creating, communicating, and applying psychological knowledge of gender identity and sexual orientation, to benefit society and improve lesbian, gay, bisexual, transgender, queer or questioning, and more (*LGBTQ+*) communities' lives (American Psychological Association, n.d.). Gender identity, much like other characteristics of potential open space users, is to be acknowledged and addressed by design professionals.

Social and demographic changes

An increasing percentage of the U.S. population identifies as LGBTQ+. A Gallup Poll reports that there is an increase of LGBT population identification (in many polls, the term utilized is "LGBT," which might not include "Q and +" communities) from 3.5% in 2012 to 4.1% in 2016 (Pew Research Center, 2017) (see Figure 6.8), and to 7.1% in 2021 (Jones, 2022). This change is reported across regions and in both urban and rural areas. The Movement Advancement Project (MAP, 2019) found that between 3% and 5% of the rural population or 15–20% of the total LGBT population lives in rural areas.

However, increases in LGBTQ+ populations in some nonurban areas, especially in conservative communities, are not always accepted or acknowledged. The LGBTQ+ population may be subject to varied challenges and amplified impacts of acceptance or rejection due to increased visibility, a ripple effect of unsupportive experiences, fewer alternatives when discriminated against, and overall, less support structure (MAP, 2019).

The LGBTQ+ rights movement continues to gain attention and focus on the needs of these individuals in the public and private realm. Various individuals, organizations, and agencies advocate and support changing norms and encourage celebrating everyone's identity by preserving LGBTQ+ spaces and histories. For example, the NYC LGBT Historic Sites Project was

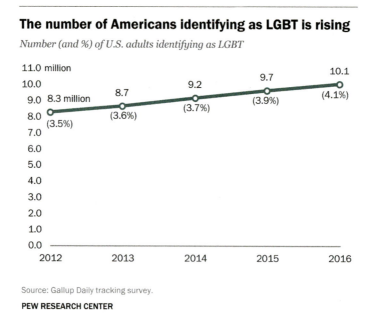

FIGURE 6.8 The number of Americans identifying as LGBT is rising (Pew Research Center, 2017).

launched in 2015 to be an educational resource by recording LGBT related historic sites in New York City (n.d.). Arup (a global sustainable development consulting firm) and the University of Westminster collaborated on exploring public spaces and queer communities (Catterall & Azzouz, 2021). In addition, the OLIN Labs (a community of practice effort of the landscape architecture and urban design practice of the OLIN Studio) launched a research initiative named PrideScapes (Olin Labs, n.d.). More discussions will continue and bring new light to innovative strategies for constructing inclusive spaces for people with any gender identity and sexual orientation.

Professional responsibilities and obligations

Addressing the needs of all genders in the design of outdoor environments is an important step toward addressing social sustainability – that is, the goal of creating places that support the well-being of people. Design professions have an obligation to address the desires and needs of all populations, including all gender minorities, in the public realm. This obligation is rooted in the professional responsibility to protect the public health, safety, and welfare in keeping with the spirit of inclusion discussed in the previous chapter.

While LGBTQ+ persons are a relatively small portion of the U.S. and other populations, their access to public spaces is vital. These spaces, along with more private places, play an important role in offering opportunities for recreation, retreat, and social encounters. They also provide important settings for social discourse and belonging (see Figure 6.9). Places for community

FIGURE 6.9 Dupont Circle, a traditionally gay neighborhood in Washington, DC, recognizes the LGBTQ+ community through rainbow-colored crosswalks. Image credit: Yiwei Huang.

GENDER AND PLACE   147

networking, such as clubs, have been shown to play a greater role in personal support within LGBTQ+ communities than do family and friends (Hulko & Hovanes, 2018). The outdoor public environment could provide the setting for those networking opportunities as well as for the representation and celebration of gender minorities.

Compared to the traditional social structures and gender identities, contemporary cultures should be more flexible to heterogeneous spatial designs. Public spaces, outdoor environments, and places people share should be more welcome to all gender identities and sexual orientations, reducing uneasiness felt by occupants. Such spaces should be designed to support the well-being of their diverse audiences and be responsive and appropriate to their users and the broader communities in which they are located. For designers, design interventions that undermine dominant narratives and encourage diversity are helpful in promoting inclusion and empowering marginalized communities like LGBTQ+ people (Catterall & Azzouz, 2021).

Preserving queer heritage is another important means of including LGBTQ+ people in public spaces (Catterall & Azzouz, 2021). Understanding both traditional and nontraditional gender identities for human-environment relations informs unique characteristics of a place. Environments must be adaptable by users (individuals or community) as society changes (norms, beliefs, relationships, technological advancements, etc.). Encouraging LGBTQ+ people to mark their own heritage and recognize their identities in places helps to counter marginalization. Applying an understanding of human and cultural factors may make this adaptation more fluid, including the acceptance of varied gender identities and their preferences and uses of public spaces.

Lastly, inclusive design practice and diversity engagement methods are also crucially important (Catterall & Azzouz, 2021). The larger community, including those individuals expected to use a new space, should acknowledge all gender identities and differences so that conflicts can be lessened during the design process. Allowing for adaptations, active engagement, and incorporating different voices will lead to a more socially sustainable environment.

GENDER-INCLUSIVE DESIGN

As society and environments change, contemporary planning and design should be more gender sensitive and gender inclusive. Ultimately, designers should create inclusive outdoor environments that address and accommodate the needs of vulnerable populations while offering opportunities for individuals to feel welcome, safe, and comfortable regardless of their gender.

Gender-inclusive urban design and planning

Recent years have brought an increase in reports and handbooks related to gender equality, especially at the urban design and city planning scales. In 2017, the Barcelona City Council published *Urban Planning with a Gender Perspective* (de Barcelona, 2017). The manual integrates gender perspectives into different aspects of urban planning, including but not limited to urban transportation mobility, accessibility and lighting, routes on foot, equality plans for companies and employment, neighborhood planning, and public space design. The city aims to achieve a barrier-free city that is fair, equal, and safe for all genders.

In 2020, the World Bank published a *Handbook for Gender-Inclusive Urban Planning and Design* (Terraza, Orlando, Lakovits, Lopes Janik, & Kalashyan, 2020) with the stance, as mentioned in this chapter, that the current city and built environment has been historically designed and planned mostly by men, and the cities work better for men than they do for women and other genders. The handbook identified six areas in the built environment that constrain or endanger women, girls, and sexual and gender minorities – access, mobility, safety and freedom from violence, health and hygiene, climate resilience, and security of tenure.

Gender-inclusive park and neighborhood design

Furthermore, some cities have taken the lead on addressing gender issues starting with efforts to provide safer and better places for all genders in public spaces and parks. In 1999, the city of Vienna, Austria redesigned two parks to specifically cater to the needs of young girls and increase their presence in public outdoor spaces (Urban Sustainability Exchange, n.d.). Specific design elements adopted in the parks include gender-neutral activity fields, clear arrangements of spaces, increased lighting, and increased visibility along main avenues, among others.

Recently in Sweden, public parks are being redesigned to be more gender-inclusive (Gardiner, 2021). During this effort, it was discovered that teenage girls do not necessarily bike to compete with others, but prefer slow biking tending to bike in groups. In this case, it was determined that the proposed public spaces should not only include a bike trail, but also places where riders can stop and chat with others. This finding may or may not be applicable to teenage girls in other communities, but it does point to the importance of understanding the needs of certain populations, an essential element of creating gender-inclusive places.

Lastly, although there might not be an established framework for gender-inclusive park design, the discoveries of park equity strategies are still applicable. Gibson, Loukaitou-Sideris, and Mukhija (2019) analyzed the outreach strategies of open space organizations that have successfully increased underprivileged populations' usage in parks and found that making parks more accessible, more welcoming, and intentionally incorporating the preferences of underserved groups are important. They propose that the tripartite framework of distribution, accessibility, and fit can be employed to create more equitable use of parks. Others note that planners and designers should think critically about gender and recognize that people of any gender carry multiple, intersecting, and dynamic identities (Chu, 2022). Participatory methods, which will be more thoroughly discussed in Chapter 7 and 8, can be used to listen to marginalized voices and counter loud dominating voices. Along with designers and planners, funding agencies and government officials need to consider a more equitable investment in parks and other open spaces. In particular, more focus on providing resources to historically under-resourced neighborhoods is needed along with creative design solutions.

CONCLUSION

Designed outdoor environments should attract and welcome all populations. Historically, these places have reflected the views and needs of males; however, various users, including all genders, have unique preferences and expectations for public places and the activities they support. Although gender biases and societal norms often disadvantage non-male populations in design and planning decisions, an increased understanding and acceptance of gender disparities promises to influence more advances in human-environment research and design. With continued interest and focus on addressing gender equality and inclusive designs, designers and planners can create more gender-sensitive and gender-inclusive places to ensure quality experiences for a broader spectrum of the public.

POTENTIAL EXERCISE AND PROJECT

A design project

How to design gender-inclusive cities? In 2020, the World Bank published *Handbook for Gender-Inclusive Urban Planning and Design* (accessible at https://www.worldbank.org/en/topic/urbandevelopment/publication/handbook-for-gender-inclusive-urban-planning-and-design). Review this handbook and conduct a gender-inclusivity analysis in a city you choose. The city should be one that you are familiar with such as the city your campus is located in your hometown or a city you visit often.

For this project, interview or have a dialogue with at least six women of different ages and different professions. During the conversation, ask about their everyday experience of the city, including their transportation mode, average travel time from one point to another, their reliance on public transit systems, and their comfort with walking on the city streets. After gathering these narratives, refer back to the handbook and produce a short proposal for increasing gender-inclusivity in this city.

SECTION III: DESIGN APPLICATIONS

7
VISUALIZING PEOPLE AND BEHAVIOR

This chapter presents methods to observe, document, and understand human perception and behavior in the outdoor environment. Before developing design recommendations, designers need to establish an understanding of the community and the specific site. Methods beyond the typical site inventory and analysis processes used by professionals are discussed. The application of these methods to various scales and project settings as well as their incorporation into different stages of the design and planning process are explored.

HISTORICAL CONTEXT

Visualizing people and behavior can be traced back to mid-20th-century work by social scientists, anthropologists, psychologists, and others. Visualizing the activities of people provides evidence that can reveal spatial issues and guide the creation of new places. Whether directly or indirectly, visualization informs scholars and practitioners on how people have used or are using the designed landscapes in both natural and built environments. Most often, the visualization of human behavior provides direct evidence to spatial planning and design inquiries. As designed spaces and landscapes evolve, visualization helps scholars and practitioners interpret the activities of people across scales and activities. Through the continued development of observation and visualization methods, spatial design efforts improve over time and become more responsive to different social and cultural contexts. These methods can inform designers of what and how landscapes can be changed or redesigned.

Numerous design *visualization methods* have been developed over the years. This chapter highlights several methods used by designers and researchers. These methods are generally presented in the same order as when they occur in a typical design process. For example, before design concept generation, commonly used visualization methods include reading the landscape and observing and documenting behavior. During design development, designers have a variety of ways to convey or visualize their ideas and the ideas of potential users. These include community mapping, photovoice, and design charrettes. After a design is implemented, visualization can be used to evaluate and document its success. Methods such as scored walks, post-occupancy evaluations (POE), and case studies create a visual record of how a place is being used and whether uses align with the designer's intent. Certainly, this does not mean that these methods cannot be used in other stages of the design, nor does it mean that there is only one method to achieve specific goals. Designers should creatively use, criticize, adapt, and combine various methods to understand places and use visualization tools to better communicate their findings and design ideas.

READING THE LANDSCAPE

When one steps into an unfamiliar site or environment, the fundamental way to understand it is to read the landscape's natural features, including landform, vegetation, hydrology, and soils, and man-made features, such as buildings, roads, and land use type. These features capture and tell the story of current and past inhabitants. *Reading the landscape* helps designers to establish cultural and historical context, understand how a place is used now, and capture design patterns and images for later phases.

Background

Mary Theilgaard Watts was an early scholar who used visualization methods to record, analyze, and help non-professionals to understand ecological and environmental characteristics. Her book, *Reading the Landscape: An Adventure in Ecology* (1957), influenced environmental designers in the 1960s and 1970s. Her artistic recordings, drawn while walking outdoors, demonstrate one means of capturing landscape stories and how to interpret clues laid down by time, natural forces, and human history (Watts, 1957, 1999, 2009).

While Watts wrote about trees, wilderness, and natural spaces, Grady Clay read urban areas. In *Close-Up: How to Read the American City* (1980), Clay proposes a method of walking in a straight line across a city – starting at one edge, crossing the center of the city, and walking all the way to the opposite edge – while observing as much as possible along the route. This *transect* method allows explorers to detect amorphous areas and unexpected adjacencies (Isenstadt, 2015), and record encounters through field sketches or photographs. Owens, LaRochelle, and McHenry (2015) build upon Clay's idea, and propose an activity called landscape stories. Similar to Clay's transect, they suggest using a relatively straight route across a landscape with frequent stops to document, observe, and question what is seen. Parker and Owens (2023) re-frame the transect as a listening experience where traversing the landscape provides an opportunity to become immersed in the landscape and the experiences of its occupants.

In addition, J.B. Jackson and Kevin Lynch, and their methods of reading the landscape, have inspired numerous designers and planners. Jackson, a cultural geographer and educator, explored the American Southwest on motorcycle and wrote prolifically about the *vernacular landscape* (Jackson, 1984, 1994). Urban planner and educator Lynch focused his work on urban settings. His book *Image of the City* (1960) examines how people experience and form mental maps of cities. The five elements he identified – path, node, landmark, edge, and districts – continue to inform how designers and planners evaluate and design cities. More of Lynch's work is discussed in Chapter 2.

Methods

While varied in scale and scope, these methods of reading the landscape allow the observer to go beyond reciting the obvious and encourages learning more about a place. Reading the landscape helps designers understand a place – how it is organized, why it looks the way it does, and the daily patterns of those living there. This method can also help designers learn how to view and learn from other places. The particulars of reading a landscape can and should vary with the individual doing the reading and the landscape being read. Designers can innovate by developing, combining, or refining methods to achieve their specific goals.

Landscape reading methods share the basic premises of *deliberately looking*, *sketching*, and *questioning the mundane*. To unearth the stories embedded within any place or landscape, time must be spent in the field observing and questioning. Three core elements of reading the landscape methods are: (1) Slow, deliberate, well-planned transportation routes with frequent lengthy stops for observation; (2) field journaling, including observational notes, sketches, and photos; and (3) follow-up research on historical and current day information (Owens, La Rochelle, & McHenry, 2015). During this process, bear in mind that both sketching and photography are symbolic representations of the landscape story that *the observer* is telling (see Figure 7.1). While sketching, the designer should ask, what is the vocabulary of the place and what are the elements under consideration? Things warranting attention range from place names to artifacts or props, from use patterns to architectural elements. Sun, Wang, and Li (2008) summarize vernacular landscape elements into three categories: the thing, the event, and the conception of vernacular. *The thing* refers to physical objects, such as architectural elements, materials, plants, or artifacts. *The event* includes local customs, ritual events, and habits; that is, those non-material representations of culture that exist in daily lives. *The conception of the vernacular* refers to the non-material symbols such as use patterns, place names, cultural atmospheres, or memories associated with the place.

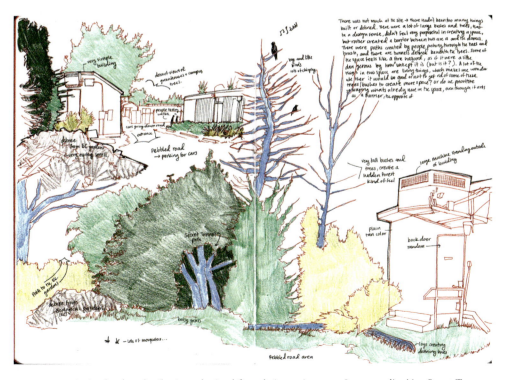

FIGURE 7.1 A site sketch and reflection submitted for a design assignment. Image credit: Aina Smart Truco.

Application and results

Designers and planners frequently use methods of reading the landscape to learn things that would not otherwise be uncovered by typical site analysis. The method highlights things that are less obviously known or understood about a place and provides a basis for forming more questions to be explored and answered. Reading the landscape also helps provide context and inspiration for later design ideas. Thus, reading landscapes provides a framework for understanding a specific place and a framework for looking at and listening to other places.

OBSERVING, DOCUMENTING, AND ANALYZING BEHAVIOR

A direct means to understand a site is to *observe* how people use it. *Behavior observations* are an important complement to other site analysis processes which often tend to focus on physical or natural features and their conditions. This section focuses on methods of observing, recording, and analyzing user behavior.

Background

Scholars across numerous fields study human behavior *in situ*. Notable methods across fields include longtime participant observation over the course of multiple years (Cushing, Green, & Eggan, 1979); sociological observations of social interactions at the individual and small group level to understand society (Frisby, 2013; Simmel, 2011); filming urban plazas in New York City to closely link the relationship between observation, documentation, and physical design (Whyte, 1980); and the use of methods including counting, mapping, tracing, tracking, photographing, journaling, and walking to study public life (Gehl & Svarre, 2013). Specific observation and recording methods are determined by the situation and the designer's goals. For example, a designer might decide to conduct observations at different time periods, compare the use of two spaces, or differentiate between the use patterns of different groups.

Behavior mapping is one of the common ways to understand the use patterns of a public space, as well as the relationship between behaviors and the built environment. Barker (1968) first advocated behavior mapping as an unobtrusive method to psychologically study behaviors in natural settings. Sanoff and Coates (1971) applied behavior mapping to understanding children's play patterns in a housing area and, in doing so, conveyed detailed behavior mapping procedures. At that time, behavior mapping was mainly used to collect data on types of activities, specific locations and places, and particular people. The resulting behavior maps showed the frequency of activity types, spatial distribution of uses, and concentrated incident locations (see Figure 7.2).

Method

The traditional method to conduct behavior mapping is relatively straightforward. A typical process is to first find or create a map of the area to be observed and divide the site into use zones or sub-areas for observation, while concurrently identifying the research questions that the behavior mapping will answer. Next, an observation plan is developed, which typically includes which activities are to be observed, when observations will occur (dates and times), what recording tools and techniques will be used, how long each round of observations will take, and what subject characteristics will be recorded (e.g., gender, age). Once the plan is

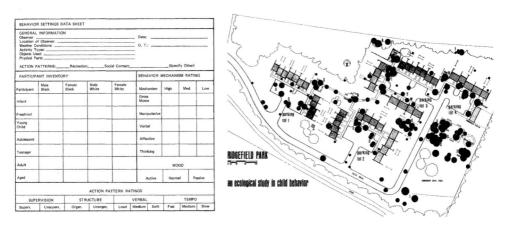

FIGURE 7.2 An example of a data collection form and the resulting behavior mapping of children in a residential setting (Sanoff & Coates, 1971).

set, observations should be conducted in a consistent and unobtrusive manner. Once on-site observations are completed, the behavior maps are compiled, compared, and analyzed with a focus on answering the research questions. For example, longitudinal studies could utilize behavior mapping to understand both seasonal change and year-round climate impact (Cosco, Moore, & Islam, 2010). Behavior mapping can also be combined with other methods to reveal more in-depth understandings of the places studied. For example, Huang and Napawan (2021) combined behavior mapping, observation, and interviews to understand the reasons behind gender separation on an urban plaza (see Figure 7.3).

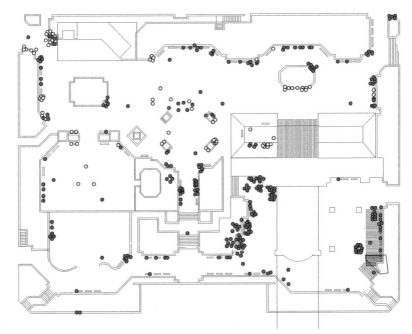

FIGURE 7.3 Digitizing behavior mapping data helped increase understanding of gender separation at one urban plaza (Huang & Napawan, 2021).

VISUALIZING PEOPLE AND BEHAVIOR   157

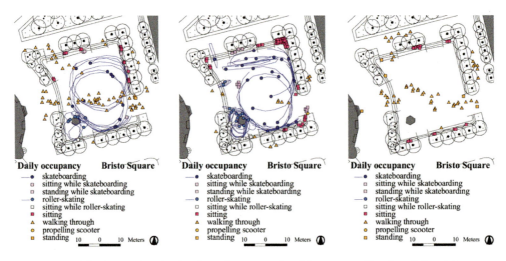

FIGURE 7.4 Behavior mapping showing dynamic patterns of spatial occupancy. Maps from left to right present daily occupancy on a weekday afternoon during poor weather, a weekend afternoon during very good weather, and a daily weekday in the early afternoon during good weather (Goličnik, 2005).

Technological innovations have brought many advances to behavior mapping. When studying children's behaviors in an outdoor playground, Cosco et al. (2010) recorded behaviors using a paper map and a handheld computer, then digitized the points or dots representing individuals in their observations and coded children's physical activity types in geographic information systems (GIS). Goličnik (2005) employed GIS using digital coding devices held by individual users to create an almost paperless data collection protocol that allowed for the coding of more variables, including the exact location of different physical activities (see Figure 7.4).

Along with behavior mapping, direct observation and sketching are straightforward ways to capture moments or elements deemed significant by the observer (see Figure 7.5, left). Digital software can also be used to create notations and conduct further analysis by integrating key interpretation measures such as stopping points, speed changes, avoidance points, and intersections (see Figure 7.5, right). Behavior can also be recorded by integrating mapping

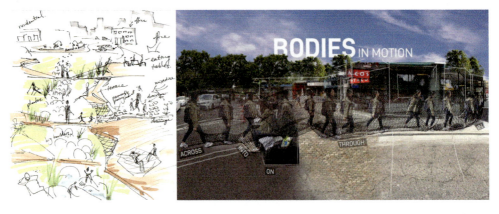

FIGURE 7.5 A student's behavior observation sketch using pen and colored markers to capture activities during one specific moment (left). Image credit: Sonia Shoji-Jeevanjee. In the "Bodies in Motion" exercise, a student used Adobe Illustrator to incorporate photo clips and notation to convey behavior (right). Image credit: Isabella Jimenez.

with walking or "go-along" interviews. Walking with an individual, the designer sees the community through another individual's eyes and captures important moments and key places on maps (Carpiano, 2009). Further behavior recording methods are discussed later in this chapter, such as online and cognitive mapping.

Application and results

Observation, behavior mapping, and other behavior recording methods are good ways to understand the current use patterns of a site and, in turn, inform design decisions. Researchers and designers may use collected data to locate both well-used and less-used places and to understand what works and what does not about a design. Behavior recording methods provide information that designers normally do not see during regular site investigations or analysis, and inform designers as to what makes a good design beyond visual aesthetics.

Behavior mapping is also an effective tool for representing environmental improvements between pre- and post-construction (Cosco et al., 2010). The Tulatoli Primary School case study in Chapter 9 illustrates this application of behavior mapping. Furthermore, behavior observations can provide critical information regarding differing use patterns among populations, difficulties and problems associated with particular user groups, and effectiveness or limitations of inclusive site designs.

Designers should keep in mind a few key points when incorporating behavior observation methods into their design process. First, behavior mapping is a strong data collection tool; however, the data itself only shows a pattern or phenomenon for a particular location, not generalizable conclusions. Designers should combine behavior mapping with other methods to verify design and use assumptions and inform recommendations. Second, the parameters of the study may limit observations and a comprehensive understanding of the use patterns may not be possible. Time constraints may limit the extent of each observation or the time span over which they occur. Seasonal or weather implications can alter use patterns. Predetermined activity lists may bias the activities recognized and noted. What researchers do not see or capture can be just as important as what is seen; studies conducted at different times of the day, week, or year, may yield very different results. Third, behavior mapping can be challenging, particularly in places with large numbers of users, highly mobile or fast activities, or where differentiations between various user groups are difficult to discern (see Koo, 2012). For instance, children running and playing or bicyclists speeding along paths can be very difficult to record or may accidentally be recorded twice. In these instances, the designer should repeat observations on multiple days and maintain a systematic approach to observing and recording. Activities that are missed while others are being recorded will likely reoccur and be recorded later. Lastly, researchers should compare and contrast the demographic data of their observations with that of the surrounding area. This step will help to ensure that targeted subjects are reflected in the behavior study; if they are not, then additional research may be necessary to determine why.

COMMUNITY AND PARTICIPATORY MAPPING

Background

A *community map* is a map produced collaboratively by residents of a particular locale, featuring local knowledge and resources (Parker, 2006). *Participatory mapping*, on the other hand, is a flexible participatory action research (PAR) approach in which researchers can study qualitative, quantitative, or mixed data collection methods (Brown, Strickland-Munro, Kobryn, & Moore, 2017) (see Chapter 7, " Digital Sources and Methods" section for a discussion of participatory GIS). People often use the two terms community mapping and participatory mapping interchangeably, as both mean a co-production of knowledge, most often maps, by local community members. Community members are solicited either to individually produce, produce with other residents, or under the direction of or in collaboration with a professional, the mapping of information which informs planning or design decisions, or research.

Various scholars and designers use community mapping for different purposes, such as to record places or features of historical, environmental, or social importance. Turnbull and Watson in *Maps are Territories* (1993) share examples of how Indigenous peoples use "ground maps" to keep a spatial representation of their own community history. Chambers (2006), a collaborator with Turnbull and Watson, highlights power relations within the mapping process, and therefore the importance of communication methods (e.g., mapping on bare ground, rather than paper) to convey information to certain communities. Hester, McNally, and Owens used community mapping as a way to enlist Sierra Club members and avid hikers in locating and mapping animal habitats (McNally, Hester, Eubanks, Hsia, & Cornwall, 1986). These community mapping examples demonstrate how designers and planners can capture and incorporate local knowledge in their decision making.

Along with representing history, location, and spatial relationships, maps are used to convey shared and individual experiences such as sensory or cognitive understanding of places. As noted earlier, Lynch's *Image of the City* aimed to analyze the mental or cognitive maps of cities by research participants, finding consistencies in the physical characteristics that influence memories of a place. On the other hand, Hayden (1995) explored how individuals' *differences* inform memories of place. She presents results from a study by the Los Angeles Department of City Planning in which residents living in three different Los Angeles neighborhoods, with different cultures and income levels, drew their cognitive maps of the Los Angeles area. A comparison of these maps reveals striking size differences in how each group perceived the city and illustrates how language, culture, and economic status impacted travel and understanding of the groups (see Figure 7.6). Furthermore, mapping the sensory perception of places has received increased attention in recent years. Researchers have used "smelly" maps, or smell-mapping, to understand participants' aromatic experiences of cityscapes (see Koo, Hustedde, & Young, 2018). In addition, sound mapping is a collaborative effort soliciting citizens to upload recorded public sounds onto a geo-based platform. The resulting map can be used to navigate cities from a different perspective, record local culture or history, identify the locations of different audible elements, or more (see The Acoustic Ecology Institute, n.d.).

Methods

Participatory maps represent community members' perception of their environment and its important characteristics. The knowledge collection process includes identifying participants, the desired knowledge, and methods of recording. A well-conceived mapping process helps to build community cohesion, raise awareness of environmental and land-related issues, empower participants to engage in resource and land-related decision-making, and ultimately, strengthen local communities and their members (Corbett, 2009).

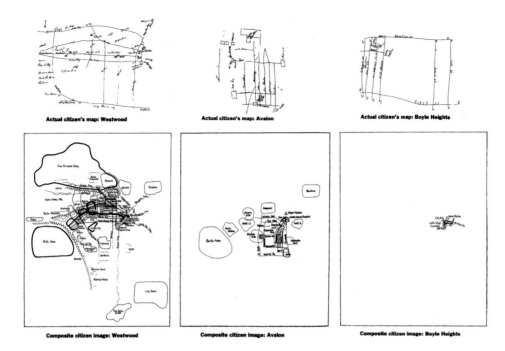

FIGURE 7.6 Cognitive maps of Los Angeles as perceived by the predominant ethnicities in different neighborhoods – white residents in Westwood, Black residents in Avalon, and Latino/a residents in Boyle Heights (Los Angeles Department of City Planning, 1971). Retrieved from Hayden (1995).

Participatory mapping strategies and approaches will vary with the design or research purpose. For example, if the researcher intends to allow residents to construct a map without any contextual references (such as a base plan), then all that is needed may be drawing tools (paper, markers, a table) and a gathering place. Participants can be guided to draw in a certain order – e.g., boundaries first, then sub-areas – then to highlight important buildings and other environmental features. Lastly, everyone provides additional information based on their knowledge. These pieces come together in a comprehensive map. If the researcher wants to observe and understand participants' priorities, they could instead allow the participants to decide what to map first and how. Participants may vary the order of mapping, the content expression, and the methods of expression, including the use of other materials (e.g., the ground, stones, or found objects). Place It! is a design process example that provides a wide assortment of objects and materials for participants to use in creating a three-dimensional expression of an important memory or a desired experience (Rojas, 2013).

Participatory mapping is also an effective tool when local knowledge is needed for complex or contentious projects. Engaging the local community will not only increase the designers' knowledge of local considerations, it will increase the residents' understanding of others' concerns and potential necessary trade-offs. In those cases, designers and researchers should make established knowledge (base maps, site inventory data, ownership maps, etc.) and mapping tools accessible and comprehensible to residents. Corbett (2009) describes two projects funded by The International Fund for Agricultural Development (IFAD) that used innovative participatory mapping techniques. In Kenya, residents used the ground as their drawing surface and stones and sticks to form boundaries and roads. In Vietnam, designers used a large-scale 3-D model to convey elevation changes and natural resources such as forests and waterways. Local residents used string, push pins, and paper to mark their ideas on the model.

Applications and results

Participatory mapping can be integrated into the site inventory and design development phases. In the Runyon Canyon master plan process (McNally et al., 1986), local knowledge mapped included invisible features and characteristics, like different user territories, and temporal occurrences, like areas which flood during big storms. A participatory mapping process may also show participants discrepancies between what people believe and what is true. For example, one group may feel that another group often occupies one piece of land, but they learn through the process that this belief is not accurate.

Participatory mapping provides a means to obtain accurate yet otherwise unavailable information, while also being cost effective. The result can be a snapshot in time or a continually evolving representation. Designers and planners should keep in mind that community maps do not have to be stagnant; they can continue to grow and represent different voices. When interpreting data, one can look at each map individually or at a compilation of all data. Additionally, maps can be digitized and combined to create a comprehensive picture.

Participatory mapping is a valuable tool for building trust between designers and residents. Seeking information from residents helps them to understand that the designer values their knowledge. In addition, the participatory mapping process opens lines of communication, provides a common base of information, and helps to build a sense of ownership in residents. As participants in the design and decision-making process, residents will more likely understand the opportunities and limitations of a site and the basis for the resulting design. However, designers and planners need to recognize that community or participatory mapping can only reflect ideas and thoughts from participants, and do not necessarily represent the entire community's perspectives.

USER-EMPLOYED PHOTOGRAPHY

Background

User-employed photography includes *photo-elicitation methods* that combine participant photographs with interviews to understand the images' significance (Balomenou & Garrod, 2019). Although he did not integrate interviews, Gesell (1934) was an early adopter of photography as a research tool and used photographs to document infant and children's behavior in the 1930s. Collier and Collier (1986) first adopted photography and photo-elicitation as a research method in the 1960s. Additionally, *auto-photography*, which is slightly different than photo-elicitation, is an ethnographic research method that allows participants to take, choose, and represent photographs themselves, thus generating authentic information and allowing researchers to look at the participants' world through the participants' eyes (Noland, 2006).

Finally, *photovoice* (closely related to auto-photography) describes a community engagement process of visually recording people's experiences and opinions. Coined by Wang and Burris

FIGURE 7.7 Members of the Sactown Heroes documented through photographs, videos, and text what they like and do not like in their community during the Youth Voices for Change project. Image credit: jesikah maria ross.

(1994, 1997), photovoice allows participants to express their personal experience and opinion on a particular topic, thus creating a sense of community ownership and expanding an individual's knowledge and validity. Likewise, Darbyshire, MacDougall, and Schiller (2005) identified how photovoice allows children to document their activities and perspective better than other methods, such as interviews, alone.

Several researchers have further integrated photographic methods with participatory mapping (Dennis, Jr., Gaulocher, Carpiano, & Brown, 2009). *Participatory photo mapping* (PPM) is a facilitated process that involves photo-elicitation interviews, inviting the public to contribute images, and public participatory mapping, resulting in a comprehensive assembly of images, narrations, and mapping data. The process engages community members in research and design decision-making in a democratic way. One such effort is Youth Voices for Change, a map created by young people in West Sacramento, California to "express their hopes and aspirations for the future" (Art of Regional Change, n.d.). Their PPM was one strategy in a multi-pronged, regional effort to understand what constitutes a healthy environment from a young person's point of view (Owens, Nelson, Perry, & Montgomery-Block, 2010) (see Figure 7.7).

Methods

Both photovoice and PPM are qualitative methods that utilize public participatory knowledge. Participants play a pivotal role in identifying and documenting issues, and share their opinions through mapping and narratives. These methods help researchers approach complex community issues without influencing the findings, while keeping the study rigorous. One multi-community approach to photovoice by Nykiforuk, Vallianatos, and Nieuwendyk (2011) had the research team partner with key stakeholders to form community working groups. Each working group then identified issues of interest in their community and implemented the method, providing an opportunity to examine the effectiveness of the method in different contexts.

The original photovoice study plan outlined by Wang and Burris (1997) consists of nine steps: (1) Select and recruit target audiences of policy makers or community leaders; (2) recruit photovoice participants; (3) introduce the concept and methodological principles to the participants; (4) obtain consent; (5) pose an initial theme; (6) distribute cameras and review feedback; (7) provide time for photography; (8) meet in a group to discuss photographs; and finally, (9) share and present those photographs to the policy makers (see also Sutton-Brown, 2014). Participants' photography can also be accompanied by written narratives or photo-journals to provide a record of personal experiences that can be shared with the community.

One of the limitations of photovoice is the likely limited sample size, and thus the applicability to larger scale community decisions. Because of costs and time demands, photovoice efforts typically recruit a select group of participants; therefore, the views of the broader community may not be captured. In addition, participants should be given direction as to the number of images to collect; otherwise, the volume of photographs may become unwieldy. The participants also need to be involved in selecting and explaining the photographs, since their intent can be easily misinterpreted.

Photovoice projects have many benefits. In addition to collecting diverse viewpoints, the process engages people in discussions and decision-making processes, helps them to learn more about their community and others, and often contributes to community change. Nykiforuk et al. (2011) reveal that one presentation to government officials resulted in immediate attention to community infrastructure issues. Likewise, the Youth Voices for Change project led the city's parks and recreation department to rethink a park master plan and their broader community participation efforts in park planning.

Applications and results

Photovoice and PPM methods provide a powerful way to articulate and share individuals' stories through images and words. These methods encompass broad sources and expressions of participants' autonomous power. Apart from being an effective tool for social science researchers, they are powerful tools for designers in terms of the richness and usefulness of the information gained and the benefits to participants and the greater community.

Residents' stories can provide valuable information to designers on the history of a site, the activities in and importance of a place for past and current residents, and the reasons for and levels of local significance or meaning, thus contributing to meaningful and appropriate design solutions. In addition, photo-elicitation methods help to build community partners for the designer. The participatory process stimulates community member's understanding of the issues and considerations leading to a final design. This knowledge will reside in the community once the designer's role ends.

SCORED WALKS

Background

Landscape architect Lawrence Halprin and his spouse, dancer Anna Halprin, first developed scored walks as a way for design students in the 1940s to increase their conscious awareness of space. Lawrence Halprin later employed *scores* in his RSVP (resources, scores, valuaction, performance) creative process (Hirsch, 2011). Based upon musical scores and their purpose of moving a performer through a composition, a scored walk actively choreographs people's movements and actions and can be used to understand and influence people's movement through environments. Halprin (1963) argues that urban areas demand participation and must be experienced through movement to come alive. In addition, a score can enable designers to record everyday movements and choreograph or score future actions.

Rae (2015) notes that scores may be either a process (the composer's intentions) or an interpretation of a process (how someone responds). By design, scores are suggestive and therefore elicit the participation of both the performer and the audience. Other landscape architects have reinterpreted and employed the concept of a scored walk. Hester (2012) notes that scores informed his 12-step participatory process. In the Runyon Canyon Master Plan, Hester incorporated a scored walk where residents experienced and listened to the site (see Figure 7.8).

Methods

The form and implementation of *a scored walk* varies with the designer and their project-specific intentions. As a design and research method, scored walks do not have clear and well-tested procedures. While Halprin used scores as a way for participants to experience a site, he also understood that engaging in a shared experience would create a common language (Hester, 2012). These two intentions – site experience and shared learning – inform the key elements of a scored walk.

Like a musical score, a scored walk should guide the experience, but can also leave opportunities for improvisation and interpretation of the performers. The score can include instructions on where to go, the path to take, and the activities to be performed once there. For example,

FIGURE 7.8 Scored walks were used during the Runyon Canyon master planning process to gain knowledge from the nearby residents and to increase their understanding of the place. Image credit: Randy Hester.

Halprin's scored walk of San Francisco includes stops at the cable car barn, Woolworth's, Union Square, and Aquatic Park at specific times. Activities to be performed at Union Square include: (1) Share your lunch and (2) at the sound of the 3 o'clock chimes, stand and face the sun. Independent participant scores were timed so that all the participants engaged in the second of these activities simultaneously. Hester's scored walk for Runyon Canyon led the participants in unison through the project site. Participants responded independently to questions posed in a workbook which they completed at each stop. One question used to challenge participants to think about the park in new ways was, "If this place could talk, what would it say?" Depending on the designer's goal for the activity, activities might contribute to learning about a place, uncovering residents' viewpoints, or design inspiration.

Applications and results

Scored walks have varied design applications. They can be an effective means for building a shared understanding of a place and community interest. Participants in a scored walk will come away with a common experience and thus understanding of a place's problems and potential. A scored walk also can allow participants to see a familiar place differently and gain a new perspective. The score may encourage participants to experience or engage with the place differently from their normal routine, see it through different lenses, or focus on specific aspects such as history or ecology. This increased participant understanding informs the designer's knowledge of the site and likely site users. In addition, this process can have a longer-term impact by contributing to a sense of local responsibility and ownership.

Along with building a general understanding about a place, scored walks can be used as a deliberate means for generating design ideas. These ideas may be derived from the non-designer participants or, as Halprin shows, design teams can participate in experiential immersions in a place. Designers may also use the concept of developing a score to guide their design decisions; that is, how will the visitor to this place experience it, and how can the design guide and shape that experience?

POST-OCCUPANCY EVALUATIONS AND THE CASE STUDY METHOD

Background

A *post-occupancy evaluation* (POE) is "a systematic evaluation of a designed and occupied setting from the perspective of those who use it" (Marcus & Francis, 1998, p. 345). POEs were first used in the field of architecture to evaluate the organization, quality, and productivity of architectural spaces (Cooper, 2001), and their use has expanded quite rapidly since the 1970s. Unlike psychological or sociological research which seeks to generate findings applicable to many situations and settings, a POE typically focuses on one type of designed setting or even just one site. The intention of most POEs is to improve the environment under study; hence, it tends to be conducted with a rigorous procedure, and only observes, records, and describes, rather than manipulates or implies (Zimring & Reizenstein, 1980). POEs help designers to address and redesign spaces and places that are reflected by users and audiences.

Francis (2001) adopted the POE method as a framework for the landscape architecture profession's *case study method*. Building upon the reliance on case studies in other professions such as law, medicine, business, and engineering, Francis argues that a similar approach to analyzing the effectiveness of particular design solutions is valuable. Case study methods advance landscape architecture knowledge and contribute to understanding project's varied contexts. A modified case study approach is used in the four projects showcased in Chapter 9.

Methods

The POE method can vary depending on the setting and purpose. For example, a POE of an urban plaza might include interviews or surveys of nearby office workers, while a POE of a nature reserve might include monitoring plant growth. In the fields of landscape architecture and environmental design, POEs often are used to evaluate the performance of parks and other outdoor spaces in terms of how well they meet the needs of their users. Several research methods are commonly utilized to understand the patterns of use, misuse, and non-uses in the setting (Marcus & Francis, 1998). Typical components of a POE and the methods used are described in Table 7.1.

TABLE 7.1 The different components of a POE method used in assessing outdoor spaces

Subjective appraisal	A recording of what is sensed in the site: What is seen (visual features, colors and textures, people and activities, who is not seen); heard (sounds and their sources); felt (temperature, materials, textures); smelled; and tasted.
Initial site observation and sketches	Sketches and maps record the site layout, key components, and surrounding environment.
Subarea analysis	A drawing that divides the site into sub-areas that have similar uses or design characteristics.
Behavior traces and behavior mapping	Behavior traces include things left behind by others, alterations, and messages (Zeisel, 2006). Behavior mapping documents the activity patterns and uses of the site.
Interviews	Interviews may be conducted with designers to uncover their intent, or with users to understand the behaviors identified in traces and mapping. Interviews with place managers or maintenance crews also offer insights. For example, how often do they come, how long do they stay, who do they come with, or what areas do they use? To get a comprehensive picture, multiple and diverse users should be interviewed.
Data summary and use analysis	The salient data should be summarized and examined for patterns, such as use of one area by one age group but not others. The collected data should be compared to information on the surrounding area's population to identify who may not be represented in the users.
Problem definition and recommendations for change	The use analysis will reveal any discrepancies between users' desired activities and the designer's intent. Recommendations will seek to determine the reasons behind misuse and non-use, and offer ways to address these shortcomings.
Final report	An integration of text and graphics which clearly presents the discoveries and recommendations.

Source: Adapted from Marcus and Francis (1998).

Additional methods have emerged that expand upon these classic POE elements. The use of videos, time-lapse photography, participant mapping, and interactive or participatory approaches such as role-playing and staged events provide additional means for learning about the current use of a place. The POE should be designed and planned with specific objectives in mind. Those objectives will inform which data collection methods will be most effective.

Applications and results

In the fields of landscape architecture and environment design, POEs are used typically in one of three ways – post-construction, on-site pre-construction, and off-site pre-construction. Following the early intent of this method, a POE is conducted after construction to determine whether a design fulfills the designer's intent and meets user's needs and offers suggestions for design alterations. A POE also may be an early step in the design process, employed to assess the current use of the site being redeveloped and to inform designers what works and what does not. In circumstances where a site is undeveloped, the designer can employ the POE method to explore how sites of a similar purpose are used. For example, a POE of an outdoor play yard at a childcare center could provide important directions for the design of a new facility.

Post-occupancy evaluations offer a systematic and quantifiable method to determine the effectiveness and suitability of a design. These findings may be used to improve the place under review, or the lessons may be applied to the creation of a new but similar place. A POE is typically focused on one location or site design, therefore findings may or may not be applicable more globally. Designers should consider the unique qualities of a place and its population when applying the findings of POEs conducted elsewhere. However, collective findings of POEs may provide guidance as to likely use patterns and other considerations. Lastly, while post-occupancy evaluations are widely acknowledged and used in many design-related fields such as architecture, landscape architecture, interior design, product design, and engineering, their adoption as an essential or required component of the design process has been limited. In particular, design competitions frequently base awards on the designer's project statements and photographs, rather than on the functioning of a design or the satisfaction of the users. One exception to this is the Great Places Award (2021) which focuses on "the experiential relationship between people and their environment."

DIGITAL SOURCES AND METHODS

The advances in and proliferation of digital means for obtaining, sharing, and analyzing information have rapidly supplanted more traditional methods of visualizing human behavior in outdoor environments. Many current research methods that rely on online data sources or computer-based media are extensions or reconfigurations of the traditional research methods already discussed. Two of those, participatory GIS mapping and the use of social media data, illustrate the incorporation and utilization of digital tools in the visualization process.

Participatory GIS mapping

Participatory geographic information systems (PGIS) or *public participatory GIS* (PPGIS) combines participatory mapping with the ArcGIS platform. This is a geo-spatial based approach that allows participants to view, edit, create, and comment on geo-spatial data through their cellphone, tablet, or computer. While traditional community meetings may not always allow for abundant community voices, PPGIS encourages and empowers diverse and extensive user engagement and deepens the understanding of local peoples' perceptions and preferences about spatial issues (Brown & Kyttä, 2014).

One project, the Franks Tract Futures project, aimed to improve the ecological, economic, and recreational condition of a California State Recreational Area. Franks Tract, a 3,000-acre property in the Sacramento-San Joaquin River Delta, is bisected by numerous active waterways and used by local and regional hunters, anglers, boaters, and others. Because numerous users are not local, traditional on-site workshops could not reach all those interested in the future of the site. PPGIS, however, provided an excellent means for gathering information on current and desired uses. The design team utilized an online map-based survey tool, Maptionnaire (2021), to solicit current users to provide information on their daily site behaviors, including where they berth, where they stay for fishing, their preferred travel route, and places which need improvement (Milligan, Kraus-Polk, & Huang, 2020). Potential participants were recruited through electronic and physical flyers which included a barcode connected to the online survey. The survey link allowed interested users, even those living far from the site, to easily communicate with the design team and contribute their knowledge to the spatial understanding of the site (see Figure 7.9).

Social media and behavior recording

Some designers and researchers have begun using social media to understand use patterns. Sourcing online data, including social media sites and video or photography sharing sites, can be an efficient method for accessing and collecting large amounts of data as compared to traditional observational methods. Today, many people, especially young people, post information about

FIGURE 7.9 PPGIS mapping, based on 728 survey responses, documents the typical boating routes and existing recreational activities in Franks Tract (Milligan, Kraus-Polk, & Huang, 2020).

their daily life on different online platforms and have therefore created a wealth of data. The analysis and application of this data to the design of varied outdoor spaces is rapidly expanding.

Researchers have employed social media data to inform park management, document use patterns of specific populations, and solicit community involvement. For example, Hamstead et al. (2018) found that Twitter and Flickr data could be used to understand human visitation dynamics for all New York parks. Barry (2014) used images on Flickr to analyze the public perception of and interests toward cattle grazing on park lands. Liang, Kirilenko, Stepchenkova, and Ma (2020) used Instagram pictures to monitor and observe unwanted visitor behaviors in national parks, aiming to achieve conservation with assurances of visitor safety. Shirtcliff (2020) presents a methodology for utilizing big data to promote youth inclusion in public spaces. Finally, researchers evaluating the success of the Seattle Freeway park mined 3,314 Instagram posts over three years and developed a method to understand park usage patterns, as well as users' emotions and activities associated with different parts of the park (Song & Zhang, 2020) (see Figure 7.10). Using social media to crowdsource data offers new possibilities for data collection on and behavior visualization of public parks.

In addition to social media, other online tools provide new methods for collecting data and engaging community members in design decisions. Game-based programs, such as Pokémon Go, can provide an excellent means to engage youth (Sadat, 2020), while on-line survey platforms allow for broader community input. Live polling, mind mapping, and photo-sharing websites also provide feedback and information that may not be accessible through traditional means to designers.

CONCLUSION

The selected visualization methods introduced in this chapter are particularly applicable to understanding people-environment relationships, including individual perceptions and experiences, behavior patterns, and place meaning. These methods can be used at various stages of the design process and modified or combined to suit the particular project circumstances. Designers should carefully consider and determine the information they want to obtain, then select the appropriate method. Designers should also consider the limitations of collecting information solely on a site within a limited timeframe and seek to maximize the understanding of a place and its population by combining various methods at different stages of the project.

Designers also must consider the accuracy and reliability of their data, ethical questions related to obtaining information, and the ownership of publicly sourced data. The accuracy of data obtained through online or digital sources should be confirmed. For example, are the GPS locations recorded in a community mapping project accurate or is the information that community members provide correct? Ethical concerns related to data collection include whether or not someone's privacy is compromised and if the sharing of this data could possibly subject them to harm. The ownership of publicly sourced data is also open to debate. Information collected from public platforms is readily available, but researchers should consider their recognition of the contributors.

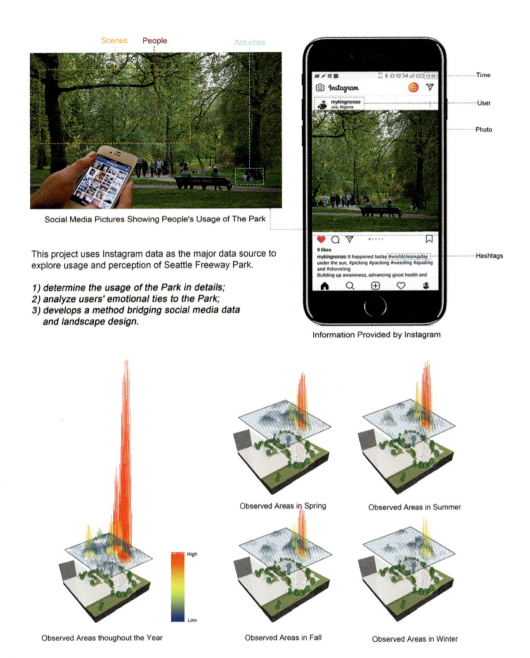

FIGURE 7.10 Social media data was used to understand park use and users' emotional connections during different seasons (Zhang & Song, 2019).

POTENTIAL EXERCISES AND PROJECT

An outdoor–indoor exercise

Behavior mapping and community mapping. This exercise combines outdoor observations with discussion and mapping to produce an evaluation of an existing outdoor space on campus.

VISUALIZING PEOPLE AND BEHAVIOR   171

Materials & setting needed:

Base map of study site(s)
8½ × 11 drawing paper
Clipboard or other writing surface
Observation template

Steps:

1. Instructor selects a study site close to the classroom. A site with a variety of activities (sitting, walking, standing, chatting, playing, reading, etc.) is ideal. Potential choices might include a courtyard, student activity center, transportation hub, or other large open space.
2. Students should first draw a plan of the site using the base map for reference. On this map, students should divide the site into observation zones if the area is too large to observe all at once.
3. Students should use the provided template as a guideline and develop their own template based on what information they hope to learn and on their initial observations. For example, if they see many users on their site playing games, they may want to develop codes for the various games.
4. Students should conduct behavior observations for approximately 30 minutes. Record your observations on the template and on the map. Move to the various sub-areas as needed.
5. At the designated time, all students return to the classroom and pin up all their completed templates and behavior maps. Everyone reviews the findings of others and makes notes as to the similarities and differences between these observations and their own.
6. The class discusses the observations.

Outdoor exercise

Photovoice exercise (journey on your way home). This exercise will give you an idea of the types of things you can learn when using photovoice.

1. The exercise begins with the class considering their campus and a route that they frequently take. What are the memorable places along this route? Why is this route used as compared to others? What things do you not like about this route?
2. Students mark their routes on a large-scale map and share their reflections.
3. The class should discuss what they envision as changes they would like for this area.
4. Using sticky notes, markers, or other means, the students should identify the things they like and want to keep and the things they do not like and want to see changes to create a community map.
5. Using a trace overlay, students should work together in groups of three or four to redesign the areas of greatest concern.
6. After a break, students should travel the route identified in the earlier discussion. They should record their route through photographs. These photos should document what they want to say about the route and places along it. Along with the images, students should make notes about their feelings and the reasons for taking the photograph.

7. Photographs should be printed or shared electronically and a reflection written about each place. Each student should share their thoughts with others.
8. Discuss this photovoice method in a class. For example: What types of things did you learn using the photovoice method that would not have been as evident during a typical site analysis? How can this method be incorporated into your design process? How might this method be adapted in different situations?
9. Compare and contrast the photovoice method with other digital engagement tools. What are the pros and cons of different visual-based methods?
10. Lastly, discuss how the community map prepared at the start of class differs from the information generated through the photovoice method.

8
ENGAGING PEOPLE IN THE PROCESS

This chapter provides an overview of how community engagement can be incorporated into the design and planning process, particularly during design development. Background on the role of community engagement in planning and design professions and governmental obligations for citizen review are discussed. The benefits and challenges of community engagement are also examined.

ROOTS OF COMMUNITY ENGAGEMENT IN DESIGN AND PLANNING

Civic duty and civic engagement

While the idea of civic duty was established by the Greeks and is embraced by many societies, the term is commonly associated with the United States and its Constitution. Civic duty is a basic tenet of a democratic society. For a democracy to function, citizens must be involved in the decision-making process through public debate and voting. In 1816, Jefferson noted, "Every man is under the natural duty of contributing to the necessities of the society; and this is all the laws should enforce on him" (Jefferson, 1903, p. 24). While civic duties extend to other obligations such as jury duty and paying taxes, the call to participate in decisions is at the root of community engagement in design and planning. Debates during the country's formation also focused on concerns that the emphasis on individual rights and capitalism would result in greed and a weakening or loss of the sense of duty and responsibilities to others (Yarbrough, 1998). The founders countered this concern with a call for community service – to get persons out of their isolated communities and to gain firsthand experience of others' needs and ideas (Tucker, 1837). Although the United States does not hold a monopoly on these civic duty principles, they have informed widely held beliefs and efforts toward civic engagement.

Current guidance from the US Citizenship and Immigration Services continues to promote these ideas of community engagement. Those seeking to become a naturalized citizen are advised that the rights and responsibilities of citizens include staying informed of the issues affecting their community, participating in the democratic process, and participating in their local community (USCIS, 2021). These responsibilities are directly aligned with civic engagement as defined by others and by those promoted in higher education. Ehrlich (2000) notes that in the context of higher education, "civic engagement means working to make a difference in the civic life of our communities and developing the combination of knowledge, skills, values and motivation to make that difference. It means promoting the quality of life in

DOI: 10.4324/9781315100036-12

a community, through both political and non-political processes" (p. vi). While citizenship is not a requirement for participation in design and planning decisions, this aspiration provides the foundation for community engagement in these endeavors.

Historical context

Several social movements and government policies in the 1960s and 1970s contributed significantly to how community involvement is currently practiced in our local governments. The civil rights movement spurred the recognition of multiple voices in public decisions. The Clean Air and Clean Water Acts and the subsequent National Environmental Policy Act (NEPA) codified the requirement to gain public input in required environmental impact statements (EISs) on federally funded projects and environmental impact reports (EIRs) on state-funded projects. Other actions, such as the Environmental Protection Agency's identification of SuperFund sites (Hird, 1993), large-scale urban renewal projects (Swyngedouw, Moulaert, & Rodriguez, 2002), and highway transportation plans (Hill, 1973) prompted affected and displaced populations to speak out, seek legal remedies, and get involved in debates around later public projects.

The long-term and institutionalized impact of required EIS and EIR completion and the accompanying public review process in particular has had significant implications for design and planning professions. Table 8.1 provides a summary and comparison of steps required in the federal EIS and California's EIR processes. The EIS and EIR processes include a

TABLE 8.1 A summary and comparison of NEPA and CEQA processes (adapted from CEQ & OPR, 2014)

	Federal environmental impact process	California's environmental impact process
Relevant Legislation	National Environmental Policy Act	California Environmental Quality Act
Initial Review	Projects are excluded if there are no extraordinary circumstances	Projects are exempt if it falls within: (a) a statutory exemption or (b) a categorical exemption
Assessment	Public engagement required	Required consultation with responsible agencies Notice of intent required Public review and comment required Agency review and comment required
Actions	If there are no significant impacts, then a *Finding of No Significant Impact* is required If mitigation is needed, then a *Mitigated Finding of No Impact* is required If there is a potential for impact, then an *Environmental Impact Statement (EIS)* is required	If no significant impacts, then a *Negative Declaration* is required If mitigation is needed, then a *Mitigated Negative Declaration* is required If there is a potential for impact, then an *Environmental Impact Report (EIR)* is required

required document containing an overview of the project, evaluations of its impacts, project mitigations, and a review of alternatives. Designers and planners often assist with the preparation of these reports. In addition, the required review and public hearing process established a model for other levels of government. Public review and comment periods are frequently required by municipalities as are alternative plans. The requisite posting of a public notice of the project hearing followed by public comments is the standard of community engagement in this context. While this process ensures that the public has access to information about a proposed project and an opportunity to voice concerns, it often does not provide a means to truly inform or shape the outcome. An evaluation of this established project review process is needed to ensure that local citizens' opinions are encouraged and heeded, not just allowed.

Social movements and public policies continue to shape the public landscape as well as citizen participation. In 2020, the Black Lives Matter movement, energized by the deaths of George Floyd, Breonna Taylor, and other Black people in the United States, led to reclaiming public spaces for public debate, recognition, and memorialization (see Figure 8.1). The COVID-19 pandemic also reshaped the public landscape, first by restricting the use of places because of possible risks of transmission and then by spurring citizen debate over reassigning and reconfiguring public spaces to reflect new behavior patterns. Playgrounds were reopened and public streets were recommissioned as outdoor eating plazas. Whereas these examples of claiming public space for public expression and use did not necessarily need the expertise of design professions, they illustrate the imperative of engaging with citizens.

FIGURE 8.1 The police killing of George Floyd prompted the creation of a memorial in his honor by community members. The memorial is located at the intersection of Chicago Ave and E 38th St in Minneapolis, Minnesota. Image credit: Fibonacci Blue, retrieved from Wiki Commons.

BEYOND LEGAL OBLIGATIONS

NEPA instituted the legal requirement for public comment, but designers and planners have led efforts beyond obligatory public hearings. These efforts include planners and designers advocating for less empowered or politically savvy citizens, community design centers, professional processes, and community-led design interventions. These forms of community engagement should not be viewed as a progression or evolution of community participation efforts but as different strategies that may be employed in various settings and situations. The focus of community-engagement work ranges from those with product-specific goals to a focus on improving social capacity, and from projects that are led by community members to those steered by experts (Wilson, 2018) (see Figure 8.2).

Advocacy planning

Influenced by Davidoff's (1965) advocacy and pluralism model of intervention, many design and planning professionals began to reject traditional practices. They fought against urban redevelopment and advocated for the rights of poor citizens, and new methods of citizen participation emerged. In addition, Arnstein's (1969) ladder of participation, which articulates progressive levels of citizen engagement from manipulation to citizen control, influenced and continues to inform the practice of community involvement. Federal programs of the 1960s, such as the Community Action Program and the Model Cities Program (Strange, 1972), encouraged citizen participation in improvement programs. With these programs, people outside the professions were allowed to voice opinions about planning and financing. Citizens were given the right to participate in planning and implementation processes through grants and technical assistance.

The 1960s and early 1970s were a time of increased community organizing and action. Many groups across the United States began to rally behind measures to prevent projects that would

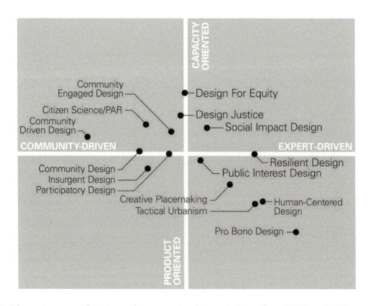

FIGURE 8.2 The various manifestations of community-driven design efforts (Wilson, 2018).

ENGAGING PEOPLE IN THE PROCESS

cause disturbance and destruction to their neighborhoods. For example, established in 1963, the Architectural Renewal Committee in Harlem fought a proposed freeway in Upper Manhattan and the Asian Neighborhood Design, established in 1973, began combating development issues faced by San Francisco's Chinatown community (Comerio, 1984). These grassroots efforts were supplemented with assistance from university efforts that mobilized students and faculty. In response to additional economic and political pressures in the 1980s, many of these community efforts evolved into project-based design assistance centers.

Community design centers

Aligned with the motivations of these earlier advocacy efforts, community design centers sought to assist communities and expand educational opportunities for university students. This model of service learning, which integrated academic objectives with community service, gained traction in the late 1980s and early 1990s. Initiated by university faculty members in design and planning programs, early community design centers sought to help communities with limited resources and those facing challenging design issues, and to train more socially conscious and responsible students. One design assistance center using this model was funded by the US Department of Education in 1988 and continues operations in the College of Architecture and Urban Studies at Virginia Tech (CDAC, n.d.). The center provides opportunities for landscape architecture, architecture, planning, and building construction students to gain experience while working in and with underserved communities. Similarly, the Hamer Center for Community Design at Penn State was established in 1996 through a private endowment and has a robust record of student and community collaborations (Hamer Center for Community Design, 2021). The Association for Community Design describes design centers as providing planning, design, and development services in low- to moderate-income communities. They expand their definition of design centers to include those operated by nonprofit and nongovernmental organizations as well as those that are university-based (ACD, n.d.).

Designer-led public planning processes

Many design educators and private practitioners integrate community participation efforts into their work outside of the design center model. As noted in Chapter 7, Halprin and Hester developed various processes for collecting data and incorporating it into the design decision process. Halprin and Burns's (1974) "Take Part" process uses the RSVP cycles discussed earlier to encourage community involvement. Hester's (1984b) "12-Step" process describes goals or milestones throughout the design process. While many practitioners do not write extensively about their participatory efforts, their efforts are no less important, and many lessons can be gleaned from examining past design award recipients. For example, the office of Moore, Iacofano, Goltsman has consistently developed and used community participation methods in their design practice. Founding partner Iacofano is a pioneer in group visual notetaking and the author of *Meeting of the Minds: A guide to successful meeting facilitation* (2001) (see Figure 8.3).

Community-based action

Public involvement in the creation of public space also includes efforts initiated and led by community members. Citizen groups and nonprofit organizations have introduced new forms of community engagement into local design and planning decisions. Community activism has led to organized and intentional efforts to reclaim public lands for the public good. Some

FIGURE 8.3 An example of group facilitation and visual note taking. Image credit: Randy Hester.

examples of community-based actions include Park(ing) Day and the Portland City Repair project. Park(ing) Day began in 2005 with the temporary conversion of a metered parking space into a mini-park by Bela, Merker, and Passmore, a group of design activists who later named themselves Rebar (Schneider, 2017). With widespread enthusiastic interest and collaboration with the Trust for Public Land, Park(ing) Day spread worldwide. The City Repair Project (n.d.) is a community-based effort to transform street intersections into public places, often through giant murals. The process of painting these intersections brings community members together through the act of co-creating and in the pride of their accomplishment. They also create gathering places, slow traffic, and make the area safer.

BENEFITS AND CHALLENGES OF COMMUNITY PARTICIPATION

The benefits of engaging residents in the design decision process are broad – from providing inspiration for design ideas, to more fully understanding a site, to building long-lasting stewards of the places being created. As noted previously, citizens can be invaluable resources in uncovering, understanding, and documenting information about a site. They are the ones with the most intimate knowledge of and often a long history with engagement with a place. They often have access to information, other users, or history that is not easily accessible to the designer. As noted in the Runyon Canyon project discussed in Chapter 7, residents may also hold valuable information about the site. There the Sierra Club members knew the canyon after years of hiking and exploring and were able to map important wildlife habitats for the design team. In addition, community members can inform designers about the cultural meaning attached to a place as well as the talents of its residents. For example, the designer might learn

180   ENGAGING PEOPLE IN THE PROCESS

that local residents have expertise they can contribute to a design-build project. In Chapter 3, some ways that designers can be more culturally competent in their work are discussed.

Community participation also ensures that the designer's decisions are relevant for the current population, their activity patterns, and their future desires. Every place and its people are different, and designers need to understand those differences. Hester (1987) describes drawing the archetypes and idiosyncrasies of a community as one of the 12 steps in his design process. The archetypes are the activity patterns that are expected, and the idiosyncrasies are those activities unique to the community. In Manteo, North Carolina, Hester found that residents regularly met at the post office to share local news and that young people in the community hung out at the docks with their friends (see Figure 8.4). Understanding these patterns contributed to a design where residents could continue long-established activities.

Lastly, a benefit of engaging residents in the design-decision process is the agency that it conveys to the participants. Engaged community members are likely to act as gatekeepers and caretakers – looking out for things out of place and either fixing things or reporting problems. During the construction phase of Runyon Canyon, a local neighbor called the designers to inform them that the park gates were the wrong color. These residents were part of the design decisions and could help monitor that their intent was honored. Citizens who are involved in design and planning processes may become long-term stewards of their community and will likely engage in other decision processes in the future. Klein (2001, p. 38)

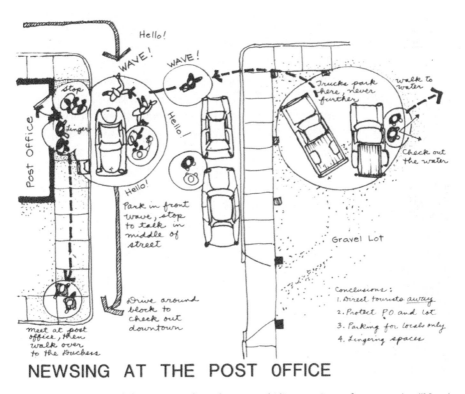

FIGURE 8.4 Diagramming daily patterns – the archetypes and idiosyncrasies – of a community. "Newsing at the post office" in Manteo, North Carolina (Hester, 1987).

goes further to suggest that projects should be evaluated on "how they catalyze participation in the development of a democratic and shared society."

The challenges of involving community members in design and planning decisions include dealing with other professionals and the public, who may not value or understand the contributions that community knowledge can make, the perceived extra time and cost of the process, and concerns that a lower-quality design will be the result. With the legal obligations to include public comment periods for publicly funded projects, more people participate in local planning than ever before. In many instances, the community engagement generated is spurred by opposition to the proposed project. Sanoff (2006) notes that powerful local interests tend to dominate over environmental or social concerns in this public discourse. He offers that "the grassroots must be empowered with the authority and responsibility for taking proactive local action, not just blocking actions" (Sanoff, 2006; Community Design Reform section, para. 4).

Designers hoping to engage locals in a design process might be faced with residents who do not trust that their opinions will be truly heard and heeded. These residents might disrupt meetings, divert discussions to the topics that concern them, or disengage from the process. Some sources, such as *Meeting of the Minds*, provide strategies for dealing with difficult participants. Distrust of the process also can be found among the professional community. Many practitioners believe that only the experts have the knowledge and skills to make these decisions, or that community members do not know what they want or need (Hester, 1983). Some designers do not want to yield their positions to those without training, they do not appreciate the expertise the residents can bring to a project, or they lack the abilities to successfully solicit that information from residents. One contributing issue to a professional mindset that downplays or rejects participatory techniques is that many designers have not received training in this area. There is a tendency to underestimate the abilities needed to successfully engage the public. Students who have been introduced to and practiced participation approaches in school were actually less confident in their ability to lead participation efforts once they entered the workforce (de la Peña, 2017). They learned enough to realize that it may not be as simple as it seems.

Community participation in design is not without issues. The community involvement in design decisions and their support for a project may be overstated. Also, community members are often hesitant to participate because their opinions have been sought but ignored previously. Designers and their paying clients often express concerns over the time and cost that adding participatory elements to the design process will bring. Although methods like surveying the community and conducting meetings have costs, they can reduce later costs by anticipating design considerations and avoiding design changes both before and after construction. Similarly, the time for developing multiple design alternatives that guess at the community's desires can be more effectively used to create focused and responsive scenarios.

Another challenge is a long-standing concern that participatory design will result in a low-quality product. While some participatory projects give residents partial control of the design or construction, the oversight of the project resides with the licensed designer. A healthy debate ensued around this point between prominent landscape architects Halprin and Hester in the early 1980s (Halprin, 1983, 1984; Hester, 1983, 1984a). Hester proposed that the process of engaging citizens would result in a design style unique to the place, while Halprin argued that the design style was the responsibility of the trained professional. This debate also informs current design award programs. In response to awards that recognize beauty, the Environmental Design Research Association and the journal *Places* joined efforts to recognize designs that combine expertise in design, research, and practice and contribute to the creation of dynamic, humane places that engage our attention and imagination. These Great Places Awards celebrate experiential relationships between people and their environment, and many include innovative and effective participatory components (EDRA, n.d.).

PARTICIPATION STRATEGIES

Many sources are available that provide excellent discussions of a variety of participatory methods for designers. One of the most recent and comprehensive, *Design as Democracy: Techniques for Collective Creativity* (de la Peña et al., 2017) shares examples from international contributors of tested participatory methods in all stages of the design process. Considering this and other sources that focus on specific techniques, this section draws attention to several key considerations for designers before and during their participatory efforts. The following sections discuss cultural norms that can influence a person's willingness to participate and how often overlooked populations should and can be engaged; the role key informants can play in understanding and making connections in a place; the importance of appropriate and accessible communication strategies; considerations in the logistics for participation from the citizen viewpoint; and nurturing agency, ownership, and power in the participants.

Cultural norms and participation methods

Much of what has been written about participation strategies has been based on work with predominantly white, middle- and upper-class residents and has been conducted by white, male designers. The processes and procedures that work in these environments do not necessarily translate well to other populations. More research is needed in this area, but there are indications that we are just beginning to recognize and respond to how diverse cultures might be better integrated into design decision-making processes (Hou & Rios, 2003). While working with a group of Hmong residents in Sacramento, a student designer had been having very active engagement from the residents in discussing the design of their community garden. Once all the next steps were identified and volunteers were sought, no one stepped forward. The designer learned through the translator that in the Hmong culture it is not appropriate to name yourself. Instead, the designer could ask someone to take on a task or could ask the residents to name one of their neighbors. A more thorough understanding of cultural norms and how they might influence participation is warranted in general and for project-specific and community-specific situations.

In addition to populations with distinct cultural identities, some people, such as those from disadvantaged or vulnerable populations, may not feel comfortable engaging in a public process or may be intentionally or unintentionally excluded from outreach efforts. People such as undocumented residents, recent immigrants, unhoused, non-English-speaking or

ESL populations, and the overemployed are often missing from mandated public hearings and designer-led workshops. These populations often depend on and use public spaces (Koo, Hustedde, & Young, 2018). Therefore, designers need to direct attention to providing information in appropriate languages and seeking the input of these populations when designing spaces that they will use or could be important in their lives.

Key informants

Key informants in a community can help a designer navigate complex relationships among other users, serve as a validating reference for the designer, and direct the design team to important information (McKenna & Main, 2013). This person may be a public official or community organizer who has been working closely with a group and earned their trust, or it can be someone who is integral to the community and is a champion for the project or cause. Designers can identify this person during the initial client and community interactions by asking for introductions to trusted members of the community. Caution should be taken to not alienate certain people because of this alliance. For example, in one community the designer learned that a local bank official supported the project and offered meeting space. The key informant let the design team know that holding a meeting in that space would ensure that members of the local labor union would not attend. Because of this knowledge, the design team held their meetings at the local high school instead.

The key informant need not be the most politically connected or powerful. In another location, the key informant was the elementary school's custodian, a woman who was known and trusted throughout the small rural community. In many small communities, the school's janitorial crew has a central role – they know the students and often the students' families, and they know the school staff. They are in touch with these community members on a daily basis. The efforts in this community were a multiyear process and began with a period of listening to the residents and identifying the issues they wanted to see addressed. Meetings were held at the school, and this custodian was always there to set up the cafeteria for the meetings. The design team spent time with her before and after meetings, learned about her concerns and ideas, and listened to her advice about individuals, meeting structure, and what could be done to get more attendees. (She suggested that instead of avoiding the dinner hour that the meeting include a potluck meal and provide childcare. This allowed participants to feed their children and still get them home in time for bed.) She became a trusted partner in the process, and once others saw this relationship, they began to feel comfortable with the design team. Such a relationship should grow out of a willingness to truly listen to someone who knows more about the community.

Communication

Communication involves how material is conveyed to individuals, including the specific languages and the outlets for sharing information (see Figure 8.5). Language issues are some of the obvious hurdles to overcome, however, some translation methods can be successful. Two venues for translation are most important for designers and planners: literature (hard copies or online) and meetings. Having someone translate meeting announcements into appropriate languages is one step in reaching all populations. Where and how these materials are disseminated can be even more important.

FIGURE 8.5 The Public Sediment Project: Alameda Creek Atlas includes participatory tools for community members which are available in multiple languages and on social media networks (SCAPE, 2019). Image credits: N. Claire Napawan, Brett Snyder, and Beth Ferguson.

One effective means of reaching diverse audiences is to identify local groups with participation from or engagement with different population groups. A local church, a women's group, a school organization, or any other number of existing institutions may be appropriate and helpful in reaching specific populations. These groups may serve as a conduit for sharing information or they can be engaged partners in design-decision making.

In addition to understanding which groups may help the designer connect with the community, it is important to understand where community members go to get their information. A local Facebook page may be an effective means to reaching citizens in one community, but it would not be successful in reaching residents who do not have a computer or Internet-enabled device. Looking for unique means of communication – such as church bulletins, information tables at local markets, or other low-tech information sources – is necessary. The key informant can help the designer understand the best means for reaching various resident groups. In addition, multi-language presentations or interpretation during meetings are critical for ensuring participation of non-English-speaking residents. Using the services of local interpreters, including known residents, can be particularly effective at helping the participants feel comfortable in sharing their ideas.

Comfort and convenience

Once the various populations in a community have been contacted, the designer should consider how to continue the engagement with them. The timing and location of meetings and the way information is shared should be thoughtfully planned. The comfort and convenience of the community participants should be prioritized.

The location of any meetings or information sharing should be convenient and should be on neutral territory (see Figure 8.6). The place should be somewhere they feel comfortable and not threatening. For example, undocumented residents might feel more comfortable attending a meeting in a church basement than at city hall. A standard practice at community meetings is a sign-in sheet. Although the purpose of this information gathering is typically to keep a

FIGURE 8.6 A design review for a senior housing project conducted at the site enabled residents to participate. Image credit: Yiwei Huang.

record of attendees for evidence that the community has been represented and to provide follow-up information, some may not want to share this information, and this practice might discourage them from staying. Alternatives to having a sign-in sheet at the entry door are (1) to begin the meeting with an explanation of why the information is being collected and how it will be used or (2) to wait until the end of the meeting and ask for anyone wanting to learn about future meetings or decisions to leave their information. In this latter approach, the total meeting attendance can be documented through a simple head count.

The timing of meetings should fit into the daily patterns of those whom the designer hopes will attend. Designers could ask to be included on the agenda for an organization's monthly meeting or to participate in a recurring community event. The weekly and monthly patterns of the community should be considered when selecting a meeting date. For example, in some locations, a Wednesday night meeting would have no one there because a large segment of the population is at choir practice. As noted earlier, an after-work meeting with childcare would allow young working parents to attend. Weekend days and alternative meeting times that are more convenient for residents should be considered.

Passing along the power

Another consideration for designers is the opportunity and obligation to move beyond sharing design alternatives or collecting ideas from residents to using the power of design to build agency among citizens (Kelkar & Spinelli, 2016; Wagner & Fernandez-Gimenez, 2009). Active engagement in a design process provides participants with knowledge that is important for making immediate decisions and has long-term implications (potentially beyond those identified with the initial project). Hester (1984b) defined this step in his design process as transferring responsibility. He explains that the designer will be leaving the project behind while the community members will be living with it. Therefore, the residents need to understand and embrace their responsibility in seeing that the project goals are honored and the project continues to fulfill the promises to the community.

Beyond this transference of project understanding and responsibilities is the opportunity to build long-lasting agency among the participants. Being engaged in a design-decision process teaches participants about how decisions are made, how to voice their opinions and ideas, how to listen to others, and other necessary skills for being an engaged citizen. This newfound agency is powerful for citizens who might not have had any previous opportunities to voice their opinions or influence decisions.

CONCLUSION

Community participation in design is an important element of creating a place that is more responsive and appropriate to a locality and its populations. The methods for how this engagement occur can and should vary with the purpose and the specific populations to be reached. For example, engaging with youth or senior populations may be very different than attempting to engage middle-aged working adults. Youth participation in particular has garnered extensive study, and numerous resources are available (i.e., Driskell, 2002; Hart, 1997; Loebach, Cox, & Little, 2020).

Designers should situate their engagement strategies in the current community context. Understanding the recent and projected changes to the population can inform the practices used to reach various populations as well as possible shifts in activity and land use patterns. Demographic changes across communities in the United States in the past few decades have influenced design considerations, such as increases in housing for older residents and alternative transportation modes. In addition, the migration of populations within the United States and increases in immigration can significantly change the composition of a community and, with that, the desired uses and preferences.

A final consideration is the changing capabilities and acceptance of digital and virtual tools. Although the capability to hold virtual meetings has been around for a while, few design practices have used these venues for gathering public input. The emergency shift to online work environments during the COVID-19 pandemic increased the availability of online platforms and the comfort of many in using these tools. Other online tools, such as shared mapping sites, provide a means of conducting participatory mapping with many people. Others combine traditional survey questions with an individual mapping of routes or places and the ability to embed photographs or videos on the map (i.e., ArcGIS Survey123; Maptionnaire).

POTENTIAL EXERCISES AND PROJECT

Indoor exercises

Role-playing in a community workshop. Designers typically experience many different personalities when conducting community meetings and workshops. Participants join in meetings because they care about what happens to a place. They bring with them these concerns and also expectations as to whether they will be heard. In addition, individual personalities can shape how a person engages with others. For this exercise, students are asked to role-play different participants in a community meeting. Each student, other than the facilitator and note-taker, will be assigned a role and a personality type (i.e., a young mother who is also a skeptic).

A design scenario should be presented to the class such as "the city is considering re-designing the neighborhood park." Participants are free to develop the specific parameters of this design effort as the discussion progresses. The class should be divided into groups of six to eight students. Roles should be randomly assigned by the instructor. Each group should have a facilitator and a note-taker. The facilitator and note-taker should take a few minutes to formulate questions for the participants to discuss. Each discussion group should meet for approximately 20 minutes and follow the lead of the facilitator. Participants should "play" the role they have been assigned.

After the group has participated in this mock workshop, they should discuss their individual and collective experiences. Consider questions such as:

- Did you feel like you had ample opportunity to express your opinion? Did you think your ideas were understood?
- Did the concerns of others change your opinions about the park design?
- Were there participants who were disruptive to the meeting? Are there things that a facilitator could do to lessen or stop these disruptions?
- Were there participants who did not contribute or who contributed very little?
- How would you handle disruptive participants? How might you entice quieter participants to share their ideas?

Some personality types:

    Observer – listens, but does not say anything
    Skeptic – does not believe anything will be done
    Know-it-all – thinks they have all the answers
    Off-topic – strays from the question asked
    Distracted – not fully engaged; checking phone
    Talker – has to interject even when it's not their turn

Some possible roles:

    Young mother of two
    Older neighbor with difficulty walking
    Teenager who likes to hang out at park with friends

Father of teenagers
Stay-at-home father of infant
Maintenance worker (currently cares for park)

Evaluating participatory techniques. Each design project will warrant and each designer will develop different techniques for engaging participants in their design or planning process. Many techniques have long-established applications; however, new techniques or adaptations of existing approaches are important for designers to consider when developing their participatory approach. Many sources provide detailed information on various participatory methods including the appropriate applications, strengths and weaknesses, or how they might be adapted to different situations. For this exercise, the class should select one or more publications featuring community engagement methods (e.g., *Design as Democracy: Techniques for Collective Creativity*) to review.

Once the publications are identified, students should work in teams of two and select one of the engagement methods. Students should prepare an in-class enactment of this method. Much like the role-playing exercise above, students can take liberties with setting the design parameters. Students should be given adequate time to prepare their demonstration, perhaps assigning the engagement techniques during one class and demonstrating them in the next.

After each presentation, students should discuss the technique and identify qualities such as:

- When would this method be appropriate
- How much time is needed to prepare this method
- How much would this cost
- What types of information is gained
- What types of information is not gained
- Who might be excluded
- What adaptations could be made

9
CASE STUDIES IN PEOPLE PLACES

INTRODUCTION

To illustrate the people-place concepts presented thus far, this chapter presents *case studies* of four design projects. These projects were identified through a review of design awards, recommendations of experts in the field, or direct experiences with the place. Each project embraces human-centered design theories and goals as well as public engagement strategies. They elucidate and further explain the theories, methods, and design practices introduced elsewhere in this book.

The four case studies represent a range of sizes, geographic locations, concepts, and design methods (Table 9.1). These projects feature places that have been designed for relaxation and restoration, community gatherings, equity and inclusion, and learning and play. The Master Plan of the Correctional Institution for Women in Iowa illustrates the concept of relaxation and restoration, showing how a place can provide an environment where incarcerated individuals will feel relaxed after spending time there. The Davis Central Park illustrates how a proactively programmed and designed space can serve as a place for the community to come together for daily tasks, celebrations, and protest throughout the past 40 years. The Vancouver Board of Parks and Recreation's Parks and Recreation Services Master Plan aims to plan an urban open space system that leads to an equitable and inclusive future for residents and visitors alike at a city scale. Lastly, the Tulatoli Primary School Outdoor Environment in Bangladesh exemplifies how learning in an outdoor space better promotes children's academic attainment, and how a school ground can become a community space that serves and attracts everyone.

A PLACE FOR RELAXATION AND RESTORATION

Case study: The Landscape Master Plan for the Iowa Correctional Institution for Women
Project location and region: Mitchellville, Iowa, United States
Project size: 30 acres
Client: Iowa Correctional Institution for Women (ICIW)
Design team: Julie Stevens, Associate Professor, Iowa State University (ISU) and ISU landscape architecture students (juniors, seniors, and graduate students)
Other key participants: Iowa Department of Corrections (IDOC), Iowa State University College of Design
Awards: 2015 American Society of Landscape Architecture (ASLA) Student Award
Time period: Research, design, and implementation from 2011 to 2017

DOI: 10.4324/9781315100036-13

TABLE 9.1 Overview of this chapter's case studies

Project title	Size	Geographic location	Key concepts involved	Design methods
A place for relaxation and restoration: **Master Plan for the Iowa Correctional Institution for Women**	30 acres (0.12 km^2)	Mitchellville, Iowa, United States	Restorative and therapeutic places (Chapter 2), people–place relationships (Chapter 6), and gender and place (Chapter 6)	Focus groups, participatory design and construction, and project evaluation
A place for gathering: **Davis Central Park**	5.8 acres (0.023 km^2)	Davis, California, United States	Cultural competency (Chapter 3), behavior mapping (Chapter 7), and engaging people in the design process (Chapter 8)	Community engagement, behavior observation, and behavior mapping
A place for inclusivity and equity: **VanPlay: Vancouver Parks & Recreation Services Master Plan**	A network of 3,212 acres of parkland (12.99 km^2)	Vancouver, British Columbia, Canada	Inclusion and access (Chapter 5), visualizing and community-engagement methods (Chapter 7), and future design influences (Chapter 10)	Benchmarking, geospatial analysis, and community, staff and stakeholder engagement
A place for learning and playing: **Tulatoli Primary School Outdoor Environment Design**	0.29 acres (1,180 m^2)	Suburban Narsingdi, Bangladesh	People and age (Chapter 4), restorative and therapeutic places (Chapter 2), and behavior mapping and post-occupancy evaluation (Chapter 7)	Interviews, questionnaires, and community-led drawing and modeling

Project abstract and context

The Iowa Correctional Institution for Women (ICIW) is a medium/minimum security prison located in rural Mitchellville, Iowa, 25 miles east of Des Moines (Iowa Department of Corrections, 2020). The institution expanded significantly, from housing 56 offenders in 1983 to 650 in 2010, thus requiring both building and landscape renovation. The State of Iowa is committed to gender-responsive practice, a growing movement to reconsider the way women are treated in prison (Shapiro, 2018). During the renovation process, the institution envisioned a new type of correctional facility, one unlike a stereotypical dark, damp, and dreary "hell-hole" prison, but instead a place that would allow women to feel safe, to reflect, and to learn (Cassidy, 2018; Shapiro, 2018). As of 2019, ICIW had become a new and revolutionary model for rehabilitating incarcerated female individuals (Cassidy, 2018).

The Landscape Master Plan for ICIW was a collaborative effort between the Department of Landscape Architecture at ISU and the correctional institution, to design and build a relaxing yet rehabilitating landscape for incarcerated individuals. In 2010, the Iowa Department of Corrections (IDOC) approached the Department of Landscape Architecture at ISU requesting assistance in preparing a simple planting plan that would be calming and relaxing for incarcerated individuals. Seeing beyond a planting design, students in Professor Julie Stevens' class instead proposed a full 30-acre campus master plan that addressed the needs of the prison's population and programmatically functioned better (Hamerlinck et al., 2015) (see Figure 9.1). Thus, a longer-term collaboration between ICIW and ISU began.

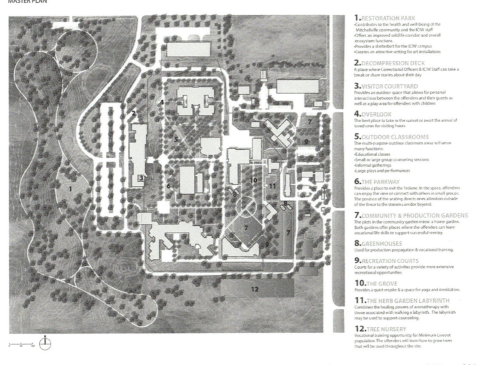

FIGURE 9.1 The Iowa Correctional Institution for Women (ICIW) master plan (Stevens, Toews, and Wagenfeld, 2018). Image credit: Hunter and Fangman.

Design process

The project was integrated into several seminars and design studio courses at ISU and included junior, senior, and graduate-level students. In spring 2011, students began exploring the issue of gardens and landscaping in prisons in a landscape architecture seminar. Students completed the master plan in a design studio in 2012. Over six years, Stevens and her students continued to work on refining site-level designs, engage with ICIW, and develop construction documents in design studios of five to 25 students and through internship programs. In 2013 and 2015, students aided on-site construction and engaged with additional projects on the site.

The design team aimed to create a calming, humane, and therapeutic environment that would support the well-being of the prison population as well as improve environmental conditions of the site. They began their efforts by researching existing literature on how landscapes can support the mental well-being of its user population. The design team started with the premise that imprisoned individuals could also experience the personal and social benefits of preferred landscape typologies which have been shown to be effective in general populations (Stevens, Toews, & Wagenfeld, 2018). Obtaining preferred landscapes (or experiencing a lack of them) is part of a complex set of factors that affects the personal and social health of humans (Stevens et al., 2018). Believing that human needs and preferences can and should be applied to a prison landscape, the master plan aimed to create a variety of spaces where incarcerated women can sit, walk, chat, explore, sense, and reflect.

To understand the target audiences' needs, the ISU design team engaged the incarcerated individuals and ICIW staff through a survey, focus group meetings, and post-occupancy evaluations (POE). Project leaders initially engaged the participants in a focus group to determine what they would like to see in the future landscape (Stevens et al., 2018). As the project progressed, those who were involved became part of the design team, became more comfortable in sharing their ideas, and helped make design decisions. During design presentations, landscape architecture faculty and student designers engaged with incarcerated individuals, prison staff, and police through focus groups and dialogues (Stevens et al., 2018). After constructing the outdoor classroom, a survey was sent to the previous participants to ask how they use and perceive the space. The design team received 149 survey results (Stucki, 2018); the outcomes of which are discussed below.

Outcomes

Through the ICIW and ISU Department of Landscape Architecture collaboration, a series of outdoor spaces were planned and designed on the ICIW campus, including a production garden, multipurpose outdoor classroom, mother/child garden, healing garden, and production garden (see Figure 9.2).

The multipurpose outdoor classroom (shown as #5 in Figure 9.1) contains five different spaces: three classrooms, a lawn mound, and an aspen grove (see Figure 9.2). The designers intentionally blended opportunities for incarcerated individuals to get out and engage with natural elements. Actions such as changing grass to turf allow prisoners the opportunity to sit on a natural material. The aspen grove provides privacy and a place to be alone, a rare experience in prison. Women can use limestone cube seating for activities such as reading, journaling,

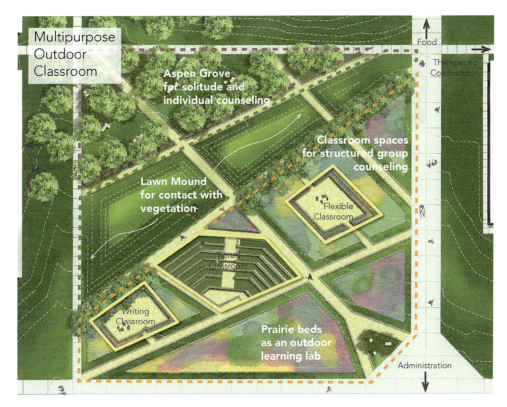

FIGURE 9.2 Multipurpose outdoor classroom design plan (Hamerlinck et al., 2015). Image credit: Julie Stevens.

and participating in counseling (Hamerlinck et al., 2015). All design considerations were well-received by those incarcerated and have cultivated a more calming and engaging environment.

The post-occupancy survey revealed that incarcerated women used the newly created spaces for reading, relaxing, hanging out with others, and personal reflection (Stucki, 2018). In follow-up interviews and focus groups, those surveyed suggested that the women were happier, calmer, and more peaceful after spending time in the new landscape (Toews, Wagenfeld, & Stevens, 2018).

Human factor elements

This project provides important information regarding several people-environment factors for designers to consider. The application of principles related to the creation of therapeutic landscapes; the use of an user-engaged design process, including observations and interviews; and a service-learning model for engaging students are briefly discussed. Each advances understanding of how these considerations can be applied to place understanding and creation.

Theoretical background on therapeutic landscapes As introduced in Chapter 2, "Health and Well-being" section, restorative place characteristics include: separation from others, comfort, a feeling of awe, opportunities for reflection, and opportunities for prospect refuges. In the ICIW project, designers prioritized using landforms and vegetation to create opportunities for privacy while ensuring users' safety. Access to gardens, horticultural features, and direct views to nature and the outdoors can positively affect people's mental health (Evans et al., 2003). Moreover, in the case of the ICIW, interaction with family members is a therapeutic process for incarcerated women. The design team therefore created a children's garden that would be fun for visiting children and provide a place that offers support and comfort for family members while they engage in tough conversations (Toews, Wagenfeld, Stevens, & Shoemaker, 2020).

Listening and learning process: Learning through observing In Chapter 7, *Visualizing people and behavior*, methods for observing, documenting, and analyzing behaviors to help designers understand site conditions and use patterns are presented. While constructing the outdoor classroom, ISU students observed the ICIW staff congregating in the parking lot during shift changes. This behavior suggested to students that a gathering place for staff was needed and would address the tremendous job stress of correctional officers and administrators. The idea of the "decompression deck" emerged as a space where staff could get away or decompress at the end of their shift (Stevens et al., 2018).

Listening and learning process: Listening through interviewing The ISU design team altered and refined the ICIW design based on interview responses received from different stakeholders. For example, focus group findings revealed that ICIW officials wanted to leave the prison grounds during their breaks and be out of sight of incarcerated individuals; however, officers and staff who work inside the secured perimeter rarely have time to leave, while staff who work outside the secured perimeter can and do go outside. The new staff decompression deck location is close enough to the entrance to easily return to work and within the line of sight of incarcerated people, but far enough away to provide a sense of privacy (Stevens et al., 2018).

Service learning and community engagement In Chapter 8, *Engaging people in the process*, we discuss the benefits of university service-learning opportunities and community participation in the design process. A community-centered design approach is essential for landscape architects to employ when reimagining community spaces, as it allows the designer to actively address the needs of the most vulnerable populations as well as of the entire community (Marcus & Sachs, 2013 cited in Stevens et al., 2018) (see Figure 9.3). Stevens reaffirmed that undertaking the ICIW landscape master plan as a student service-learning project opened the door for students to adapt their design skills, engage with a population with which they would not typically interact, and develop proposals that would likely help them obtain future employment opportunities (Stevens, Wagenfeld, Toews, & Wachtendorf, 2016).

Reflections and discussion

The ICIW design project is an excellent example of actively applying environmental psychology theory, listening to and incorporating input from community members, empowering vulnerable groups by engaging them in the design process, and refining a design based on a community's special needs. This project illustrates the belief that everyone is worthy and in need of access to nature and the outdoors. This experience increased student designers' awareness of the ways in which addressing environmental and social justice in their designs

FIGURE 9.3 Community effort during the building process (Hamerlinck et al., 2015). Image credit: Julie Stevens.

can address social problems and increase their knowledge and investment in community issues while also seeking solutions to identified issues (Stevens et al., 2018). For the instructor, the project re-centered the importance of forming relationships with individuals and communities affiliated with a design project (here, incarcerated individuals, prison staff, and administrators). These relationships contributed to the project progressing smoothly. In addition, spending time with a project's users is essential to understanding and incorporating their needs and concerns into design recommendations. Stevens also pointed out the political aspect of working on a prison landscape and with incarcerated people. The ISU design team encountered pushback from people who did not want their tax money spent on prisons and from prison officers who were not convinced of the need to build a better landscape for incarcerated people (Stucki, 2018). Stevens stated in an email as a self-reflection that "the pushback we received in the beginning was probably, in part, due to the naivety of our message. We learned to communicate differently with the media by underscoring the importance of every human life and the evidence-based research upon which we based the designs. We have gained a lot more support over the years through outreach, public presentations and communication."

A PLACE FOR GATHERING

Case study: Davis Central Park
Project location and region: Davis, California
Project size: 5.8 acres

Client: City of Davis

Design team: CoDesign (subsequently MIG): Mark Francis, Professor, University of California, Davis and landscape architect and principal; James Zanetto, architect and principal; Skip Mezger, landscape architect and principal, and Cheryl Sullivan, landscape architect

Other key participants: Save Open Space (SOS)[1]

Awards:

1999 Centennial Medallion, American Society of Landscape Architects (ASLA)

1999 Ahwahnee Merit Award for one of the Best Projects Built in the Past Ten Years, Local Government Commission, American Institute of Architects, and American Planning Association

Time period: Research from 1983 to 1987; design and construction from 1987 to 1994

Publications featuring project:

Hester, R.T. 2006. *Design for Ecological Democracy.* Cambridge, MA: MIT Press.

Project abstract and context

Davis Central Park is located along the main vehicular thoroughfare, Russell Boulevard, adjacent to the commercial core of the city of Davis, a college town 20 miles west of Sacramento, CA. The project site was at one time two distinct properties bisected by Fourth Street. In 1937, the city created Davis City Park in this location through a federal Work Progress Administration investment ("Central Park," n.d.; "Davis Central Park," n.d.). After the Regents of the University of California declared the former University Farm as the University of California, Davis (UC Davis) in 1959, the city of Davis became a growing university town (Scheuring, 2001). The population growth along with the political upheaval of the 1960s saw the park site used for festival gatherings, particularly among youth counterculture communities. Local activists also had attempted for several years to establish a community farmers' market at the park.

Proposals to develop the southern portion of the site for commercial interests emerged in 1984 but were opposed by the community group Save Open Space (SOS) and most voters (Francis, 1999). City leadership then sought proposals to extend and develop the park. A local design office, CoDesign, secured the contract. Project co-lead Francis had identified the potential of this site as a central gathering space for the growing Davis community, and saw an opportunity to integrate tradition and innovation to serve a mixed-life urban park in a burgeoning environmentally sustainable and socially responsible city (Francis, 2010; "Central Park and Davis Farmer's Market," n.d).

Design process

Prior to securing the contract to design the park, Francis led UC Davis students in surveying the community to understand the potential desired uses for the re-designed park. They found a strong interest in increasing its size. These survey results formed the basis for opposing commercial development proposals for a portion of the site and contributed to getting on the ballot a city referendum asking voters to approve the expansion of Central Park. This referendum passed in 1984 (Francis, 1999; Francis, n.d.).

In 1987, the City of Davis hired CoDesign to develop a park master plan. The design team proposed a community participatory approach. A diverse design program was proposed,

FIGURE 9.4 Davis Central Park community workshop ("Central Park and Davis Farmer's Market," n.d.). Image credit: Mark Francis.

including a permanently covered pavilion and a market plaza for the farmers' market, a large public garden, a teen center, two children's play areas, a central lawn area, and an interactive children's fountain (Francis, 1999; Francis & Griffith, 2011).

During the process, the design team believed that a wide range of community engagement processes were essential to better understand the existing site, its "sacred places," and the needs and hopes of developing a larger park for Davis residents. The designers led numerous walking tours and workshops, observed how the park was used, built models and simulations, and conducted community surveys to better integrate the ideas of Davis residents into designs. One of the most useful methods he employed was a design workshop in the park near the existing farmers' market on a busy Saturday (see Figure 9.4), because it allowed the wider community already attending the market to participate (Project for Public Spaces, 2008).

Project result and impact

The Davis City Council approved the Central Park Master Plan in 1988. Fourth Street, which separated the existing park from the new park expansion, was replaced with a broad sloping lawn which reinforced the park's original sycamore grove (Project for Public Spaces, 2008) (see Figure 9.5). The farmers' market also relocated to its new home, an open-air pavilion in the southeastern part of the park. A "heritage" oak tree on the northern end of the pavilion was surrounded with a deck, while just beyond it lies a picnic area which includes an artist-designed water basin with several pipes and spigots so that people can get a drink, rinse their hands and feet, or wash off produce. At the southwest corner of the park exists a former youth center (currently home to the Bicycle Hall of Fame) and a public garden planted by community members. Between the youth center and the market space is a large ground level fountain, which local children call a "beach." On hot days, children and parents bring towels and picnics and spend the day playing in the geysers that spring up from the ground. One playground is adjacent to the pavilion, and another is at the northeast edge of the site. Along with more traditional climbing structures and swings, this area includes a manual pedal-powered carousel. The carousel (built with in-kind donations) is physically powered by volunteers and is popular with young children. Community groups sign up to operate the carousel and collect donations (typically one dollar) from riders to support their organizations.

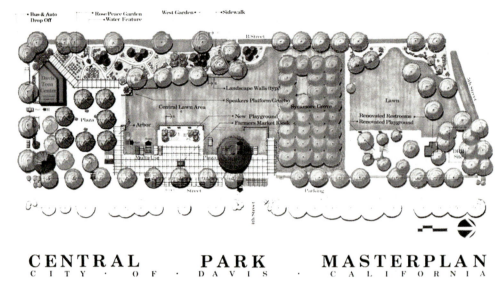

FIGURE 9.5 Central Park Master Plan (Francis & Griffith, 2011). Image credit: CoDesign Inc.

Farmers, local bakeries, and other food producers participate in farmers' markets twice each week on Wednesdays and Saturdays. The farmers' market is popular, attracting an estimated 4,000 and 7,000 residents respectively weekly ("Davis Farmers' Market," 2021). The Saturday morning market also attracts large regional crowds. The Wednesday market is held in the late afternoon during winter months (November–March) and early evening during the rest of the year. The early evening market is called "Picnic in the Park," and includes food trucks and live music performances which attract local families and university students alike (see Figure 9.6).

People of all ages frequent the park. The addition of the fountains and carousel led the local newspaper to call the park a "children's paradise" (Enterprise staff, 2006). In an annual reader's poll of the local newspaper, the park and the market are frequently named as "the best place for a picnic," "the best place to meet up with friends," and "the best place to take an out-of-towner."

FIGURE 9.6 Central Park in 2005 (Francis, 2010) and 2018. Image credits: Mark Francis (left), Yiwei Huang (right).

Human factor elements

Three findings related to person-environment relations and their application to design decisions are evident in this case study. The Davis Central Park project provides an excellent example of how designers can and should engage in proactive practice, how public spaces can be designed for diverse groups of people, and illustrates various research and participatory methods. These lessons can be adapted to any number of design efforts and are not limited to park designs.

Proactive practice One of the factors that makes this project different from others is its proactive practice approach, particularly in terms of the implementation of community engagement strategies. Francis proactively sought the visions of the community while working with students through a class, then promoted those visions to local citizens and officials. This approach surveyed and prioritized community desires, then used that understanding to advocate for change rather than responding to predetermined, mandated requirements (Francis, 1999). Francis and his students lead efforts to understand and inform the park planning goals for the community rather than responding to a typical call for proposals.

Activating public spaces for all The success of Davis Central Park can be attributed to some of the principles that have been mentioned in previous chapters in the book. Davis Central Park is designed as an inclusive, accessible, and welcoming place (Chapter 5). The location of the park makes it convenient for all residents and students; its design features provide access for varied abilities; and the activity programming appeals to a wide range of cultural and personal preferences as well as ages (Chapters 3, 4, and 6). The Park is also a dynamic and active place wherein a wide range of programs, events, and activities meet the needs and interests of the community.

Other features at the park contribute to its accessibility and inclusiveness. The Park and its farmers' market operate year-round, with a schedule of seasonal celebrations that cater to different cultural groups as well as weekly activities (see Figure 9.7). In response to community desires, the Park has provided Wi-Fi access since 2006 ("Central Park," n.d.). As a gathering space, it allows for a mixed-life center in which diverse user groups can share the place with less conflict (Francis, 2010).

FIGURE 9.7 A special powwow performance on Central Park's main lawn (left) and the weekly inclusion of bounce houses (right). Image credit: Yiwei Huang.

Research and participatory methods Methods to engage with local community members included surveys, behavior observations, and walking tours during the first phase. Later, behavior observations and community workshops were integral to the design development process (Chapters 7 and 8). As noted previously, community surveys were an effective tool in identifying community desires and to generate interest and support for the development of a park. The walking tours allowed the designer to experience the site through the residents' eyes. Lastly, the workshops provided an opportunity for community members to think creatively about what the park may look like in the future and how it might function.

Reflections and discussion

Davis Central Park provides excellent guidance on design considerations for creating a gathering place. A gathering place needs to reflect the interests and desires of the local community. The initial community survey laid the foundation for shifting the future of the site from a commercial development to the expansion of an existing park. This proactive approach prioritizes the needs of the residents over the ambitions or goals of public officials or developers and can serve as a model for other designers. Instead of waiting for a call for qualifications or proposals, designers can serve as advocates for the local community.

This project also highlights the need to bring activities that will attract users to a space. The design team identified program elements that would activate the space and contribute to creating a community gathering place. Moving the small weekly gathering of local farmers to sell their goods from an existing street to the park was a key element to attract the community. Providing a permanent structure that accommodated more vendors led to the further expansion of the market. This, in turn, prompted other activities adjacent to the market activity, such as listening to music, relaxing, being with others, and children playing.

As discussed in Chapter 8, there are numerous benefits of engaging residents in the design-decision process, from providing inspirations for design ideas, to more fully understanding a site, to building longlasting stewards of the places we create. Davis Central Park is an excellent example of a project developed with community-engaged practices, one that highlights important characteristics of a successful gathering place. In comparison to the other case studies in this chapter, Davis Central Park is a mature landscape design and includes ongoing updates to reflect changes in local needs. For example, the playgrounds have been re-designed, seating areas updated, WiFi access added, and the youth center converted to the Bicycle Hall of Fame. More than three decades after its initial design and construction, the Davis community continues to cherish and utilize Davis Central Park as part of their everyday lives.

A PLACE FOR INCLUSIVITY AND EQUITY

Case study: VanPlay, Vancouver's Parks and Recreation Services Master Plan
Project location and region: Vancouver, British Columbia, Canada
Project size: A network of 1,300 hectares (3,212 acres) of parkland, 28 kilometers (17 miles) of seawall and 175 neighborhood facilities

Consultant team: Design Workshop, Modus Planning, Design & Engagement, Lees + Associates, HCMA Architecture + Design, Urban Design 4 Health, Rand Corporation, ETM Associates, University of Victoria, Applied Ecological Services, Urban Food Strategies

Client and key participants for engagement: Vancouver Board of Parks and Recreation (Park Board)

Awards: 2018 ASLA Professional Award (Honor Award, Communication Category), 2020 ASLA Colorado Chapter Award (Honor Award, Equity, Inclusion & Diversity Category)

Time period: Planning and design from May 2017 to October 2019

Project abstract and context

In 2016, the City of Vancouver's Board of Parks and Recreation (Park Board) started to develop Vancouver's new master plan including a 100-year vision, 25-year outlook, and 10-year implementation strategy for the city. VanPlay serves as a guide for developing and redeveloping parks and recreational facilities used by more than 630,000 residents of and countless visitors to Vancouver. The consultant team led by Design Workshop used extensive community engagement strategies and both traditional and innovative methods throughout the process. They focused on delivering an equitable park and recreational system, improving everyone's park experience, and integrating nature, recreation, and culture into everyday life (Vancouver Board of Parks and Recreation, 2020). The purpose of this master plan is to ensure that all Vancouver citizens, regardless of their ethnicity, gender, religion, race, financial status, sexual orientation, age, or ability levels, benefit from access to high quality, connected parks and recreation opportunities (Vancouver Board of Parks and Recreation, 2020).

Methodology and process

Officially launched in 2017 and completed in 2019, VanPlay had five phases of engagement and content development: (1) satisfaction, big ideas, and priority setting; (2) challenges and opportunities; (3) goals for the futures and roles and responsibilities; (4) testing the goals; and (5) level of service, big moves, and operationalization of the big ideas (Vancouver Board of Parks and Recreation, 2018) (see Table 9.2).

TABLE 9.2 VanPlay's five phases of engagement and content development (adapted from Vancouver Board of Parks and Recreation, 2018).

Phase 1	Process: ongoing data collection, analysis, precedent research, technical work, and mapping Development: papers on themes they envisioned shaping the master plan conversations and a video to generate interest in participating in the effort
Phase 2	A series of five community presentations that attracted more than 600 participants
Phase 3	Brought together stakeholders and city partners in small workshops and explored the city with three elementary school groups
Phase 4	Drafted goal statements that were shared and revised with the community through online surveys
Phase 5	Developing success metrics with the community through workshops and a survey

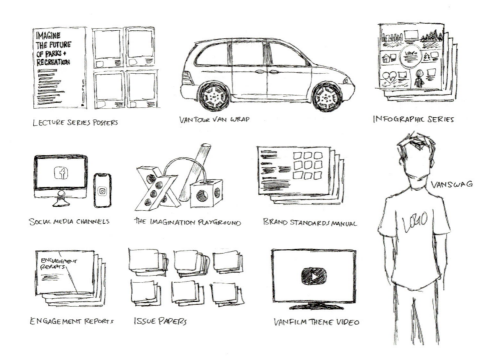

FIGURE 9.8 Novel forms of community engagement. Image credit: Copyright © 2018 by Design Workshop, Inc. for Vancouver Board of Parks and Recreation.

The engagement effort of VanPlay started in June 2017. By December 2017, the VanPlay process had initiated 30,000 community conversations. The Park Board and the consultant team shared the process and gathered feedback through the project website, VanPlay videos, issue papers, the VanPlay Tour (a tour of 15 events throughout the city with a pop-up Imagination Playground), the VanPlay Smart City Talk series (a collaboration with Urbanarium, University of British Columbia School of Architecture and Landscape Architecture), the VanPlay Community Dialogue series, various social media outlets (e.g., YouTube, Facebook, Twitter), Community Center Association meetings, stakeholder meetings, and the VanPlay external advisory group (Design Workshop, 2018) (see Figure 9.8).

On July 23, 2018, the Park Board Commissioners unanimously approved Reports 1 and 2 and on October 9, 2019, approved Reports 3 and 4. Highlights of the four reports follow.

Outcomes

The strategies the Park Board and the consultant team used during the development of VanPlay have sweeping positive implications for Park Board's daily operations, as well as for the future of park and facility planning and allocations writ large (City of Vancouver, 2020). The project's online engagement tools and videos were accessed more than 10,000 times; 50% of responses were from youth under the age of 18 (Design Workshop, 2018). The approaches used during the development of this master plan marked a paradigm shift in how community engagement could be conducted today, demonstrating how embodying the client's values and goals and empowering the community to share their dreams for the future can be achieved at the same time.

VanPlay identifies ten aspirational goals and three "strategic bold moves" – equity, asset needs, and connectivity – each of which have accompanying policies and tools for use by decision-makers (Howard & Culbertson, 2020). In total, five reports have been successfully released: Report 1: Inventory and Analysis; Report 2: 10 Goals to Shape the Next 25 Years; Report 3: Strategic Bold Moves; Report 4: The Playbook: Implementation Plan; and Report 5: The Framework. Together, these reports constitute a policy framework placing these strategies at the core of Park Board activities and decisions. Specifically, the master plan proposes a new approach titled "Equity Initiative Zones" to accomplish the goal of more equitable provision (Vancouver Board of Parks and Recreation, 2019).

During the 2018 TalkVancouver survey phase, 92% of respondents supported the goal of "prioritizing the delivery of resources where they are needed most" (Vancouver Board of Parks and Recreation, 2019, p. 19). Park Board also heard from community members and stakeholders that they did not understand why some projects received higher priorities in money allocations (Howard & Culbertson, 2020). Thus, the first strategy addressed was *equity*, using the "Initiative Zones" equity tool. Historically, planners used two-dimensional distance mapping to regulate park development (for example, in the 1928 Plan for Vancouver, the metric for urban park siting was one park per square mile). However, this metric was flawed due to differential neighborhood density as well as landform variations. VanPlay's new strategy uses geospatial data to identify underserved areas in which to target increased investment in parks (see Figure 9.9). VanPlay

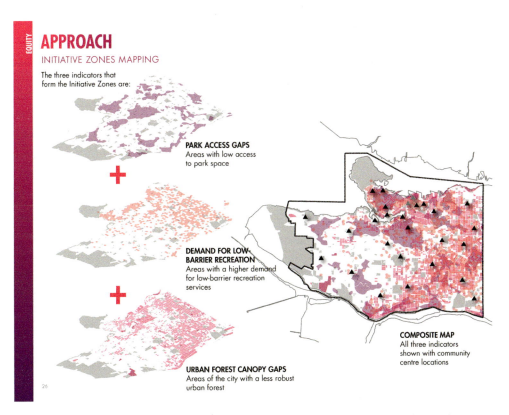

FIGURE 9.9 Equity approaches to mapping initiative zones. Image credit: Copyright © 2019 by Design Workshop, Inc. for Vancouver Board of Parks and Recreation.

utilizes three indicators to determine the Initiative Zones: (1) park access gaps; (2) demand for low-barrier recreation; and (3) urban forest canopy gaps (Vancouver Board of Parks and Recreation, 2019). Overlaying the three indicators together, the Initiative Zones maps highlight historically underserved areas where the Park Board can set priorities on allocating programs and resources geographically.

Human factor elements

The VanPlay project illustrates two important people-environment considerations. As a comprehensive planning document, the project enlisted the participation of many populations using innovative tools and methods. In addition, VanPlay embraced an equity approach to data collection and application.

Engagement methods In their community engagement policy, framework planning, and final playbook, VanPlay prioritized engaging often under-served groups, who they identified as persons with culturally diverse backgrounds, low-income persons, individuals with disabilities, and youth. Some specific actions worth highlighting include using inclusive plan graphics that intentionally represent people of different ages, sizes, gender identifications; utilizing all different tools and communication methods to allow maximum participation; aligning with the city's ongoing engagement with Musqueam, Squamish, and Tsleil-Waututh First Nations and decolonizing the vision plan language. As discussed in Chapter 8, designers cannot rely on only one method or use one common tool to truly understand and analyze the unique problems of communities. VanPlay's process is in keeping with this notion.

Equity, spatial planning, and data collection VanPlay successfully achieved its *equity* approach by acknowledging the biases and gaps created by solely relying on quantitative data, particularly missing pieces from historically underrepresented groups. VanPlay Report 3 "Strategic Bold Moves" collected both quantitative and qualitative data and represented both visually. Consultants collaborated directly with partners, equity-seeking groups, and others to make sure that communities voices were heard. This approach sharply contrasts to the typical colonial methods that reinforce systemic oppression (Vancouver Board of Parks and Recreation, 2019, p. 25).

Reflections and discussion

Chapter 5 addresses the need to approach projects with a spirit of inclusion. The intent is that aspiring designers practice with an inclusive mindset – how can this project provide a place for anyone who wants to use it? It may be convenient to design for the status-quo or the most obvious potential users; however, people with varied backgrounds, abilities, ages, and interests all must share public outdoor environments. Without a concerted effort to understand all possible populations and their desires, a successful long-term design will be impossible to achieve.

The last lessons from VanPlay come from its visualization and community-engagement methods, as discussed in Chapter 7. There is no one-size-fits-all type of engagement method that can be used universally. As illustrated by this project, a combination of approaches is often needed to reach multiple populations. Designers need to be trained in participatory techniques and cognizant of the benefits and challenges of the different methods for engaging residents in the design-decision process. The VanPlay project offers a range of different tactics flexibly pulled together to gain input from varied potential user groups.

A PLACE FOR LEARNING AND PLAYING

>**Case study**: Tulatoli Primary School Outdoor Environment Design
>**Project location and region:** Raipura, Narsingdi, Bangladesh
>**Project size**: School parcel size: 1,180 square meters (0.29 acres); building area: 294 square meters (3165 sq. ft)
>**Client:** Tulatoli Primary School (358 students in total)
>**Design team**: Matluba Khan, Lecturer, Cardiff University; Fuad Abdul Quaium, Ghorami Jon and the students and teachers at Tulatoli Primary School
>**Other key participants (faculty advisors):** Simon Bell (Edinburgh College of Art and Estonian University of Life Sciences); Sarah McGeown (University of Edinburgh); Eva Silveirinha de Oliveira (University of Edinburgh)
>**Awards:**
>2017 Global Health Day Poster Award
>2017 ASLA Student Award (Student Community Service category)
>2016 Environmental Design Research Association (EDRA) Great Places Award (Place Design category)
>2014 EDRA Best Student Paper Award
>**Time period:** Design and construction from October 2014 to January 2015

Project abstract and context

Bangladesh was one of the signatories to the United Nations (UN) Millennium Declaration in 2000. Bangladesh committed to the goals identified at the summit, with a target to remain faithful to achieving universal primary education by 2015 (Rabbi, 2008). Bangladesh's primary education (ages 6–11) enrollment rate increased after signing the Declaration and had reached 100% by 2018 (UNESCO Institute for Statistics, 2020). However, only half of enrolled students graduated, with an average drop-out rate of 45.1% (Khan, 2012). Khan, a trained architect in Bangladesh, noticed this issue and began to question how the physical school environment might influence student learning outcomes and school completion. She started to rethink learning spaces in Bangladesh and how indoor and outdoor spaces impact childhood learning and development (Project for Public Spaces, 2016). Khan engaged in the Tulatoli Government Primary School project while pursuing her doctoral degree in landscape architecture at the University of Edinburgh. She conducted a research project that evaluated the learning outcomes of students both before and after outdoor environmental improvements were implemented.

Tulatoli Government Primary School is in the sub-district of Raipura, 80 miles from the capital of Dhaka. Similar to other government primary schools in Bangladesh, the school consists of several classrooms, an office, a toilet block, and a barren unsurfaced dirt schoolyard (see Figure 9.10). Like many other primary schools, the outdoor environment is not integrated into the students' learning experience or fully utilized due to a lack of design (Khan, 2017).

FIGURE 9.10 Tulatoli Primary School before and after the design interventions (Khan, 2017). Image credit: Matluba Khan.

According to Khan, most students attending Talutoli Government Primary School are from low- to middle-income families. The classrooms were poorly lit and had poor ventilation, leading the children to feel uncomfortable and bored. In addition, most children would not return to school after lunch breaks at home (Khan, 2017). School enrollment at the time of the project was 358 students (52% boys and 48% girls). Of the entire student population, 61 children, all aged between 8 and 11 years old, and from four grade levels, participated in the research to test the impact of outdoor environments on academic attainment (Khan, McGeown, & Bell, 2020).

Methodology and process

To achieve a school landscape that enhances children's learning experiences and motivates them to learn, the designers first examined several theoretical models and evidence from previous research. Some of the research that informed this project includes work on the positive impact of greenness on educational attainment, affordance theory, and behavior settings (Khan et al., 2020). The designers incorporated these concepts with the desires of the school's children and teachers and the local community. Different groups contributed their opinions in various ways. Children had opportunities to share their ideas through drawings and children-led model-making workshops (Khan, Bell, McGeown, & de Oliveira, 2020). Students and teachers also participated in focus group meetings to explain their preferences for proposed learning areas. Meetings to share the aims and goals of the project were also held with parents and members of the community.

After an intensive engagement process, a preliminary design was produced that contained a combination of different learning areas, including a natural learning area, water area, an area with loose materials, play area, gardens, and an amphitheater (see Figure 9.11) (Khan, 2017). The project was under construction between October 2014 to January 2015 with active participation by the children and community members. The school children carried bricks and cured them, constructed the garden beds, sowed seeds, and grew plants. They also painted the school walls and drew murals on them. Local community members contributed bamboo for planting, while local carpenters and students from leading architectural institutions volunteered their skills and knowledge. The new school landscape was completed in January 2015 and the children and teachers have actively used it for outdoor education and informal play since then (Khan, 2017).

FIGURE 9.11 Design plans showing the school's outdoor environment before and after the intervention (Khan, McGeown, & Bell, 2020).

Outcomes

The project team gathered feedback through focus group meetings, semi-structured interviews, post-occupancy evaluations, behavior mapping, and a questionnaire, as well as the mathematics and science exam scores since the courses were taught outdoors (Khan, 2017; Khan et al., 2020). Analysis of pre- and post-intervention data shows that the new landscape design had a positive impact on children's academic performances, motivation, school attitude, and campus activities (see Figures 9.12 and 9.13). Analysis of data from the focus group meetings with parents showed that most children who used to go home for lunch but did not return in the afternoon now asked their mothers to pack their lunches to eat at school. Children who typically left school immediately after the last bell rang began to spend time on campus after school was dismissed. As of 2017, the school environment has been recognized as a community place, a meeting space, and an engaged learning playground, by students, their parents, and other community members (Khan, 2017).

Human factor elements

The Tulatoli Primary School project provides unique lessons for applying human factors research to design decisions. Theories related to child development, loose parts, and affordances guided the design process and goals. In addition, through a post-occupancy examination, the designers provide evidence that design choices had the anticipated impacts on the children's enjoyment and learning.

Child development and the environment The needs of children and how those needs are addressed in the outdoor environment are discussed in Chapter 4. Children need places where they can explore, be connected with nature, be physically active, and socialize with their friends. This project revealed similar theoretical themes. The children's drawings created

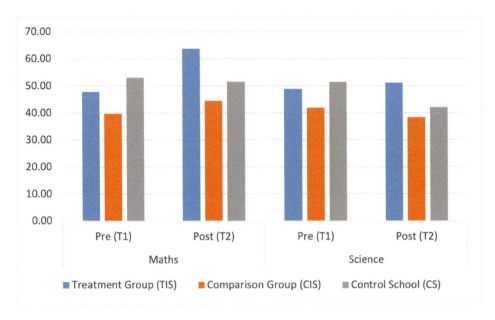

FIGURE 9.12 Tulatoli Primary School academic performance comparisons: Differences in mathematics and science attainment between the treatment group (students using the outdoor environment for learning), the comparative group (students at this school not using the outdoor environment for learning), and a control school (a school in the region without outdoor learning) (Khan et al., 2020).

during the design process illustrated these desires and the designer subsequently built upon these themes in the design.

Loose parts and affordance theory The concept of affordances describes how individuals perceive how they might use an environment and is discussed in greater detail in Chapter 2 (see "Affordances" section). The project team for the Tulatoli Primary School Outdoor Environment

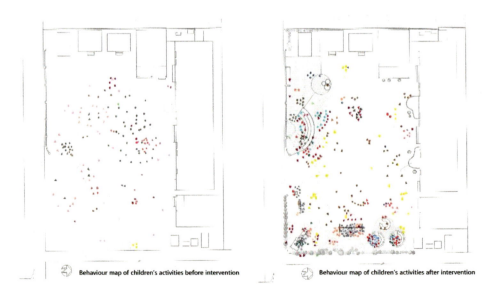

FIGURE 9.13 Behavior mapping showing student activities before and after the design intervention (Khan, 2017).

Design project actively applied affordance theory to their design understanding and recommendations. One application was through incorporating loose natural and manufactured materials into the site. These materials offer the children the affordance of interpreting and using the materials however they desire. According to Khan, "[The children] buil[t] houses in the open yard fetching materials from the area with loose materials" (Khan, McGeown, & Bell, 2020, p. 1095). The students also benefited from loose materials in that it aided their memorization of science concepts and theories. For instance, one student described how "Madam uses seeds to teach us counting, division, subtraction…" while another expressed that "[w]e can understand better when the teacher uses different elements. Even if we forget, we can remember when we look outside at these settings" (p. 1095).

Outdoor spaces and relaxation From the quasi-experimental research, the authors found that the children's science and math scores increased when these subjects were taught outside, which supports the hypothesis that learning in re-designed school grounds can improve children's academic attainment. Moreover, children also expressed that they enjoyed their outdoor classes as they felt more physically comfortable there (Khan et al., 2020). The newly designed outdoor space took advantage of direct sunlight, better ventilation, fresher air, and a direct connection to green plants and cultivated areas. The new school landscape provides a calm and restorative environment for the primary school's students, and also benefits teachers and community members.

REFLECTIONS AND DISCUSSION

Places to learn and play are needed everywhere, yet their design is often limited to meeting purely functional demands and are relegated to an area set aside for specific purposes. With a few notable exceptions, schools have seldom considered their outdoor spaces as educational opportunities. The Tulatoli School landscape provides an excellent example of how a landscape can provide a foundation for play and learning activities without being overly prescriptive. Using an affordance-based understanding of their design allowed the designers to create places that are interpreted and used differently by students, teachers, and community members. In addition, the project team's incorporation of loose parts also promotes individualized interpretation and activities.

While this project is located on a school property, opportunities to learn and to play can happen almost anywhere. Landscapes provide limitless venues for learning about the history of a place, the cultures of its occupants, natural systems in operation, and even the space to reflect and learn about ourselves. Likewise, landscapes can hold joy for people. Opportunities to be free from behavioral expectations and to both create and experience a place are limited. Much like the creativity seen when a young child discovers a large, discarded box, outdoor environments can encourage the imagination. The challenge that this project addresses and exemplifies for others is how to create a place that will encourage and nurture that joy and imagination.

NOTE

1 Save Open Space (SOS) was a local campaign to protect the land from development. The organization is no longer active.

SECTION IV: LOOKING AHEAD

10
PEOPLE AND CHANGE

While it is impossible to predict which advances and societal shifts will most influence design decisions in the future, this chapter examines several changes poised to shape how design practice is conducted and several issues likely to transform design decisions and impact human behaviors. Prominent in contemporary design foci are the physical and social impacts of sustainability in planning and design, the connections between place and well-being, and the application of technology in design practice focused on the human scale (see Table 10.1). These three topics and some of their influences on behavior and design decisions are discussed as illustrations of societal influences. The topics were identified based on continuing and current practices and do not attempt to address all possible scenarios or influences on design. Instead, these topics are offered as a means for considering how changes in society are linked to changes in human behavior and environmental decisions. With time, new concerns and innovations will assuredly continue to influence people–environment relationships.

The reciprocal relationship between people's changing needs and their environment affects the design of outdoor environments as well as human behavior. Among various broad societal influences, technological advancements enable social and infrastructure enhancements that aim to improve people's livelihoods at local to global scales. New technology is shaping behaviors such as reliance on personal smart devices (phones, watches, and other wearable devices), influencing how people navigate the landscape, record their experiences, and share those experiences. In addition, social and environmental challenges are changing due to advanced technology affecting human behaviors. As an illustration, increased production and reliance on personal vehicles and expanded infrastructure increased unsustainable and unhealthy behaviors resulting in partial impacts on climate change and public health concerns that warrant broader attention. These associated relationships will likely influence design decisions in the future and continue to reflect and respond to contemporary issues, users' evolving interests and concerns, and the need for responsive placemaking decisions. Designers should consider, anticipate, and respond to societal shifts to encourage functional, pleasing, and sustainable places.

SUSTAINABLE PLANNING, DESIGN, AND PEOPLE

Background

Prior to the widespread adoption of the concept of sustainability, many scholars and advocates worked to increase awareness of the overuse of natural resources and the accompanying

DOI: 10.4324/9781315100036-15

TABLE 10.1 Examples of potential physical and social environment impacts due to projected societal shifts

Impacts of societal shifts

		Physical environment	Social environment
Sustainable Planning, Design, and People	Land use	Mixed land use with higher densities, such as transit-oriented development (TOD), smart growth approaches	Human-centric patterns such as denser, more compact development and effective pedestrian routes at comfortable scales
	Transportation	Design for multiple transportation modes and incorporation of advanced technology (e.g., autonomous vehicles)	Attention to accessibility and inclusion for diverse populations as well as alternative transportation modes
	Site design	Comprehensive design practices addressing human use and sustainability goals	Human-scaled and human-centric designs, increased user engagement, and attention to social interactions and well-being
Health and Well-being	Active living	Inclusive and well-connected environments supporting physical activity (e.g., trail systems) and increased access and activity choices	Opportunities for formal and informal social relationships, supportive recreation, and increased social capital supporting health and well-being
	Role of nature for social and mental health	Visual and physical access to green space in residential, educational, and work settings	Incorporation of activities such as community walks, gardening programs, citizen science opportunities, nature prescription programs
	Increasing reliance on technology	Advanced technology to visualizing physical activity behaviors, self-monitoring activity levels (e.g., wearable devices and trackers)	Technology as a means for increasing and accessing recreational and social opportunities contributing to better health
Virtual Influences in Design	Virtual space and connected experiences	Increase of access to digitally connected networks and virtual experiences	Increased online communities of support and interest, expanded experiences with new people, and opportunities to experience and learn about new places
	Visualization, engagement, and experiential tools	Development of virtual platforms and tools for design simulations, social networks, and communication (e.g., virtual reality tools, QR codes, gaming applications)	Increased augmented and virtual reality experiences, access to engagement tools, and access to decision-making information such as alternative designs

unintended negative environmental impacts. The "Tragedy of the Commons" popularized by Hardin (1968), writings such as Carson's *Silent Spring* (1962), and the environmental movement beginning in the 1960s alerted people to the negative consequences of society's pattern of environmental disregard. The Earth Summit in 1992 established a global partnership embracing a sustainable approach to improving the environment and people's lives and has since led to the creation of 17 Sustainable Development Goals (United Nations, n.d.). The overall goals of living within the environmental means of the planet and employing a sustainable approach to decision-making have become more prevalent in planning and design education than in the past.

Despite recent increases in environmental awareness and sustainable development efforts, negative environmental impacts continue to cause harm. In general, human decisions and behaviors have contributed to the diminishment of the Earth's natural capacity to heal and replenish in a timely manner (Whitmee et al., 2015). The UNESCO Courier (2018) published *Welcome to the Anthropocene!,* a periodical documenting a debate among scientists about the many impacts humans have had on the planet and questioning whether a new epoch, the Anthropocene, should be added after the Holocene. For example, these scientists identify that reliance on fossil fuels as a source of energy is a cause of climate change; therefore, they propose to separate the current period from earlier epochs because of these human impacts. While the contributing factors to climate change are complex, they are intrinsically linked to human systems and behaviors. Industrial and development practices harm the environment with impacts such as pollution, global warming, sea-level rise, loss of biodiversity, and increased natural hazards. Scholars also found that vulnerable populations tend to suffer greater burdens from unsustainable behaviors (Cassella, 2019; Salem, 2020).

Designers anticipate and respond to shifting sustainability concerns as their decisions relate to mitigating negative impacts on the environment in the short and long term. Societies should approach the three pillars of sustainability – environmental, economic, and social – holistically and simultaneously at various scales. While a great deal of focus has been placed on the environmental elements of sustainability, addressing the economic and social aspects is critical. Sound decisions should balance the economic costs and benefits with the environmental and social gains. Increasingly, environmental awareness and sustainability education provide practitioners with tools to assess their potential impacts on the environment. These efforts can contribute to creating long-term stewardship of a place, spur a proactive approach to place-based decisions, and lead to behavior changes among individuals.

Current practices

Since the late 20th century, societies are more conscious of sustainable practices. This increased attention is spurred by a better understanding of ecosystems and their role, the resilience and recovery capabilities of various environments, and the benefits of minimizing environmental impacts. These current practices provide opportunities to test and learn new ways of doing things and offer alternative models to more established but less sustainable approaches. Often, recent trends and practices emphasize and address people's needs and people-centric behaviors to steward positive and sustainable long-term environmental changes.

Land use planning and policies The shift in practices from 1980 to 2010 offers a narrow window to examine the relationships between physical planning and human behaviors. Unlike cultures based on compact urban design, urban and suburban American cities segregated building types and land uses as many expanded outward during the mid-20th century. In contrast, contemporary land use planning has been and continues to shift toward greater incorporation of mixed land uses and denser development (Calthorpe, 1993).

Several concepts and strategies, such as *transit villages*, *transit-oriented development* (TOD), *New Urbanism*, and *smart growth*, have emerged in response to uncontrolled growth and environmental impacts of human developments. Transit villages and TOD focus on planning mixed-use communities and neighborhoods centered around quality public transportation systems such as transit stops and stations. Often, they are walkable and pedestrian-oriented (Cervero, 1994; National Academy of Science, Engineering, and Medicine (NASEM), 2004; US GAO, 2014) (see Figure 10.1). New Urbanism, a movement founded in 1993, aims to inform development practices and policies with the goal of creating more livable communities. New Urbanist principles include making neighborhood populations and uses more diverse, integrating public transit and pedestrian ways into communities, celebrating the local context, and organizing the community around public places (Charter of the New Urbanism (CNU), 2001, 2018; Talen, 2006). Smart growth is an approach aiming to mitigate development

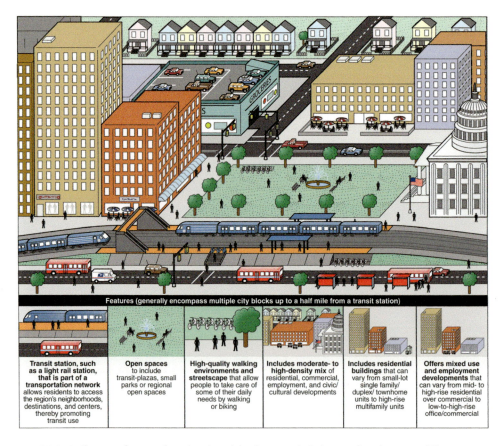

FIGURE 10.1 Common features of transit-oriented developments include a transit station near public open spaces and quality pedestrian-focused environments with mixed land use of medium to high density. Image credit: U.S. Government Accountability Office.

impacts through policies encouraging "a mix of building types and uses, diverse housing and transportation options" within existing neighborhoods, and robust community engagement (Smart Growth America, 2022, para. 4). New Urbanism and smart growth are interrelated and often perceived as similar in that both efforts focus on mitigating growth impacts. Smart growth practices came from a "community of environmentalists and policy planners" while New Urbanism was much more influenced by "architects and physical planners" (Knaap & Talen, 2005, 109). All of these approaches advocate for mixed-use developments with more reliance on public transportation and alternative travel modes by reducing vehicle miles traveled. These types of development integrate human-scale planning and design strategies that encourage pedestrian-centered activities such as walking and biking instead of relying on personal vehicles. Examples of TODs are present in numerous US communities, such as Arlington County, Virginia; Boston, Massachusetts; and Portland, Oregon (NASEM, 2004; Jacobson & Forsyth, 2008).

Transportation planning and modes of travel With advances in technology and infrastructure, transportation decisions and travel behaviors have focused on creating expanded transportation networks to accommodate faster and increased movement of people and goods. Despite efforts to improve public transit options, the primary mode of travel in the United States and many developed cultures continues to be the automobile. People's travel preferences are influenced by the options available to them and by personal priorities. In many locations, the result is continued reliance on the car. Road design reflects the desire to move these vehicles between places as quickly and safely as possible and results in a road network or hierarchy based on speed, width, and the number of lanes. Streets predominantly designed for vehicular travel make driving more convenient but deter pedestrians and cyclists who subsequently need to seek safer and more comfortable routes elsewhere. In many situations, people are driving cars even for short-distance errands that can otherwise be done on foot or on bicycles because the environment is more supportive of the automobile (Park, Ewing, Sabouri, & Larsen, 2019).

Transportation planning often considers the impact of travel decisions on individuals' quality of life as well as impacts on the broader community. Current transportation planning efforts aim to increase alternative travel modes, such as pedestrians and cyclists, to diversify travel behavior, despite that much of the funding in the United States remains devoted to the automobile (HR 3684 Infrastructure Investment and Jobs Act, 2021). An approach which prioritizes the different levels of travel and transport behaviors at the personal, community, and regional scales can improve human–environment relationships and further support infrastructure decisions for people's health and well-being (Global Designing Cities Initiative (GDCI), n.d.). At a narrower scope, *complete streets* is a concept and strategy to ensure meeting diverse travelers' needs, regardless of age, ability, or transportation mode (Smart Growth America, 2013). These streets can allow easier access to places and destinations while emphasizing safety, comfort, and access. Complete streets include designated lanes for various travel modes that are connected at local to regional scales (see Figure 10.2).

Site design and sustainability With an increased interest in sustainability, development efforts have focused on smarter choices in site selection, material use, and design process. Many planners and designers have become more aware of potential impacts of

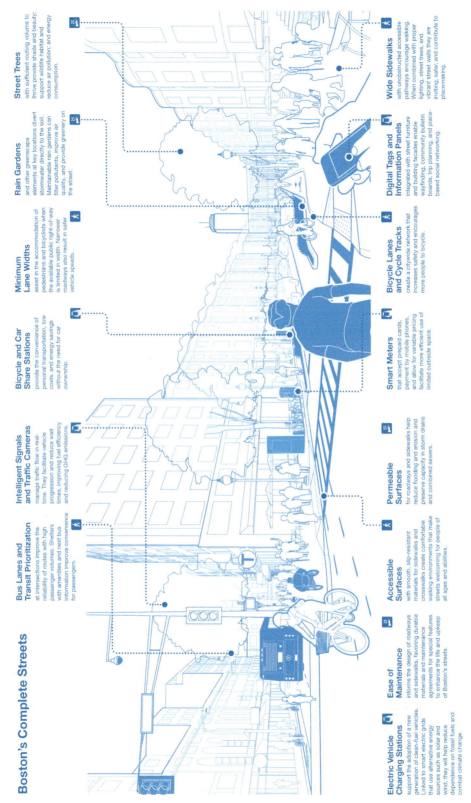

FIGURE 10.2 Complete streets consider all users by including designated lanes or areas for vehicles, bicycles, service providers, and pedestrians. Image credit: Boston Transportation Department.

FIGURE 10.3 Washington Canal Park in Washington, DC earned recognition as a SITES Platinum level pilot project in 2013. Originally used for school bus parking, the OLIN Studio and collaborators designed a public park for the site which embraced sustainable principles and emphasized user experience. Image credit: OLIN (left) and OLIN/Sahar Coston-Hardy (right).

developments on environmental conditions and are more accountable for the sustainable performance and functioning of the designed outdoor environments they influence (Garde, 2009; Steiner, 2020; Wessel, 2021). Performance standards have been developed for design practices such as the Leadership in Energy and Environmental Design (LEED) and the Sustainable SITES Initiative (SITES) rating systems. The former is a green building rating system and the latter is its equivalent focusing on sustainable landscapes. The practices contained within LEED ND (Neighborhood Development) (one of several subtopic standards of LEED) and SITES aim to reflect positive human-oriented behaviors for the use, experience, and understanding of places (see Figure 10.3). Both standards are voluntary, market-driven, consensus-based tools that serve as a guideline and assessment mechanism for site development of varied sizes, contexts, and environmental characteristics and seek measurable and accountable actions to lessen human-induced burdens on natural ecosystems and continue to evolve (Calkins, 2012; GBCI, 2014; Sustainable SITES Initiative, 2014; U.S. GBC, 2014, 2017). They also help inform and educate practitioners, educators, community leaders, and the public to make design decisions that enhance ecosystem services for long-term coexistence between humanity and the planet.

Overall, a greater accountability of the functions and performances of outdoor environment designs are expected today than in the past. Planners and designers have tools to measure the environmental, social, and economic performance of their designed outdoor environments and contribute toward greater sustainability goals. By quantifying and comparing the performance of outdoor environment designs with past projects, designers can contribute to improving and sustaining the function and health of outdoor environments.

Projections for the future

If current trends continue, the future will focus on land use planning and practice emphasizing denser, resourceful, and compact design, mixed-use, and integrating more sustainable transportation planning strategies. Some growing transportation mode trends include sharing programs for bicycles and e-scooters as well as driverless autonomous vehicles (personal and commercial) (see Figure 10.4). Driverless technology integrates science, engineering, and artificial intelligence, and with its adoption, will influence the design of outdoor environments (Guerra, 2016;

FIGURE 10.4 A rendering of a future transit stop in a mixed-use neighborhood which will accommodate walking, cycling, and driverless vehicles (Hilburg, 2018). Image credit: Kohn Pedersen Fox Associates.

Guerra & Morris, 2018; Parkin, Clark, Clayton, Ricci, & Parkhurst, 2018). Likewise, e-scooters and bike-sharing programs are being piloted for short-distance travel (Bordenkircher, O'Neil, & Scott Smith, 2018; Scott Smith & Schwieterman, 2018) and their presence is already beginning to impact many urban areas by contributing to congested sidewalks, conflicts with other transportation modes, and safety concerns. Moreover, owning personal flying devices or hoverboards, as portrayed in movies, may become a reality. The implications of these innovations for future land use and transportation planning and designs warrant consideration.

Sustainable practices have and will continue to evolve with time. These practices inform large-scale planning decisions and development patterns. Technological advancements, consumer purchasing trends, innovative thinking, and visioning influence planning priorities. The focus on sustainability places more attention on efforts that are responsive to specific contexts and that consider people–environment relationships. As transportation systems, land use, and development practices continue to evolve, the outcomes will likely be more environmentally conscious and address considerations for adopting renewable energy, artificial intelligence, and their applications for efficiency. Concerns and issues in the future may revolve around living within limited environmental means while adapting to decisions that influence how the outdoor environments are designed and how their performance impacts peoples' behaviors in and toward sustaining them.

HEALTH AND WELL-BEING

The design of outdoor places and healthy behaviors influence each other. In recent years, more people have become aware and concerned about their health, and are making lifestyle changes to support their well-being. As discussed in Chapter 2, outdoor environments designed with such wellness in mind can be beneficial to people's physical, mental, and social health and well-being.

Background

People's wellness and healthy communities can be improved when the outdoor environment is designed to encourage physical activity, facilitate interaction with others, and restore mental health. Unfortunately, reductions in physical labor, reliance on automobiles, and changes to diet during the late 20th century have contributed to current public health issues in the United States. With these shifts, obesity and related chronic disease rates have increased over the past four decades. The Centers for Disease Control and Prevention have identified that social determinants of health, including food choices, economic stability, and neighborhood and built environment, partly contribute to the obesity epidemic (CDC, n.d.). The design of cities and towns, amount of physical activity, shifting demographics, and lifestyle changes are other contributors (Frumkin, 2002; Jackson & Sinclair, 2012; ULI, 2013; Robert Wood Johnson Foundation, 2013). In addition, mental health concerns, including increases in stress, anxiety, and addiction, are continuing to increase. Designers can help alleviate these health impacts through creating safe, convenient, and comfortable environments.

Moreover, a growing reliance on technology, and along with accompanying changes in outdoor leisure activities, has altered people's behaviors and attitudes toward the landscape. In particular, the widespread ownership of personal electronic devices has changed how people experience outdoor environments. For example, Americans' smartphone ownership increased from 35% in 2011 to 85% in 2021 (Pew Research Center, 2021). Verbal conversations are replaced by silent texting or social media exchanges, often while in the physical presence of someone else. While civic and cultural gathering places are also important for people's social and mental health (ULI, 2013), such behaviors contribute to decreased socialization in the traditional sense. Furthermore, the expansion of television, internet, and WiFi networks has opened an era of virtually endless entertainment (e.g., movies, music, gaming) both in terms of where it can be accessed and when. Excess screen time, passive recreation, and a common obsession with personal communication devices are influencing a lack of physical activity, sedentary lifestyles, and isolated social relationships, among other concerns across all ages.

Current practices

A focus on designing places to support physical activity and participation in outdoor environments has received increased attention by public health disciplines. In addition, multidisciplinary efforts continue to address the reciprocal relationship between land use and built environment patterns and active behaviors. Prescriptive recommendations, such as spending more time in nature, are emerging and highlight the importance of expanding beyond traditional means of addressing health concerns. Moreover, efforts to use technology to improve healthy behaviors such as tracking activity or prompting movement are contributing to healthier lifestyles.

Design for active living Various interventions have come about that aim to increase physical activities and improve health in the United States such as Active Living by Design, a program supported by the Robert Wood Johnson Foundation. This foundation along with the CDC, the National Institute of Health (NIH), and others are hoping to address the increase in chronic diseases such as cardiovascular disease and type 2 diabetes (Robert Wood Johnson Foundation,

2013; ULI, 2012). This movement aims to overcome sedentary lifestyles through design interventions from a community, policy, and environment perspective (Day, 2006; Robert Wood Johnson Foundation, 2013). Active Living by Design advocates and researchers have identified reasons for physical inactivity, offered policy recommendations, and designed resolutions to support increased physical activity. These researchers have identified environmental characteristics that support increased physical activity such as shorter distances to destinations, denser parcels, strengthening connectivity, and perceived social support for walking (Day, 2006; Brownson, Hoehner, Day, Forsyth, & Sallis, 2009; Moudon et al., 2007). In addition, others have found that an individual's level of actively engaging in the outdoor environment, motivation, incentives, and inspiration are affected by environmental conditions (Fraser, Munoz, & MacRury, 2019).

The physical environment can support active living by providing active transportation and recreational features. Pedestrian-focused designed environments that naturally integrate physical activity into daily routines as recreation are an effective means to contribute to increased physical activity (ULI, 2013; US DOT, 2015). Additionally, when outdoor environments are designed to support physical activity, individuals who regularly exercise outdoors have lower anxiety levels (Lawton, Brymer, Clough, & Denovan, 2017). Trail systems, such as the Atlanta BeltLine, are a valuable example of long-term community investment toward the health and well-being of communities. This pedestrian–bicycle–transit loop links neighborhoods around Atlanta's perimeter (Davidson, 2011). Originally proposed by Georgia Tech graduate student Gravel, the Atlanta BeltLine concept was more fully developed and described in the 2004 report by Alex Garvin and Associates (2004) (see Figure 10.5).

FIGURE 10.5 Atlanta BeltLine Eastside Trail near Ponce City Market connects people to parks and destinations around the urban greenway. Image credit: Christopher T. Martin.

Role of nature for social and mental health Access to nature and its qualities are vital for people's emotional, psychological, and physical health (Coppel & Wüstemann, 2017). In particular, the presence of nature can contribute to preventing stress, helping people cope with distress, and accessing nature. Research finds that with higher levels of "nature-connectedness," people are happier in life and "have lower levels of depression and anxiety" (Mental Health Foundation, 2021, p. 9). The role of nature is essential for social and mental health, as evidenced during the COVID-19 pandemic when people often alleviated stress and anxiety by spending time outdoors to combat isolation due to business closures and community lockdowns (Mental Health Foundation, 2021). The importance of being able to safely access nature and open spaces while socially distancing highlighted a variety of health and well-being benefits.

With the increased attention to the importance of spending time in nature for health benefits, nature prescription programs have emerged. Two such programs, *park prescription* (ParkRx) and *nature prescription* (Nature Rx), aim to improve behavioral and physical health. Physicians or healthcare providers counsel their patients to spend time engaging in activities in nature and green spaces to address or prevent varied medical conditions such as stress or obesity (Institute at the Golden Gate, 2020; James, Christiana, & Battista, 2019). Nature prescription programs provide patients with opportunities to gain health benefits through experiences in local parks and green spaces (Kondo et al., 2020). Many ParkRx programs are designed for the general public, and those providing flexible activities that can be easily done are more popular (Institute at the Golden Gate, 2020). Other researchers share that parks are community resources for pediatric resilience and that park prescriptions are a way to address pediatric stress (Razani et al., 2019). Researchers are trying to determine how to best increase opportunities for children living in low-resource neighborhoods, as these audiences are often most vulnerable and could greatly benefit from increased nature access (Sefcik et al., 2019).

Technology effects on behavior and design While increased reliance on technology has contributed to sedentary lifestyles, digital technology can offer solutions to increasing populations' engagement with outdoor environments. Smartphone apps, tech-enabled site furnishings, and wearable devices such as fitness trackers are some tools that encourage physical activity and can facilitate social encounters. Likewise, educational apps, such as those used to promote nature exploration in parks, and facilitate children's exploration of the outdoors in fun, non-formal settings. Children participating in such activities have been shown to retain the knowledge learned during their outdoor experience and can have independent educational opportunities in nature as often as they like (Crawford, Holder, & O'Connor, 2017).

Attracting people to the outdoors is another step toward increasing physical activity. Site furniture and design features that incorporate technology, such as QR codes to online information and internet access, can entice people to visit a public place and encourage their stay (Kimic, Maksymiuk, & Suchocka, 2019). Furthermore, fitness trackers allow users to not only measure their physical activity but also share this information with others. Visitors to an unfamiliar place can access information from others about hiking, running, and biking trails or to find others to join them. Bicycling routes and user-intensity information gathered through cycling and running apps can inform the planning and design of formally designated cycling routes that can support people's outdoor recreation (Jestico, Nelson, & Winters, 2016). This technology also makes it possible to collect information which can inform design and policy decisions, including data over multiple years and from different locations for longitudinal studies of use patterns. For example, MapMyFitness helped researchers assess differences in outdoor physical activity in parks in St. Louis, Missouri (Adlakha, Budd, Gernes, Sequeira, & Hipp, 2014) and Winston-Salem, North Carolina (Hirsch et al., 2014).

Integrating people's interests in virtual experiences with the outdoor environment can also be used to increase participation in physical activity. For example, the location-based augmented reality (AR) game Pokémon GO integrates in-app activities with the immediate landscape. The game promotes physical and social activities and inspires multiple generations of users to explore public places. Researchers found that physical activity increased with Pokémon GO users walking a total of 4.6 billion kilometers in the two months after its initial release in 2016 (Althoff, White, & Horvitz, 2016). Although the game's popularity and the endurance of people's connection with the game may be limited, green space has a positive relationship with daily walking and running distances, of which AR games like Pokémon GO have the potential to link people and their environments to enhance public health (Lee, Zeng, Oh, Lee, & Gao, 2021; Ma et al., 2018; Potts, Jacka, & Yee, 2017) (see Figure 10.6).

FIGURE 10.6 A person using the Pokémon GO app (augmented reality) for recreation in the outdoors. Image credit: Jayoung Koo.

Although certain aspects of technological advancements have resulted in unhealthy behaviors, when utilized to its advantage, technology can positively influence people engaging in physical activity in outdoor settings. Social media, gaming, and other tech-focused activities have and can continue to positively influence the use of outdoor places. Designers can also use digital information regarding behavior patterns, activities, and more to inform design decisions which enhance health and well-being. Ultimately, aiming for healthier lifestyles will require new landscape designs that support ongoing changes to how people receive and share information.

Projections for the future of healthy places

The thoughtful design of physical environments can also bring about improved health and well-being by supporting the social capital of individuals and communities. Frumkin, Frank, and Jackson define *social capital* as "a feature of communities, corresponding at the individual level to a person's network of social relationships" (2004, p. 166). Attitudes of trust and reciprocity, and behaviors of social networking and civic participation are essential features of social capital that help bind communities together. People living in communities with high social capital may behave healthier, and high social capital may also lead to policies protecting health. On the other hand, the decline of social capital is concerning as sprawling regions may miss opportunities to promote lifelong health benefits (Frumkin, Frank, & Jackson, 2004). Others have found that community-level characteristics are associated with increased life expectancy such as places with a "growing population, better quality primary care, and greater social cohesion" (Dobis, Stephens, Skidmore, & Goetz, 2020, p. 9). Overall, social capital is vital in supporting increasing physical activity, bolstering active living lifestyles, and supporting social and mental health through friends and groups exercising together in outdoor environments where they feel comfortable and safe.

Along with considering the needs of the general populations, designers should give directed attention to making outdoor places welcoming and supportive of older residents. Aging populations are maintaining active lifestyles longer; therefore, designers need to consider how older populations might access recreational opportunities (see Chapter 4,"Designing for older adults" section for further discussion). Designs that are flexible and adaptable to multiple purposes have the potential to enhance health and well-being for wider age spans more so than environments designed for single purposes or ages. Embedding simple features like shade, drinking fountains, and seating can promote healthy behaviors. The addition of other conveniences such as WiFi access and charging outlets may also contribute to increased use. As noted in the Atlanta BeltLine, multi-use paths or greenways can function as alternative transportation corridors supporting walking and biking away from vehicular traffic. Such transportation infrastructure can connect neighborhoods and districts safely while also offering access to nature and recreational amenities, thus supporting improved health all around.

Today, individuals often receive health-related information and recommendations through online communities. While some shared information may not be accurate or relevant, this source of information can be an effective and convenient way for people to learn about outdoor activities in their community. For example, opportunities for outdoor activities shared through social media and smartphone apps allow for sending out reminders of event times and locations. In addition, advances in and widespread use of wearable technology has the potential to further enhance the quality of life (Lee, Kim, Ryoo, & Shin, 2016) as well as informing designers as to the places and actions that can help remediate negative influences on health. Lastly, as evidenced during the COVID-19 pandemic, technologies enabled some jobs to be performed away from the traditional office. As more people work from home or at remote locations, community and neighborhood planning may need to pay more attention to increasing recreational opportunities close to residential areas in order to offset sedentary work habits.

In general, physical design decisions should seek to incorporate active living strategies. What, why, and how outdoor environments are planned, designed, and function are essential for enhancing human–environment relationships and people's health and well-being. Ultimately, lifestyle change depends on a person's decision to actively engage in outdoor environments; therefore, the challenge exists to make these places attractive and supportive of their needs and interests. The creation of outdoor environments that support and enhance a populations' physical, mental, social, and emotional well-being will significantly contribute to positive health outcomes.

VIRTUAL INFLUENCES IN DESIGN

The introduction of virtual space has prompted various lifestyle changes and raised concerns about what impact these changes might have on outdoor environments. New technologies have brought opportunities for designers to visualize and simulate designs through visual displays and virtual spaces. The idea of providing virtual representations of space is not new to the design world although the techniques are. Early landscape architecture simulations were static manipulations of hand-drawn scenes, photographs, and scaled models. Next, movement through design proposals was represented using fly-through animations and videos. While these earlier tools remain in use, emerging technologies provide designers with increasing realism and accuracy in demonstrating their proposals. Further, advances in virtual experiences are expanding recreational and entertainment opportunities for people. Software, communications networks, and supporting infrastructure innovations have strengthened the foundations for new virtual and recreational opportunities (Portman, Natapov, & Fisher-Gewirtzman, 2015).

Background

Experiences and relationships in virtual space are not limited by physical boundaries, geographical locations, or previously known people. Remote work and isolation prompted by the COVID-19 pandemic boosted further conversation on virtual experiences and pushed societies to rethink how to embrace technology more. Work meetings, education delivery, family gatherings, and other social events moved to on-line virtual spaces during this time. These virtual gathering spaces, long used by gamers and others, were quickly embraced by the wider population. During this period, design practitioners, educators, and students increasingly used online platforms to engage with their clients, consult with constituents, and share ideas. The awareness of the effectiveness and efficiency of virtual reality as a community engagement tool increased. Increasingly, designers are utilizing the technology to showcase immersive virtual experiences of their design proposals and to engage residents and others. Design technologies have evolved from large-scale visual simulation laboratories to portable visual communication tools used to test and gain feedback for design ideas (Portman et al., 2015).

Milgram and Kishino introduced the virtuality continuum, in which *augmented reality* (AR) "which refers to all cases in which the display of an otherwise real environment is augmented by means of virtual (computer graphic) objects" and the "*virtual reality* (VR) environment is one in which the participant observer is totally immersed in, and able to interact with, a completely synthetic world" (1994, p. 2). AR and VR are part of *mixed reality* (MR) or the merging of real and virtual worlds. As a contrast to previous design simulations and representations, MR and its incorporation into design practice will likely continue to impact design development, community participatory methods, and design decision-making. As in recent years, the design process will evolve to take advantage of emerging AR and VR tools and designers will look for new applications of these technologies (see Figure 10.7).

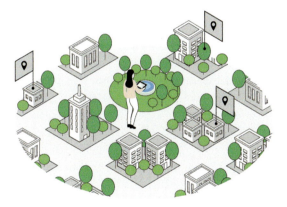

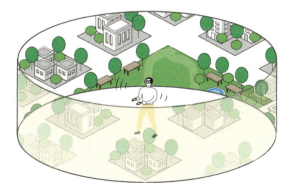

FIGURE 10.7 Diagram of augmented reality and virtual reality where design is simulated over a physical environment (AR) or communicated through virtual tools (VR).

Current practices

Society has become more globally connected and people increasingly communicate with others far away through the support of technology. Such changes continue to influence what is important to people and how they choose to spend their time. As more people are exposed to and engage in virtual experiences, the function of outdoor environments will change. Designers, in particular, are increasingly utilizing virtual spaces to help communicate and present their design proposals to potential audiences. Through varied forms of augmented, virtual, and mixed reality (AR/VR/MR), collecting information, feedback, and presentation of design alternatives is becoming more affordable, accessible, and entertaining. The use of such space, process, and modes of visual communication and experiences are expanding opportunities for people to participate more effectively in design development processes than in the past.

Virtual space and connected experiences The proliferation of ownership and access to personal computers and devices has expanded the opportunities for virtual activities on social media platforms. Many people already interact in virtual spaces including completing errands and information gathering, such as checking emails and news, forming social relationships, and varied forms of on-line recreation. Virtual spaces can enhance interactions that may otherwise be limited to the physical environments by overcoming physical distances (Schroeder, 2006). Virtual social spaces have increased as places for communities to relate to one another and provide an environment for people to share knowledge and experiences. Chatrooms and social media are also effective means to share ideas, communicate, and socialize. In many ways, virtual space overlaps with the functions of the physical environment in this regard. Applications such as Pokémon GO were a phenomenon that instantly gained popularity through AR. The MR experience of this app successfully situated gaming in outdoor settings. Pokémon GO exemplified how human–environment relationships can be integrated with virtual space. The app motivated gamers to move about in the real landscape and offered opportunities for socializing (Humphreys, 2010, 2017; Lee et al., 2021; Perry, 2016; Wang & Hsieh, 2018).

Virtual spaces have contributed to societies creating new forms of human–environment relationships. For example, social media networks enable visual sharing, such as photographs of travel, along with tips and resources. The spatial dimension of virtual social space is similar to that of a physical environment where people can gather and interact, ultimately these relationships give meaning to the virtual space. An increasing number of hobbyists, artisans, community activists, and others use social media to share their design ideas and experiences, and influence others through their examples shared on platforms such as Instagram, Pinterest, Facebook, and Snapchat. The reach of these exchanges can be measured through "likes" as a response to the information shared. This type of nontraditional space illustrates the opportunities that virtual spaces can play in addressing human–environment relationships and merging physical and virtual spaces.

Visualization, engagement, and experiential tools Virtual space can be an effective and efficient means for designers to share design ideas and gain feedback. Through AR/VR, designers can simulate and experiment with visualization in three dimensions using visually

FIGURE 10.8 Using AR, a B&O Railroad Museum (Baltimore, Maryland) visitor explores elements of a three-dimensional model through an iPad camera. The camera app provides more detailed information on buildings and other features. Image credit: HighRock/highrock.com.

realistic detail and offering immersed experiences (Portman et al., 2015; Virtual Reality Society, 2017). Designers can assist audiences in reading the designed landscapes through iterative, responsive engagement processes thereby serving as "catalyst[s] of a social process" (Danahy quoted in Barth, 2015). Public participation can occur in cyber-space such as through on-line community design engagement, gaming, and learning. Applications can be used to test and share design proposals in real-time or over extended periods, and on-site or remotely. The virtual experience provides a level of spatial cognizance that is highly visual with three-dimensional depth of scales, distances, angles, and other aspects of designs. AR/VR offers dynamic, immersive, and convincing experiences through the fabrication of materials and situations that enable an accurate portrayal (Barth, 2015; Kerr & Lawson, 2020; Portman et al., 2015; Stouhi, 2021) (see Figure 10.8).

Increasingly, designers are utilizing AR/VR technologies and virtual space in their projects, inviting clients and potential users to immerse themselves in the design development and feedback processes. Stakeholders can share their input with local governments, institutions, corporations, or others (see Figure 10.9). These technological advances allow for an improved understanding of design proposals.

Advances in technology have addressed earlier criticisms related to the costs associated with producing and accessing virtual environments. Early visualization experiments often occurred in a few large laboratory settings or were limited to practices that had the means for the technology (Portman et al., 2015). Current AR/VR equipment and software programs

PEOPLE AND CHANGE   231

FIGURE 10.9 Community members experience design alternatives through a virtual reality (VR) headset during a presentation by students. Image credit: Jayoung Koo.

are more accessible and affordable as both stand-alone tools such as headsets or through on-line services.

While innovations and increasing interests in utilizing advanced technologies are shaping current design practice, some concerns regarding the impact this might have on people's actual experience of places exist. One such concern is that the time spent on screens and in virtual space takes away from the time in outdoor environments. Individuals may become so immersed in online, virtual environments that they have difficulty adjusting to the real physical or social environment. They may also elect to spend time in virtual spaces where other like-minded people can be found. This behavior could contribute to social polarization. In addition, some may choose to visit virtual places because they find them more visually appealing.

Projections for the future

Increasingly, people are psychologically and physically dependent on virtual experiences and these experiences continue to grow in popularity. The use of visualizations and simulations can augment human–place relationships. For example, experiential tools, such as QR codes and gaming, can enable access to information. In addition, supporting infrastructure, such as increased WiFi access and charging stations, can improve experiences in the outdoor environment.

Designers will likely increasingly integrate virtual experiences into the places they create and into their design practices. The continued development of AR/VR/MR technology will further help clients and users better understand design proposals and experiences, and will help practitioners imagine and test new design ideas. Three-dimensional rendering software is already becoming more accessible to designers for the creation and presentation of their ideas. Technology which supports virtual social spaces and recreation continues to evolve. Such advancements will contribute to strengthening and sustaining human–environment relationships through the creation of supportive virtual and outdoor environments.

Access to broadband and wireless networks has moved from a nicety to an expectation, and will possibly become a requirement in public spaces. Arguments persist that not all places have to be constantly connected to mobile communication systems, however, concerns for safety, access to directions and other information, and more make compelling justifications for connecting even the most remote locations. In addition, income disparities, both locally and globally, provide additional motivation for creating accessible networks. Designers will likely play a role in bringing this access to more populations through the inclusion of such services in the outdoor environment.

CONCLUSION

While predicting the future is not without challenges, it is possible to observe and project how social shifts may impact the places designers create while also being open to new advancements. Designers have a long tradition of responding to new knowledge and changes in environmental conditions as well as adapting new technologies to their work. The human experience is an important consideration for designers – how might future interests and innovations impact how people engage in the landscapes around them?

Human–environment relationships reflect past, current, and changing social and environmental conditions; therefore, it is vital to observe and anticipate societal shifts that will influence this relationship in the future. A focus on sustainability goals as well as climate change response has implications for many realms of design practice. From small-scale decisions such as material selection to regional scale planning like transportation systems, choices are shaped by current concerns and new information. Likewise, public health concerns have long informed decisions by landscape architects, however, those concerns persist and have intensified. Research is continuing to shed light on the role that the physical environment plays in healthy lifestyle choices and in direct contributions to adverse or positive health outcomes. Similarly, advances in technology and their impact on human activities is not new. While the advent of the personal computer and phone have significantly changed how people access and share information, so did the telegraph, telephone, and television. While designers are often at the forefront of technology adoption in their practices, they also have an opportunity to incorporate these advances into their place designs.

Careful and ongoing consideration of how these and other concerns are influencing changes in environmental behaviors is needed. Designers should be proactively addressing current issues and incorporating new knowledge into their design decisions. While accurately forecasting potential new issues or societal shifts in understanding is impossible, continued monitoring and consideration of the human–environment relationship is essential. The thoughtful evaluation of landscape impacts on individuals and communities, from personal satisfaction to the effective management of systems, will provide important measures for improving the outdoor environment.

POTENTIAL EXERCISE AND PROJECT

An indoor exercise
Site analysis and round table discussions

1. Assign a city that everyone in the class is familiar with (a nearby city or the city where campus is located).
2. Divide students into groups.
3. Find historical data (maps, pictures, written oral history, newspapers, etc.) and try to draw out the lifestyle or daily experience of residents 50, 20, and 10 years ago.
4. Present findings to the class in groups.
5. Conduct a roundtable discussion afterward:
   - What do you see or predict changing in the future of this city?
   - What will be the biggest issue or element that may change the city's form (again)?
   - What do you think will change between people and their environmental relationships with these changes?

Potential project

A future city Note: Continues from the previous indoor exercise.

Write a scenario of the future vision of a city using two of the following assumptions:

- 50% of automobiles are self-driving
- 50% of the transportation modes are something other than personal cars (bikes, scooters, skateboards, on foot, or other)
- 50% of population works from home
- Local regulations require 50% of the city's land cover to be pervious materials
- Active living principles are embraced by the city and residents
- Nature prescriptions are supported
- Solar power becomes the city's main energy source
- Sea level rises by 2 feet

REFERENCES

Abass, Z. I., Andrews, F., & Tucker, R. (2020). Socializing in the suburbs: Relationships between neighbourhood design and social interaction in low-density housing contexts. *Journal of Urban Design, 25*(1), 108–133.

Adlakha, D., Budd, E. L., Gernes, R., Sequeira, S., & Hipp, J. A. (2014). Use of emerging technologies to assess differences in outdoor physical activity in St. Louis, Missouri. *Frontiers in Public Health, 2*, 41. doi:10.3389/fpubh.2014.00041

Adlakha, D., Marquet, O., Hipp, J. A., & Tully, M. A. (2017). Pokémon GO or Pokémon Gone: How can cities respond to trends in technology linking people and space? *Cities & Health, 1*(1), 89–94. doi:10.1080/23748834.2017.1358560

Agyman, J. (2010, October 17). *Inclusive or exclusive spaces?* Retrieved from https://julianagyeman.com/2010/10/17/inclusive-or-exclusive-spaces/

Alex Garvin & Associates, Inc. (2004, December 15). *The Beltline Emerald Necklace: Atlanta's new public realm.* Atlanta, GA: Trust for Public Land. Retrieved from https://beltline.org/wp-content/uploads/2012/04/Emerald-Necklace-Study1.pdf

Allee, W. C. (1938). *The social life of animals.* New York, NY: Norton.

Allen, D. J. (2014). *Operating within "transit deserts:" The application of just, open and equitable circulator systems within outer urban residential neighborhoods.* Doctoral dissertation, Proquest Digital Dissertations (3626225).

Allen, D. J. (2017). *Lost in the transit desert: Race, transit access, and suburban form.* London: Routledge.

Altman, I. (1975). *The environment and social behavior.* Monterey, CA: Brooks/Cole.

Altman, I. (1976). Privacy: A conceptual analysis. *Environment and Behavior, 8*(1), 7–29.

Altman, B. (2001). Disability definitions, models, classification schemes, and applications. In G. Albrecht, K. Seelman, & M. Bury (Eds.), *Handbook of disability studies* (pp. 97–122). New York, NY: Sage Publications.

Althoff, T., White, R. W., & Horvitz, E. (2016). Influence of Pokémon Go on physical activity: Study and implications. *Journal of Medical Internet Research, 18*(12), e315. doi:10.2196/jmir.6759

American Academy of Pediatrics. (n.d.). Ages and stages. *Healthy Children.* Retrieved from https://www.healthychildren.org/english/ages-stages/pages/default.aspx

American Psychological Association. (n.d.). *Sexual orientation and gender diversity.* Retrieved from https://www.apa.org/pi/lgbt

American Society of Landscape Architects (ASLA). (2018). *Professional licensure policy statement.* Washington, DC.

American Society of Landscape Architects (ASLA). (n.d.a). *Professional practice network: Children's outdoor environments.* Retrieved from https://www.asla.org/children.aspx

American Society of Landscape Architects (ASLA). (n.d.b). *Professional practice network: Universal design: Playgrounds.* Retrieved from https://www.asla.org/universalplaygrounds.aspx

Amin, A. (2009). Collective culture and urban public space. *Public Space.* Retrieved from https://www.publicspace.org/multimedia/-/post/collective-culture-and-urban-public-space

Amster, R. (2003). Patterns of exclusion: Sanitizing space, criminalizing homelessness. *Social Justice, 30*(1), 195–221.

Angeles, L., & Roberton, J. (2020). Empathy and inclusive public safety in the city: Examining LGBTQ2+ voices and experiences of intersectional discrimination. *Womens Studies International Forum, 78*, 102313.

Appleton, J. (1975). *The experience of landscape.* London: Wiley.

Appleyard, D., & Lintell, M. (1972). The environmental quality of city streets: The residents' viewpoint. *Journal of the American Institute of Planners, 38*(2), 84–101.

Armstrong, T. (2020). The twelve stages of the human life cycle. *American Institute for Learning and Human Development*. Retrieved from https://www.institute4learning.com/resources/articles/the 12-stages-of-life/

Arnstein, S. R. (1969). A ladder of citizen participation. *Journal of the American Planning Association, 35*(4), 216–224.

Art of Regional Change. (n.d.). *Youth Voices for Change*. Retrieved from http://artofregionalchange.ucdavis.edu/?page_id=38

Arthur, P., & Passini, R. (2002). *Wayfinding: People, signs, and architecture* (Limited Commemorative Edition). Ontario, Canada: Focus Strategic Communications.

Ashton, N. L., & Shaw, M. E. (1980). Empirical investigations of a reconceptualized personal space. *Bulletin of the Psychonomic Society, 15*(5), 309–312.

Association for Community Design. (n.d.). *About*. Retrieved from https://www.communitydesign.org/about

Balomenou, N., & Garrod, B. (2019). Photographs in tourism research: Prejudice, power, performance and participant-generated images. *Tourism Management, 70*, 201–217.

Barcelona, A. de (2017). Mesura de govern: Urbanisme amb perspectiva de genere. *L'urbanisme de la vida quotidiana.Area d'Ecologia, Urbanisme i Mobilitat*, Barcelona.

Barker, R. G. (1968). *Ecological psychology*. Stanford, CA: Stanford University Press.

Barry, S. J. (2014). Using social media to discover public values, interests, and perceptions about cattle grazing on park lands. *Environmental Management, 53*(2), 454–464.

Barth, B. (2015). *Virtual reality is making a leap. Will landscape architects be ready?* Retrieved from https://landscapearchitecturemagazine.org/2015/12/08/get-real/

Baum, A., & Paulus, P. B. (1987). Crowding. In D. Stokols & I. Altman (Eds.), *Handbook of environmental psychology* (pp. 533–570). New York, NY: Wiley.

Boardman, J. D., Barnes, L. L., Wilson, R. S., Evans, D. A., & Mendes de Leon, C. F. (2012). Social disorder, APOE-E4 genotype, and change in cognitive function among older adults living in Chicago. *Social Science and Medicine, 74*(10), 1584–1590.

Bordenkircher, B., O'Neil, R., & Scott Smith, C. (2018). Managing the sharing economy: Municipal policy responses to homesharing, ridesharing and bikesharing in Illinois. *Illinois Municipal Policy Journal, 3*(1), 17–48.

Brooklyn Bridge Park Development Corporation & Michael Van Valkenburgh Associates, Inc. (2005). *Brooklyn Bridge Park 2005 master plan: A framework for design*. Retrieved from https://www.brooklynbridgepark.org/wp-content/uploads/2022/01/Brooklyn-Bridge-Park-MP_2005.pdf

Bronfenbrenner, U. (1977). Toward an experimental ecology of human development. *American Psychologist, 32*(7), 513–531. doi:10.1037/0003-066X.32.7.513

Brown, G., & Kyttä, M. (2014). Key issues and research priorities for public participation GIS (PPGIS): A synthesis based on empirical research. *Applied Geography, 46*, 122–136.

Brown, G., Strickland-Munro, J., Kobryn, H., & Moore, S. A. (2017). Mixed methods participatory GIS: An evaluation of the validity of qualitative and quantitative mapping methods. *Applied Geography, 79*, 153–166.

Brown, J. H., Buono, T., Burke, M., Delaplane, T., Jones, J. P., & Wewer, D. (2021). *National Park Service campground design guidelines*. Cultural Landscape Guidance Documents. U.S. Department of the Interior, National Park Service. Retrieved from https://irma.nps.gov/DataStore/Reference/Profile/2286534

Brownson, R. C., Boehmer, T. K., & Luke, D. A. (2005). Declining rates of physical activity in the United States: What are the contributors? *Annual Review of Public Health, 26*, 421–443.

Brownson, R. C., Hoehner, C. M., Day, K., Forsyth, A., & Sallis, J. F. (2009). Measuring the built environment for physical activity: State of the science. *American Journal of Preventive Medicine, 36*(4), Supplement, S99–S123.E12. doi:10.1016/j.amepre.2009.01.005

Cadórniga, H. F., & de la Peña, D. (2017). El carrito: Rolling out the cart. In D. de la Peña, D. J. Allen, R. T. Hester, J. Hou, L. J. Lawson, & M. J. McNally (Eds.), *Design as democracy: Techniques for collective creativity* (pp. 64–67). Washington, DC: Island Press.

Calkins, M. (2012). *The sustainable sites handbook: A complete guide to the principles, strategies, and best practices for sustainable landscapes*. John Wiley & Sons, Inc.

Calthorpe, P. (1993). *The next American metropolis: Ecology, community, and the American dream*. New York, NY: Princeton Architectural Press.

Calthorpe, P., Corbett, M., Duany, A., Moule, E., Plater-Zyberk, E., & Polyzoides, S. (n.d.). Ahwahnee principles for resource-efficient communities. *Local Government Commission*. Retrieved from https://www.lgc.org/who-we-are/ahwahnee/principles/

Capaldi, C. A., Passmore, H. A., Nisbet, E. K., Zelenski, J. M., & Dopko, R. L. (2015). Flourishing in nature: A review of the benefits of connecting with nature and its application as a wellbeing intervention. *International Journal of Wellbeing, 5*(4), 1–16. doi:10.5502/ijw.v5i4.449

Carpiano, R. M. (2009). Come take a walk with me: The "go-along" interview as a novel method for studying the implications of place for health and well-being. *Health & Place*, 15(1), 263–272.

Carson, R. (1962). *Silent spring*. Boston, MA: Houghton Mifflin.

Cassella, C. (2019). There's a climate threat facing Pacific islands that's more dire than losing land, *Science Alert*, [on-line], Available at: https://www.sciencealert.com/pacific-islanders-are-in-a-climate-crisis-as-rising-sea-levels-threaten-water

Cassidy, R. (2018). Rethinking prison design: Iowa Correctional Institution for Women. *Building Design + Construction*. Retrieved from https://www.bdcnetwork.com/rethinking-prison-design-iowa-correctional-institution-women

Catterall, P., & Azzouz, A. (2021). *Queering public space: Exploring the relationship between queer communities and public spaces*. Retrieved from https://www.arup.com/perspectives/publications/research/section/queering-public-space

Center for Active Design. (n.d.). *Designing for workplace wellbeing*. Retrieved from https://web.archive.org/web/20210921061139/https://centerforactivedesign.org/designingforworkplacewellbeing

Center for Community Health and Development. (n.d.). Building culturally competent organizations. In *The community tool box* (Chapter 27, Section 7), University of Kansas. Retrieved from https://ctb.ku.edu/en/table-of-contents/culture/cultural-competence/culturally-competent-organizations/main

Center for Disease Control (CDC). (n.d.). *Overweight & obesity: Causes of obesity*. Retrieved from https://www.cdc.gov/obesity/basics/causes.html

Central Park. (n.d.) Retrieved July 6, 2021 from DavisWiki: https://localwiki.org/davis/Central_Park

Central Park and Davis Farmer's Market. (n.d.). Department of Human Ecology, University of California, Davis. Retrieved from https://humanecology.ucdavis.edu/market

Cervero, R. (1994). Transit villages: From idea to implementation. *Access*, 5, 8–13. University of California Transportation Center (UCTC). Berkeley, CA. Retrieved from https://www.accessmagazine.org/wp-content/uploads/sites/7/2016/07/access05-02-Transit-Villages.pdf

Cervero, R. (1995). Planned communities, self-containment and commuting: A cross-national perspective. *Urban Studies*, 32(7), 1135–1161.

Chambers, R. (2006). Participatory mapping and geographic information systems: Whose map? Who is empowered and who disempowered? Who gains and who loses? *The Electronic Journal of Information Systems in Developing Countries*, 25(1), 1–11.

Chappell, C. (2018, November 26). Climate change in the US will hurt poor people the most, according to a bombshell federal report. *CNBC*. Retrieved from https://www.cnbc.com/2018/11/26/climate-change-will-hurt-poor-people-the-most-federal-report.html

Chatterjee, K., Chng, S., Clark, B., Davis, A., De Vos, J., Ettema, D. ... Reardon, L. (2020). Commuting and wellbeing: A critical overview of the literature with implications for policy and future research. *Transport Reviews*, 40(1), 5–34.

Chawla, L. (Ed.). (2002). *Growing up in an urbanizing world*. Paris and London: UNESCO Publishing and Earthscan.

Chawla, L., Keena, K., Pevec, I., & Stanley, E. (2014). Green schoolyards as havens from stress and resources for resilience in childhood and adolescence. *Health & Place*, 28, 1–13.

Chinurum, J. N., Ogunjlmi, L. O., & O'Neill, C. B. (2014). Gender and sports in contemporary society. *Journal of Educational and Social Research*, 4(7), 25–25.

Chu, C. (2022). *Gender-Inclusive Planning and Design for Los Angeles Parks*. UCLA eScholarship. https://escholarship.org/uc/item/4ht60519#page=30

City of Fremantle. (n.d.) *Esplanade Youth Plaza*. Retrieved from https://www.fremantle.wa.gov.au/community/sport-and-recreation/esplanade-youth-plaza

City Repair Project. (n.d.). Retrieved from https://cityrepair.org/

City of Vancouver. (2020). VanPlay: Vancouver's Parks and Recreation Services Master Plan. Retrieved from https://vancouver.ca/parks-recreation-culture/vanplay-parks-and-recreation-strategy.aspx

Clark, C., & Uzzell, D. L. (2002). The affordances of the home, neighbourhood, school and town centre for adolescents. *Journal of Environmental Psychology*, 22(1–2), 95–108.

Clarke, P. J., Weuve, J., Barnes, L., Evans, D. A., & Mendes de Leon, C. F. (2015). Cognitive decline and the neighborhood environment. *Annals of Epidemiology*, 25(11), 849–854.

Clay, G. (1980). *Close-up: How to read the American City*. Chicago, IL: The University of Chicago Press.

Climate Central. (2019, October 29). *Flooded future: Global vulnerability to sea level rise worse than previously understood*. Retrieved from https://assets.ctfassets.net/cxgxgstp8r5d/6mRq4VMSLqgzGJ5lfjPfld/45c4e5e20ed1985b75ac680cde40cb27/2019CoastalDEMReport.pdf

Cohen, S., Underwood, L. G., & Gottlieb, B. H. (Eds.). (2000). *Social support measurement and intervention: A guide for health and social scientists*. Oxford: Oxford University Press.

Collier, J., & Collier, M. (1986). *Visual anthropology: Photography as a research method*. Albuquerque, NM: University of New Mexico Press.

Comerio, M. C. (1984). Community design: Idealism and entrepreneurship. *Journal of Architectural and Planning Research, 1*(4), 227–243.

Community Design Assistance Center. (n.d.). *About CDAC*. College of Architecture and Urban Studies, Virginia Tech. Retrieved from https://cdac.caus.vt.edu/about-cdac/

Congress for the New Urbanism (CNU). (2001). *Charter of the New Urbanism*. Retrieved from https://www.cnu.org/who-we-are/charter-new-urbanism

Congress for the New Urbanism (CNU). (2018). 25 *Great ideas of New Urbanism*. Retrieved from https://www.cnu.org/sites/default/files/25-great-ideas-book.pdf

Conn, M. K. (1988). Adolescence and the environment: Editor's introduction. *Children's Environments Quarterly, 5*(2), 2–3.

Cooper, C. (2014). *Human spaces report: Biophilic design in the workplace*. Singapore: Interface. Retrieved from https://interfaceinc.scene7.com/is/content/InterfaceInc/Interface/AsiaPac/WebsiteContentAssets/Documents/Press%20Releases/Human%20Spaces%20Report/wc_ap-humanspacesreport2015.pdf

Cooper, I. (2001). Post-occupancy evaluation - where are you? *Building Research & Information, 29*(2), 158–163.

Coppel, G., & Wüstemann, H. (2017). The impact of urban green space on health in Berlin, Germany: Empirical findings and implications for urban planning. *Landscape and Urban Planning, 167*, 410–418. doi:10.1016/j.landurbplan.2017.06.015

Corbett, J. (2009). *Good practices in participatory mapping: A review prepared for the International Fund for Agricultural Development (IFAD)*. Retrieved from https://www.ifad.org/documents/38714170/39144386/PM_web.pdf/7c1eda69-8205-4c31-8912-3c25d6f90055

Cordell, H. K., & Super, G. R. (2000). Trends in Americans' outdoor recreation. In W.C. Gartner & D. W. Lime (Eds.), *Trends in outdoor recreation, leisure and tourism* (pp. 133-144). New York, NY: CABI Publishing.

Cosco, N. G., Moore, R. C., & Islam, M. Z. (2010). Behavior mapping: A method for linking preschool physical activity and outdoor design. *Medicine & Science in Sports & Exercise, 42*(3), 513–519.

Costall, A. (1995). Socializing affordances. *Theory & Psychology, 5*(4), 467–481.

Council on Environmental Quality (CEQ) & California Governor's Office of Planning and Research (OPR). 2014, February 14. *NEPA and CEQA: Integrating State and Federal Environmental Reviews*. Retrieved from https://www.energy.gov/nepa/downloads/nepa-and-ceqa-integrating-state-and-federal-environmental-reviews-final

Cranz, G. (1982). *The politics of park design: A history of urban parks in America*. Cambridge, MA: The MIT Press.

Cranz, G. (1980). Women in urban parks. *Signs: Journal of Women in Culture and Society, 5*(3), S79–S95.

Crawford, M. R., Holder, M. D., & O'Connor, B. P. (2017). Using mobile technology to engage children with nature. *Environment and Behavior, 49*(9), 959–984. doi:10.1177/0013916516673870

Crowe, T. (1991). *Crime prevention through environmental design*. Boston, MA: National Crime Prevention Institute – Butterworth Heinemann, Boston, 1991.

Cushing, F. H., Green, J., & Eggan, F. (1979). *Zuñi: Selected writings of Frank Hamilton Cushing*. University of Nebraska Press.

Darbyshire, P., MacDougall, C., & Schiller, W. (2005). Multiple methods in qualitative research with children: More insight or just more? *Qualitative Research, 5*(4), 417–436.

Davidoff, P. (1965). Advocacy and pluralism in planning. *Journal of the American Institute of Planners, 31*(4), 331–338.

Davidson, E. (September/October 2011). The Atlanta BeltLine: A green future. *Public Roads, September/October 2011, Vol. 75.* FHWA-HRT-11-006. Retrieved from https://highways.dot.gov/public-roads/septemberoctober-2011/atlanta-beltline-green-future

Davis Central Park (n.d.). The Living New Deal. Retrieved from https://livingnewdeal.org/projects/davis-central-park-davis-ca/

Davis Farmers Market. (n.d.). Retrieved from https://www.davisfarmersmarket.org/about-us/

Day, K. (2000). The ethic of care and women's experiences of public space. *Journal of Environmental Psychology, 20*(2), 103–124. doi:10.1006/jevp.1999.0152

Day, K. (2006). Active living and social justice: Planning for physical activity in low-income, black, and Latino Communities. *Journal of the American Planning Association, 72*(1), 88–99. doi:10.1080/01944360608976726

D'Costa, K. (2017). The American obsession with lawns. *Scientific American*. Retrieved from https://blogs.scientificamerican.com/anthropology-in-practice/the-american-obsession-with-lawns/

de la Peña, D. (2017). *Sowing seeds of political engagement: The value of contentious projects in design studios*. Voices of place: Proceedings of the 48th Environmental Design Research Association Conference. Madison, WI: EDRA.

de la Peña, D., Allen, D. J., Hester, R. T., Hou, J., Lawson, L., & McNally, M. J. (Eds.). (2017). *Design as democracy: Techniques for collective creativity*. Washington, DC: Island Press.

Dennis, S. F. Jr., Gaulocher, S., Carpiano, R. M., & Brown, D. (2009). Participatory photo mapping (PPM): Exploring an integrated method for health and place research with young people. *Health & Place, 15*(2), 466–473.

Design Workshop. (2018). *ASLA Professional Awards: VanPlay: Plan to Play*. Retrieved from https://www.asla.org/2018awards/455350-VanPlay.html

Devlin, A. S. (Ed.). (2018). *Environmental psychology and human well-being: Effects of built and natural settings*. London: Academic Press.

Dillon, I., & Green, J. (2019a). *Universal design*. Retrieved from https://www.asla.org/universaldesign.aspx

Dillon, I., & Green, J. (2019b). *Universal design: Parks and plazas*. Retrieved from https://www.asla.org/universalparksandplazas.aspx

Di Masso, A., Williams, D. R., Raymond, C. M., Buchecker, M., Degenhardt, B., Devine-Wright, P. ... Von Wirth, T. (2019). Between fixities and flows: Navigating place attachments in an increasingly mobile world. *Journal of Environmental Psychology, 61*, 125–133.

Disability Rights Education & Defense Fund. (n.d.). *International disability rights: International laws*. Retrieved from https://dredf.org/legal-advocacy/international-disability-rights/international-laws/

Dobis, E. A., Stephens, H. M., Skidmore, M., & Goetz, S. J. (2020). Explaining the spatial variation in American life expectancy. *Social Science & Medicine, 246*, 112759. doi:10.1016/j.socscimed.2019.112759

Driskell, D. (2002). *Creating better cities with children and youth: A manual for participation*. Paris: UNESCO.

Duzenli, T., Bayramoglu, E., & Özbilen, A. (2010). Needs and preferences of adolescents in open urban spaces. *Scientific Research and Essays, 5*(2), 201–216.

Environmental Design Research Association (EDRA). (n.d.). *EDRA Great Places Award*. Retrieved from https://www.edra.org/page/greatplaces

Ehrlich, T. (2000). Preface. In T. Ehrlich (Ed.), *Civic responsibility and higher education*. Westport, CT: American Council on Education and Oryx Press.

Eisenmann, J. C., Gentile, D. A., Welk, G. J., Callahan, R., Strickland, S., Walsh, M. ... Walsh, D. A. (2008). SWITCH: Rationale, design, and implementation of a community, school, and family-based intervention to modify behaviors related to childhood obesity. *BMC Public Health, 8*, 223.

England, K. V. L. (1993). Changing suburbs, changing women: Geographic perspectives on suburban women and suburbanization. *Frontiers: A Journal of Women Studies, 14*(1), 24–43.

Enterprise staff. (2006, September 24). More powerful than a burrowing owl, it's Davis, A to Z. *The Davis Enterprise*. Retrieved from https://infoweb.newsbank.com/apps/news/document-view?p=WORLDNEWS&docref=news/114611F528FD83D8/

Ericksen, J. A. (1977). An analysis of the journey to work for women. *Social Problems, 24*(4), 428–435.

Erikson, E. H. (1963). *Youth: Change and challenge*. New York, NY: Basic Books.

Evans, G. W. (2001). Environmental stress and health. In A. Baum, T. Revenson, & J. E. Singer (Eds.), *Handbook of health psychology* (pp. 571–610). Mahwah, NJ: Erlbaum.

Evans, G. W. (2003). The built environment and mental health. *Journal of Urban Health: Bulletin of the New York Academy of Medicine, 80*(4), 536–555.

Evans, G. W., & Kantrowitz, E. (2002). Socioeconomic status and health: The potential role of environmental risk exposure. *Annual Review of Public Health, 23*, 303–331.

Evans, G. W., Wells, N. M., & Moch, A. (2003). Housing and mental health: A review of the evidence and a methodological and conceptual critique. *Journal of Social Issues, 59*(3), 475–500.

Evans, W. P., Owens, P. E., & Marsh, S. C. (2005). Environmental factors, locus of control, and adolescent suicide risk. *Child and Adolescent Social Work, 22*(3–4), 301–319.

Faber Taylor, A., Kuo, F. E., & Sullivan, W. C. (2002). Views of nature and self-discipline: Evidence from inner city children. *Journal of Environmental Psychology, 22*, 49–63.

Fenster, T. (2005). The right to the gendered city: Different formations of belonging in everyday life. *Journal of Gender Studies, 14*(3), 217–231.

Fisk, D. M. (2001). American Labor in the 20th century. *Compensation and Working Conditions, 6*(3), 3–8.

Foster, A. C. (2016). A closer look at spending patterns of older Americans. *US Bureau of Labor Statistics: Beyond the Numbers, 5*(4). Retrieved from https://www.bls.gov/opub/btn/volume-5/spending-patterns-of-older-americans.htm

Frost, J. L., & Wortham, S. C. (1988). The evolution of American playgrounds. *Young Children, 43*(5), 19–28.

Francis, M. (1989). Control as a dimension of public-space quality. In I. Altman & E. H. Zube (Eds.), *Public places and spaces* (pp. 147–172). Boston, MA: Springer.

Francis, M. (1999). Proactive practice: Visionary thought and participatory action in environmental design. *Places, 12*(2), 60–67.

Francis, M. (2001). A case study method for landscape architecture. *Landscape Journal, 20*(1), 15–29.

Francis, M. (2010). Mixed-life places. In T. Banerjee & A. Loukaitou-Sideris (Eds.), *The Routledge companion to urban design* (pp. 432–445). New York, NY: Routledge.

Francis, M., & Griffith, L. (2011). The meaning and design of farmers' markets as public space: An issue-based case study. *Landscape Journal, 30*(2), 261–279.

Francis, M., Koo, J., & Ramirez, S. (2010). *Just a comfortable place to sit: Davis sittable space study*. Department of Environmental Design, University of California, Davis. Retrieved from https://humanecology.ucdavis.edu/sites/g/files/dgvnsk161/files/inline-files/Just%20A%20Comfortable%20Place%20to%20Sit%20Final%20Report.pdf

Franck, K. A. (1989). Women and urban public space: Research, design, and policy issues. In I. Altman & E. H. Zube (Eds.), *Public places and spaces*. Human Behavior and Environment. Boston, MA: Springer.

Fraser, M., Munoz, S. A., & MacRury, S. (2019). What motivates participants to adhere to green exercise? *International Journal of Environmental Research and Public Health, 16*(10), 1832. doi:10.3390/ijerph16101832

Fredericksen, E. (2002). Architecture that shreds (designing skateboarding parks). *Architecture, 91*(4), 46–+.

Frey, W. (2020). The nation is diversifying even faster than predicted, according to census data. *Brookings*. Retrieved from https://www.brookings.edu/research/new-census-data-shows-the-nation-is-diversifying-even-faster-than-predicted/

Frisby, D. (2013). *Georg Simmel*. New York, NY: Routledge.

Frumkin, H. (2001). Beyond toxicity: Human health and the natural environment. *American Journal of Preventive Medicine, 20*(3), 234–240.

Frumkin, H. (2002). Viewpoint: Urban sprawl and public health. *Public Health Reports, 17*, 201–217.

Frumkin, H., Frank, L., & Jackson, R. J. (2004). *Urban sprawl and public health: Designing, planning, and building for healthy communities*. Washington, DC: Island Press.

Gade, D. W. (1976). The Latin American Central plaza as a functional space. *Publication Series (Conference of Latin Americanist Geographers), 5*, 16–23.

Garde, A. (2009) Sustainable by design? Insights from U.S. LEED-ND pilot projects. *Journal of the American Planning Association, 75*(4), 424–440. doi:10.1080/01944360903148174

Gardiner, J. (2021, June). Public spaces that girls want to use: A design problem. *The Possible: Healthier Places*. Issue 7. https://www.the-possible.com/public-spaces-that-girls-want-to-use-a-design-problem/

Gaster, S. (1991). Urban children's access to the neighborhood: Changes over three generations. *Environment and Behavior, 23*(1), 70–85.

Gehl, J., & Svarre, B. (2013). *How to study public life* (Vol. 2). Washington, DC: Island Press.

Gesell, A. (1934). *An atlas of infant behavior: A systematic delineation of the forms and early growth of human behavior patterns*. Normative series (with H. Thompson and C. S. Amatruda). Naturalistic series (with A. V. Keliher, F. L. Ilg, and J. J. Carlson). New Haven, CT: Yale University Press.

Gibson, D. (2009). *The wayfinding handbook: Information design for public places*. New York, NY: Princeton Architectural Press.

Gibson, J. J. (1979). *The theory of affordances: The ecological approach to visual perception*. Boston, MA: Houghton-Mifflin.

Gibson, J. J. (1979). *The ecological approach to visual perception*. New York, NY: Houghton Mifflin.

Gibson, S., Loukaitou-Sideris, A., & Mukhija, V. (2019). Ensuring park equity: A California case study. *Journal of Urban Design, 24*(3), 385–405.

Gieseking, J. J., Mangold, W., Katz, C., Low, S., & Saegert, S. (Eds.). (2014). *The people, place, and space reader*. New York, NY: Routledge.

Ginsburg, K. R. (2007). The importance of play in promoting healthy child development and maintaining strong parent-child bonds. *Pediatrics, 119*(1), 182–191.

Global Designing Cities Initiative. (n.d.). *Global street design guide*. Retrieved from https://globaldesigningcities.org/publication/global-street-design-guide/

Gobster, P. H. (2002). Managing urban parks for a racially and ethnically diverse clientele. *Leisure Sciences, 24*(2), 143–159.

Godtman Kling, K., Margaryan, L., & Fuchs, M. (2020). (In)equality in the outdoors: Gender perspective on recreation and tourism media in the Swedish mountains. *Current Issues in Tourism, 23*(2), 233–247.

Goličnik, B. (2005). *People in place: A configuration of physical form and the dynamic patterns of spatial occupancy in urban open public space*, PhD Thesis, School of Landscape Architecture, Edinburgh College of Art/Heriot-Watt University.

Golledge, R. G. (Ed) (1999). *Wayfinding behavior: Cognitive mapping and other spatial processes*. Baltimore, MD: The Johns Hopkins University Press.

Goltsman, S. M., Gilbert, T. A., Wohlford, S. D., & Kirk, N. L. (1993). *The accessibility checklist: An evaluation system for buildings and outdoor settings second edition: User's guide*. Berkeley, CA: MIG Communications.

Goltsman, S., & Iacofano, D. (Eds). (2007). *The inclusive city: Design solutions for buildings, neighborhoods, and urban spaces*. Berkeley, CA: MIG Communications.

Gray, P. (2017, September). Plenary. Talk presented at International Play Association Conference, Calgary, Canada.

Great Places Award. (2021). 2021 Great Places Award brochure. Environmental Design Research Association. Retrieved from https://www.edra.org/page/greatplaces

Green Business Certification Inc. (GBCI). (2014). *SITES v2 reference guide for sustainable land design and development*. Green Business Certification Inc.

Greeno, J. G. (1994). Gibson's affordances. *Psychological Review, 101*(2), 336–42.

Grimm-Pretner, D. (2011). Engendered spaces. In L. Mozingo & L. Jewell (Eds). *Women in landscape architecture: Essays on history and practice*, 174–180.

Guerra, E. (2016). planning for cars that drive themselves: Metropolitan planning organizations, regional transportation plans, and autonomous vehicles. *Journal of Planning Education and Research, 36*(2), 210–224. doi:10.1177/0739456X15613591

Guerra, E., & Morris, E. A. (2018). Cities, automation, and the self-parking elephant in the room. *Planning Theory & Practice, 19*(2), 291–297. doi:10.1080/14649357.2017.1416776

Haas, M. (1996). Children in the junkyard. *Childhood Education, 72*, 345–351.

Hale, K., & Provenzan, K. (2021). *Inclusive design for outdoor spaces*. Retrieved from https://www.greenschoolyards.org/inclusive-design

Hall, E. T. (1990a edition). *The hidden dimension*. New York, NY: Anchor Books.

Hall, E. T. (1990b edition). *The silent language*. New York, NY: Anchor Books.

Hall, G. (2013, January 17). Why DreamWorks is such a great place to work. *L.A. Biz*. Retrieved from https://www.bizjournals.com/losangeles/news/2013/01/17/dream-job-dreamworks-animation-places.html

Halprin, L. (1963). *Cities*. New York, NY: Reinhold.

Halprin, L. (1983, September/October). Cuts and fills (letters to the editors). *Landscape Architecture Magazine, 30*.

Halprin, L. (1984, May/June). Cuts and fills (letters to the editor). *Landscape Architecture Magazine, 24*, 26–27.

Halprin, L., & Burns, J. (1974). *Taking part: A workshop approach to collective creativity*. Cambridge, MA: MIT Press.

Hamer Center for Community Design. (n.d.). *About*. Stuckeman School, College of Arts and Architecture, Pennsylvania State University. Retrieved from https://sites.psu.edu/hamercenter/about/

Hamerlinck, K., Buescher, T., Javellana, A., Iversen, L., Bounds, T., Brouillette, J. … Stevens, J. (2015). Landscapes of Justice: Redefining the prison environment. 2015 ASLA Student Awards. Retrieved from https://www.asla.org/2015studentawards/95349.html/

Hamstead, Z. A., Fisher, D., Ilieva, R. T., Wood, S. A., McPhearson, T., & Kremer, P. (2018). Geolocated social media as a rapid indicator of park visitation and equitable park access. *Computers, Environment and Urban Systems, 72*, 38–50.

Hansel Bauman Architect. (2010). *Gallaudet University DeafSpace design guidelines volume 1*. (Working draft, August 31, 2010). Retrieved from https://app.dcoz.dc.gov/Exhibits/2010/ZC/15-24/Exhibit95.pdf

Hasenbush, A., Flores, A. R., & Herman, J. L. (2019). Gender identity nondiscrimination laws in public accommodations: A review of evidence regarding safety and privacy in public restrooms, locker rooms, and changing rooms. *Sexuality Research and Social Policy, 16*, 70–83. doi:10.1007/s13178-018-0335-z

Hardin, G. (1968). The tragedy of the commons. *Science, 162*(3859), 1243–1248. http://www.jstor.org/stable/1724745

Hardin, M., & Greer, J. D. (2009). The influence of gender-role socialization, media use and sports participation on perceptions of gender-appropriate sports. *Journal of Sport Behavior, 32*(2), 207.

Harris, K. (2007). The impact of aging populations on outdoor recreation. *American Trails*. Retrieved from https://www.americantrails.org/resources/the-impact-of-aging-populations-on-outdoor-recreation

Hart, R. A. (1997). *Children's participation: The theory and practice of involving young citizens in community development and environmental care*. London: Earthscan.

Hartig, T., Evans, G. W., Jamner, L. D., Davis, D. S., & Gärling, T. (2003). Tracking restoration in natural and urban field settings. *Journal of Environmental Psychology, 23*(2), 109–123.

Hartig, T., Mang, M., & Evans, G. W. (1991). Restorative effects of natural environment experiences. *Environment and Behavior, 23*(1), 3–26.

Hasenbush, A., Flores, A. R., & Herman, J. L. (2019). Gender identity nondiscrimination laws in public accommodations: A review of evidence regarding safety and privacy in public restrooms, locker rooms, and changing rooms. *Sexuality Research & Social Policy, 16*(1), 70–83.

Hatzenbuehler, M. L. (2009). How does sexual minority stigma "get under the skin"? A psychological mediation framework. *Psychological Bulletin, 135*(5), 707.

Hayden, D. (1995). *The power of place: Urban landscapes as public history*. Cambridge, MA: The MIT Press.

Hayduk, L. A. (1983). Personal space: Where we now stand. *Psychological Bulletin, 94*(2), 293–335.

Hediger, H. (1955). *Studies of the psychology and behavior of animals in zoos and circuses*. New York, NY: Criterion.

Heft, H. (1988). Affordances of children's environments: A functional approach to environmental description. *Children's Environments Quarterly, 5*(3), 29–37.

Heft, H. (2001). *Ecological psychology in context: James Gibson, Roger Barker, and the legacy of William James's radical empiricism*. Mahwah, NJ: Lawrence Erlbaum Associates, Inc.

Heft, H., & Chawla, L. (2005). Children as agents in sustainable development: The ecology of competence. In C. Spencer & M. Blades (Eds.), *Children and their environments* (pp. 199–216). Cambridge: Cambridge University Press.

Helft, M. (2007, March 10). Google, master of online traffic, helps its workers beat the rush. *The New York Times*. Retrieved from https://www.nytimes.com/2007/03/10/technology/10google.html

Helphand, K. I. (1979, July 16-20). *Environmental autobiography*. Paper presented at the International Conference on Environmental Psychology, University of Surrey, England.

Hendrey, L. B., Glendinning, A., Shucksmith, J., Love, J., & Scott, J. (1994). The developmental context of adolescent life-styles. In R. K. Silbereisen & E. Todt (Eds.), *Adolescence in context: The interplay of family, school, peers, and work in adjustment* (pp. 66–81). New York, NY: Springer-Verlag.

Henley, N. (1977). *Body politics: Power, sex, and nonverbal communication*. Englewood Cliffs, NJ: Prentice Hall.

Herek, G. M., & McLemore, K. A. (2013). Sexual prejudice. *Annual Review of Psychology, 64*, 309–333.

Herrington, S. (1997). The received view of play and the subculture of infants. *Landscape Journal, 16*(2), 149–160.

Herrington, S., & Studtmann, K. (1998). Landscape interventions: New directions for the design of children's outdoor play environments. *Landscape and Urban Planning, 42*(2–4), 191–205.

Hester, R. T. (1979). A womb with a view: How spatial nostalgia affects the designer. *Landscape Architecture, 69*, 475–581.

Hester, R. T. (1983, May/June). Process can be style: Participation and conservations in landscape architecture. *Landscape Architecture Magazine*, no page numbers.

Hester, R. T. (1984a, September/October). Cuts and fills (letters to the editor). *Landscape Architecture Magazine, 20*, 22–24.

Hester, R. T. (1984b). *Planning neighborhood space with people*. New York, NY: Van Nostrand Reinhold.

Hester, R. T. (1985). Subconscious landscapes of hearts. *Places Journal, 2*(3), 10–22.

Hester, R. T. (1987). Community design: Making the grassroots whole. *Built Environment (1978-)*, 45–60.

Hester, R. T. (2012). Scoring collective creativity and legitimizing participatory design. *Landscape Journal, 31*(1/2), 135–143.

Hester, R. T., McNally, M. J., Hale, S., Lancaster, M., Hester, N., & Lancaster, M. (1988). We'd like to tell you …': Children's views of life in Westport, California. *Small Town, 18*(4), 19–24.

Heylighen, A., Van der Linden, V., & Van Steenwinkel, I. (2017). Ten questions concerning inclusive design of the built environment. *Building and Environment, 114*, 507–517. doi:10.1016/j.buildenv.2016.12.008

Hilburg, J. (2018, April 12). What role do architects have in a driverless future? *The Architect's Newspaper*. Retrieved from https://www.archpaper.com/2018/04/driverless-future-architects-role/

Hill, M. (1973). *Planning for multiple objectives: An approach to the evaluation of transportation plans*. Philadelphia: Regional Science Research Institute.

Hird, J. A. (1993). Environmental policy and equity: The case of Superfund. *Journal of Policy Analysis and Management, 12*(2), 323–343.

Hirsch, A. B. (2011). Scoring the participatory city: Lawrence (& Anna) Halprin's take part process. *Journal of Architectural Education, 64*(2), 127–140.

Hirsch, J. A., James, P., Robinson, J. R. M., Eastman, K. M., Conley, K. D., & Laden, F. (2014). Using MapMyFitness to place physical activity into neighborhood context. *Frontiers in Public Health*, 2(19), 1–9. doi:10.3389/fpubh.2014.00019

Ho, C. H., Sasidharan, V., Elmendorf, W., Willits, F. K., Graefe, A., & Godbey, G. (2005). Gender and ethnic variations in urban park preferences, visitation, and perceived benefits. *Journal of Leisure Research*, 37(3), 281–306.

Hood, W., & Basnak, M. (2015). Diverse truths: Unveiling the hidden layers of the shadow catcher commemoration. In B. Tauke, K. Smith, & C. Davis (Eds.), *Diversity and design: Understanding hidden consequences* (pp. 37–53). New York, NY: Routledge.

Horwitz, J., & Klein, S. (1978). An exercise in the use of environmental autobiography for programming and design of a day care center. *Childhood City Newsletter*, 14, 18–19.

Hou, J. (Ed.). (2013). *Transcultural cities: Border crossing and placemaking*. New York, NY: Routledge.

Hou, J. (2013). Transcultural participation: Designing with immigrant communities in Seattle's International District. In J. Hou (Ed.), *Transcultural cities: Border crossing and placemaking* (pp. 222–236). New York, NY: Routledge.

Hou, J., & Rios, M. (2003). Community-driven place making: The social practice of participatory design in the making of Union Point Park. *Journal of Architectural Education*, 57(1), 19–27.

Howard, E. (1920). *Territory in bird life*. London: John Murray.

Howard, K., & Culbertson, K. (2020, June 22). More equitable access to open space? Vancouver has a plan for that. *The City Fix*. Retrieved from https://thecityfix.com/blog/equitable-access-open-space-vancouver-plan-katherine-howard-kurt-culbertson/

Howland, L. (2019a, February 20). *Modesto homeless get a fresh start under 9th Street Bridge*. ABC 10. Retrieved from https://www.abc10.com/article/news/modesto-homeless-get-a-fresh-start-under-9th-street-bridge/103-3aa485ff-16ee-431f-9bc8-6267271a1683

Howland, L. (2019b, March 11). *'It's only me doing it': Modesto's homeless forced to clean up and move as city closes Beard Brook Park*. ABC10. Retrieved from https://www.abc10.com/article/news/modesto-closes-beard-brook-park-homeless-camp/103-73e60b4d-c441-4411-bfe2-d04300f98e6c

H.R.3684–117th Congress (2021–2022): Infrastructure Investment and Jobs Act. (2021, June 4). https://www.congress.gov/bill/117th-congress/house-bill/3684

Huang, Y., & Napawan, N. C. (2021). "Separate but equal?" Understanding gender differences in urban park usage and its implications for gender-inclusive design. *Landscape Journal*, 40(1), 1–16.

Hulko, W., & Hovanes, J. (2018). Intersectionality in the lives of LGBTQ youth: Identifying as LGBTQ and finding community in small cities and rural towns. *Journal of Homosexuality*, 65(4), 427–455.

Humphreys, L. (2010). Mobile social networks and urban public space. *New Media & Society*, 12(5), 763–778. doi:10.1177/1461444809349578

Humphreys, L. (2017). Involvement shield or social catalyst: Thoughts on sociospatial practice of Pokémon GO. *Mobile Media & Communication*, 5(1), 15–19. doi:10.1177/2050157916677864

Hutchison, R. (1994). Women and the elderly in Chicago's public parks. *Leisure Sciences*, 16(4), 229–247.

Hyde, J. S., Bigler, R. S., Joel, D., Tate, C. C., & van Anders, S. M. (2019). The future of sex and gender in psychology: Five challenges to the gender binary. *The American Psychologist*, 74(2), 171–193.

Iacofano, D. S. (2001). *Meeting of the minds: A guide to successful meeting facilitation*. Berkeley, CA: MIG Communication.

IAPS. (2021). *About IAPS: Some history*. Retrieved from https://iaps-association.org/about-iaps/some-history/

Institute for Human Centered Design (IHCD). (2018). *Inclusive design: History*. Retrieved from https://www.humancentereddesign.org/inclusive-design/history

Institute at the Golden Gate (IGG). (2020). *Reflecting on ParkRX models: 2020 ParkRx Census results*. Retrieved from http://instituteatgoldengate.org/parkrx-2020-census

Iowa Department of Corrections (IDOC). (2020). Retrieved from https://doc.iowa.gov/

Isenstadt, S. (2015). Metropolis regained. *Places Journal*, November.

Israel, T. (2003). *Some place like home: Using design psychology to create ideal places*. Hoboken, NJ: Wiley-Academy.

Jackson, J. B. (1984). *Discovering the vernacular landscape*. New Haven, CT: Yale University Press.

Jackson, J. B. (1985). Discovering the vernacular landscape. *Landscape Journal*, 4, 57–60.

Jackson, J. B. (1994). *A sense of place, a sense of time*. New Haven, CT: Yale University Press.

Jacobs, J. (1961). *The death and life of great American cities*. New York, NY: Random House.

Jacobson, J., & Forsyth, A. (2008). Seven American TODs: Good practices for urban design in Transit-Oriented Development projects. *Journal of Transport and Land Use*, 1(2). doi:10.5198/jtlu.v1i2.67

Jackson, R. J., & Sinclair, S. (2012). *Designing healthy communities*. San Francisco, CA: John Wiley & Son, Inc.

James, J. J., Christiana, R. W., & Battista, R. A. (2019). A historical and critical analysis of park prescriptions. *Journal of Leisure Research*, *50*(4), 311–329. doi:10.1080/00222216.2019.1617647

Jefferson, T. (1903). *The writings of Thomas Jefferson* (Vol. 20). Issued under the auspices of the Thomas Jefferson memorial association of the United States.

Jestico, B., Nelson, T., & Winters, M. (2016). Mapping ridership using crowdsourced cycling data. *Journal of Transport Geography*, *52*, 90–97. doi:10.1016/j.jtrangeo.2016.03.006

Jiang, J. (2018, November 28). Teens who are constantly online are just as likely to socialize with their friends offline. *Factank: News in the numbers*. Pew Research Center. https://www.pewresearch.org/fact-tank/2018/11/28/teens-who-are-constantly-online-are-just-as-likely-to-socialize-with-their-friends-offline/

Jim, C. Y., & Chen, W. Y. (2006). Impacts of urban environmental elements on residential housing prices in Guangzhou (China). *Landscape and Urban Planning*, *78*(4), 422–434.

Jones, J. M. (2022). LGBT identification in U.S. ticks up to 7.1%. *Gallup News*. Retrieved online https://news.gallup.com/poll/389792/lgbt-identification-ticks-up.aspx

Jones, S., & Graves, A. (2000). Power plays in public space: Skateboard parks as battlegrounds, gifts, and expressions of self. *Landscape Journal*, *19*, 136–148.

Jorgensen, L. J., Ellis, G. D., & Ruddell, E. (2012). Fear perceptions in public parks: Interactions of environmental concealment, the presence of people recreating, and gender. *Environment and Behavior*, *45*(7), 803–820.

Kaiser, P., Diez Roux, A. V., Mujahid, M., Carnethon, M., Bertoni, A., Adar, S. D. … Lisabeth, L. (2016). Neighborhood environments and incident hypertension in the multi-ethnic study of atherosclerosis. *American Journal of Epidemiology*, *183*(11), 988–997.

Kaitz, M., Gar-Haim, Y., Lehrer, M., & Grossman, E. (2004). Adult attachment style and interpersonal distance. *Attachment & Human Development*, *6*(3), 285–304.

Kane, M. J. (1990). Female involvement in physical recreation—Gender role as a constraint. *Journal of Physical Education, Recreation & Dance*, *61*(1), 52–56.

Kaplan, R., & Herbert, E. J. (1987). Cultural and sub-cultural comparisons in preferences for natural settings. *Landscape and Urban Planning*, *14*, 281–293.

Kaplan, R., & Kaplan, S. (1984). *The experience of nature*. Cambridge, MA: Cambridge University Press.

Kaplan, R., Kaplan, S., & Ryan, R. L. (1998). *With people in mind: Design and management of everyday nature*. Washington, D.C: Island Press.

Kaplan, S. (1995). The restorative benefits of nature: Toward an integrative framework. *Journal of Environmental Psychology*, *15*(3), 169–182.

Katz, M. (2011, October 28). Factoria Joven Skate Park. *Design Milk*. Retrieved from https://design-milk.com/factoria-joven-skate-park/

Kelkar, N. P., & Spinelli, G. (2016). Building social capital through creative placemaking. *Strategic Design Research Journal*, *9*(2), 54–66.

Kerr, J., & Lawson, G. (2020). Augmented reality in design education: Landscape architecture studies as AR experience. *The International Journal of Art & Design Education*, *39*(1), 6–21. doi:10.1111/jade.12227

Kimic, K., Maksymiuk, G., & Suchocka, M. (2019). The application of new technologies in promoting a healthy lifestyle: Selected examples. *Bulletin of Geography. Socio-Economic Series*, *43*(43), 121–130. doi:10.2478/bog-2019-0008

Khan, M. (2012). *Outdoor as learning environment for children at a primary school of Bangladesh* [Unpublished master's thesis]. Bangladesh University of Engineering and Technology, Dhaka, Bangladesh.

Khan, M. (2017). *An outdoor learning environment for and with a primary school community in Bangladesh*. 2017 ASLA Student Awards. Retrieved from https://www.asla.org/2017studentawards/334970.html

Khan, M., Bell, S., McGeown, S., & de Oliveira, E. S. (2020). Designing an outdoor learning environment for and with a primary school community: A case study in Bangladesh. *Landscape Research*, *45*(1), 95–110.

Khan, M., Bell, S., & Wood, J. (Eds.). (2020). *Place, pedagogy and play: Participation, design and research with children*. London: Routledge.

Khan, M., McGeown, S., & Bell, S. (2020). Can an outdoor learning environment improve children's academic attainment? A quasi-experimental mixed methods study in Bangladesh. *Environment and Behavior*, *52*(10), 1079–1104.

Khan, R. L., & Antonucci, T. C. (1980). Convoys over the life course: Attachment, roles and social support. In P. B. Baltes & O. G. Grim (Eds.), *Life-span development and behavior* (Vol. 3, pp. 253–286). New York, NY: Academic Press.

King, M., & de Jong, E. (2016). Legibility and continuity in the built environment. In R. H. Hunter, L. A. Anderson, & B. L. Belza (Eds.), *Community wayfinding: Pathways to understanding* (pp. 61–79). New York, NY: Springer.

Klein, S. (2001). Participation in place: EDRA/Places awards, juror comment. *Places*, *14*(1), 38–40.

Klotz, A., & Bolino, M. C. (2021). Bringing the great outdoors into the workplace: The energizing effect of biophilic work design. *Academy of Management Review*, *46*(2), 231–251.

Knaap, G., & Talen, E. (2005). New urbanism and smart growth: A few words from the academy. *International Regional Science Review*, *28*(2), 107–118. doi:10.1177/0160017604273621

Kneebone, E., & Holmes, N. (2015). *The growing distance between people and jobs in metropolitan America*. Washington, DC: Brookings Institution.

Koo, J. (2012). *Re-created urban landscapes: Brownfields as sustainable public open spaces*. PhD dissertation, University of California, Davis.

Koo, J., Hustedde, R., & Young, R. (2018). Radical walking: Tool, practice, and implications for community development. *Community Development Practice, Fall 2018*, (22), 17–28.

Kondo, M. C., Oyekanmi, K. O., Gibson, A., South, E. C., Bocarro, J., & Hipp, J. A. (2020). Nature prescriptions for health: A review of evidence and research opportunities. *International Journal of Environmental Research and Public Health,*, *17*(12), 4213. doi:10.3390/ijerph17124213

Korpela, K. M. (1989). Place-identity as a product of environmental self-regulation. *Journal of Environmental Psychology*, *9*(3), 241–256.

Korpela, K. M. (1992). Adolescents' favourite places and environmental self-regulation. *Journal of Environmental Psychology*, *12*(3), 249–258.

Krenichyn, K. (2004). Women and physical activity in an urban park: Enrichment and support through an ethic of care. *Journal of Environmental Psychology*, *24*(1), 117–130. doi:10.1016/S0272-4944(03)00053-7

Krenichyn, K. (2006). The only place to go and be in the city': Women talk about exercise, being outdoors, and the meanings of a large urban park. *Health & Place*, *12*(4), 631–643.

Kruger, L. E., Hall, T. E., & Stiefel, M. C. (2008). *Understanding concepts of place in recreation research and management*. Portland OR: USDA Forest Service, Pacific Northwest Research Station.

Kuo, F. E., Sullivan, W. C., Coley, R. L., & Brunson, L. (1998). Fertile ground for community: Inner-city neighborhood common spaces. *American Journal of Community Psychology*, *26*(6), 823–851.

Kuo, M. (2015). How might contact with nature promote human health? Promising mechanisms and a possible central pathway. *Frontiers in Psychology*, *6*, 1093.

Kyttä, M. (2004). The extent of children's independent mobility and the number of actualized affordances as criteria for child-friendly environments. *Journal of Environmental Psychology*, *24*(2), 179–198.

Ladd, F. C. (1977). Residential history: You can go home again. *Landscape*, *21*(2), 15–20.

Ladd, F. C. (1978). City Kids in the absence of… In R. Kaplan, & S. Kaplan (Eds.), *Humanscape: Environments for people* (pp.77–81). North Scituate, MA: Duxbury Press.

Lawton, E., Brymer, E., Clough, P., & Denovan, A. (2017). The relationship between the physical activity environment, nature relatedness, anxiety, and the psychological well-being benefits of regular exercisers. *Frontiers in Psychology*, *8*, 1058. doi:10.3389/fpsyg.2017.01058

Lee, C. (2016). Promoting walking via ease of wayfinding. In R. H. Hunter, L. A. Anderson, & B. L. Belza (Eds.), *Community wayfinding: Pathways to understanding* (pp. 171–193). New York, NY: Springer.

Lee, J., Kim, D., Ryoo, H., & Shin, B. (2016). Sustainable wearables: Wearable technology for enhancing the quality of human life. *Sustainability*, *8*, 466.

Lee, J. E., Zeng, N., Oh, Y., Lee, D., & Gao, Z. (2021). Effects of Pokémon GO on physical activity and psychological and social outcomes: A systematic review. *Journal of Clinical Medicine*, *10*(9), 1860. doi:10.3390/jcm10091860

Leventhal, G., Schanerman, J., & Matturro, M. (1978). Effect of room size, initial approach distance and sex on personal space. *Perceptual and Motor Skills*, *47*(3), 792–794.

Leventhal, T., & Brooks-Gunn, J. (2000). Neighborhoods they live in: The effects of neighborhood residence on child and adolescent outcomes. *Psychological Bulletin*, *126*(2), 309–337.

Lewicka, M. (2011). Place attachment: How far have we come in the last 40 years? *Journal of Environmental Psychology*, *31*(3), 207–230.

Li, D., & Sullivan, W. C. (2016). Impact of views to school landscape on recovery from stress and mental fatigue. *Landscape and Urban Planning*, *148*, 149–158.

Li, J., & Nassauer, J. I. (2020). Cues to care: A systematic analytical review. *Landscape and Urban Planning*, *201*, 103821.

Lieberg, M. (1995). Teenagers and public space. *Communication Research*, *22*(6), 720–744.

Liang, Y., Kirilenko, A. P., Stepchenkova, S. O., & Ma, S. (2020). Using social media to discover unwanted behaviours displayed by visitors to nature parks: Comparisons of nationally and privately owned parks in the Greater Kruger National Park, South Africa. *Tourism Recreation Research*, *45*(2), 271–276.

Loebach, J., Cox, A., & Little, S. (2020). Behavior mapping to support the development of youth-friendly public outdoor spaces. In J. Loebach, S. Little, A. Cox, & P. E. Owens (Eds.), *The Routledge handbook of designing public spaces for young people: Processes, practices and policies for youth inclusion* (pp. 308–328). New York, NY: Routledge.

Loebach, J., Little, S., Cox, A., & Owens, P. E. (Eds.). (2020). *The Routledge handbook of designing public spaces for young people: processes, practices and policies for youth inclusion*. New York, NY: Routledge.

Los Angeles City Planning Department. (1971). *The visual environment of Los Angeles*. Los Angeles, CA: Los Angeles City Planning Department.

Loukaitou-Sideris, A. (1995). Urban form and social context: Cultural differentiation in the uses of urban parks. *Journal of Planning Education and Research, 14*(2), 89–102.

Loukaitou-Sideris, A. (2005). Is it safe to walk here: Design and policy responses to women's fear of victimization in public places. *Research on Women's Issues in Transportation*, 102–112.

Louv, R. (2008). *Last child in the woods: Saving our children from nature-deficit disorder*. Chapel Hill, NC: Algonquin Books.

Lovering, M. J. (1990). Alzheimer's disease and outdoor space: Issues in environmental design. *American Journal of Alzheimer's Care and Related Disorders & Research, 5*(3), 33–40.

Low, S. M., Taplin, D., Scheld, S., & Fisher, T. (2002). Recapturing erased histories: Ethnicity, design, and cultural representation—A case study of Independence National Historical Park. *Journal of Architectural and Planning Research, 19*(4), 131–148.

Low, S. M., Taplin, D., & Scheld, S. (2005). *Rethinking urban parks: Public spaces and cultural diversity*. Austin, TX: University of Texas Press.

Lucas, B. (1995). Learning through landscapes: An organization's attempt to move school grounds to the top of the educational agenda. *Children's Environments, 12*(2), 233–244.

Lund, H. (2003). Testing the claims of new urbanism: Local access, pedestrian travel, and neighboring behaviors. *Journal of the American Planning Association, 69*(4), 414–429.

Lutz, R. (2018, September 7). *Get to know Santa Monica's newest universally accessible North Beach playground*. Retrieved from https://www.santamonica.gov/blog/get-to-know-santa-monica-s-newest-universally-accessible-north-beach-playground

Lynch, K. (1960). *The image of the city*. Cambridge, MA: MIT Press.

Lynch, K. (1977). *Growing up in cities: Studies of the spatial environment of adolescence in Cracow, Melbourne, Mexico City, Salta, Toluca, and Warszawa*. Cambridge, MA: MIT Press.

Lynch, S. M. (2003). Cohort and life-course patterns in the relationship between education and health: A hierarchical approach. *Demography, 40*(2), 309–331.

Ma, B. D., Ng, S. L., Schwanen, T., Zacharias, J., Zhou, M., Kawachi, I. … Sun, G. (2018). Pokémon GO and physical activity in Asia: Multilevel study. *Journal of Medical Internet Research, 20*(6), e217.

Maas, J., Verheij, R. A., de Vries, S., Spreeuwenberg, P., Schellevis, F. G., & Groenewegen, P. P. (2009). Morbidity is related to a green living environment. *Journal of Epidemiology & Community Health, 63*(12), 967–973.

MacGregor, S. (1996). Deconstructing the man-made city: Feminist critiques of planning thought and action. In *Change of plans: Towards a non-sexist sustainable City* (pp. 25–50). Toronto: University of Toronto Press.

Mäkinen, K., & Tyrväinen, L. (2008). Teenage experiences of public green spaces in suburban Helsinki. *Urban Forestry & Urban Greening, 7*(4), 277–289.

Malone, K. (2002). Street life: Youth, culture and competing uses of public space. *Environment and Urbanization, 14*(2), 157–168.

Manzo, L. (2005). For better or worse: Exploring the multiple dimensions of place meaning. *Journal of Environmental Psychology, 25*(1), 67–86.

Manzo, L. C., Kleit, R. G., & Couch, D. (2008). "Moving once is like having your house on fire three times": The experience of place and displacement among residents of a public housing site. *Urban Studies, 45*(9), 1855–1878.

Manzo, L. C., & Devine-Wright, P. (2021). *Place attachment: Advances in theory, methods, and applications*. New York, NY: Routledge.

Manzo, L. C., & Perkins, D. D. (2006). Finding common ground: The importance of place attachment for community participation and planning. *Journal of Planning Literature, 20*(4), 335–350.

Maptionnaire. (2021). Retrieved from https://maptionnaire.com/

Marcus, C. C. (1995). *House as a mirror of self: Exploring the deeper meaning of home*. Berkeley, CA: Conari Press.

Marcus, C. C. (2007). Alzheimer's garden audit tool. *Journal of Housing for the Elderly, 21*(1–2), 179–191.

Marcus, C. C. (2014). Environmental autobiography. *Room One Thousand, 2*. Retrieved from https://escholarship.org/uc/item/1rr6730h

Marcus, C. C., & Francis, C. (1998). *People places: Design guidelines for urban open space* (2nd ed.). Hoboken, NJ: John Wiley & Sons.

Marcus, C. C., & Sachs, N. A. (2013). *Therapeutic landscapes: An evidence-based approach to designing healing gardens and restorative outdoor spaces.* Hoboken, NJ: John Wiley & Sons.

Marshall, N. J. (1972). Privacy and environment. *Human Ecology, 1*(2), 93–110.

Marušić, B. G., & Marušic, D. (2012). Behavioural maps and GIS in place evaluation and design. In (Ed.), *Application of Geographic Information Systems.* IntechOpen. doi:10.5772/47940

Mather, M., & Scommegna, P. (2017, February). How neighborhoods affect the health and well-being of older Americans. *Population Reference Bureau* (35). Retrieved from https://www.prb.org/todays-research-aging-neighborhoods-health/#

Matthews, M. H. (1987). Gender, home range and environmental cognition. *Transactions of the Institute of British Geographers, 12*, 32–56.

Maxwell, L. E., Mitchell, M. R., & Evans, G. W. (2008). Effects of play equipment and loose parts on preschool children's outdoor play behavior: An observational study and design intervention. *Children Youth and Environments, 18*(2), 36–63.

Mays, V. M., & Cochran, S. D. (2001). Mental health correlates of perceived discrimination among lesbian, gay, and bisexual adults in the United States. *American Journal of Public Health, 91*(11), 1869–1876.

Mayerson, A. (1992). *The history of the Americans with Disabilities Act: A movement perspective.* Retrieved from https://dredf.org/abut-us/publications/the-history-of-the-ada/

Mazumdar, S., & Mazumdar, S. (1993). Sacred space and place attachment. *Journal of Environmental Psychology, 13*, 231–242.

McCamant, K., & Durrett, C. (1994). *Cohousing: A contemporary approach to housing ourselves.* Berkeley, CA: Ten Speed Press.

McElroy, J. C., & Morrow, P. C. (1994). Personal space, personal appearance, and personal selling. *Psychological Reports, 74*(2), 425–426.

McKenna, S. A., & Main, D. S. (2013). The role and influence of key informants in community-engaged research: A critical perspective. *Action Research, 11*(2), 113–124.

McKendrick, J. H. (2000). The geography of children: An annotated bibliography. *Childhood, 7*(3), 359–387.

McNally, M. J., Hester, R. T., Eubanks, P. L., Hsia, H., & Cornwall, C. M. (1986). *Runyon Canyon Master Plan design guidelines.* City of Los Angeles Recreation and Parks Commissioners. Retrieved from http://libraryarchives.metro.net/dpgtl/lacity/1986-Runyon-Canyon-Master-Plan-Design-Guidelines.pdf

Meadows, D. (1998). *Indicators and information systems for sustainable development.* Hartland Four Corners, VA: The Sustainability Institute.

Mental Health Foundation. (2021). *Nature: How connecting with nature benefits our mental health.* Retrieved from https://www.mentalhealth.org.uk/sites/default/files/2022-06/MHAW21-Nature-research-report.pdf

Merriam-Webster. (n.d.). Culture. *Merriam-Webster Dictionary.* Retrieved July 1, 2019, from https://www.merriam-webster.com/dictionary/culture

MIG, Inc. (n.d.). *About us.* Retrieved July 21, 2022, from https://www.migcom.com/about-us.

MIG, Inc. (2019). *A day at the beach: North Beach Park.* Retrieved from https://www.migcom.com/work/north-beach-park

Milgram, P., & Kishino, F. (1994). A taxonomy of mixed reality visual displays. *IEICE Transactions on Information and Systems, 77*(12), 1321–1329.

Mishra, S., Mazumdar, S., & Saur, D. (2010). Place attachment and flood preparedness. *Journal of Environmental Psychology, 30*(2), 187–197.

Miller, Y. D., & Brown, W. J. (2005). Determinants of active leisure for women with young children—an "ethic of care" prevails. *Leisure Sciences, 27*(5), 405–420.

Milligan, B., Kraus-Polk, A., & Huang, Y. (2020). Park, fish, salt and marshes: Participatory mapping and design in a watery uncommons. *Land, 9*(11), 454.

Mitchell, D. (2003). *The right to the city: Social justice and the fight for public space.* New York, NY: Guilford Press.

Moffat, R. (1983). Crime prevention through environmental design: A management perspective. *Canadian Journal of Criminology, 25*(4), 19–31.

Moore, R. (1997). The need for nature: A childhood right. *Social Justice, 24*(3), 69, 203–220.

Moore, R., & Cosco, N. (2000, September). Developing an earth-bound culture through design of childhood habitats. In *Conference on people, land, and sustainability: A global view of community gardening,* Nottingham, UK.

Morville, P. (2005). *Ambient findability: What we find changes who we become.* Sebastopol, CA: O'Reilly Media, Inc.

Moudon, A. V., Lee, C., Cheadle, A. D., Garvin, C., Johnson, D. B., Schmid, T. L. ... Weathers, R. D. (2007). Attributes of environments supporting walking. *American Journal of Health Promotion, 21*(5), 448–459. doi:10.4278/0890-1171-21.5.448

Movement Advancement Project (MAP). (April 2019). *Where we call home: LGBT people in rural America.* Retrieved from www.lgbtmap.org/rural-lgbt

Mozingo, L. (1989). Women and downtown open spaces. *Places 6*(1), 38–47. Retrieved from http://escholarship.org/uc/item/7jd71866

Mozingo, L. (2016). *Pastoral capitalism: A history of suburban corporate landscapes.* Cambridge, MA: The MIT Press.

Nasar, J. L., & Julian, D. A. (1995). The psychological sense of community in the neighborhood. *Journal of the American Planning Association, 61*(2), 178–184.

Nassar, H., & Duggan, P. (2017). Village talk. In D. de la Peña, D. J. Allen, R. T. Hester, J. Hou, L. J. Lawson, & M. J. McNally (Eds.), *Design as democracy: Techniques for collective creativity* (pp. 52–56). Washington, DC: Island Press.

National Academies of Sciences, Engineering, and Medicine (NASEM). (2004). *Transit-Oriented Development in the United States: Experiences, challenges, and prospects.* Washington, DC: The National Academies Press. doi:10.17226/23360

National Academies of Sciences, Engineering, and Medicine (NASEM). (2020). *Understanding the well-being of LGBTQI+ populations.* Washington, DC: The National Academies Press. doi:10.17226/25877

National Center for Health Statistics. (2021). Health, United States, 2019: Table 25. Hyattsville, MD: Centers for Disease Control and Prevention. Retrieved from https://www.cdc.gov/nchs/hus/contents2019.htm

National Park Service. (n.d.). *About us.* Retrieved August 2, 2021, from https://www.nps.gov/aboutus/index.htm

National Trust. (n.d.a). *How we are run.* Retrieved August 2, 2021, from https://www.nationaltrust.org.uk/features/how-we-are-run

National Trust. (n.d.b). *Our constitution.* Retrieved August 2, 2021, from https://www.nationaltrust.org.uk/features/our-constitution

NCSU Center for Universal Design. (2011). *Principles of universal design.* Retrieved from https://web.archive.org/web/20130401103302/http://design-dev.ncsu.edu/openjournal/index.php/redlab/article/viewFile/130/78

Neudel, E. (Director). (2011). *Lives worth living* [Film; 1 disc on DVD]. PBS Social Justice. Storyline Motion Pictures, LLC.; Independent Television Service (ITVS).

Neuts, B., & Vanneste, D. (2018). Contextual effects on crowding perception: An analysis of Antwerp and Amsterdam. *Tijdschrift voor Economishce en Sociale Geografie, 109*(3), 402–419.

Newman, O. (1972). *Defensible space: Crime prevention through urban design.* New York, NY: Macmillan.

Noack, P., & Silbereisen, R. (1988). Adolescent development and choice of leisure settings. *Children's Environments Quarterly, 5*(2), 25–33.

Noland, C. M. (2006). Auto-photography as research practice: Identity and self-esteem research. *Journal of Research Practice, 2*(1), Article M1.

Norris, C., McCahill, M., & Wood, D. (2004). Editorial. The growth of CCTV: A global perspective on the international diffusion of video surveillance in publicly accessible space. *Surveillance & Society, 2*(2/3), 110–135.

Norris, F. H., Stevens, S. P., Pfefferbaum, B., Wyche, K. F., & Pfefferbaum, R. L. (2008). Community resilience as a metaphor, theory, set of capacities, and strategy for disaster readiness. *American Journal of Community Psychology, 41*(1), 127–150.

NYC LGBT Historic Sites Project. (n.d.). *Making an invisible history visible.* Retrieved from https://www.nyclgbtsites.org/

Nykiforuk, C. I. J., Vallianatos, H., & Nieuwendyk, L. M. (2011). Photovoice as a method for revealing community perceptions of the built and social environment. *International Journal of Qualitative Methods, 10*(2), 103–124.

O'Brien, D. T., Farrell, C., & Welsh, B. C. (2019). Looking through broken windows: The impact of neighborhood disorder on aggression and fear of crime is an artifact of research design. *Annual Review of Criminology, 2*(1), 53–71.

Okoro, C. A., Hollis, N. D., Cyrus, A. C., & Griffin-Blake, S. (2018). Prevalence of disabilities and health care access by disability status and type among adults – United States, 2016. *Morbidity and Mortality Weekly Report (MMWR) 2018, 67,* 882–887. doi:10.15585/mmwr.mm6732a3

Olin Labs. (n.d.) *PrideScapes.* Retrieved from https://olinlabs.com/pridescapes

Owens, P. E. (1988). Natural landscapes, gathering places, and prospect refuges: Characteristics of outdoor places valued by teens. *Children's Environments Quarterly*, *5*(2), 17–24.

Owens, P. E. (1994). Teen places in Sunshine, Australia: Then and now. *Children's Environments*, *11*(4), 292–299.

Owens, P. E. (2001). Recreation and restrictions: Community skateboard parks in the United States. *Urban Geography*, *22*(8), 782–797.

Owens, P. E. (2002). No teens allowed: The exclusion of adolescents from public spaces. *Landscape Journal*, *21*(1–2), 156–163.

Owens, P. E. (2005). Healthy teen turfs: Belonging, safety and territories at high school. In *Design for diversity: Proceedings of the 36th annual conference of the Environmental Design Research Association* (p. 237). Vancouver.

Owens, P. E. (Ed.). (2010). *Youth voices for change: Opinions and ideas for the future of West Sacramento*. Davis, CA: Center for Regional Change, University of California.

Owens, P. E. (2017). A place for adolescents: The power of research to inform. The built environment. In K. Bishop & L. Corkery (Eds.), *Designing cities with children and young people: Beyond playgrounds and skate parks* (pp. 65–78). New York, NY: Routledge.

Owens, P. E. (2018). "We just want to play": Adolescents speak about their access to public parks. *Children, Youth and Environments*, *28*(2), 146–158.

Owens, P. E. (2020). A fundamental need: Linking adolescent development to the public realm. In J. Loebach, S. Little, A. Cox, & P. E. Owens (Eds.), *Fostering the inclusion of youth in the public realm: Design practices, processes and policies for the creation of youth-inclusive public outdoor environments* (pp. 7–22). New York, NY: Routledge.

Owens, P.E. & Hafer, N. (2004, November). *You, your community, your view: Youth images of community*. Session presented at Assets in action, making a difference: Healthy communities-healthy youth, the 8th annual Search Institute conference. St. Paul, MN.

Owens, P. E., LaRochelle, M., & McHenry, J. L. (2015). Landscape stories: Unearthing the culture of agricultural communities in the Central Valley. In B. Tauke, K. Smith, & C. Davis (Eds.), *Diversity and design: Understanding hidden consequences* (pp. 55–77). New York, NY: Routledge.

Owens, P. E., LaRochelle, M., Nelson, A., & Montgomery-Block, K. (2011). Youth voices influencing local and regional change. *Children, Youth Environments*, *21*(1), 253–274.

Owens, P. E., Nelson, A. A., Perry, A., & Montgomery-Block, K. F. (2010). *Youth voice matters: Toward healthy youth environments*. Davis, CA: Center for Regional Change, University of California. Retrieved from https://regionalchange.ucdavis.edu/sites/g/files/dgvnsk986/files/inline-files/Youth_Voice_Matters.pdf.

Oxford University Press. (2016). *Inclusivity, n.* Oxford English Dictionary Online (OED Online). Oxford University Press. December 2021, www.oed.com/view/Entry/93584. Accessed February 8, 2022.

Özgüner, H. (2011). Cultural differences in attitudes towards urban parks and green spaces. *Landscape Research*, *36*(5), 599–620.

Pain, R. (1991). Space, sexual violence and social control: Integrating geographical and feminist analyses of women's fear of crime. *Progress in Human Geography*, *15*(4), 415–431.

Park, K., Ewing, R., Sabouri, S., & Larsen, J. (2019). Street life and the built environment in an auto-oriented US region. *Cities*, *88*, 243–251.

Parker, B. (2006). Constructing community through maps? Power and praxis in community mapping. *The Professional Geographer*, *58*(4), 470–484.

Parker, C. (2021). Homelessness in the public landscape: A typology of informal infrastructure. *Landscape Journal*, *40*(1), 49–61.

Parker, C., & Owens, P. E. (2023). A line through a city: Using transects to uncover patterns, experiences and histories of everyday landscapes. In L. Corkery & K. Bishop (Eds.), *Routledge handbook of urban landscape research* (pp. 415–429). New York, NY: Routledge.

Parkin, J., Clark, B., Clayton, W., Ricci, M., & Parkhurst, G. (2018). Interactions involving autonomous vehicles in the urban street environment: A research agenda. *Proceedings of the Institution of Civil Engineers: Municipal Engineer*, *171*(1), 15–25. ISSN 0965-0903. Available from: http://eprints.uwe.ac.uk/33654

Passini, R. (1992). *Wayfinding in architecture*. New York, NY: Van Nostrand Reinhold.

Paulus, P. B. (1988). *Prison crowding: A psychological perspective*. New York, NY: Springer.

Pedersen, D. M. (1987). Sex differences in privacy preferences. *Perceptual and Motor Skills*, *64*(3_suppl), 1239–1242.

Peinhardt, K., & Storring, N. (2019a, July 12). *Inclusive by design: Laying a foundation for diversity in public space*. Retrieved from https://www.pps.org/article/inclusive-by-design-laying-a-foundation-for-diversity-in-public-space

Peinhardt, K., & Storring, N. (2019b, July 2). *Programming for inclusion: Enhancing equity through public space activation*. Retrieved from https://www.pps.org/article/programming-for-inclusion-enhancing-equity-through-public-space-activation

Peinhardt, K., & Storring, N. (2019c, October 18). *Public space management and the brass tacks of inclusive placemaking*. Retrieved from https://www.pps.org/article/public-space-management-and-the-nitty-gritty-of-inclusive-placemaking

Perkins, D. D., & Long, D. A. (2002). Neighborhood sense of community and social capital. In A. T. Fisher, C. C. Sonn, & B. J. Bishop (Eds.), *Psychological sense of community: Research, applications, and implications* (pp. 291–318). Boston, MA: Springer.

Perrin, A., & Anderson, M. (2019, April 10). *Share of U.S. adults using social media, including Facebook is mostly unchanged since 2018*. Pew Research Center. https://www.pewresearch.org/fact-tank/2019/04/10/share-of-u-s-adults-using-social-media-including-facebook-is-mostly-unchanged-since-2018/

Perry, A., Nichiporuk, N., & Knight, R. T. (2016). Where does one stand: A biological account of preferred interpersonal distance. *Social Cognitive and Affective Neuroscience, 11*(2), 317–326.

Perry, F. (2016, July 22). Urban gamification: Can Pokemon GO transform our public spaces? *The Guardian*. Retrieved from https://www.theguardian.com/cities/2016/jul/22/urban-gamification-pokemon-go-transform-public-spaces

Pew Research Center. (2015, December 17). *Parenting in America: Outlook, worries, aspirations are strongly linked to financial situation*. Retrieved from https://www.pewsocialtrends.org/2015/12/17/1-the-american-family-today/

Pew Research Center. (2017). *The number of Americans identifying as LGBT is rising*. Data source: Gallup Daily tracking survey. Retrieved from https://www.pewresearch.org/fact-tank/2017/06/13/5-key-findings-about-lgbt-americans/ft_17-06-12_lgbtamericans_rise/

Pew Research Center. (2020, April). *Worldwide optimism about future of gender equality, even as many see advantages for men*. Retrieved from https://dspace.ceid.org.tr/xmlui/bitstream/handle/1/824/Worldwide%20Optimism%20About%20Future%20of%20Gender%20Equality.pdf?sequence=1&isAllowed=y

Pew Research Center. (2021, April 7). *Mobile fact sheet*. Retrieved from https://www.pewinternet.org/fact-sheet/mobile/

Piaget, J. (2013). *Play, dreams and imitation in childhood*. New York, NY: Routledge (Original work published 1951).

Picheta, R. (2021, January 27). New Zealand tells tourists to stop copying other people's travel photos. *CNN Travel*. Retrieved from https://www.cnn.com/travel/article/new-zealand-tourist-photos-campaign-scli-intl/index.html

Podobnik, B. (2011). Assessing the social and environmental achievements of New Urbanism: Evidence from Portland, Oregon. *Journal of Urbanism: International Research on Placemaking and Urban Sustainability, 4*(2), 105–126.

Porteous, J. D. (1977). *Environment & behavior: Planning and everyday urban life*. Reading, MA: Addison-Wesley.

Portman, M., Natapov, A., & Fisher-Gewirtzman, D. (2015). To go where no man has gone before: Virtual reality in architecture, landscape architecture and environmental planning. *Computers, Environment and Urban Systems, 54*, 376–384. doi:10.1016/j.compenvurbsys.2015.05.001

Potts, R., Jacka, L., & Yee, L. H. (2017). Can we 'Catch 'em All'? An exploration of the nexus between augmented reality games, urban planning and urban design. *Journal of Urban Design, 22*(6), 866–880. doi: 10.1080/13574809.2017.1369873

Project for Public Spaces. (2008, December 31). *Community Defines a New Model for A Park*. Retrieved from https://www.pps.org/article/successdavis

Project for Public Spaces. (2016, May 23). *Announcing the recipients of EDRA's 17th annual Great Places Awards*. Retrieved from https://www.pps.org/article/edra2016

Proshansky, H. M., Ittelson, W. H., & Rivlin, L. G. (Eds.). (1970). *Environmental psychology: Man and his physical setting*. New York, NY: Holt, Rinehart and Winston.

Rabbi, A. F. M. (2008). *Primary education in Bangladesh: Viability of millennium development goals* [Master's thesis, Dhaka, Bangladesh: BRAC University]. Retrieved from http://hdl.handle.net/10361/595

Rae, J. (2015). *A landscape of paths: Seeing, being, moving, making* [Master's thesis, Lincoln University].

Rana, R. S. J. B., & Piracha, A. L. (2007). Cultural frameworks. In M. Nadarajah & A. T. Yamamoto (Eds.), *Urban crisis: Culture and the sustainability of cities* (pp. 13–50). New York, NY: United Nations University Press.

Rands, M., & Levinger, G. (1979). Implicit theories of relationship: An intergenerational study. *Journal of Personality and Social Psychology, 37*(5), 645.

Rapoport, A. (1969). *House form and culture*. Englewood Cliffs, NJ: Prentice-Hall.

Rapoport, A. (1980). Cross-cultural aspects of environmental design. In I. Altman, A. Rapoport, & J. F. Wohlwill (Eds.), *Environment and culture* (pp. 7–46). Boston, MA: Springer US.

Razani, N., Niknam, K., Wells, N. M., Thompson, D., Hills, N. K., Kennedy, G. … Rutherford, G. W. (2019). Clinic and park partnerships for childhood resilience: A prospective study of park prescriptions. *Health & Place*, 57, 179–185. doi:10.1016/j.healthplace.2019.04.008

Razmjouei, J., Tehrani, G. M., Alibabaei, A., Tanjani, P. T., & Razmjouei, N. (2017). Effect of urban sidewalk safety on pedestrian's health indicators. *Special Issue of International Review*, 2(Part II), 181.

Reed, E. S. (1996). *Encountering the world: Toward an ecological psychology*. Oxford: Oxford University Press.

Richards, C., Bouman, W. P., Seal, L., Barker, M. J., Nieder, T. O., & T'Sjoen, G. (2016). Non-binary or genderqueer genders. *International Review of Psychiatry*, 28(1), 95–102.

Riley, J. G., & Jones, R. B. (2007). When girls and boys play: What research tells us. *Childhood Education*, 84(1), 38–43.

Rishbeth, C. (2001). Ethnic minority groups and the design of public open space: An inclusive landscape? *Landscape Research*, 26(4), 351–366.

Rivlin, L. (1978). Environmental autobiography. *Childhood City Newsletter, 14*.

Rogers, J. (2018, August 9). [Online post photograph]. Retrieved from https://ggwash.org/view/68633/skateboarding-is-good-for-cities.-so-why-is-it-a-crime-in-dc

Roberto, E. (2008). *Commuting to opportunity: The working poor and commuting in the United States*. Washington, DC: Brookings Institution.

Robert Wood Johnson Foundation. (2013). *Active living by design: An RWJF national program [Program Result Reports]*. Retrieved from https://web.archive.org/web/20170628190116/http://www.rwjf.org/content/dam/farm/reports/program_results_reports/2013/rwjf71184

Rojas, J. (2013). Children are natural-born urban planners! *Journal of Applied Research on Children, 4*.

Ruggeri, D. (2021). The agency of place attachment in the contemporary co-production of community landscapes. In L. C. Manzo & P. Devine-Wright (Eds.), *Place attachment: Advances in theory, methods, and applications* (pp. 243–260). New York, NY: Routledge.

Ryan, R. (2012). Human health and well-being for sustainable sites. In M. Calkins (Ed.), *The sustainable sites handbook: A complete guide to the principles, strategies, and best practices for sustainable landscapes* (pp. 429–478). New York, NY: Wiley.

Rydström, J. (2019). Disability, socialism and autonomy in the 1970s: Case studies from Denmark, Sweden and the United Kingdom. *Disability & Society*, 34(9–10), 1637–1659. doi:10.1080/09687599.2019.1605883

Sack, R. D. (1986). *Human territoriality: Its theory and history*. New York and Cambridge: Cambridge University Press.

Sadat, R. (2020). Fluid inquiry: Investigating a re-imagination of youth friendly public places in the era of a rapidly changing technology. In J. Loebach, S. Little, A. Cox, & P. E. Owens (Eds.), *The Routledge handbook of designing public places for young people: Processes, practices and policies for youth inclusion* (pp. 222–236). New York, NY: Routledge.

Sadeghi, A. R., & Jangjoo, S. (2022). Women's preferences and urban space: Relationship between built environment and women's presence in urban public spaces in Iran. *Cities*, 126, 103694. doi:10.1016/j.cities.2022.103694

Saegert, S., & Hart, R. (1978). The development of sex differences in the environmental competence of girls and boys'. In P. Stevens, Jr. (Ed.) *Studies in the anthropology of play*. West Point, NY: Leisure Press.

Salem, S. (January 9, 2020). *Climate change and the sinking island states in the Pacific*. Retrieved from https://www.e-ir.info/pdf/80990

Sallis, J. F., Burns, J., Owen, N., & Veitch, J. (1997). Physical activity promotion for male factory workers: A realistic option? *Health Promotion Journal of Australia: Official Journal of Australian Association of Health Promotion Professionals*, 7(3), 169.

Salmani, A., Saberian, O., Amiri, H., Bastami, M., & Shemshad, M. (2015). Study on urban parks environmental safety in women viewpoints based on crime prevention through environmental design approach (Case study: Valiasar Park, Shahr-e-Qods, Tehran, Iran). *Bulletin of Environment, Pharmacology and Life Sciences*, 4, 95–102.

Sando, O. J., Kleppe, R., & Sandseter, E. B. H. (2021). Risky play and children's well-being, involvement and physical activity. *Child Indicators Research*, 14, 1435–1451.

Sanoff, H., & Coates, G. (1971). Behavioral mapping: An ecological analysis of activities in a residential setting. *International Journal of Environmental Studies*, 2(1–4), 227–235.

Sanoff, H. (2006, January 2). Origins of community design. *PN: Planners Network*. Retrieved from http://www.plannersnetwork.org/2006/01/origins-of-community-design/.

Sasidharan, V., And, F. W., & Godbey, G. (2005). Cultural differences in urban recreation patterns: An examination of park usage and activity participation across six population subgroups. *Managing Leisure*, *10*(1), 19–38.

Sassen, S. (2000). New frontiers facing urban sociology at the millennium. *The British Journal of Sociology*, *51*(1), 143–159.

Scannell, L., & Gifford, R. (2010a). Defining place attachment: A tripartite organizing framework. *Journal of Environmental Psychology*, *30*, 1–10.

Scannel, L., & Gifford, R. (2010b). The relations between natural and civic place attachment and pro-environmental behavior. *Journal of Environmental Psychology*, *30*, 289–297.

SCAPE. (2019). Public sediment for Alameda Creek: 2019 ASLA Professional Award. Retrieved from https://www.asla.org/2019awards/640057-Public_Sediment_For_Alameda_Creek.html.

Schaeffer, K. (2019, August 23). Most U.S. teens who use cellphones do it to pass time, connect with others, and learn new things. *Factank: News in the Numbers*. Pew Research Center. Retrieved from https://www.pewresearch.org/fact-tank/2019/08/23/most-u-s-teens-who-use-cellphones-do-it-to-pass-time-connect-with-others-learn-new-things/.

Scheuring, A. F. (2001). *Abundant harvest: The history of the University of California, Davis*. Davis, CA: UC Davis History Project.

Schiebinger, L. (2014). Scientific research must take gender into account. *Nature*, *507*(7490), 9–9.

Schneider, B. (2017, September 15). How Park(ing) Day went global. *Bloomberg CityLab*. Retrieved from https://www.citylab.com/life/2017/09/from-parking-to-parklet/539952/.

Schroeder, R. (2006). Being there and the future of connected presence. *Presence: Journal of Teleoperators and Virtual Environments*, *15*(4), 438–454.

Scraton, S., & Watson, B. (1998). Gendered cities: Women and public leisure space in the 'postmodern city'. *Leisure Studies*, *17*(2), 123–137.

Scommegna, P., Mather, M., & Kilduff, L. (2018, November 12). Eight demographic trends transforming America's older population. *Population Reference Bureau*. Retrieved from https://www.prb.org/eight-demographic-trends-transforming-americas-older-population/.

Scott Smith, C., & O'Neil, R. (2018). *Dimensions of DIVVY: Exploring the social, spatial and temporal performance of bikesharing in a period of growth and expansion*. Retrieved from https://las.depaul.edu/centers-and-institutes/chaddick-institute-for-metropolitan-development/research-and-publications/Documents/ChaddickInstitute_DivvyReport_Feb2018.pdf.

Scott Smith, C., & Schwieterman, J. (2018). *E-Scooter scenarios: Evaluating the potential mobility benefits of shared dockless scooters in Chicago*. Retrieved from https://las.depaul.edu/centers-and-institutes/chaddick-institute-for-metropolitan-development/research-and-publications/Documents/E-ScooterScenariosMicroMobilityStudy_FINAL_20181212.pdf

Sefcik, J. S., Kondo, M. C., Klusaritz, H., Sarantschin, E., Solomon, S., Roepke, A. … Jacoby, S. F. (2019). Perceptions of nature and access to green space in four urban neighborhoods. *International Journal of Environmental Research and Public Health*, *16*(13), 2313. doi:10.3390/ijerph16132313

Sewell, J. E. (2011). *Women and the everyday city: Public space in San Francisco, 1890–1915*. Minneapolis, MN: University of Minnesota Press.

Shammas, B. (2019, March 7). Time to play: More state laws require recess. *Edutopia*. Retrieved from https://www.edutopia.org/article/time-play-more-state-laws-require-recess.

Shapiro, J. (2018, October 17). In Iowa, a commitment to make prison work better for women. *NPR*. https://www.npr.org/2018/10/17/656972806/in-iowa-a-commitment-to-make-prison-work-better-for-women.

Shirtcliff, B. (2015). Big data in the Big Easy: How social networks can improve the place for young people in cities. *Landscape Journal*, *4*(2), 161–176.

Shirtcliff, B. (2020). How to use big data for youth inclusion: Lessons and insights from video-based social media research on adolescent free play in cities. In J. Loebach, S. Little, A. Cox, & P. E. Owens (Eds.), *The Routledge handbook of designing public places for young people: Processes, practices and policies for youth inclusion* (pp. 237–249). New York, NY: Routledge.

Shuter, R. (1976). Proxemics and tactility in Latin America. *Journal of Communication*, *26*(3), 46–52.

Silverstein, M., & Giarrusso, R. (2010). Aging and family life: A decade review. *Journal of Marriage and the Family*, *72*(5), 1039–1058.

Simmel, G. (2011). *Georg Simmel on individuality and social forms*. Chicago and London: University of Chicago Press.

Singer, A. (2013). Contemporary immigrant gateways in historical perspective. *Daedalus: The Journal of the American Academy of Arts & Sciences*, *142*(3), 76–91. doi:10.1162/DAED_a_00220

Skenazy, L. (2008, April 1). Why I let my 9-Year-old ride the subway alone. *The New York Sun*. Retrieved from https://web.archive.org/web/20190227225508/https://www.nysun.com/editorials/why-i-let-my-9-year-old-ride-subway-alone.

Smart Growth America. (2013). *Taking action on complete streets: Implementing processes for safe, multimodal streets*. Retrieved from https://docslib.org/doc/12839576/taking-action-on-complete-streets-implementing-processes-for-safe-multimodal-streets

Smart Growth America. (2022). *What is smart growth?* Retrieved from https://smartgrowthamerica.org/what-is-smart-growth/

Smith, A. D. (1990). Towards a global culture? *Theory, Culture & Society*, 7(2–3), 171–191.

Smith, A. S., & Trevelyan, E. (2019, October 22). In some states, more than half of older residents live in rural areas. *U.S. Census Bureau*. Retrieved from https://www.census.gov/library/stories/2019/10/older-population-in-rural-america.html

Sneed, T. (2014, July 31). What's behind the arrests of mothers for leaving their children unattended? *U.S. News & World Report*. Retrieved from https://www.usnews.com/news/articles/2014/07/31/whats-behind-the-arrests-of-mothers-for-leaving-their-children-unattended

Sommer, R. (1965). Further studies of small group ecology. *Sociometry*, 28(4), 337–348.

Sommer, R. (1969). *Personal space: The behavioral basis of design*. Englewood Cliffs, NJ: Prentice-Hall (Spectrum).

Song, Y., & Zhang, B. (2020). Using social media data in understanding site-scale landscape architecture design: Taking Seattle Freeway Park as an example. *Landscape Research*, 45(5), 627–648.

Sonnenfeld, J. (1967). Environmental perception and adaptation level in the arctic. In D. Lowenthal (Ed.), *Environmental perception and behavior* (pp. 42–53). Chicago, IL: University of Chicago.

Sorokowska, A., Sorokowski, P., Hilpert, P., Cantarero, K., Frackowiak, T., Ahmadi, K. ... Pierce, J. D. Jr. (2017). Preferred interpersonal distances: A global comparison. *Journal of Cross-Cultural Psychology*, 48(4), 577–592.

Spain, D. (2014). Gender and urban space. *Annual Review of Sociology*, 40, 581–598.

Spielberger, C. (2004). *Encyclopedia of applied psychology*. New York, NY: Academic Press.

Steiner, F. (2020). Landscape governance: The prospects for the SITES rating system. *Socio-Ecological Practice Research*, 2, 301–310. doi:10.1007/s42532-020-00068-x

Steinfeld, E., & Maisel, J. L. (2012). *Universal design: Creating inclusive environments*. Hoboken, NJ: John Wiley & Sons, Inc.

Stenou, K. (2002). *UNESCO Universal declaration on cultural diversity: A vision, a conceptual platform, a pool of ideas for implementation, a new paradigm*. Retrieved from https://unesdoc.unesco.org/ark:/48223/pf0000127162

Stevens, J. L., Toews, B., & Wagenfeld, A. (2018). Designing the correctional landscape: An invitation to landscape architecture professionals. *Landscape Journal*, 37(1), 55–72.

Stevens, J. L., Wagenfeld, A., Toews, B., & Wachtendorf, P. (2016). Creating well-rounded designers of prison environments: Transdisciplinary action research, design and teaching. *Bridging the Gap. ECLAS Conference 2016, Rapperswil, Switzerland* (14), 201–3.

Stine, S. (1997). *Landscapes for learning: Creating outdoor environments for children and youth*. Somerset, NJ: John Wiley & Sons, Inc.

Stokols, D. (1972). On the distinction between density and crowding: Some implications for future research. *Psychological Review*, 79(3), 275–77.

Stokols, D. (1977). Origins and directions of environment-behavioral research. In D. Stokols (Ed.), *Perspectives on environment and behavior: Theory, research, and applications* (pp. 536). New York, NY: Plenum Press.

Stokols, D., & Altman, I. (Eds.). (1987). *Handbook of environmental psychology* (Vol. 2). New York, NY: Wiley.

Stokols, D., & Shumaker, S. A. (1981). People in places: A transactional view of settings. In J. Harvey (Ed.), *Cognition, social behavior, and the environment* (pp. 441–488). Hillsdale, NJ: Erlbaum.

Stouhi, D. (2021, April 21). Layering of realities: VR, AR, and MR as the future of environmental rendering. *ArchDaily*. Retrieved from https://www.archdaily.com/960330/layering-of-realities-vr-ar-and-mr-as-the-future-of-environmental-rendering

Strange, J. H. (1972). Citizen participation in community action and model cities programs. *Public Administration Review*, 32, 655–669.

Stucki, L. M. (2018). *Prison landscapes: An exploration of therapeutic landscapes in women's prison facilities* [Master's thesis, Manhattan, KS: Kansas State University]. Retrieved from https://krex.k-state.edu/dspace/handle/2097/38545.

Sun, X. W., Wang, H., & Li, X. (2008). Vernacular and landscape architecture: Application of vernacular landscape elements in landscape architecture. *Chinese Landscape Architecture, 8*, 37–40.

Sustainable Sites Initiative® (SITES). (2013) *SITES certified project: Washington Canal Park*. Retrieved from https://www.sustainablesites.org/sites/default/files/legal/Case%20Studies_WA%20Canal%20Park.pdf

Sustainable Sites Initiative® (SITES). (2014). *SITES v2 rating system for sustainable land design and development.* Green Business Certification Inc.

Sutton-Brown, C. A. (2014). Photovoice: A methodological guide. *Photography and Culture, 7*(2), 169–185.

Swyngedouw, E., Moulaert, F., & Rodriguez, A. (2002). Neoliberal urbanization in Europe: Large-scale urban development projects and the new urban policy. *Antipode, 34*(3), 542–577.

Takano, T., Nakamura, K., & Watanabe, M. (2002). Urban residential environments and senior citizens' longevity in megacity areas: The importance of walkable green spaces. *Journal of Epidemiology and Community Health, 56*(12), 913–918.

Talen, E. (2006). Connecting new urbanism and American planning: An historical interpretation. *Urban Design International, 11*(2), 83–98. doi:10.1057/palgrave.udi.9000166

Taylor, A. F., Kuo, F. E., & Sullivan, W. C. (2001). Coping with ADD: The surprising connection to green play settings. *Environment and Behavior, 33*(1), 54–77.

Taylor, A. F., Kuo, F. E., & Sullivan, W. C. (2002). Views of nature and self-discipline: Evidence from inner city children. *Journal of Environmental Psychology, 22*(1–2), 49–63.

Taylor, R. B., & Stough, R. R. (1978). Territorial cognition: Assessing Altman's typology. *Journal of Personality and Social Psychology, 36*(4), 410–423.

Terraza, H., Orlando, M. B., Lakovits, C., Lopes Janik, V., & Kalashyan, A. (2020). *Handbook for gender-inclusive urban planning and design*. Washington, DC: The World Bank Publication. https://openknowledge.worldbank.org/handle/10986/33197

The Acoustic Ecology Institute. (n.d.) *Soundscapes links*. Retrieved from https://aeinews.org/aeiarchive/soundscapelinks.html

The Cultural Landscape Foundation (TCLF). (2020). *Vernacular landscapes*. Retrieved from https://tclf.org/category/landscape-category/vernacular-landscape

Thompson, C. W. (2002). Urban open space in the 21st century. *Landscape and Urban Planning, 60*(2), 59–72.

Tinsley, H. E., Tinsley, D. J., & Croskeys, C. E. (2002). Park usage, social milieu, and psychosocial benefits of park use reported by older urban park users from four ethnic groups. *Leisure Sciences, 24*(2), 199–218.

Toews, B., Wagenfeld, A., & Stevens, J. (2018). Impact of a nature-based intervention on incarcerated women. *International Journal of Prisoner Health, 14*(4), 232–243.

Toews, B., Wagenfeld, A., Stevens, J., & Shoemaker, C. (2020). Feeling at home in nature: A mixed method study of the impact of visitor activities and preferences in a prison visiting room garden. *Journal of Offender Rehabilitation, 59*(4), 223–246.

Torres, J. (2020). Why is it important to provide child- and youth-friendly streets? In J. Loebach, S. Little, A. Cox, & P. E. Owens (Eds.), *The Routledge handbook of designing public spaces for young people: Processes, practices and policies for youth inclusion* (pp. 52–63). New York, NY: Routledge.

Transport for London. (2007). *Legible London: Yellow book: A prototype wayfinding system for London*. London: Applied Information Group for Transport for London.

Tranter, P., & Doyle, J. (1996). Reclaiming the residential street as play space. *International Play Journal, 4*, 81–97.

Tryon, G. S., & Tryon, W. W. (1982). Issues in the lives of dual-career couples. *Clinical Psychology Review, 2*, 49–65.

Tuan, Y. F. (1974). *Topophilia: A study of environmental perception, attitudes, and values*. Englewood Cliffs, NJ: Prentice Hall.

Tucker, G. (1837). *The life of Thomas Jefferson, third president of the United States*. Philadelphia, PA: Carey, Lea & Blanchard.

Turnbull, D., & Watson, H. (1993). *Maps are territories: Science is an atlas: A portfolio of exhibits*. Chicago, IL: The University of Chicago Press.

Tylor, E. B. (1871). *Primitive culture: Researches into the development of mythology, philosophy, religion, art, and custom* (Vol. 1). London, UK: John Murray Albemarle Street.

Ulrich, R. S. (1983). Aesthetic and affective response to natural environment. In I. Altman & J. Wohlwill (Eds.), *Behavior and the natural environment* (pp. 85–125). Boston, MA: Springer.

Ulrich, R. S. (1984). View through a window may influence recovery from surgery. *Science, 224*(4647), 420–421.

Ulrich, R. S. (1991). Effects of interior design on wellness: Theory and recent scientific research. *Journal of Health Care Interior Design, 3*, 97–109.

United Nations. (2000). *Millennium Declaration*. Retrieved from https://www.un.org/en/development/devagenda/millennium.shtml

United Nations. (2022). *Convention on the rights of persons with disabilities (CRPD)*. Retrieved from https://www.un.org/development/desa/disabilities/convention-on-the-rights-of-persons-with-disabilities.html

United Nations. (n.d.). *Sustainable development goals*. Retrieved from https://sustainabledevelopment.un.org/?menu=1300

United Nations Educational, Scientific and Cultural Organization (UNESCO). (2016). *Culture, urban, future: Global report on culture for sustainable urban development*. Retrieved from https://unesdoc.unesco.org/ark:/48223/pf0000245999

United Nations Educational, Scientific and Cultural Organization (UNESCO). (2018). Welcome to the Anthropocene! *Courier*. Retrieved from https://unesdoc.unesco.org/ark:/48223/pf0000261900

United Nations Educational, Scientific and Cultural Organization (UNESCO). (n.d.). *Cultural diversity*. Retrieved from https://wayback.archive-it.org/10611/20171126022411/http://www.unesco.org/new/en/social-and-human-sciences/themes/international-migration/glossary/cultural-diversity/

United Nations Educational, Scientific and Cultural Organization (UNESCO) Institute for Statistics. (n.d.) *School enrollment, primary (% gross) – Bangladesh*. Retrieved April 18, 2023, from https://data.worldbank.org/indicator/SE.PRM.ENRR?locations=BD

United Nations General Assembly. (1948, December). *Universal Declaration of Human Rights*. United Nations. Paris. https://www.un.org/en/about-us/universal-declaration-of-human-rights

United Nations Women. (1995, September). The Beijing Declaration and the Platform for Action. In *Fourth World Conference on Women*. Retrieved from https://www.icsspe.org/system/files/Beijing%20Declaration%20and%20Platform%20for%20Action.pdf

U. S. Access Board. (n.d.). *Laws*. Retrieved from https://www.access-board.gov/law/

U. S. Access Board. (2014 May). *Outdoor developed areas: A summary of accessibility standards for federal outdoor developed areas*. Retrieved from https://www.access-board.gov/files/aba/guides/outdoor-guide.pdf

U. S. Access Board. (2015). *Architectural Barriers Act (ABA) accessibility guidelines: Outdoor developed areas standards*. Federal Register 36 CFR Part 1191. RIN 3014-AA22. Retrieved September 26, 2013 from https://www.access-board.gov/files/aba/ABAstandards.pdf

U. S. Access Board. (2018). *Guidelines and standards*. Retrieved from https://www.access-board.gov/guidelines-and-standards

U.S. Census Bureau. (2019, June 20). *Population estimates show aging across race groups differs* (release number CB 19-90). https://www.census.gov/newsroom/press-releases/2019/estimates-characteristics.html

U.S. Census Bureau. (2021, September 30). *Living with disabilities*. Retrieved from https://www.census.gov/library/visualizations/2021/comm/living-with-disabilities.html

U.S. Census Bureau. (2022, July 11). *Change in childhood disability rates by disability type: 2008 and 2019*. Retrieved from https://www.census.gov/library/visualizations/2022/comm/childhood-disability-rates-by-type.html

U.S. Citizenship and Immigration Services. (2021). *Rights and Responsibilities*. Retrieved from https://my.uscis.gov/citizenship/information.

U.S. Department of Justice (DOJ). (1990). Americans with Disabilities Act of 1990, Statute at Large 104 Stat. 327 – Public Law 101-336 (07/26/1990). Retrieved from https://www.congress.gov/101/statute/STATUTE-104/STATUTE-104-Pg327.pdf

U.S. Department of Justice (DOJ). (1994). *ADA standards for accessible design title III regulation 28 CFR Part 36 (1991)*. Revised as of July 1, 1994. Retrieved from https://www.ada.gov/law-and-regs/design-standards/1991-design-standards/

U.S. Department of Justice (DOJ). (2010a). *2010 ADA standards for accessible design*. Retrieved September 15, 2010 from https://archive.ada.gov/regs2010/2010ADAStandards/2010ADAStandards.pdf

U.S. Department of Justice (DOJ). (2010b). *Guidance on the 2010 ADA standards for accessible design*. Retrieved September 15, 2010 from https://archive.ada.gov/regs2010/2010ADAStandards/Guidance_2010ADAStandards.pdf

U.S. Department of Transportation (US DOT). (2015). *Active transportation*. Retrieved from https://www.transportation.gov/mission/health/active-transportation

U.S. Department of Transportation (US DOT). (2022). *Moving to a complete streets design model: A report to Congress on opportunities and challenges*. Retrieved from https://highways.dot.gov/sites/fhwa.dot.gov/files/2022-03/Complete%20Streets%20Report%20to%20Congress.pdf

U.S. Green Building Council (US GBC). (2014). *LEED Reference guide for neighborhood development*. Retrieved from https://www.usgbc.org/resources/leed-reference-guide-neighborhood-development-0

U.S. Green Building Council (US GBC). (2017). *LEED ND projects*. Retrieved from https://www.usgbc.org/projects?SearchResultsortOption=%22Featured+Projects%22&Rating+System=%5B%22Neighborhood+Development+plan%22%5D

U.S. Government Accountability Office (GAO). (2014, November 18). *Public transportation: Multiple factors influence extent of Transit-Oriented Development*. GAO-15-70. Retrieved from https://www.gao.gov/assets/gao-15-70.pdf

Urban Land Institute (ULI). (2013). *Intersections: Health and the built environment*. Washington, DC: Urban Land Institute.

Urban Sustainability Exchange. (n.d.). *Gender sensitive park design*. Accessed October 24, 2022 from https://use.metropolis.org/case-studies/gender-sensitive-park-design#casestudydetail.

Valine, K. (2018, September 19). Modesto opens up Beard Brook Park to the homeless. *Modesto Bee*. Retrieved from https://www.modbee.com/news/article218608835.html

Van Andel, J. (1990). Places children like, dislike, and fear. *Children's Environments Quarterly*, 24–31.

Vancouver Board of Parks and Recreation. (2018). *Vancouver's parks and recreation: Inventory and analysis (Report 1)*. Retrieved from https://vancouver.ca/files/cov/vanplay-report-1-chapter-1-introduction.pdf

Vancouver Board of Parks and Recreation. (2019). *Vancouver's parks and recreation: Strategic bold moves (Report 3)*. Retrieved from https://parkboardmeetings.vancouver.ca/2019/20191009/REPORT-VanPlay-Report3-StrategicBoldMoves-AppendixA-20191009.pdf

Vancouver Board of Parks and Recreation. (2020). *Vancouver's Park and Recreation Framework*. https://vancouver.ca/files/cov/vanplay-framework.pdf

Vaughn, A. (2018). DeafScape: Applying DeafSpace to landscape. *Ground Up Journal* (07), 100–103. Retrieved from https://issuu.com/alexavaughn/docs/deafscape_groundupjournal_avb

Vaughn-Brainard, A. (2020, July 24). The ADA at 30: The battle for an accessible and inclusive future continues. *The Dirt: Uniting the built and natural environments*. Retrieved from https://dirt.asla.org/2020/07/24/the-ada-at-30-the-battle-for-an-accessible-and-inclusive-future-continues/

Verstrate, L., & Karsten, L. (2015). Development of nature playgrounds from the 1970s onwards. In B. Evans, J. Horton, & T. Skelton (Eds.), *Play, recreation, health and well being* (pp. 1–19). Singapore: Springer Singapore.

Vespa, J., Medina, L., & Armstrong, D. M. (2020). Demographic turning points for the United States: Population projections for 2020 to 2060. *Current population reports* (P25-1144). Washington, DC: U.S. Census Bureau. Retrieved from https://www.census.gov/content/dam/Census/library/publications/2020/demo/p25-1144.pdf

Virden, R. J., & Walker, G. J. (1999). Ethnic/racial and gender variations among meanings given to, and preferences for, the natural environment. *Leisure Sciences*, *21*(3), 219–239.

Virtual Reality Society. (2017). *What is virtual reality?* Retrieved from https://www.vrs.org.uk/virtual-reality/what-is-virtual-reality.html

Vischer, J. C. (2008). Towards an environmental psychology of workspace: How people are affected by environments for work. *Architectural Science Review*, *51*(2), 97–108.

Wachs, T. D., & Gruen, G. (1982). *Early experience and human development*. New York, NY: Plenum.

Wagner, C. L., & Fernandez-Gimenez, M. E. (2009). Effects of community-based collaborative group characteristics on social capital. *Environmental Management*, *44*(4), 632–645.

Walmsley, D. J., & Jenkins, J. M. (1992). Tourism cognitive mapping of unfamiliar environments. *Annals of Tourism Research*, *19*(2), 268–286.

Wandersman, A., & Nation, M. (1998). Urban neighborhoods and mental health: Psychological contributions to understanding toxicity, resilience, and interventions. *American Psychologist*, *53*(6), 647–656.

Wang, C., & Burris, M. A. (1994). Empowerment through photo novella: Portraits of participation. *Health Education Quarterly*, *21*(2), 171–186.

Wang, C., & Burris, M. A. (1997). Photovoice: Concept, methodology, and use for participatory needs assessment. *Health Education & Behavior*, *24*(3), 369–387.

Wang, S. S., & Hsieh, C.-T. (2018). Ubiquitous Pokémon Go: Human–environment relationships and the location-based augmented reality game. *Environment and Behavior*. doi:10.1177/0013916518817878

Ward, C. (1990). *The child in the city*. London, UK: Bedford Square Press.

Watts, M. T. (1957). *Reading the landscape: An Adventure in ecology*. New York, NY: Macmillan.

Watts, M. T. (1999). *Reading the landscape of America*. Rochester, NY: Nature Study Guild Publishers.

Watts, M. T. (2009). *Reading the landscape of Europe*. Rochester, NY: Nature Study Guild Publishers.

Wells, N. M. (2000). At home with nature: Effects of "greenness" on children's cognitive functioning. *Environment and Behavior*, *32*(6), 775–795.

Wells, N. M., & Evans, G. W. (2003). Nearby nature: A buffer of life stress among rural children. *Environment and Behavior*, *35*(3), 311–330.

Wells, N. M., & Rollings, K. A. (2012). The natural environment in residential settings: Influences on human health and function. In S. D. Clayton (Ed.), *The Oxford handbook of environmental and conservation psychology* (pp. 509–523). Oxford: Oxford University Press.

Wener, R. (2008). History and trends in environmental design research (EDR). *Journal of Architectural and Planning Research*, *25*(4), 282–297. Retrieved from www.jstor.org/stable/43030844

Wessel, P. (2021, March). Gauging the value of the SITES rating system. *Parks & Recreation Magazine*, 26–27.

Westin, A. (1967). *Privacy and freedom*. New York, NY: Atheneum.

Whitmee, S., Haines, A., Beyrer, C., Boltz, F., Capon, A. G., de Souza Dias, B. F. ... Yach, D. (2015). Safeguarding human health in the Anthropocene epoch: Report of the Rockefeller Foundation-Lancet Commission on planetary health. *The Lancet*, *386*(10007), 1973–2028. doi:10.1016/S0140-6736(15)60901-1

Whyte, W. (1980). *The social life of small urban spaces*. Washington, DC: Conservation Foundation.

Wilson, B. B. (2018). A short history of community-driven design. In *Resilience for all: Striving for equity through community-driven design* (pp 15–28). Washington, DC: Island Press.

Wilson, J. Q., & Kelling, G. L. (1982). Broken windows. *Atlantic Monthly*, *249*(3), 29–38.

Withagen, R., & Michaels, C. F. (2005). On ecological conceptualizations of perceptual systems and action systems. *Theory & Psychology*, *15*(5), 603–620.

Wolfinbarger, K. G., & Shehab, R. L. (2000, July). A survey of ramp and stair use among older adults. In *Proceedings of the Human Factors and Ergonomics Society Annual Meeting* (Vol. 44, No. 24, pp. 4–76). Los Angeles, CA: SAGE Publications.

Woolley, H., Hazelwood, T., & Simkins, I. (2011). Don't skate here: Exclusion of skateboarders from urban civic spaces in three northern cities in England. *Journal of Urban Design*, *16*(4), 71–487. doi:10.1080/13574809.2011.585867

World Commission on Environment and Development (WCED). (1987, August 4). *A/42/427-Report of the World Commission on Environment and Development: Our Common Future*. Retrieved from https://sustainabledevelopment.un.org/milestones/wced

World Health Organization (WHO). (2001). *International classification of functioning, disability, and health: ICF*. Geneva, Switzerland: World Health Organization. Retrieved from https://apps.who.int/iris/handle/10665/42407

World Health Organization (WHO). (2017). *What do we mean by 'sex' and 'gender'?* Retrieved from https://web.archive.org/web/20170130022356/https:/apps.who.int/gender/whatisgender/en/

World Health Organization and the World Bank (WHO & WB). (2011). *World report on disability*. Retrieved from https://www.who.int/teams/noncommunicable-diseases/sensory-functions-disability-and-rehabilitation/world-report-on-disability

Wunderlich, R. E., & Cavanagh, P. R. (2001). Gender differences in adult foot shape: Implications for shoe design. *Medicine and Science in Sports and Exercise*, *33*(4), 605–611.

Yarbrough, J. M. (1998). *American Virtues: Thomas Jefferson on the character of a free people*. Lawrence, KS: University of Kansas Press.

Yellen, J. (2020). The history of women's work and wages and how it has created success for us all. *Brookings Institution, May*. https://www.brookings.edu/essay/the-history-of-womens-work-and-wages-and-how-it-has-created-success-for-us-all/

Young, N. (2021, March). *Childhood disability in the United States: 2019*. American Community Survey Briefs. ACSBR-006. Retrieved from https://www.census.gov/content/dam/Census/library/publications/2021/acs/acsbr-006.pdf

Zhang, B., & Song, Y. (2019). *Using social media data to understand site-scale landscape architecture design*. Retrieved from https://www.asla.org/2019awards/629092-Using_Social_Media_Data_To_Understand_Site.html

Zeisel, J. (1974). Fundamental values in planning with the non-paying client. In J. Lang, C. Burnette, W. Moleski, & D. Vachon (Eds.), *Designing for human behavior: Architecture and the behavioral sciences* (pp. 293–301). Stroudsburg, PA: Dowden, Hutchinson and Ross.

Zeisel, J. (2006). *Inquiry by design: Environment/behavior/neuroscience in architecture, interiors, landscape, and planning*. New York, NY: W.W. Norton & Company.

Ziersch, A. M., Baum, F. E., MacDougall, C., & Putland, C. (2005). Neighbourhood life and social capital: The implications for health. *Social Science & Medicine*, *60*(1), 71–86.

Zimring, C. M., & Reizenstein, J. E. (1980). Post-occupancy evaluation: An overview. *Environment and Behavior*, *12*(4), 429–450.

Zube, E. H. (1984). Themes in landscape assessment theory. *Landscape Journal*, *3*(2), 104–110.

INDEX

Note: *Italicized* and **bold** page numbers refer to figures and tables. Page numbers followed by "n" refer to notes.

AAP *see* American Academy of Pediatrics (AAP)
accessibility 47; definition of 118; outdoor *122*, *123*
accessible design 124–125, *126*
ACD *see* Association for Community Design (ACD)
active living, design for 223–224, *224*
Active Living by Design 223–224
activity support 53–54, 55, *55*
actual safety 53
adolescents, places for 95–100; application to design 99–100, *100*; background of 95–97; being with nature 97; places for fun 97, 99; places to be with others 97; reasons for valuing 97–99, *98*; restoration 97
advocacy planning 178–179
aesthetic qualities of place 45–47
affordances 12; actualized 42; application to design 43–44, *43*; background of 42; definition of 42; developmental 42; key findings 42–43; observations on children's playground 63
AGAT *see* Alzheimer's Garden Audit Tool (AGAT)
age: and interpersonal distances 29
"aging in place" model 109
AHBE 114
Ahwahnee Principles 104
Alex Garvin and Associates 224
al-Haram Mosque, Medina, Saudi Arabia 70
Allen, D. J. 102–103, 260
Altman, I. 8, 34, **35**
Alzheimer's Garden Audit Tool (AGAT) 109, **110**
American Academy of Pediatrics (AAP) 89
American Society of Landscape Architects (ASLA) 95
anonymity 39
Appleton, J. 45
AR *see* augmented reality (AR)
Arab Spring 16

Architectural Renewal Committee, Harlem 179
Arnstein, S. R.: ladder of participation 178
ASLA *see* American Society of Landscape Architects (ASLA)
Association for Community Design (ACD) 179
Atlanta BeltLine 224, *224*, 227
attire: and interpersonal distances 30
augmented reality (AR) 226, 229–232, *229*, *231*
auto-photography 162

baby-boomers 13
Barcelona City Council: *Urban Planning with a Gender Perspective* 148
Barker, R. G. 156
Barry, S. J. 170
behavior: analysis 156–159; documenting 156–159; exerting one's personal space 41; historical context 153–154; mapping 156, *157*, *158*, 171–172; nonverbal 41; observations 156–159; territorial 41; verbal 41; visualizing 153–173
Beijing Declaration and the Platform for Action 137, 138
bisexual 145
#BlackLivesMatter movement 16, 177, *177*
BlueCross BlueShield headquarters, Tennessee 105
B&O Railroad Museum, Baltimore, Maryland *231*
Bowling Green, Kentucky *116*
branding 58
British Standards Institute: inclusive design, definition of 125
Bronfenbrenner, U.: socio-ecological model 2, *3*, 8, 90
Brooklyn Bridge Park, New York City 114, *115*
Brunson, L. 44–45
Burris, M. A. 162–164
butterfly wings painting, Nashville *18*

Cadórniga, H. F. 81
California Environmental Quality Act (CEQA) **176**

259

Carson, R.: *Silent Spring* 217
case study method: applications and results 170; background of 165–166; methods 166–167, **166**
CDC *see* Centers for Disease Control and Prevention (CDC)
Centers for Disease Control and Prevention (CDC) 89, 223
CEQA *see* California Environmental Quality Act (CEQA)
Chambers, R. 160
Charles Schwab campus, Austin *104*
Chawla, L. 97
children, environments for 89–95; activities 90–93; application to design 93–95, **96**; background of 89–90; learning, places for 93, *94*; play, places for 93; playgrounds, evolution of 91–93, *92*; purpose of play 90–91, **90**, *91*
civic duty 175–176
civic engagement 175–176
civic space design 79
Clay, G.: *Close-Up: How to Read the American City* 154
climate change 17–19
Coates, G. 156
co-housing *38*
Coley, R. L. 44–45
College of Architecture and Urban Studies, Virginia Tech 179
Collier, J. 162
Collier, M. 162
Community Action Program 178
community-based action 179–180
community design centers 179
community engagement in design and planning *178*; advocacy planning 178–179; civic duty 175–176; civic engagement 175–176; community-based action 179–180; community design centers 179; designer-led public planning processes 179; historical context 176–177; roots of 175–177
community mapping: applications and results 162; background of 159–160; indoor exercise 171–172; methods 160–162; outdoor exercise 172–173
community participation: benefits of 180–183; challenges to 180–183; comfort and convenience 185–186, *186*; communication 184–185, *185*; cultural norms 183–184; evaluation of 189; indoor exercises 188–189; key informants 184; methods 183–184; passing along the power 186–187; strategies 183–187
connectivity 58
constrained action 42
continuity 58
Convention on Rights of Persons with Disabilities (CRPD) 119

Cooper, C. 103
Corbett, J. 161
Cosco, N. G. 93, 95
Costall, A. 42
Cox, A. 95
CPTED *see* Crime Prevention Through Environmental Design (CPTED)
Cranz, G. 78; *Politics of Park Design, The* 79
crime, safety and fear of: gender differences in 141–143, *142*
Crime Prevention Through Environmental Design (CPTED) 53–56, *54*, *55*, 142
crowding 38–41; application to design 41; background of 38–39; *versus* density 39; key findings 39–41
CRPD *see* Convention on Rights of Persons with Disabilities (CRPD)
culture 67–87; applications to design 77–82; characteristics of 68–71; civic space design 79; contemporary uses of open spaces 72–74, *75*; core interests and concerns 76; cultural awareness 83; cultural competency, development of 82–84, *83*; cultural knowledge 82; culturally inclusive design 78; cultural sensitivity 83; definition of 67–68; elements and design features, importance of 79–80, *80*; ever-changing 68–69; geographically influenced 69; geographic location and 69; in global cities 70–71; group project 85–86, *85*; historical and cultural uses of spaces 71–72, *71–73*; importance of 67–68; indoor exercise 84; institutional knowledge 77–78; and interpersonal distances 29–30; and landscape preferences 74; multicultural impacts and culturally sensitive engagement strategies 80–82, *82*; outdoor exercise 84–85; recreational activities 74, 76; spiritual 70, *70*; variance across scales 69; vernacular landscapes, cultural aesthetics and cultural representation in 76–77

Darbyshire, P. 163
Davidoff, P. 178
Davis Central Park, California 197–202; design process 198–199, *199*; human factor elements 201–202, *201*; project abstract and context 198; project result and impact 199–200, *200*; reflections 202
Davis City Council 199
de la Peña, D. 81; *Design as Democracy: Techniques for Collective Creativity* 183
demographic change 13, 15
density: *versus* crowding 39; social 39, *40*; spatial 39, 40, *40*
designer-led public planning processes 179
designers, roles and responsibilities of: background 118–120; design considerations 123–124; levels of compliance 120–123
design for all 125

design program 12–13
Devine-Wright, P. 50
disability: definition of 118–119; U.S. Census 119, *120*
districts 57, 58
DreamWorks 102
Duggan, P. 81
Dupont Circle, Washington, DC *147*

edges 57
EDRA *see* Environmental Design Research Association (EDRA)
Ehrlich, T. 175
EIRs *see* Environmental Impact Reports (EIRs)
EISs *see* Environmental Impact Statements (EISs)
el carrito 81
Ellis, G. D. 142
environmental autobiography 21–22; indoor exercise 24–25; outdoor exercise 25–26
Environmental Design Research Association (EDRA) 183
Environmental Impact Reports (EIRs) 176–177
Environmental Impact Statements (EISs) 176–177
Environmental Protection Agency 176
Environment and Behavior 9
environment–behavior relationships 7, 9; definition of 8
equity, place for 202–207, **203**, *204*, *205*
Erikson: stages of psychosocial development 89
Esplanade Youth Plaza, Fremantle, Australia *100*
Evans, G. W. 40, 44, 49, 91
exclusion, landscapes of 115–117, *116*, *117*

familiarity: and interpersonal distances 30
family structure 15
Fenster, T. 136
Fisher, T. 79
fit 24
floating water markets, Thailand *71*
Fort Mason farmers' market, San Francisco, CA *33*
Fourth World Conference on Women, Beijing, China 136–137
Francis, M. 1, 166–167
Frank, L. 227
Franks Tract Futures project 169
free action 42
freedom 22
Frumkin, H. 227

gathering, place for 197–202, *199–201*
Gehl, J. 156
gender: bias in built environment 134–136; definition of 133–134; equality 136–138, *137*, *138*; identities 145–148; inclusivity 136–138; and interpersonal distances 29; professional responsibilities and obligations 147–148, *147*; sexual orientations 145–148; social and demographic changes and 146–147, *146*
gender differences 134, *135*; design features 144–145; recreational choices 139–141, *140*; safety and fear of crime 141–143, *142*; social and cultural ties 143–144, *143*, *144*
gender-inclusive design: park and neighborhood design 149; project 150; urban design and planning 148–149
genderqueer 134
geographic information systems (GIS) 158, 168; participatory 169
geographic proximity 50
Gesell, A. 162
Gibson, J. J. 42, 58
Gibson, S. 149
Gifford, R. 49
GIS *see* geographic information systems (GIS)
Gobster, P. H. 76
Goličnik, B. 158
Goltsman, S. 93, 114
Google Maps 17
Gray, P. 90, 91
Great Places Award 168
Greeno, J. G. 42
Greer, J. D. 140
Gruen, G. 41

Haas, M. 91
Hall, E. T. 27, 29–30, 40
Halprin, A. 165
Halprin, L. 165, 166, 182
Hamer Center for Community Design, Penn State 179
Hamstead, Z. A. 170
Hardin, G. 217
Hardin, M. 140
Hart, R. 139
Hayden, D. 160
health 222–228; application to design 47–49, **48**; background of 223; current practices 223–227, *224*; key findings 47–47, *46*; physical 45; projections for the future 227–228; social 44
heath: background of 44–45
Heft, H. 42
Henley, N. 139–140
Herrington, S. 91, 95
Hester, R. 95, 160, 182–183, 187; Runyon Canyon Master Plan 165, *165*, 181, *181*; sacred structure mapping 51, *52*; user-needs checklist 22, **23**, 26
heterosexual 145
hierarchy 58
Ho, C. H. 141
homosexual 145
Hou, J. 78
Huang, Y. 1, 141, 144, 157
human–environment relations 2, 3, 7–11

human factors, in design process 7–9; importance of 9–11; situating 11–13, *12*
human factors in societal context, situating: climate change 17–19; demographic change 13, 15; family structure 15; technology 15–17, *16*
Hunt Hall, University of California, Davis *122*

Iacofano, D. 93, 114; *Meeting of the Minds: A guide to successful meeting facilitation* 179, 182
IAPS *see* International Association of People-Environment Studies (IAPS)
ICIW *see* Iowa Correctional Institution for Women (ICIW)
IDOC *see* Iowa Department of Corrections (IDOC)
IFAD *see* International Fund for Agricultural Development (IFAD)
image/maintenance 54
inclusion 9; definition of 113; design considerations 125–129, *126–129*; designers, roles and responsibilities of 118–124, *120*, **121**, *122*, *123*; indoor exercise 131; in outdoor environments 113–118, **114–118**; place for 202–207, *203*, *204*, *205*; potential project 131–132; requirements 124–129, *126–129*
inclusive design *126*; choices, offering 130; comply with legal standards 130; definition of 125; engagement with potential user groups 130; flexibility in 130–131; proactive thinking 130
Independence National Historical Park, Philadelphia, Pennsylvania 79–81, **80**
Indianapolis Cultural Trail *127*
institutional knowledge 77–78
interconnectivity 58
International Association of People-Environment Studies (IAPS) 9
International Fund for Agricultural Development (IFAD) 161
interpersonal distances *28*
intimacy 39
intimate spaces 48
intimate zone 32
Iowa Correctional Institution for Women (ICIW): The Landscape Master Plan 191–200, **192**, *193*, *195*, *197*
Iowa Department of Corrections (IDOC) 193
Islam, M. Z. 95
Ittelson, W. H. 50

Jackson, J. B. 76, 77, 154
Jackson, R. J. 227
Jacobs, J. 54, *54*, 55
Jangjoo, S. 145
Jenkins, J. M. 59
Jorgensen, L. J. 142
justice: social 9

Kaplan, R. 142
Kaplan, S. 142
Khan, M. 211
Kirilenko, A. P. 170
Kishino, F. 229
Koo, J. 1, 159, 160, 184
Krenichyn, K. 141
Kuo, F. E. 44–45

landmarks 57, 58
landscape: of exclusion 115–117, *116*, *117*; of inclusion 114–115, *114*, *115*; preferences 74; vernacular 154, 155
landscape, reading: application and results 156; background 154; methods 154–155, *155*
Landscape Master Plan for the Iowa Correctional Institution for Women, The 191–197, **192**; design process 194; human factor elements 195–196, *197*; outcomes 194–195, *195*; project abstract and context *193*; reflections 196–197
landscape values: formation of 19–21, *20*; uncovering 21–22, *21*; value-based criteria 22–24, **23**
LaRochelle, M. 45, 154
learning, places for 93, *94*, 207–211, *208–210*
legibility 58
Levi Strauss Plaza, San Francisco, CA *43*
Li, X. 155
Liang, Y. 170
life-cycle stage 89–112; adolescents, places for 95–100, *98*, *100*; children, environments for 89–95, **90**, *91*, *92*, *94*, *96*; indoor exercise 109, 111; older adults, designing for 105–109, *105*, **108**, **110**; outdoor exercise 111; potential project 112; worker needs 101–105; workplace design 101–105
Little, S. 95
Loebach, J. 95
Los Angeles Department of City Planning 160, *161*
Loukaitou-Sideris, A. 76, 149
Louv, R. 93; *Last Child in the Woods* 99
Low, S. 78, 79, 80, **80**
Lynch, K. 56–57; *Image of the City, The* 56, 154, 160

Ma, S. 170
MacGregor, S. 136
Manteo, NC *52*
Manzo, L. C. 50
MAP *see* Movement Advancement Project (MAP)
MapMyFitness 226
Marcus, C. C. 21, 25; Alzheimer's Garden Audit Tool (AGAT) 109, **110**; "Social Factors in Landscape Architecture" 1
Maxwell, L. E. 91
McHenry, J. L. 154
McNally, M. J. 160

Meadows, D. 11
"melting pot" model 74
#MeToo movement 16
Mexican Heritage Cultural Center, San Jose, CA: gates and paving design 13, *14*
Michael Van Valkenburgh Associates, Inc. (MVVA) 114
Milgram, P. 229
Millennium Square, Sheffield, England *117*
Mission Dolores Park, San Francisco, CA *32*
Mitchell, M. R. 91
mixed reality (MR) 229, 230, 232–233
mobility 47, 126–128
Moch, A. 44
Model Cities Program 178
Montgomery-Block, K. 45
Moore, R. C. 93, 95, 114
Movement Advancement Project (MAP) 146
Mozingo, L. 102, 142, 144
MR *see* mixed reality (MR)
Mukhija, V. 149
multisensory experiences 48–49
MVVA *see* Michael Van Valkenburgh Associates, Inc. (MVVA)

Nadaka Park, Gresham, Oregon *94*
Napawan, N. C. 141, 144, 157
Nassar, H. 81
National Environmental Policy Act (NEPA) 176, **176**; legal requirement for public comment 178
National Institute of Health (NIH) 223
nature-deficit disorder 93
nature prescription (Nature Rx) 225
Nelson, A. 45
NEPA *see* National Environmental Policy Act (NEPA)
Netherlands, the: woonerf or living yard 95
Neudel, E.: *Lives Worth Living* 119
Newman, O. 37, 54–56, *54*
New Urbanism 104, 218, 219
Nieuwendyk, L. M. 164
NIH *see* National Institute of Health (NIH)
nodes 57
nonbinary 134
nonverbal behavior 41
North Beach Playground, Santa Monica, CA 114, *114*
NYC LGBT Historic Sites Project 146–147
Nykiforuk, C. I. J. 164

older adults, designing for 105–109; application to design 107–109, **108**; background of 105–106, *105*; community planning 107–108; disability, presence of 106; environments and activities 106–107; geographic distribution 106; racial and ethnic background 106; residential alternatives 108–109; socio-economic conditions 106
OLIN Labs 147

OLIN Studio 147
outdoor environments, inclusion in 113–118; background of 113–114; design considerations 117–118, *118*; landscapes 114–115, *114*, *115*
Owens, P. E. 36, 42, 44, 45, 47, 51, 93, 96, 97, 99, 100, 116, 154, 160, 163

PAR *see* participatory action research (PAR)
Parker, C. 154
Park Guell, Barcelona, Spain 75
park prescription (ParkRx) 225
participatory action research (PAR) 160
participatory geographic information systems (PGIS) 169
participatory mapping: applications and results 162; background of 159–160; methods 160–161
participatory photo mapping (PPM) 163–164
Passini, R. 56–59
paths 57, 58
Patrick Tighe Architecture 114
people–place relationships 2, 27–63; affordances 42–44; crowding 38–41; health and well-being 44–49; indoor exercise 59, 62; outdoor exercise 62; personal spaces 27–33, *28*, *31–33*; place attachment 49–52, *49*, *52*; privacy 38–41; proxemics 27–33; research project 63; safety and security 53–56, *54*, *55*; territoriality 34–38, **35**, *36*, *38*; wayfinding 56–59, *57*
perceived safety 53
personal spaces 27–33, *28*, *31–33*; application to design 31–33; background 27–29; characteristics of individuals 29–30; definition of 28; familiarity 30; key findings 29; marking and defending 30; relationships 30; setting or situation, type of 30
Pew Research Center 15, *16*, 135, 146, *146*, 223; on gender equality 137–138, *138*
PGIS *see* participatory geographic information systems (PGIS)
photo-elicitation methods 162, 164
photovoice 162–163, 172–173
physical access to nature 48
physical activity, design considerations for **48**
physical health 45
physical qualities of place 45–46
Piaget, J. 89, 90
place attachment 49–52, *49*, *52*; application to design 51; background of 49–50; key findings 50–51
place identity 50
Places 183
play: characteristics of **90**; developmental functions of **90**; places for 93; purpose of 90
playgrounds: evolution of 91–93, *92*; universally designed, elements of **96**
Plaza Mayor, Salamanca, Spain 73
Pleasure Garden 139
POE *see* post-occupancy evaluation (POE)

Pokémon Go 170, 226, *226*, 230
post-occupancy evaluation (POE): applications and results 167; background of 165–166; methods 166–167, **166**
PPGIS *see* public participatory GIS systems (PPGIS)
PPM *see* participatory photo mapping (PPM)
privacy: application to design 41; background of 38–39; key findings 41; types of 39
private backyard **35**
proactive thinking 130
promoted action 42
Proshansky, H. M. 50
Prospect Park, Brooklyn, New York City 141
proxemics 27–33; application to design 31–33; background 27–29; characteristics of individuals 29–30; familiarity 30; key findings 29; relationships 30; setting or situation, type of 30
proximity 58
psychological process 50
psychosocial development: stages of 89
public outdoor dining **35**
public participatory GIS systems (PPGIS) 169, *169*
Public Sediment Project, Alameda Creek Atlas *185*
public zone 32

Rae, J. 165
Rapoport, A. 20, 74–75
recreational activities 74, 76
recreational choices, gender differences in 139–141, *140*
redundancy 58
reflection 45
reform parks 79, 139
relationships: and interpersonal distances 30
relaxation, place for 191–197, *192*, *193*, *195*, *197*
reserve 39
restoration 45, **48**, 97; place for 191–197, *192*, *193*, *195*, *197*
Rishbeth, C. 125
Rivlin, L. G. 50
Robert Wood Johnson Foundation 223
role-playing, in community workshop 188–189
Ruddell, E. 142
Ruggeri, D. 51
Runyon Canyon Master Plan 165, *165*
Ryan, R. 47–49
Ryan, R. L. 142

sacred space 59
sacred structure mapping 51, *52*
Sadeghi, A. R. 145
Saegert, S. 139
safety 53–56, *54*, *55*; actual 53; application to design 54–56; background of 53; key findings 53–54; perceived 53
"salad bowl" approach 74
Sanoff, H. 9, 156, 182

Save Open Space (SOS) 211n1
Scannell, L. 49
Scheld, S. 79
Schiller, W. 163
scored walks *165*; applications and results 166; background of 165; methods 165–166
secure spaces 48
security 53–56, *54*, *55*; application to design 54–56; background of 53; key findings 53–54
sense of belonging 129, *129*
sense of community 50
sense of place 50
sex: definition of 133
shared courtyard **35**
Shirtcliff, B. 170
social and mental health, role of nature for 225
social capital 44, 227
social density 39, *40*
social distancing 32, **32**, *33*
"Social Factors in Landscape Architecture" 1
social health 44
social justice 9
social media and behavior recording 169–170, *171*
social zone 32
socio-ecological model 2, *3*, 8, *8*, 90
sociofugal space 31, **31**, 32
sociopetal space 31, **31**, 32
solitude 39
Sommer, R. 28
SOS *see* Save Open Space (SOS)
spaces: historical and cultural uses of 71–72, *71–73*; open, contemporary uses of 72–74, *75*; spatial density 39, *40*, *40*; spatial orientation 56
Stepchenkova, S. O. 170
Stokols, D. 8, 39
student housing site, evaluation of 26
Studtmann, K. 91
subjective appraisal 25
Sullivan, W. C. 44–45
Sun, X. W. 155
surveillance 55; community 54
sustainability 11, 219, 221
sustainable development 11
Sustainable Development Goals 217
sustainable planning, design, and people: background of 215–26, *216*; current practices 217–221, *218*, *220*, *221*; projections for the future 221–222, *222*
Svarre, B. 156

Taplin, D. 79
target hardening 54
TCLF *see* The Cultural Landscape Foundation (TCLF)
technology 15–17, *16*, *18*; effects on behavior and design 225–227
Temple of Heaven, Beijing, China *73*
territorial behavior 41

territoriality 27, 34–38, *36*, *38*; application to design 37–38; background of 34; definition of 34; key findings 34–37; types of **35**
The Cultural Landscape Foundation (TCLF) 78
Thompson, C. W. 74
Torres, J. 91
Tragedy of the Commons 217
transect method 154
transgender 145
Tulatoli Primary School Outdoor Environment Design, Raipura, Narsingdi, Bangladesh 159, 207–211; human factor elements 209–211; methodology and process 208, *209*; outcomes 209, *210*; project abstract and context 207–208, *208*
Turnbull, D.: *Maps are Territories* 160

UK *see* United Kingdom (UK)
UN *see* United Nations (UN)
UNESCO *see* United Nations Educational, Scientific and Cultural Organization (UNESCO)
United Kingdom (UK): Learning through Landscapes program 93, *94*; National Trust 77, 78
United Nations (UN): Millennium Declaration 207
United Nations Educational, Scientific and Cultural Organization (UNESCO) 67, 77; Courier's *Welcome to the Anthropocene!* 217; *Global Report on Culture for Sustainable Urban Development* 78; Universal Declaration on Cultural Diversity 78
United States (US): American National Standards Institute (ANSI) A117.1 **121**; Americans with Disabilities Act (ADA) 119–125, **121**; Architectural Barriers Act (PL-90-480) (ABA) 3 **121**; Census Bureau, on disability 119, *120*; Citizenship and Immigration Services (CIS) 175; Clean Air Act 176; Clean Water Act 176; Department of Education 179; Department of Interior 78; Education Amendments of 1972, Title IX 136, 140; National Park Service (NPS) 77, 78; No Child Left Behind Act (NCLB) of 2001 93; Rehabilitation Act (PL-93-112) Section 504 **121**; Sun City and Trilogy residential developments 108
universal design 125, *126*
US *see* United States (US)
user-employed photography *163*; applications and results 164; background of 162–163; methods 163–164

Vallianatos, H. 164
Van Andel, J. 90–91
VanPlay, Vancouver's Parks and Recreation Services Master Plan 202–207; human factor elements 206; methodology and process 203–204, **203**, *204*; outcomes 204–206, *205*; project abstract and context 202; reflections 206–207
verbal behavior 41
vernacular landscape 154, 155
vernacular landscapes, cultural aesthetics and cultural representation in 76–77, *77*
village talk 81
Virden, R. J. 144
virtual influences, in design 228–233; background of 228–229; current practices 230–232, *229*, *232-232*; projections for the future 232–233
virtual reality (VR) 229, *229*, 232, 230–233, *232*
virtual space 230
visual access to nature 48
visual and hearing challenges, accommodating for 128–129, *128*
visual quality 54, 56
VR *see* virtual reality (VR)

Wachs, T. D. 41
Walker, G. J. 144
Walmsley, D. J. 59
Wang, C. 162–164
Wang, H. 155
Ward, C.: *Child in the City, The* 91
Watson, H.: *Maps are Territories* 160
Watts, M. T.: *Reading the Landscape: An Adventure in Ecology* 154
wayfinding 56–59, *57*; application to design 58–59; background of 56–57; communication strategies 59, **60–61**; definition of 56; key findings 57–58
well-being 222–228; application to design 47–49, **48**; background of 44–45, 223; current practices 223–227, *224*; key findings 45–47, *46*
Wells, N. M. 44
Whyte, W.: *Social Life of Small Urban Space* 10, *10*
Woolwich Square, London *127*
worker needs 101–105; background of 101–102
workers needs: application to design 104–105
workplace design 101–105; application to design 104–105; background of 101–102; changes in 101–102; history of 101; in outdoor environments 102–104, *103*, *104*; role of 102–104
workplace disparities 102
World Bank: *Handbook for Gender-Inclusive Urban Planning and Design* 149, 150
World Health Organization: gender, definition of 133; sex, definition of 133

Youth Voices for Change 163, *163*

Zeisel, J. 22, 24, **35**
Zube, E. H. 74